Africa's Economic Partnership with China

This book examines how increasing Africa-China relations in the fields of trade, development finance, and investment have impacted productive capacities and structural economic transformation in sub-Saharan Africa (SSA).

The book argues that statistical and empirical evidence show that China's influence has not substantially altered the fundamentals in Africa, and instead outlines a framework of policy conclusions and recommendations to help achieve transformational growth and development. Despite increased Chinese investments in transport, energy, communications, and manufacturing, sub-Saharan Africa is yet to see tangible economic and development benefits according to the multidimensional Productive Capacities Index (PCI). External trade is dogged by the same problems as during the colonial era, with primary commodities dominating exports to China, and industrial or manufacturing products dominating imports, thereby leaving the region exposed to external economic shocks. The book considers whether there are lessons to be learned from the experience of Asian countries such as Vietnam, proposing pragmatic, coordinated, non-ideological, and non-confrontational policy approaches to development.

This book will be of interest to researchers, policymakers, advisors, academics, and practitioners with an interest in development in Africa, and China's increasing role in the continent.

Mussie Delelegn Arega (PhD), A/Head, Productive Capacities and Sustainable Development Branch, United Nations Conference on Trade and Development (UNCTAD).

Routledge Studies in African Development

Responding to Mass Atrocities in Africa
Protection First and Justice Later
Raymond Kwun-Sun Lau

Politics in The Gambia and Guinea-Bissau
Precolonial Influence on the Postcolonial State
Mariama Khan

Engendering Democracy in Africa
Women, Politics and Development
Niamh Gaynor

Social Protection, Pastoralism and Resilience in Ethiopia
Lessons for Sub-Saharan Africa
Edited by Zeremariam Fre, Bereket Tsegay, Araya M. Teka, John Livingstone and Nicole Kenton

Sustainable Development in Post-Pandemic Africa
Effective Strategies for Resource Mobilization
Edited by Fred Olayele and Yiagadeesen Samy

Socioeconomic Shocks and Africa's Development Agenda
Lessons and Policy Directions in a Post-COVID-19 Era
Edited by Evans Osabuohien, Gbadebo Odularu, Daniel E. Ufua and Romanus A. Osabohien

Africa's Economic Partnership with China
An Holistic Analysis
Mussie Delelegn Arega

For more information about this series, please visit: www.routledge.com/Routledge-Studies-in-African-Development/book-series/RSAD

Africa's Economic Partnership with China

An Holistic Analysis

Mussie Delelegn Arega

Routledge
Taylor & Francis Group
LONDON AND NEW YORK

First published 2023
by Routledge
4 Park Square, Milton Park, Abingdon, Oxon OX14 4RN

and by Routledge
605 Third Avenue, New York, NY 10158

Routledge is an imprint of the Taylor & Francis Group, an informa business

British Library Cataloguing-in-Publication Data
A catalogue record for this book is available from the British Library

Library of Congress Cataloging-in-Publication Data
Names: Arega, Mussie Delelegn, author.
Title: Africa's economic partnership with China: an holistic analysis/Mussie Delelegn Arega.
Description: New York, NY: Routledge, 2023. |
Series: Routledge studies in african development | Includes bibliographical references and index. |
Identifiers: LCCN 2022023937 (print) | LCCN 2022023938 (ebook) | ISBN 9781032281070 (hardback) | ISBN 9781032281087 (paperback) | ISBN 9781003295334 (ebook)
Subjects: LCSH: Africa, Sub-Saharan–Foreign economic relations–China. | China–Foreign economic relations–Africa, Sub-Saharan.
Classification: LCC HF1611.Z4 C617 2023 (print) | LCC HF1611.Z4 (ebook) | DDC 337.6073–dc23/eng/20220824
LC record available at https://lccn.loc.gov/2022023937
LC ebook record available at https://lccn.loc.gov/2022023938

ISBN: 978-1-032-28107-0 (hbk)
ISBN: 978-1-032-28108-7 (pbk)
ISBN: 978-1-003-29533-4 (ebk)

DOI: 10.4324/9781003295334

Typeset in Goudy
by Deanta Global Publishing Services, Chennai, India

Contents

Figures

Tables

Preface

This book provides an alternative narrative to the Africa-China partnership and its impact on Africa's economic development and structural transformation. It challenges the widely accepted mainstream wisdom that the impact of China's emergence as a major investor and trading partner of African countries has been to reinforce Africa's traditional role as supplier of commodities and importer of manufactured products. In contrast, this book uses the Productive Capacities Index (PCI) – a tool specifically designed to measure the level of development of productive capacities – to demonstrate whether the impact of the Africa-China partnership has been qualitatively different from those experienced with traditional development partners. The PCI is an innovative and multidimensional composite index that maps the development of capabilities that countries require to produce a wide range of products and services, foster structural transformation, and develop.

In Africa, decades of reforms in economic policies and institutions and development partnerships with traditional development partners such as the EU, USA, and Japan have not reversed the region's lag in socioeconomic progress and marginalization from the global economy. The pitfalls of the reform processes implemented since the 1980s, in many cases externally imposed, were their excessive focus on narrow objectives of macroeconomic stabilization, reducing the role of the state in economic development and short-term political outcomes. Most often, the primary goals of the reforms and adjustment programmes prescribed to countries of SSA were to secure donor approval of policies, acquire adjustment funds, and articulate market-driven narratives without due attention to country-specific circumstances, resources endowments, and the capacity to implement such policy reforms.

The economic growth performance of African countries in the post-structural adjustment period, particularly since the new millennium, has been relatively better as demonstrated by a steady and high-level growth experienced in many African countries. The problem was governments were obsessively focused on generating higher (quantity) growth while ignoring the form, quality, sustainability, and impact of such growth on employment creation and poverty reduction. Consequently, economic growth in Africa, when it occurred, remained enclave-based and failed to lead to capital accumulation, build economic resilience to shocks, and foster productive capacities and structural economic transformation.

In a bid to foster industrialization and structural economic transformation, African countries began to pursue investement and an export-led industrialization strategy hoping to replicate the rapid growth and economic development achieved by the newly industrialized Asian economies some six decades ago. To that end, many African countries built (at colossal costs) industrial parks, export processing zones, or special economic zones to attract efficiency-seeking FDI and produce low-value manufactured goods for export. However, to date, only South Africa, Mauritius, Morocco, and Tunisia have made significant progress in building dynamic economies based on investment and export-led strategies. Otherwise, Africa's share in global FDI flows remains negligible (although significant when compared to their economic size). In 2020, the region's combined average manufactured value-added (in dollar terms) was below one-tenth of the average for developing countries. The manufactured value-added as a percentage of GDP remains below 10 percent against the average of about 17 percent for other developing countries. These trends are clear manifestations of "premature deindustrialization" of SSA and dominance of primary commodities in their export baskets.

The question is why Africa (notably SSA) continues to remain locked in low-level equilibrium traps (weak productive capacities, underdevelopment, poverty, and destitution) while other developing regions managed to make socioeconomic progress over the years? Will unprecedented expansion in Africa-China partnership change the socioeconomic fundamentals and dynamics of SSA? China's engagements with Africa through international trade, investment, and development finance have grown in extent, scale, and magnitude in recent years. This new trend has generated euphoria, negative narratives, and even campaigns against the close Africa-China economic relationship, particularly in the Western media.

This book provides unbiased, data-driven, and evidence-based analysis of the evolution of the Africa-China partnership and the impact on African countries' aspirations to build productive capacities, kick-start the process of structural economic transformation, address the region's continued socioeconomic woes, and reverse the dependence on external finance for development. It also articulates how best to harness Africa's natural resource endowments by recalibrating factors of production, entrepreneurship, and ICT and by putting in place the right mix of institutions, policies, legal, and regulatory frameworks. The book argues that African countries, particularly those in SSA, need to put in place endogenous and nationally owned development policies that maximize comparative advantages and relieve key binding constraints to growth and development. This includes harnessing the potential of global and regional trade, finance, and market opportunities in the same way as the East Asian economies such as Vietnam. The book squarely places the primary responsibilities of Africa's development on the shoulders of political and policymaking elites, technocrats, private sector, and civil society actors of the continent. Developing African countries is neither the responsibility of China nor the obligation of traditional development partners but Africans themselves who should be in the "driving seat", taking their countries in the right direction.

Africa's growth and development must rely on home-grown deliberate policies that mobilize and recalibrate key enablers and drivers of growth and transformation. Taking advantage of global opportunities, without doubt, requires fostering developmental partnership by selectively picking what works best for Africa and tacitly rejecting what does not. In so doing, those responsible for Africa's development, at both national and regional levels, should avoid confrontational or ideological approaches in forging partnerships. Africa's policymakers also need to change long-standing attitudes of assuming responsibilities or obligations in multilateral trade, finance, and development architectures based on political expediency only. They must incorporate effective cost-benefit analysis in enterprising development and pursuing multilateral, bilateral, and regional trade, investment, and finance agreements. They need to put in place business models and functioning institutions that allow business and the private sector to thrive, innovate, competitively produce, and grow.

Learning from vibrant development economies such as Vietnam, policymaking in Africa should be guided by pragmatism and forward-looking strategies centred not only on learning from others and imitation but also on experimentation, including the self-discovery of locally suitable development policies. These should also include technological catch-up, innovation, and applying provisions of the concept of the Developmental State, which, while respecting indigenous policy formulation, advocates for the active and facilitative role of the state. The key lesson emerging from the analysis conducted in this book is that no nation has ever developed without nationally owned policies that foster productive capacities and structural economic transformation. What distinguishes successful countries from the less successful ones is the former's abilities to formulate and implement home-grown, pragmatic, and forward-looking development strategies, which are aligned with their respective explicit (revealed) and implicit (latent) comparative advantages and serve as a key to relieve the most pervasive binding constraints to development. Such policies, particularly in Asia, have accelerated economic growth, improved living standards of the populations, enhanced human, and physical capital formation, facilitated growth of their respective domestic private sectors, and accelerated the transfer of technology and innovation for production transformation including through industrialization.

As noted above, this book applies the Productive Capacities Index (PCI) to examine the impact of increasing Africa-China partnership. In addition to the PCI, supplementary data from various secondary sources[1] are used to analyze trends in trade, development finance, and investment. The primary objective is to explore whether there is a qualitative shift in the structure of SSA's socioeconomic landscape because of Africa-China partnership. In this context, the book closely examines whether there are relationships between the "rising China" and the "rising Africa" narratives that have been promulgated recently in academic writings and the media. More importantly, the book sheds light on whether the "Africa rising" narrative is a myth or reality. In view of the lack of progress in the commodity-based and aid-driven growth model, a paradigm shift is necessary to replace Africa's traditional (short-term) approaches to development by programmatic, long-term, multisectoral, and coherent home-grown development policies.

The book further discusses the outcome of policy reforms pursued by countries in the SSA region, comparing them with the experiences of East Asian economies, particularly Vietnam. It examines whether there are policy lessons for SSA from the Asian experiences in fostering productive capacities and structural economic transformation. In synthesizing the lessons from Asia, the focus of the book is not on "what" East Asian economies and Vietnam have achieved but "how" they have achieved it or what have they done differently that African countries have failed to do. Understanding how Asian economies that are not as endowed with natural resources as African countries have recalibrated key drivers and enablers of growth through pragmatic, home-grown, and development-driven policies, provides useful lessons for developing countries, particularly those in SSA.

Many books have been written on Africa-China economic relations in recent years, most of them focusing on the socioeconomic transformation in China itself and how the strengthening of South-South cooperation is contributing to China's emergence as a global economic powerhouse. This book takes the discussion in a different direction and sheds new light on the question of whether the growing Africa-China partnership is any different from the long-standing partnership that Africa had with traditional development partners. In so doing, the book offers conceptually sound, rigorous, evidence-based, and holistic analysis of Africa-China partnership with a focus on trade, finance, and investment. It is designed to serve as a guide to reshape Africa's development policies and the region's broader partnerships in the years ahead. The aim is to facilitate the formulation and implementation of consistent and coherent policies centred on the development of productive capacities and fostering structural economic transformation in the region. In view of the new dynamism coming from the Asian Dragon and in the absence of holistic analysis on Africa-China partnership, the book brings new perspectives on the challenges and opportunities for Africa in its engagements with China. Building on the PCI and drawing practical policy lessons from the experiences of successful developing countries such as Vietnam, the book aims to bridge huge analytical, conceptual, and statistical gaps on the role of China in Africa. The conclusions, findings, and the new orientation of policies articulated in the book serve as a guide to formulate and implement forward-looking and multisectoral development policies that will help SSA to address structural impediments, harness comparative advantages, and accelerate the fostering of productive capacities and structural economic transformation as key for achieving inclusive growth and sustainable development.

Note

1 These include the UNCTADstat, global Productive Capacities Index (PCI), UNCTAD Data on Foreign Direct Investment (FDI), COMTRADE, World Trade Organization (WTO) database, the International Trade Centre UNCTAD/WTO (ITC), IMF, World Bank Database, and the World Development Indicators of the World Bank. Key indicators of productive capacities and structural economic transformation, including Manufacturing Value Added as percentage of GDP, Export Concentration and Diversification Indices, and Gross Fixed Capital Formation are used to assess the impacts of SSA's engagements with China. On Chinese loan, credit, and other financial flows, data from Johns Hopkins SAIS China Africa Research Initiative is used.

Acknowledgements

Writing analytical study is challenging, demanding, and frustrating but writing a book such as this one is even harder, more complex, and nerve-wracking. It is more so for someone so engulfed and consumed by professional commitments as me and yet audacious to undertake such a task. My academic field of studies, vast professional experience, and extensive duty travels across the world as well as countless dialogues and deliberations at national, regional, and global levels on key development policy issues are clearly discernible in every line, paragraph, and chapter of the book.

Interestingly, this book project would not have come to fruition without the direct and indirect support of so many academics, experts, and individuals in every step of the process. I am deeply and sincerely grateful to every one of them. My very special thanks and appreciation are to the anonymous reviewers and Dr Taffere Tesfachew for their thought-provoking and substantive feedback on subsequent drafts. I am equally thankful to Alberto Munisso and Sonia Bouali for their statistical assistance during the conceptualization phase of the book. My gratitude and sincere thanks also go to the Routledge team, consisting of Alexandra de Brauw, Helena Hurd, and Rosie Anderson for their superb work and tireless guidance from conception to the end. I am also grateful to Deanta Global Publishing, Chennai, India Team for desktop publishing and layout of the book.

My wife Zerthun and our two children – Ammanuel and Mahlet – taught me exceptional discipline. They gave me unimaginable strength, undiminishing love, and unconditional moral support that have helped me to achieve my long-awaited and grandiose project of writing a book.

Although this book is the fruition of many known and anonymous individuals' opinions, the responsibility for any errors and omissions is solely my own.

1 Introduction

Countries in sub-Saharan Africa (SSA) hold significant potential for sustained and inclusive growth, given the untapped natural and human resources the region possesses. The region is home to about "30 percent of the world's total mineral reserves and significant share of the global production of economically important minerals" (UNECA: 2011a, Nordic Africa Institute–NAI: 2018). According to the 2014 US Geological Survey, SSA possesses 50 percent of global chromium, 53 percent of cobalt, 53 percent of diamonds, 20 percent of gold, 65 percent of manganese, 15 percent of uranium reserves (US Geological Survey: 2014, NAI: 2018), and vast agricultural lands. However, harnessing such potential has proven daunting due to the complex internal and external development challenges the region has been facing for several decades. This notwithstanding, natural capital continues to drive economic growth, international trade, and livelihoods in SSA. While international trade brought more interest, value, and intense rivalry in natural resources among economically powerful nations, the benefits from such resources are not equitably shared along the supply chain. For instance, how much can countries producing and exporting oil or precious minerals such as diamonds earn and benefit from the production and processing along the value chain? In addition to the skewed share of benefits from such resources, the overconsumption of such vital minerals could have impacts on natural habitat, climate, and intergenerational capital accumulation. How should these "exploitative" relationships between the custodians of natural capital and those who benefit the most be sustained?

As argued in the various chapters of this book, natural resource endowments and the overdependence of SSA on such resources have further exacerbated socioeconomic vulnerability, inequality and problems of governance in the region. Unlike other developing regions, economic growth in SSA, when it occurred, failed to create jobs, and reduce poverty. Nor could it generate or contribute to aggregate savings, investments, and overall capital accumulation which are foundational for production transformation. The natural resources of SSA made economic growth enclave-based (commodity-driven) and, hence, the cause of poverty, inequalities, conflicts, anaemic corruption, and cronyism. Consequently, SSA remains underdeveloped and the last frontier in the fight against poverty, destitution, and overall socioeconomic marginalization. The region's growth

DOI: 10.4324/9781003295334-1

pattern remains fragile, and vulnerable to negative external shocks (economic, political, environmental, health, etc.). These are the cause and consequence of weak productive capacities and the lack of structural economic transformation, which constitute the main binding constraints to socioeconomic growth and development in SSA. This, in turn, heightened the region's continued uncertainties and vulnerability[1] to negative internal and external shocks such as COVID-19 as well as overdependence on external assistance.

The capacity to withstand the knock-on impacts of the current global health crisis caused by the COVID-19 pandemic depends, to a large extent, on economic, human resources, institutional and technological capabilities, and the overall productive capacities of nations. COVID-19 has already caused havoc with devastating ramifications for the global economy, particularly the poorest economies such as those in SSA. Preliminary assessments and forecasts indicate that the bouts of the pandemic in SSA will be colossal. The impact will be serious and costly in terms of lost lives and livelihoods of citizens, overburdened health systems, and healthcare delivery capacities. Beyond impacts on health and healthcare systems, the crisis is also causing serious disruptions in investment, trade, production, and supply networks with unprecedented job losses, food insecurity, and an increase in poverty while drastically cutting aggregate output and global demand for exports from SSA. The COVID-19 pandemic has also brought back the role of governments not only in terms of fiscal response, bailout, and economic stimulus packages but also in rethinking global interdependence, production and supply networks, and weighing the cost-benefit of these. What would be the future of the relocation of production of basic key supplies such as facemasks, hand-sanitizer, and personal protective equipment (PPE) in search of production efficiency of investments? Should these be considered as vital strategic goods in the future and produced in every county – rich or poor? Moreover, global crises (economic, financial, health-related, or otherwise) can have disproportionate impacts on poor and vulnerable economies such as those in SSA. Such crises particularly tend to penalize investments into the future due to the systemic uncertainties they cause (Hepburn et al.: 2020), which will have direct and substantial negative impacts on capital flows to SSA – the region often considered or perceived as risky for such flows. What should the post-COVID-19 policies and strategies of African governments be?

Despite the negative socioeconomic consequences on SSA, the book does not dwell much on COVID-19 due to four main reasons. First, the research for the book had already advanced a lot before the outbreak of the pandemic, and its ravaging consequences were predicted or estimated. Second, statistics and accurate information on the scale, extent, and scope of the impact of the pandemic is still unfolding, with no end yet in sight to contain the pandemic. Third, SSA has not become the epicentre of the pandemic as the spread of the virus has penetrated the region slower than expected. Finally, the question which the book is poised to address deals with the underlying causes of the underdevelopment, socioeconomic uncertainties, and vulnerabilities of SSA and not the symptoms per se. The expected socioeconomic impact of the pandemic on SSA confirms the prevailing fragility and vulnerability of the region, and its inability to contain the spread of the disease or withstand its negative socioeconomic consequences. The key message from the book is that the COVID-19 pandemic is a wake-up call for the countries of SSA, as it is for the major economies of the world. They must foster their respective domestic productive capacities and transform their economies to accelerate socioeconomic development and withstand unexpected negative shocks such as those emanating from the current pandemic. The post-COVID19 domestic development policies and strategies of SSA should focus on laying the foundation for broad-based and inclusive growth and resilience-building by fostering their productive capacities and structural economic transformation. Therefore, development policymakers of African countries and their development partners should seriously consider the recommendations provided in Chapter 9 of this book which aim to relieve key structural weakness and foster production transformation in SSA.

In investigating the Africa-China partnership, this book recognizes the importance of heterogeneity. Lumping together all 48 countries[2] of SSA as one can mask heterogeneity of economic performances, diversity and uniqueness of local conditions, resources base, institutions, and sociocultural set-ups. Nevertheless, there are several commonalities across the countries of SSA. Almost all the countries of the region face similar challenges in achieving transformative economic growth and development. Therefore, the analysis is based on the aggregate development experiences of SSA. This is further corroborated by country-specific case studies, which provide insights into understanding the country-specific development challenges, experiences, and contexts of the Africa-China partnership.

As indicated earlier in this section, SSA is a region endowed with some of the world's most critically important natural resources, including oil, natural gas, and precious stones as well as other mineral and non-mineral resources. It has some of the fastest-growing economies in the developing world in recent years together with expanding markets, a growing middle class, and bulging young populations. Moreover, for several decades, the countries of the region have been undertaking wide-ranging policy and institutional reforms – some prescribed from outside; others, home-grown; and still some others, reciprocal (bilateral) or multilateral in nature often undertaken in the context of trade and investment agreements. There are further regional economic grouping commitments which create opportunities but also challenges. In parallel with domestic policy and institutional reform as well as regional and global integration efforts, SSA has also seen substantial increases in international trade, investment, and development finance, including with rising economic powers from the developing South, notably the People's Republic of China. The region's natural capital (natural resources), as it had been the cause for the "Scramble for Africa" and the rush for the "partition and conquest of the dark continent" by the European colonial powers between 1871 and 1914 (Brooke-Smith: 1987, Pakenham: 1991, Hopkins: 1993, Michalopoulos and Papaioannou: 2011), there is now a concern that the same resources could lead to the "new Scramble for Africa" in the 21st century (Carmody: 2007, Ouma: 2012).

Since the 1960s, developed countries poured aid (development, humanitarian or emergency aid, and technical assistance) to Africa, notably SSA. Some estimates put the combined allocation of aid to Africa surpassing USD 1 trillion over the last five to six decades (Moyo: 2009). If external development finance flows from non-traditional donors and multilateral sources (the World Bank, the International Monetary Fund, the United Nations, and the African Development Bank) are included, the estimate of combined aid inflows to Africa to date can be well above USD 2 trillion. Only in 2017, net aid disbursement to the African continent amounted to USD 51.8 billion of which nearly USD 44 billion was to countries in SSA (OECD: 2019). Besides aid flows, investment relationships between the West and Africa have also increased in absolute terms, although the relative share of Africa in both in world investment flows and stocks remains negligible. For instance, in 2017, the total foreign direct investment (FDI) inflows to Africa were USD 32 billion, accounting for 2.9 percent of global flows compared to 49.8 percent share of developed economies, 33.3 percent share of developing Asia and 10.6 percent share of Latin America and the Caribbian (UNCTAD: 2020c).

There is a concern regarding the mismatch between massive financial and investment inflows and lack of commensurate socioeconomic progress in SSA. This has led to arguments and counterarguments that Africa's trade, finance, and investment relations with developed countries over the years, have not brought about substantial socioeconomic transformation. In fact, the West's partnerships with Africa have been largely exploitative (Oyeranti et al.: 2010), facilitating capital drain (Naoroji: 1969) and perpetuating dependency on external growth factors (Hettne: 1983). The intensity and prevalence of abject poverty in SSA remain a daunting challenge; fragility or collapse of its economic growth is recurrent; and an overall underdevelopment of the region is a constant phenomenon despite increased international support measures and aid inflows.

In addition to aid and investment flows, most SSA countries have also been enjoying preferential market access to developed country markets (the EU, Japan, and the USA) for several decades. However, the region's share in world exports remains negligible (less than one percent) and, at times, in precipitous decline. Against substantial amounts of aid and investment flows (relative to their economic sizes) and preferential market access for the region's exports to major markets, SSA remains the poorest of all the developing regions of the world. Thirty-three out of 54 countries in Africa are least developed (classified as such by the United Nations) and many show little sign of catching up with middle-income and emerging economies. Aid-dependent African countries have recorded an average annual growth rate of 0.2 percent (Moyo: 2009), with little or no impact on poverty reduction. Moyo's arguments against malfunctioning and patronizing "development aid" and a pro-private sector approach to development raised serious criticisms from some corners. Moorsom (2010) claims that Moyo's assessment of African entrepreneurs were "fictional, that she confused markets and capitalism, and that her analysis missed a point by omitting oppressive African States, whose bad governance and dictatorship held back the growth of entrepreneurs and entrepreneurship". Moyo also portraits all the wrongs in development aid without critically examining how aid resources have been used by recipient countries or whether the problem is the aid itself or its utilization. It is also wrong to assume that all forms of external aid failed to bring about desired changes on the ground. For instance, humanitarian aid saved lives during times of national distress (such as famine or other natural catastrophes) in recipient countries. Moreover, aid resources that went to the health and education sectors have also played an important role in improving universal access to these vital sectors, particularly of the poor in many countries of SSA. This is to argue that the glaring and miserable failure of aid is pronounced in the field of economic development. Further research, such as that by Collier (2007) provides comprehensive evidence as to why impoverished countries fail to progress despite international development aid and support (see also Figure 1.1).

The last few decades have opened new avenues and opportunities for SSA's growth and transformation, with the region forging robust development partnership with "rising China". The Africa-China partnership covers areas such as trade, investment, and development finance as well as preferential market access for exports of the region. The unprecedented expansion in the Africa-China economic partnership has generated euphoria, particularly among Africa's political

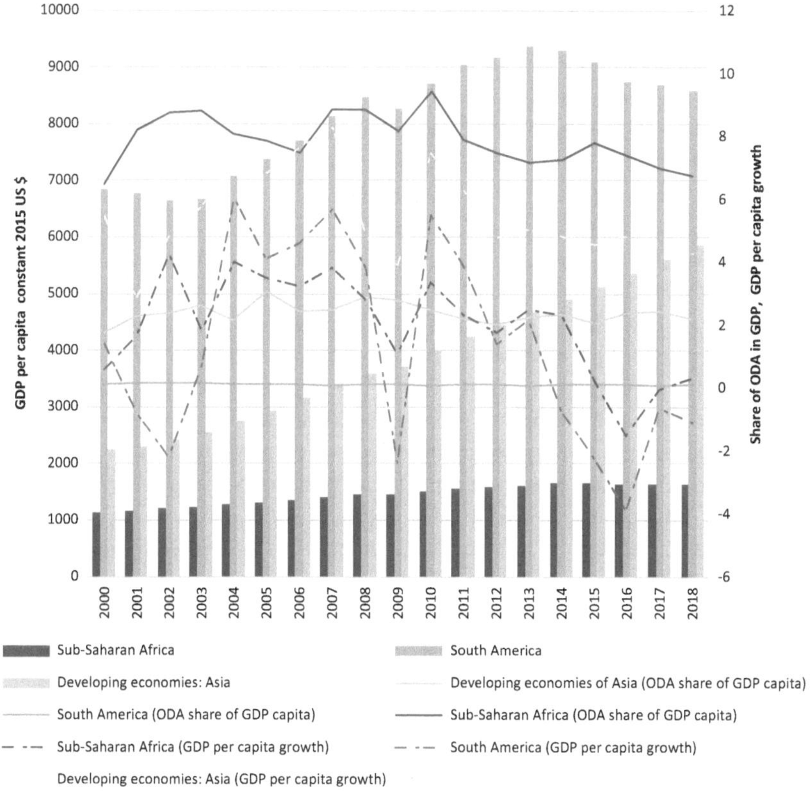

Figure 1.1 Regional ODA distribution and economic performance (2000–2018).

Source: OECD Aid Database and World Bank Development Indicators (2019).

elites, analysts, and policy practitioners. Some scepticism has also emerged on the real or actual benefits of the new partnership of Africa with China. For many observers, the new partnership offers a renewed hope and momentum for Africa's trade and investment expansion as well as helping to address the root causes of underdevelopment and continued marginalization of the continent in the global economy. For others, China's insatiable appetite for extractive resources is the motivation behind the expanded Africa-China partnership. Hence, according to the latter groups, the Africa-China partnership is between two unequal players with little or no intention to transform or develop Africa. China's robust engagements in Africa have also brought about intense competition and rivalry, not only between China and the West but also with other emerging economies in the developing South (Brazil, India, and Turkey) and major economies in the former Eastern Bloc such as Russia. The rivalry between the old and the new entrants into Africa has raised apprehension as to whether such stiff competition leads to "a new Scramble for Africa" (Carmody: 2007, Ouma: 2012). This concern is reinforced by the recent wave of new partnership arrangements and summits held between Africa and its traditional and non-traditional trade and development partners.[3] Of these expanded relations, this book's main interest is to investigate the growing Africa-China partnership and whether this will transform the economies of SSA and help the region to achieve inclusive and sustained economic growth and development.

In the area of international trade, merchandise trade (both exports and imports) between China and SSA has skyrocketed in the last three decades, with the region maintaining a positive balance until 2013 (Figures 1.3 and 1.4). Chinese FDI – both inflows to SSA and stocks in the region have also substantially increased (Chapters 3 and 4). Country-by-country reviews of FDI flows provide interesting insights into the magnitude and direction of Chinese FDI flows. During the 2010–2017 period, nearly 78 percent of FDI inflows to Niger and 70 percent of those to Angola originated from China. Likewise, during the same period 72 percent of FDI inflows to Zimbabwe, 82 percent to Botswana, and 44 percent to Ethiopia originated from China. This distribution shows that Chinese FDI inflows to SSA also, though targeted on countries with natural endowments, are not exclusively limited to extractive sector-driven economies only.

As with the Africa-China partnership on trade and investment, Chinese development finance in Africa has also been constantly increasing, although available data and statistical information in such flows is neither consistent nor reliable. Different sources report different data and statistical information on Chinese development aid or finance to Africa. The absence of official data on Chinese development aid (in all forms) has contributed to growing suspicion (particularly in developed countries) on the motivation and transparency of the robust Chinese presence in and engagement with Africa. According to the China-Africa Research Initiative (CARI) at Johns Hopkins University's Paul H. Nitze School of Advanced International Studies,[4] during 2000–2017, combined Chinese development finance to Africa was about USD 143 billion. More than 96 percent of this was destined for SSA (excluding South Africa), with Angola being the top recipient (USD 42.8 billion) over the 17-year period (see Table 4.2, Chapter 4). However, despite a substantial expansion in trade, development finance and FDI inflows (from traditional and non-traditional partners), SSA remains the locus of generalized and widespread poverty.

SSA further benefits from continued and targeted support from the United Nations, which mobilizes political (policy), technical assistance, and financial support in favour of Africa. For instance, the UN General Assembly established the category of Least Developed countries (LDCs)[5] in 1971, with the view to mobilizing international partnerships in support of these structurally weak economies. Countries are categorized by the General Assembly as LDCs based on threshold levels of low Gross National Income per capita (less than USD 1,290 in 2018 triennial review), low Human Assets Index (HAI)[6] (less than 66) and high Economic Vulnerability Index (EVI)[7] (higher than 32). When LDCs reach or surpass these benchmarks, they are recommended to "graduate" or exit the group (as per the graduation criteria and rule)[8] and become middle income (developing) countries. This can be regarded as a sign of socioeconomic progress. While there is no direct relationship between international support measures and progress towards graduation, a combination of sustained economic growth, increased investments (domestic and international), sustained peace and stability, favourable international economic environment, and international support measures are key drivers of the graduation process. In principle, graduated countries depend less on external or international support mechanisms than LDCs particularly if they reach upper middle-income[9] status. However, even after graduation, there still are uncertainties and systemic or structural vulnerability, which can make graduating or graduated countries to fall back into the list of LDCs. The socioeconomic crisis caused by the COVID-19 pandemic is expected to delay or postpone the graduation of recommended countries to exit the group of LDCs in the next few years.[10] It is in this context, that countries are advised to foster productive capacities and structural economic transformation to make their graduation from LDCs more sustainable and irreversible.

Unfortunately, in nearly 50 years of the group of LDCs' existence, while only six countries have managed to graduate to date, more than 22 new countries have regressed and joined the group of the poorest countries (LDCs) since the official establishment of the group in 1971. Currently there are 46[11] countries categorized as LDCs, with a combined estimated population of 1 billion, 33 of which are in SSA. The increasing number of poorest countries in the world (from the original 25 to 46 currently), is a result of the continued deterioration of their socioeconomic trends and weak productive capacities, particularly in SSA. More importantly, it is the consequence of failure in domestic policies and international support mechanisms to transform the socioeconomic landscape of these countries. Overall, in SSA, economic growth and massive development aid and investment flows failed to have an impact on job creation, poverty reduction, and sustained economic growth and development. Economy-wide productivity remains low and productive capacities sluggish, making economic growth too weak to generate decent jobs, reduce poverty, and withstand negative external or internal shocks. Several countries in SSA were also caught in perpetual cycles of conflict and political instability as well as facing problems related to governance, corruption, and mismanagement of productive resources. Moreover, demographic changes and transitions, as well as the population growth rates of SSA countries outstripping their real economic growth rates, make them the locus of generalized poverty, which, in turn, acts as a deterrent to economic growth and production transformation (UNCTAD: 2002).

The internal structural handicaps of Africa's economic growth coupled with systemic microeconomic and macroeconomic instability, low investment, poor technological capability, and low capital accumulation translate into weak productive capacities and lack of structural economic transformation. These render economic growth fragile and less inclusive, unsustainable, and vulnerable to external shocks, with heightened risks and uncertainties. These also indicate that partnerships in support of Africa have failed to change the dismal socioeconomic conditions prevailing in the region. Poor economic performance locks countries in a low-level equilibrium (low income, technology, capital accumulation, weak productive capacities, and poverty) which in turn has increased the overdependence of these countries on external assistance, with no impact on structural economic transformation. Dependence on external finance limits the role of sovereign states in formulating and implementing development policies. External resources by their nature are unpredictable, unsustainable, and subject to conditionality and changes in the priorities of donors. Weak states, in turn, are characterized by weak institutions, bad governance, underdeveloped infrastructure, and poor human resources, which collectively make them unable to formulate and implement transformational policies. Such a vicious circle continues unabated if nations fail to foster economy-wide productive capacities and kick-start structural transformation (Chapter 2). Such is the case in SSA.

Available evidence shows that the economies of SSA are the most aid-dependent and yet they are the weakest performers in terms of Gross Domestic Product (GDP) and GDP per capita growth rates (Figure 1.1). For SSA, the Official Development Assistance (ODA) to GDP share is higher than the ratio of the region's export to GDP. On the other hand, top performing South American and Asian regions are the least aid-dependent when compared based on the share of ODA in their respective GDP. During the 2000–2018 period, the average ODA to GDP ratio of SSA was nearly 8 percent, while that of South America and Asia remained at 0.2 and 2 percent, respectively (Figure 1.1). If aid-dependent weaker economies such as Afghanistan, Bangladesh, Cambodia, Lao PDR, Myanmar, Nepal, and Yemen (Asia's LDCs) are removed from the dataset, the Asian region's average ODA to GDP ratio can be as low as that of South America. SSA's overdependence on ODA is even the highest of all the regions when compared with the respective countries' total government expenditures, where the ratio in some cases reaches as high as 65–70 percent on average (see the case studies of Angola and Ethiopia in Chapter 6).

The continuous deterioration of socioeconomic conditions in SSA can be attributed to domestic policy failures and misguided international support measures, which are badly designed or misaligned with the development objectives and priorities of recipient countries. Unfavourable global aid architecture, stringent aid conditionality, complex aid channels, and unfair trade policies, collectively or individually, undermine domestic efforts to foster productive capacities and structural economic transformation. These are parts of the equation in the region's persistent development problems (for more details on this, see also Easterly: 2002, Mkandawire: 1998, 2005a, Moyo: 2009).

Misalignment of development aid results from the motivation behind granting such aid. In most cases development aid is driven by donors' political, diplomatic, or strategic interests (Lumsdaine: 1993). In some other cases, aid is more influenced by moral or ethical considerations than concerns to facilitate the development processes. Development aid itself tends to focus more on addressing short-term imbalances, humanitarian emergencies, crises, and instabilities as opposed to relieving binding constraints to long-term development (Lancaster: 2007). UNCTAD (2006) also argues that development aid has increasingly been concentrated on social sectors, often at the expense of productive sectors of the economy, such as agriculture, industry, or physical infrastructure. This is not to suggest that social sectors are less important than economic sectors but rather to argue that the increasing support provided to social sectors should not be at the expense of economic sectors. Donors and recipient countries must endeavour to rebalance sectoral distribution of development resources (external or domestic) between the social and economic sectors of the economy, with due emphasis on productive sectors to help the fostering of productive capacities and structural economic transformation in recipient countries.

The inherently unbalanced aid allocation, combined with the impact of perennial external economic shocks, has contributed to weak productive capacities and lack of structural economic transformation in SSA. However, the sluggish and dismal socioeconomic performance of the region and its persistently weak productive capacities cannot and should not be attributed to external factors only. There are several internal conditions that contribute to the lack of substantial economic transformation in SSA. These include weak policy formulation and implementation capacities, fragmentation of policies and lack of coordination, inefficient resource allocation and weak institutions, bad governance and macroeconomic instabilities, overdependence on the production and exports of primary commodities, mismanagement of scarce development resources, corruption, and the "natural resources' curse" (Collier and Hoeffler: 2005). Further adverse factors hampering inclusive and sustained economic growth with little or no structural economic transformation include political conflicts and civil strife, ethnic polarization or inter-ethnic conflicts and heightened impact of climate change (World Bank: 2000, 2007, Collier: 2007, Mkndawire: 2015). Consequently, Africa has exhibited slow growth, high capital flight, a risky business and investment environment, weak social capital formation, and dilapidated physical infrastructure (Gunning and Collier: 1999). Unlocking these binding constraints on development through fostering productive capacities and structural transformation, requires concerted efforts to simultaneously address adverse external and internal factors to minimize their impacts on socioeconomic performance of SSA.

The question is: will the emergence of new development partners such as China, result in a different outcome both in terms of Africa's growth prospects and the potential for productive capacities building and structural transformation? The responses to this question depend on careful examination of the uniqueness, specificities, and development experiences of individual African countries and their respective engagements with China. Every country in SSA has its own unique characteristics: geographical, political, historical, demographic, and social circumstances. Resource endowment and starting conditions also vary widely between countries, with potentially important implications for growth and structural transformation. These variations, in combination or singularly, shape or influence the development trajectories of countries. Each country also has different governance systems and structures, different patterns of production and consumption, different sets of micro and macroeconomic conditions, and different productive capacities and capabilities. Therefore, to consider Africa or SSA as a homogeneous group, is tantamount being "reductionist" (Mkandawire: 2015). Their heterogeneity should be recognized that the growth and development paths, as well as experiences of each country, are unique and the factors that influence them negatively or positively are complex and varied.

However, heterogeneity does not prevent the countries of SSA from learning from each other's experiences and from other advanced developing countries. For instance, Asian countries are not homogeneous. However, variations among and between them have not prevented them from learning from one another. South Korea, Singapore, Taiwan, and Hong Kong followed the footsteps of Japan, whereas Malaysia, Thailand, China, and now Vietnam all drew important lessons and benefits from South Korea, and Japan itself. Moreover, the countries of SSA have important similarities, common characteristics, and often identical development challenges. Therefore, for the purpose of this book, SSA is considered as a group throughout the book with emphasis on the aggregate experience of the region rather than an individual country's development experience (henceforth, in the book "Africa" refers to SSA). Case-based examination and deep-dive analysis of the experiences of Angola and Ethiopia[12] are included to complement analysis of regional (aggregate) experience and to minimize potential bias or errors of interpretation in the analysis of aggregate experiences. More individual countries' experiences are also used to illustrate or provide country-specific contexts, challenges, and prospects in fostering productive capacities and structural economic transformation. A deep-dive analysis of Vietnam (Chapters 7 and 8) is intended to draw policy and operational lessons for SSA from its fresh and vast experience in fostering productive capacities and structural transformation. The focus is on how Vietnam identified comparative advantages, and relieved binding constraints to its socioeconomic transformation. Vietnam's experience is particularly needed to see whether there was any role for international support in its development process and how the country tapped bilateral regional and global opportunities, including with China? It is also relevant for the discussions of SSA's development challenges and prospects given historical, political, economic, and ideological similarities with many countries of SSA and China, as well as the relative "freshness" of the country's accelerated growth and transformation.

The main objective of embedding case-based analysis is to minimize selectivity and confirmation bias (Bennett: 2012). It is also intended to avoid the potential risk of misinterpretation that may arise from bundling (as homogenous) the otherwise diverse growth and development experiences of countries of SSA and their economic relations with China. The case-based approach is key to enriching the analysis by providing historical explanations and country-specific context of transformation challenges. By using the World Bank's Enterprise Survey database, the book further discusses firm-level challenges, undermining production transformation and competitiveness in Angola and Ethiopia. This is to assess whether the Africa-China partnership is qualitatively different from the continent's long-standing partnerships with traditional partners such as the EU, USA, or Japan in unlocking challenges at the level of firms or enterprises.

1.1 Changing Development Narratives

Africa's policy or political ambitions have always been to achieve higher economic growth and a stable macroeconomic framework, which were thought to be indispensable for substantial poverty reduction. The focus has been on generating higher growth rates (7 percent or above), with the intention of lifting up GDP and the income of the population. Closer examination and reviews of recent national policies, development plans, and vision documents of several countries in the region still show the heavy emphasis placed on the quantity of growth as opposed to the quality. Such a preoccupation with high economic growth is not accidental. Rather, it is in line with mainstream thinking in development studies that high economic growth increases national output and creates jobs, which, in turn, increase the incomes of households, reduce poverty, and accelerate capital accumulation.

However, exclusive focus on quantitatively higher growth can be misleading. During the commodities super-cycles or boom periods (2001–2007), several countries in SSA indeed achieved higher economic growth rates (exceeding 7 percent on average). These growth rates were short-lived and remained too weak to raise aggregate domestic income or demand, create decent jobs, and substantially reduce extreme poverty. There are several limitations with "quantity-centred" economic growth approaches to development, particularly in SSA: first, achieving higher economic growth rates (quantity) has become the mantra of the political agenda and policymaking process. This has led to an excessive "politicization of growth" and hence growth has become a short-term goal or preoccupation of African political leadership and the policy of governments. For several years, this has undermined efforts to plan for the broad, long-term, sustained, and inclusive growth and development of the region. In short, economic growth was perceived as an end by the policymakers of SSA. There is nothing wrong with this as it has been the case in many developed and newly industrialized economies. As argued by Myrdal, "economic growth, defined as an increase in

GDP per capita, naturally, and necessarily became to the forefront of policy preoccupation" (Myrdal: 1973, p. 182). However, it poses a systemic problem when the importance of the quality of growth is ignored by policymakers. Second, little attention was given to the sources and forms of growth as well as inclusivity and the sustainability of such growth. Africa's growth has generally been "commodity-driven", enclave-based, and vulnerable to the vagaries of external shocks, with little social or economic gains. As a result, African countries have not been successful in substantial job creation, expansion of aggregate income, capital formation, and sustained poverty reduction. Third, the quantity of growth, when attained, leads to "complacency" and shifts the attention of policymakers away from improving the quality of growth and its distributional aspect. It undermines opportunities to catalyze sources and drivers of growth and address the real causes of underdevelopment. Fourth, without appropriate income distribution policies, high economic growth can lead to inequalities. Finally, "growth-centric" approaches have inherent limitations and systemic bias as they are defined in arbitrary and exclusionary ways (Myrdal: 1973). For instance, in the African context, household activities, cross-border trade, or even environmental costs have not been captured in the calculations of national income or GDP. In short, the relationship between high economic growth and substantial poverty reduction is neither automatic nor linear (World Bank: 2000/2001).

In recognition of these limitations, there has been a visible shift in the recent discourses and economic development narratives of SSA. The shift is from focusing on the quantity of growth per se towards paying greater attention to the quality of growth. Achieving quality growth can be facilitated by productive transformation and the dynamics of the growth process (Nubler and Ernst: 2013). High performing growth and transformation processes can be achieved only through interrelated and integrated approaches to develop social capabilities, productive transformation, productive jobs (employment), and domestic enterprises. Such a paradigm shift in development narratives is part and parcel of the quest for long-term and inclusive economic growth and development. This has also been at the centre of domestic policies and strategies of several countries of SSA. Economic transformation through industrialization and capacity development have been integral components of development policies of Botswana, Ethiopia, Kenya, Namibia, Nigeria, and Rwanda, to name but a few countries[13] (UNCTAD and UNIDO 2011, Altenburg: 2010). The Organisation of African Unity (now the African Union) has also put in place a regional initiative in 2001 – the New Partnership for Africa's Development (NEPAD).[14] NEPAD emphasized the need for structural transformation of the continent through investment, industrialization, and economic integration to achieve sustainable growth[15] and development in the region. Internationally, within the United Nations,[16] there has been increasing focus on the fostering of productive capacities and structural economic transformation in weaker developing economies.

Despite the shift in development discourses and corresponding national, regional, and international commitments, effective implementation of these has continued to pose daunting challenges. Consequently, available socioeconomic indicators show that SSA has been continuously lagging behind other developing regions in achieving sustainable and inclusive growth, reducing poverty and improving the livelihoods of the population (Ocampo et al.: 2009, Lin: 2013). The World Bank's poverty data[17] shows that during 1990–2015, the percentage of poor people in SSA has declined from 59.6 percent to 41.4 percent. However, the absolute number of poor people has increased from 303.6 million to 412 million during the same period. Moreover, recent growth data show persistent fragility and vulnerability in the economies of SSA. During 2001–2018, GDP per capita growth collapsed from an average of about 7 per cent before the 2008–2009 global financial economic and financial crises, to an average of about 3.9 per cent, which is about 1 per cent in real growth terms in the post-crises period. The deepest growth collapse in decades SSA was observed during the 2008–2009 crises when GDP per capita grew by less than 4 per cent or about 1 per cent in real terms.This trend has repeated it self during 2015–2016 due to the collapse of international commodity prices. (Figure 1.2).

SSA's persistent vulnerability of growth to external economic shocks reflects a typical "commodity-driven" growth model characterized by weak productive capacities and an absence of structural economic transformation. Such a model also means that the benefits of growth tend to be highly concentrated in a few sectors, undermining the impact on poverty reduction even during the boom period of 2001–2007. The commodities sector (particularly the mining and oil sector) is also rigid and capital-intensive with less propensity to absorb labour or create employment opportunities, further undermining the impact of economic growth on jobs, household income, and poverty reduction. The 2008–2009 financial and economic crises and the resulting growth collapse of SSA show the limit and inherent volatility of the commodity-driven growth model to the vagaries of external shocks. This also makes industrialization and structural economic

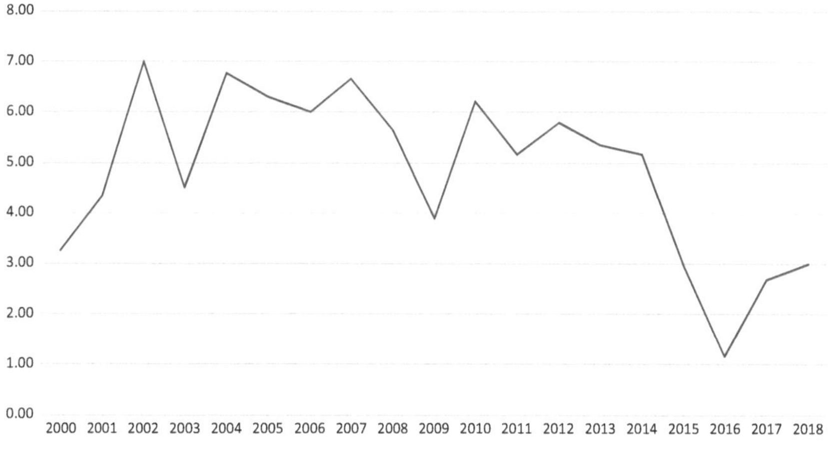

Figure 1.2 Average GDP per capita growth in SSA, constant USD 2010 (2001–2018).
Source: UNCTADstat (2019).

transformation harder to achieve as it leads to the overvaluation of exchange rates, penalizing other sectors of the economy ("Dutch Disease"),[18] high unemployment, and the crowding out of investment opportunities.

The impact of the COVID-19 pandemic and inability of SSA's economies to withstand adverse socioeconomic shocks is the outcome of persistent development challenges facing the region. Although there is no end yet in sight to contain the ravaging consequences of the pandemic, various estimates put the human, healthcare system, and overall socioeconomic cost of COVID-19 on SSA too big to bear, given the already weak socioeconomic foundations of the region. Recent estimates by the United Nations Economic Commission for Africa put the export revenue loss for African oil exporting countries (which includes the largest oil economies from SSA) between USD 65 billion and USD 130 billion for 2020, while up to 3.3 million people could lose their jobs (UNECA: 2020). A further forecast by the World Bank shows that the pandemic will cost SSA between USD 37 billion and USD 79 billion in output loss only in 2020, driving the region into a recession for the first time in more than 25 years, and reversing the modest gain in poverty reduction of the last several decades (World Bank: 2020a). Other estimates (e.g., by OXFAM International: 2019, UNCTAD: 2020c) indicate, respectively, the challenges of food security and significant reduction in FDI inflows to SSA. The severity of the impact of the COVID-19 pandemic is a clear sign of the fragility and vulnerability of SSA's weak socioeconomic fundamentals (i.e., productive capacities and structural economic transformation). While the pandemic has impacted all nations and economies, including major developed economies, the impact on SSA could be severe and may take a significantly longer time for the economy to rebound. Even prior to the COVID-19 pandemic, economic growth per capita in SSA had been volatile and consistently declining (Figure 1.2).

Against the severe impact of a negative external economic environment, SSA's externally imposed policy prescriptions of the 1980s and the 1990s placed heavy emphasis on the domestic causes of poor economic growth in SSA and, hence, prescribed radical policy and institutional reforms. For instance, the focus of trade liberalization policies prescribed and imposed on the countries of SSA was to address domestic gaps and limitations such as policy and institutional inadequacies, administrative weakness, overvalued exchange rates, and prohibitive trade restricting or distorting regulations. That is, adjustment policies placed heavy responsibility for Africa's dismal socioeconomic performance squarely on domestic causes (World Bank: 1981).[19] Excessively inward-looking liberalization policies dogmatically prescribed and implemented in SSA have indeed failed to address external shocks, such as commodity price volatility, recurring oil, and debt crises as well as the 2008–2009 "triple-F" (Food, Fuel, and Financial) crises, which hit Africa's trade and development prospects hard at periodic or intermittent intervals. Surprisingly, after the 1980s and 1990s policy prescriptions and two decades later, the World Bank in its *World Development Report 2000/2001* recognized that market reforms entirely failed in SSA, principally, due to inadequate public investment and excessive bureaucracy, which undermined market reforms (World Bank: 2000/2001, pp. 61–95).

External policy prescriptions widely implemented in SSA were premised on simplified assumptions of the complex factors affecting economic growth trajectories in SSA and by confining them to domestic policy and institutional environments. Undoubtedly, the weakness of Africa's institutional and human resources capacities have had a negative impact on the continent's socioeconomic performances (Franceman: 1998). But these are not the only challenges facing SSA. For instance, the root causes of sluggish economic performance in Africa are the lack of capital accumulation (Darga: 1998), technology, innovation, and productive investment. These factors, which positively or negatively influence the dynamics of economic growth, cannot be fixed by simply embracing the free-market mantra, which has guided SSA's policymaking environment for more than three decades. UNCTAD (2008a) further argues that SSA's weak and vulnerable economic performance is the outcome of erroneous and misguided external policy prescriptions often by the International Financial Institutions (IFIs).

A more perplexing or paradoxical feature of Africa's socioeconomic performance is that, even with the historically high economic growth driven by the commodities boom (Figures 1.1 and 1.2) of the early 2000s, its development trajectories have not shown substantial socioeconomic transformation. This has heightened the search for explaining Africa's economic growth paths and pointed to the inadequacy of the existing conception of development, which in turn, calls for a new development framework (Lin: 2013). Such discourses on development policies signal a paradigm shift away from excessive preoccupation to generate higher growth (quantity) towards a greater emphasis on the quality and sustainability of economic growth. The latter is anchored in "structural fundamentals" – "building productive capacities", and "fostering structural economic transformation". Productive capacities and structural transformation (for more details on the two concepts, see Section 1.2. below) are viewed as key not only for generating broad-based and inclusive economic growth (quality) but also for sustaining it for a longer period (Ocampo et al.: 2009, Lin and Monga: 2014, McMillan and Rodrik: 2011, UNCTAD: 2006).

The increasing focus on productive transformation and related approaches is consistent with earlier works (such as Kuznets: 1966), which argue that sustained economic growth cannot happen without structural transformation. According to Kuznets, countries that remain poor are those which have failed to achieve structural transformation in their economies. Kuznets defined the economic growth of a country as a "long-term rise in capacity to supply increasingly diverse economic goods to its population based on technology, institutional and ideological adjustments that the growing capacity demands". Building on the works of Kuznets and Solow's growth model (Solow: 1956), Acemoglu (2007) provides extensive analysis and empirical evidence on variations in income and development across and between nations. For Acemoglu the difference in income and development between nations is explained by investment in physical capital, human capital, and technological differences. Furthermore, differences in technology between nations reflect genuine differences in the techniques of production and the quality of machines used, as well as differences in production organization, productive efficiency, or "calibrated total factor productivity" (Acemoglu: 2007).

Despite changes in the development discourses towards qualitative growth, the domestic development policies of several countries of SSA are still driven by quantity of growth, and largely focused on incremental poverty reduction approaches as opposed to achieving transformational, inclusive, and sustainable growth and development. Similarly, international support mechanisms such as ODA, market access, and FDI facilitation are not geared towards reducing dependency on aid and transforming economies. Against this backdrop, the question, is: has the recent shift in Africa's trade, development finance, and investment patterns towards China brought qualitative changes in its economic transformation? The book particularly attempts to examine the Africa-China partnership and whether such a shift has positively impacted the continent's growth and development trajectory, anchored in the building of productive capacities, and fostering structural economic transformation, conceptualized as follows.

1.2 What Is Meant by Productive Capacities[20] and Structural Transformation?

There are no universally accepted definitions of the concepts of productive capacities and structural transformation or factors driving the two processes. The two concepts are viewed differently in different theoretical, operational, or analytical contexts. However, this book argues that there are direct relationships and interactions between the two concepts. That is, while productive capacities serve as the foundation for kick-starting the process of structural transformation, it is the latter that augments and sustains productive capacities in the long run. The processes of fostering productive capacities and structural transformation should not be viewed as a sequence or a phenomenon where one follows the other. It should rather be considered as twin processes that go in parallel in a gradual, incremental, and mutually reinforcing manner.

The lack of an agreed definition of productive capacities emanates from the complexity of the processes and the diversity of factors driving the fostering of such capacities and capabilities. It is, for instance, not obvious to what extent productive capacities should refer to existing or potential capabilities. Should fertile, yet uncultivated land, be considered a productive capacity or not? Can untapped natural resources be considered as productive capacities? Can a large population with abundant yet unemployed labour be considered as part of the productive capacities of nations irrespective of income, knowledge, skills, or educational levels? Similarly, institutional[21] conceptualization of the notion is also heterogenous, each institution providing functional definitions within its areas of expertise. Moreover, different schools of thought variously view productive capacities from technological, innovation, and learning systems as key to boosting sectoral or economy-wide productivity, employment, and growth.

A more comprehensive conceptualization of productivities that captures the broadness of the term and diversity of factors influencing it, which is used in this book as a basis, is the one provided by the United Nations Conference on Trade and Development (UNCTAD). UNCTAD defines productive capacities as "the productive resources, entrepreneurial capabilities and production linkages which together determine the capacity of a country to produce goods and services and enable it to grow and develop" (UNCTAD: 2006). Thus, the UNCTAD definition stresses three distinct but interrelated dimensions – productive resources, entrepreneurial capabilities, and production linkages – that make up fundamental elements or pillars of productive capacities. The relevance of each of the pillars is discussed further in later chapters.

The concept of structural transformation,[22] as Kruger (2008) has put it, has often been neglected in theories of economic development. As such, to date, there is not a single unified theory of structural change. Nor is there a universally accepted definition. In this book, the emphasis is on qualitative changes or structural and long-term shifts in productive resources from low value-added, low-technology, and low-productivity economic activities (or sectors) to higher value-added, knowledge-, and technology-intensive higher-productivity economic activities or sectors. These are collectively regarded as structural economic transformation. Therefore, the definition adopted in the book for the concept refers to a qualitative, deep, and long-term shift of productive resources from low productivity, low value-added sectors into efficient production and export of higher value-added, technologically sophisticated goods and services. It is also used to connote a shift from the production and export of low-value primary commodities into higher value-added, from lower-productivity sectors to higher-productivity sectors, etc. The process can take place across different sectors and/or within a given sector of the economy. This broad conceptual foundation is in line with earlier theoretical or empirical approaches to structural economic transformation which emphasize the gradual shift in the employment contributions of sectors, and their relative importance in economic growth, wellbeing, and overall development of nations. Fisher (1939), with his classification of industries based on a hierarchy of needs, and Clark (1957), with a listing of industries based on their common characteristics, provided sector-specific analytical approaches to understand structural transformation. They both argued that a gradual shift in employment and value-added from primary and secondary (usually agricultural and industrial) sectors to the tertiary sector (usually the services sector) is inherent in the process of economic development and structural transformation. The underlying assumption of the Fisher-Clark approaches was that "most services have higher income and lower price elasticity than agricultural or industrial products". The income-price elasticity analogy of the Fisher-Clark model, as a core of structural transformation, can be characterized as a demand phenomenon. That is, with rising income levels, the demand for inferior goods (agriculture and industry) will inevitably be saturated eventually, while the demand for superior services will continue to grow (Kruger: 2008).

A further work on structural transformation, which is directly relevant to the discussions in this book is the one by Vries et al. (2013). The authors' analysis squarely focuses on structural transformation in SSA. Despite the lack of consistent and analytically relevant data, the authors offered conceptual and methodological insights into and perspectives on the process and patterns of structural transformation in Africa over a relatively longer period (1960–2010). According to the authors, the process of structural transformation in Africa has been inconsistent over time and too weak to withstand the impacts of external economic shocks and crises, such as the oil and debt crises of the 1970s and 1980s and the global financial and economic crisis of 2008–2009. Hence, the process and pattern of transformation seen in Africa has not been in line with transformational development as observed in other developing countries, especially Asia. As discussed in Chapters 7 and 8, what has been observed in East Asian economies and recently in Vietnam is the right type of structural transformation, as opposed to the wrong type seen in SSA.

1.3 China in Africa Discourses: What Is New?

The Africa-China partnership, although viewed as new in most recent literature, it is not actually new. Even during the Cold War,

> while the old colonial powers sought to strengthen the special relationship they had formed mostly with their former colonies, the Eastern bloc [the Soviet Union and China] embarked on a major campaign to gain new influence in the new States of Africa.
>
> (Meredith: 2005)

The new features of the current Africa-China partnership, however, is the sheer magnitude, extent, form, and nature, amplified by increasing trade, development finance, and investment flows (in absolute terms). The last couple of decades have also witnessed fundamental shifts within the Africa-China partnership – from old ideological and geopolitical relations to a post-Mao economic partnership (RAND Corporation: 2015). Such a paradigm shift puts trade, development aid, and investment as the "primary drivers of Africa-China relations" and reflects China's growing dominance in global trade and investment. The Africa Centre for Economic Transformation (ACET) (2009) views the growing economic ties between Africa and China as the most significant shift in the continent's economic partnerships in recent history. As indicated in the preceding sections, between 2000 and 2017, Chinese development finance (including loans, grants, and export credits) to African countries surpassed USD 143 billion, with nearly 96 percent destined for SSA.

Regarding international trade, Figure 1.3 shows astronomical increases in merchandise trade between Africa and China. Two and half decades earlier (in 1995), the total exports from SSA to China were less than USD 1 billion, with the share of total exports in GDP of about 1.5 percent. In subsequent years, the total exports from SSA to China have shown steady and exponential growth, reaching the peak of USD 67 billion in 2014, nearly 4 percent of the GDP of the region. Such a rapid expansion in exports to China in recent years was not

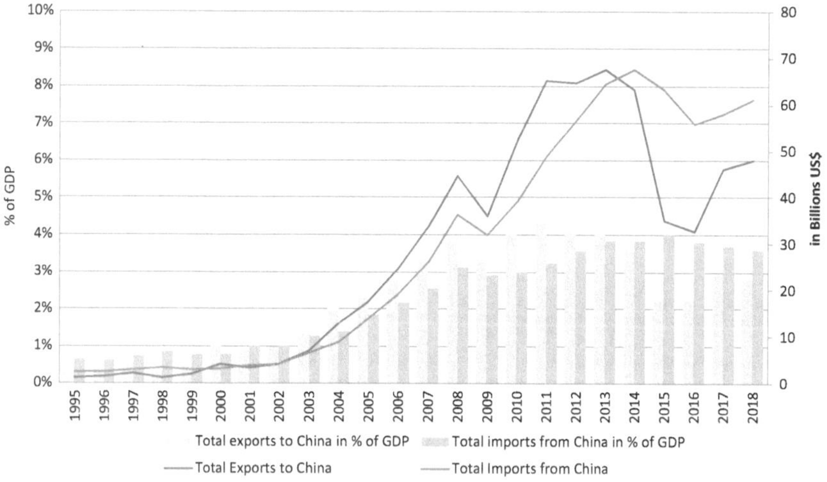

Figure 1.3 SSA's merchandise trade with China (1995–2018), USD billions.
Source: UNCTADstat (2020).

sustained for long. There was a decline after 2012, hitting as low as USD 32.8 billion in 2016 (the lowest level in a decade), although slightly recovered to USD 48.9 billion in 2018. The export share of GDP also declined from the peak of 4 percent in 2012 to a mere 2.2 percent in 2015 and 2.8 percent in 2018. As with exports, imports from China to SSA also shown a steady and exponential growth from relatively the same level as exports in 1995 (less than USD 1 billion) to a whopping USD 67.5 billion in 2015. In recent years, the total value of SSA's merchandise imports from China has decelerated to USD 55.8 billion in 2016 (the lowest level in a decade), which quickly rebounded in 2018 to USD 61.2 billion. Likewise, the import share to GDP climbed from less than 1 percent in 1995 to about 4 percent in 2014 before its modest decline to 3.6 percent in 2018. For almost a decade (2003–2013), Africa had maintained a positive balance in its trade with China. However, in recent years this trend has changed, with China consistently recording a positive balance since 2014. Such instabilities in the international trade of SSA are the outcomes of supply and demand-side problems or challenges. On the supply side, the main ones include low economy-wide productivity, lack of export diversification, absence of value addition or transformation in goods exported, and the continued dependence of SSA on exports of primary commodities, which are vulnerable to the vagaries of negative exogenous and endogenous shocks. On the demand side, the decline in SSA's exports to China is due to sluggish global demand for its unprocessed (primary) commodities and the collapse of international prices of petroleum oil – the commodity which accounts, on average, for more than 40 percent of SSA's merchandise exports to China (see Figure 1.4). The negative trade balance of SSA is expected to be further aggravated as the adverse socioeconomic impact of COVID-19 deepens. Addressing both supply- and demand-side constraints

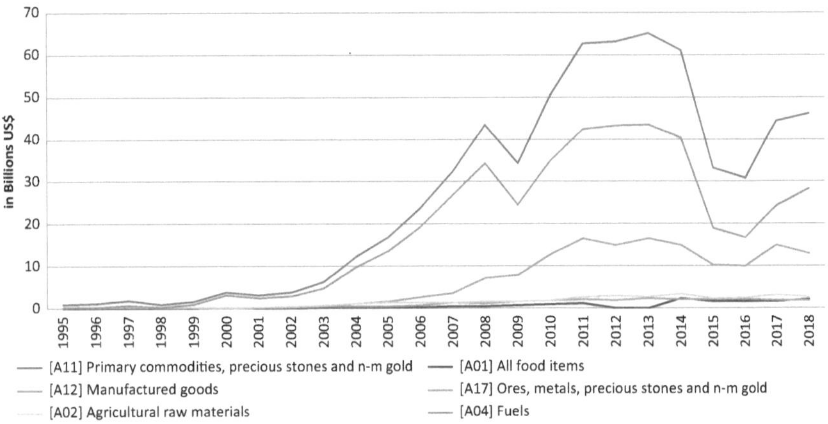

Figure 1.4 Composition of SSA's merchandise exports to China (1995–2018), USD billions.

Source: UNCTADstat (2020).

on SSA's international trade requires the fostering of productive capacities and structural economic transformation. This is vital not only as an economic resilience-building measure but also key to ensure the sustainability of economic growth with significant social outcomes and to reduce excessive dependence of the region on external supports.

For the period 2003–2013, aided by a commodities boom and strong demand from China, SSA had indeed registered a positive trade balance with China, albeit with varying magnitude. However, such a trend paints a different picture in a country-by-country analysis (Osakwe: 2017). The author found that, if Angola is excluded from the panel trade data between China and Africa, the trade balance between SSA and China is in favour of the latter. Angola is the second largest exporter of oil in Africa after Nigeria and the largest trading partner of China from SSA. Without Angola, SSA indeed would incurs a large and growing trade imbalance with China even during 2009–2013. As of 2014, SSA as a region runs trade deficit with China. These growing trade imbalances mean that export earnings are unable to pay for import bills. Therefore, excess imports over exports had to be financed through ODA, direct borrowing, commodity-backed loans, or FDI. The growing trade deficit and the deterioration of the terms of trade of SSA are the result of increasing commoditization of the export structure of the region, which itself is the consequence of weak productive capacities and the absence of structural economic transformation. Heavy and persistent dependence on the primary commodities exports of SSA and the resulting trade deficit heightens the problems of capital outflows, increased indebtedness, persistent poverty, and job losses.

Irrespective of the direction of trade balance of SSA, there is consensus now that China, being the second largest source of world FDI inflows (UNCTAD:2014) and trade after the USA, has emerged as a global economic powerhouse to be reckoned with.

> China's spectacular growth over the past three decades has made the country not only a driver for world trade, investment and development but also a stabilizing force in the world economy as demonstrated by China's role during the East Asian financial crisis of late 1990s and the recent global economic crisis.
> (Lin: 2013)

The key driver of China's unprecedented growth and the convergence of income and prosperity with industrialized economies is the "fostering of structural transformation, characterized by continuous technological innovation, industrial upgrading, capable institutions, including robust role of the State in policy formulation and implementation and well-functioning market conditions" (Lin: 2013).

Africa has undoubtedly been benefiting from a Chinese economic bonanza, despite a growing trade imbalance in favour of China (Obiorah: 2008, Lin: 2013, UNCTAD: 2014, Lopes: 2016). In terms of trade, according to the World Bank, total trade (exports plus imports including trade in services) between China and SSA has grown over 100-fold since 1990. In 2014, Africa-China trade hit USD 222 billion – an amount that is about three times larger than the continent's trade with the USA. This analysis is consistent with the trade figures provided in Figure 1.3, except that the latter shows merchandise exports and imports of SSA to China and vice versa. Regarding the composition of exports, the bulk of merchandise exports from SSA to China are still in primary (high volume, low value) commodities such as precious stones, non-manufactured gold, fuel, agricultural raw materials, and some food items (see Figure 1.4). Production and exports, particularly of agricultural commodities such as coffee, horticulture, and cotton, like manufacturing exports, are key in maximizing dynamic gains in the form of technological learning and upgrading (Hausmann and Rodrik: 2003), generating much-needed foreign currency, and attracting FDI to the agriculture sector. However, there is no disagreement that overdependence on such products for a long time can have adverse impacts on the socioeconomic development of nations and that SSA needs to lower its dependence on exporting primary commodities to stagnant markets (export destinations) to fully harness the potential of trade for improved socioeconomic performance. Africa-China trade relations are still based on African countries exporting primary commodities to and importing value-added technologically sophisticated products from China. Such a trend reinforces the traditional division of labour between the two partners, with SSA continuously supplying raw materials and China serving as a source of value-added, light, or technologically sophisticated manufactured products to SSA. In short, the Africa-China trade pattern and composition is the same as the pattern of trade flows between SSA and traditional developed country partners. Nevertheless, trade between the two has shown unprecedented growth both in terms of volume and value. "Africa-China economic relations are generally of greater importance to African States than to China as China-Africa trade accounts for 15 percent of African States' total but just 5 percent of China's total trade" (RAND Corporation: 2015). However, there is no doubt, that SSA needs to build its productive capacities and export competitiveness, lower trade and transport costs, and modernize its infrastructure in order to maximize socio-economic benefits from the growing relations with China (Mbekeani: 2007).

The increasing magnitude (both in volume and value) of trade between China and Africa is also driving Chinese FDI inflows to SSA. However, the real impact of these on industrial outputs and manufacturing exports from SSA is yet to materialize on a substantial scale. Data show that during 2001–2015 Chinese FDI flows to Africa increased from USD 1 billion to USD 5.6 billion, before declining to less than USD 3 billion in subsequent years. In 2017–2018, the annual flows rebounded, reaching close to USD 4 billion. In terms of FDI stock, in 2016, with USD 42 billion on aggregate (see Table 4.1, Chapter 4), China was the second largest investor in Africa after the European Union (EU28). In a country-by-country review, the main (historically) FDI home countries of SSA (the United Kingdom and France) have lost substantial ground to China in recent years. In terms of FDI,[23] the United Kingdom and France each accounted for 5 percent in 2017, while the share of China amounted to 23.9 percent in the same year. As with exports, FDI inflows from China to SSA are still heavily concentrated in extractive sectors, although the share of infrastructure has been on the rise in recent years. During 2006–2014, the sectoral distribution of China's total FDI in SSA shows 41.3 percent in metals, 40.2 percent in energy, 9.2 percent in finance, 5.7 percent in real estate, 1.8 percent in transport, 0.6 percent in agriculture, and 1.1 percent others. Such a pattern in trade and investment reveals starkly similar patterns with long-standing trade and investment relations with the European Union, the USA, and Japan.

The most recent data (see Table 4.1, Chapter 4, and Figure 5.8, Chapter 5) shows that Chinese FDI stocks and flows have been evenly distributed across the countries of SSA, irrespective of extractive resource endowments. Moreover, according to the 2018 figures by the American Enterprise Institute's Chinese Investment Tracker, sectoral distribution of Chinese investment in SSA has changed in recent years. In 2018, the share of transport, power and metals, and real estate accounted for 33 percent, 33 percent, and 11 percent, respectively. A further interesting trend to be noted relates to the Chinese development finance (grants, concessional loans, and export credits), which amounted to about USD 135 billion during 2000–2017 (see Table 4.2, Chapter 4). Not only the sheer magnitude but the sectoral distribution of development finance (as defined in this book) has shown a significant shift, with the transport, communications, power (electricity), and mining sectors accounting for a substantial share (see Figure 4.6, Chapter 4). In addition to increasing Africa-China economic ties, are there any policy lessons that African countries can draw from the new and fast-growing relationship with China? China's successful experience in lifting more than half a billion people from abject poverty in a short period of time is exemplary for many developing countries including those in SSA (Obiorah: 2008).

Africa-China economic relations have shown an unprecedented increase in volume and value terms. However, it should be noted that, as opposed to the quantity, it is the quality of trade and investment and development finance that drives and sustains growth in output and exports with substantial impact on job creation and poverty reduction. Therefore, it is timely to investigate if these growing partnerships are any different from the continent's long-standing relations with developed economies. Are Africa-China relations qualitatively different form the continent's relations with EU, USA, and Japan? Will China's engagement in Africa facilitate or hinder "productive capacity building" and "structural economic transformation" in SSA? What are the policies and strategies needed to make Africa-China economic relations robust and mutually beneficial?

1.4 SSA and Its Traditional Development Partners (EU, USA, Japan)

SSA has been receiving substantial development and humanitarian (emergency) aid, as well as technical assistance, over the years from bilateral and multilateral sources. However, massive aid flows have not changed the socioeconomic fundamentals of recipient countries, with a huge gap between aid inflows and economic performance (Figure 1.1). SSA's trade and investment relations with the EU, USA, and Japan are also one of the oldest, which are further discussed and closely examined in Chapter 5. Besides financial aid, the countries of SSA also enjoy preferential trade and facilitated investment relations with the European Union, including through the EU-African Caribbean Partnership (ACP) Agreements, the legislative mandate, which dates to the 1957 Treaty of Rome. The underlying aim in granting Africa preferential treatment appears to be to strengthen post-colonial "bondage" between Africa and European colonial powers so that the continent's "directed specialization" as a source of raw materials remains unchanged (Oloruntoba: 2011).

Following in the footsteps of the EU, the USA also provides preferential investment and trade benefits to Africa through the Africa Growth and Opportunity Act (AGOA) mainly to maintain and strengthen its global dominance and hegemony in the continent but more importantly to ensure and protect its broader political, security, and economic interests (Congress Research Service [CRS] Report: 2008). The USA is also an important source of ODA to several countries of SSA, with increasing allocations to the social sectors. The US Millennium Challenge Account (MCA), which initially targeted 24 developing countries, includes 12 countries from SSA[24] (CRS: 2006, Owusu: 2007). The target countries are selected on the basis of a complex set of criteria, which consist of 16 indicators,[25] covering three broad areas: good governance, investing in people (education and health), and fostering economic freedom (by promoting open markets, sustainable budget, private sector, and entrepreneurship). While the MCA has been viewed as an important US initiative in support of developing countries since the Marshall Plan[26] (or European Recovery Programme) of 1948 and the Latin America-focused Alliance for Progress[27] of the 1960s, it suffers from a series of systemic problems. These include complex eligibility criteria, cumbersome bureaucratic processes to apportion and release resources, inadequacy of funds, and excessive lethargy (US House of Representative, 28 June 2007). As with the EU and the USA, Japan also provides substantial economic assistance to the countries of SSA with the view to supporting the region's socioeconomic transformation. The relationship between Japan and Africa is more "experimental" than economic or trade-based relations (Wild: 2011), where the former devotes more attention to the transfer of its successful development experiences whereas the latter remains the market for a transfer of such experiences. Notwithstanding substantial development aid flows, preferential market access for exports, and investment arrangements through various schemes,[28] the socioeconomic performance of SSA has generally remained poor, weak, and vulnerable. Aid, investment flows, and preferential market access granted to SSA by traditional development partners have failed to boost the region's productive capacities and structural economic transformation and trigger socioeconomic benefits to the continent. This is due to structural impediments facing SSA but more importantly due to several additional factors, such as problems in the design and composition of international support mechanisms; increasingly complex technical or non-trade barriers, selection bias and stringent conditionality attached to development aid, and the preferential trade arrangements offered to the region by its trading or development partners. These are discussed in greater detail in Chapter 5 of the book.

Against this backdrop, it seems now that the emergence of some countries of the South, notably China, gives a fresh and renewed hope to the growth and development prospects of SSA. As hinted above, China has increasingly become an important trade and development partner for many countries of SSA. At a time when global trade policies have stalled, protectionism is rising, and global investment confidence remains shaky, such dynamism from China is remarkable and unprecedented. It is also vital for SSA's production transformation centred on or driven by productive capacities and structural economic transformation. However, as much as there are opportunities, there are also challenges that should be overcome for SSA to take full advantage of its growing trade and investment ties with China. Putting in place the right policies and strategies (at micro and macroeconomic levels), building institutions, improving governance and the quality of partnership should be among the main issues that need to be addressed at the national and international levels (Chapter 9). SSA should use such growing partnerships with China to lay the foundation for transformation with the aim of achieving inclusive and sustainable growth with decent jobs creation and significant poverty reduction.

Notes

1 Conceptually, vulnerability to shocks is used throughout the book to denote systemic risks and uncertainties as well as fragility that result from multidimensional external or internal shocks – be they economic, financial, or health related – that adversely impact economic growth or output, export earnings, government revenues, production and supply networks, employment, health, and education outcomes, as well as income opportunities in an economy including firms, households, and individuals. Often, systemic or structural vulnerability can be regarded as paranormal and beyond the control of sovereign economic entities.

2 For this book, SSA consists of 48 countries: Angola, Benin, Botswana, Burkina Faso, Burundi, Cameroon, Cape Verde, Central African Republic, Chad, Comoros, Congo, Côte d'Ivoire, Democratic Republic of Congo (DRC), Djibouti, Equatorial Guinea, Eswatini, Ethiopia, Gabon, The Gambia, Ghana, Guinea, Guinea-Bissau, Kenya, Lesotho, Liberia, Madagascar, Malawi, Mali, Mauritania, Mauritius, Mozambique, Namibia, Niger, Nigeria, Rwanda, Sao Tome and Principe, Senegal, Seychelles, Sierra Leone, Somalia, South Africa (is not included in the analysis), South Sudan, Sudan, Tanzania, Togo, Uganda, Zambia, Zimbabwe. Mayotte, Reunion, St Helena, and Western Sahara are not considered in the list in the context of the present book.

3 These include: the US-Africa Leaders and Business summits, European Union-African Union summits, Canada-Africa Business summits, India-Africa summits, Forum on Africa China Cooperation (FOCAC) summit, Tokyo International Conference on Africa's Development (TICAD), Russia-Africa summits Arab-Africa summits, and Turkey-Africa Summit.

4 Detailed data is available at http: //www.sais-cari.org/data-chinese-loans-and-aid-to-africa.

5 The concept of least developed countries was developed during the inception stages of the United Nations Conference on Trade and Development (UNCTAD), whose earlier work documented that not all developing countries are at the same or comparable level of economic development. Differentiation within the developing countries led to the identification of the weakest and most vulnerable groups of countries called least developed countries (LDCs), a significant majority of which are in SSA. UNCTAD's seminal work ultimately recognized by the United Nations General Assembly, which officially established the group by its resolution 2768 (XXVI) of 18 November 1971.

6 The Human Assets Index (HAI) is a composite index consisting of six health- and education-related indicators: under-five mortality rate, maternal mortality rate, percentage of people undernourished, gross secondary school enrollment, and adult literacy rates.

7 The Economic Vulnerability Index (EVI) is composed of demographic, geographic, and economic indicators: size of population, share of population in low elevation coastal areas, remoteness, merchandise export concentration index, export instability, and instability of agricultural production.

8 As a rule, countries that meet or exceed the threshold levels for at least two of the three criteria at two consecutive triennial reviews are recommended to graduate (or exit) the group of LDCs. In exceptional circumstances, when the GNI per capita exceeds the threshold level by two-fold, irrespective of progress or lack thereof on the other two criteria (HAI and EVI), countries can also be recommended to graduate by an "income only" criterion.

9 The World Bank does not use or follow the United Nations classification of countries such as LDCs. Instead, the Bank uses its own classification which is based on Gross National Income per head (GNI per capita) calculated by the Bank's Atlas method. Accordingly, for the 2021 fiscal year, low-income economies were defined as those with a GNI per capita of USD 1,035 or less in 2019; lower middle-income economies between USD 1,036 and USD 4,045; upper middle-income economies between USD 4,046 and USD 12,535; high-income economies with USD 12,536 or more in the same year (www.data.worldbank.org).

10 Angola is scheduled to graduate in 2021 (but was extended by one year due to the impact of COVID-19), Bhutan (2023), Sao Tome and Principe (2024), Solomon Islands (2024), and Vanuatu (2020).

11 The current list of LDCs include Afghanistan, Angola, Bangladesh, Benin, Bhutan, Burkina Faso, Burundi, Cambodia, Central African Republic, Chad, Comoros, Democratic Republic of Congo (DRC), Djibouti, Eritrea, Ethiopia, Gambia, Guinea, Guinea-Bissau, Haiti, Kiribati, Lao People's Democratic Republic, Lesotho, Liberia, Madagascar, Malawi, Mali, Mauritania, Mozambique, Myanmar, Nepal, Niger,

Rwanda, Sao Tome and Principe, Senegal, Sierra Leone, Solomon Islands, Somalia, South Sudan, Sudan, Timor-Leste, Togo, Tuvalu, Uganda, United Republic of Tanzania, Yemen, and Zambia (see www.unctad.org, www.undesa.org, or www.un.org/ohrlls).

12 Angola and Ethiopia are chosen because of their robust partnership with China, their historical and socioeconomic similarities as well as differences (see the discussions in Chapter 6).

13 The Growth and Transformation Plans (GTPs of Ethiopia), The Rwanda We Want Vision 2050 document of the Government of Rwanda, and the Sustainable Development Agenda of Botswana are but a few of domestic policy documents and visions in SSA that articulate sustainable and inclusive economic growth through productive capacities and structural transformation.

14 The New Partnership for Africa's Development (NEPAD) was adopted at the 37th session of the Assembly of African Head of States and Governments in July 2001 in Lusaka, Zambia. NEPAD was designed to provide a coherent and consistent framework for the formulation and implementation of policies and strategies aimed at accelerating economic growth, enhancing cooperation, and deepening economic integration among African countries.

15 Sustainable development conceptually is understood as socioeconomic development that meets the needs of the present generation through judicious use of existing resources, without compromising the ability of future generations to meet their own needs (for more details, see the Report of the World Commission on Environment, usually called the Brundtland Report but formally entitled *Our Common Future*, available at www.sustainabledevelopment.un.org).

16 The Programme of Action for Least Developed Countries (LDCs) for the Decade 2011–2020, adopted by the Fourth United Nations Conference on LDCs held in 2001 (A/Conf.2019./3/Rev.1), and that of the Landlocked Developing Countries (Vienna Programme of Action for LLDCs for the Decade 2014–2014) adopted by the Second UN Conference held in 2014, identified productive capacities and structural economic transformation as key to achieving inclusive and sustainable economic growth and development in the two groups of countries.

17 The World Bank's poverty data are based on primary household surveys obtained from governmental statistics agencies and World Bank country offices. The Bank computes the poverty headcount ratio at USD 1.90 a day in 2011 PPP (percentage of population).

18 In economics, "Dutch Disease" refers to an economic instability or crisis that arises because of the discovery of vast natural resources, such as oil, natural gas, and other minerals, and when such newfound wealth leads to currency appreciation, a decline in exports, and an increase in imports as well as job losses. The paradox penalizes sectors such as agriculture, manufacturing, and tourism by making the production and services costly and uncompetitive internationally. The term entered economics literature in the mid-1970s when the discovery of natural gas in the Netherlands in 1959 caused the value of the Dutch Guilder to rise sharply, making Dutch exports of all non-oil products less competitive on the world market.

19 The World Bank's 1981 study entitled *Accelerated Development in Sub-Saharan Africa*, usually referred to as the Berg report (named after its main author, the US economist Elliot Berg), prescribed significant currency devaluation, deregulation, and trade liberalization including elimination of what was then perceived as distortions on agricultural production, industrial goods, and trade. Consequently, Structural Adjustment Programmes (SAPs) and Poverty Reduction Strategy Papers (PRSPs) widely prescribed and implemented in SSA, respectively, in the 1980s and 1990s.

20 Throughout the book productive capacities are used in plural form to denote different capacities in an economy.

21 For instance, the World Trade Organization (WTO) views productive capacities from trade-centric approaches. For the United Nations Industrial Development Organization (UNIDO) the concept is viewed as industry or manufacturing sector focused as measured by global industrial or manufacturing competitiveness indices developed by UNIDO. The conceptual analysis of productive capacities by the United Nations Economic Commission for Africa (UNECA) focus more on the role of regional trade integration and inter-regional infrastructure as the foundations for building productive capacities. The United Nations Development Programme (UNDP) and the World Bank meanwhile work with approaches and perspectives that are more centred on human resource capacities or social capabilities.

22 In this book, the phrases "structural economic transformation", "structural transformation", "production transformation", or "transformation" are used interchangeably. Whenever "structural change" is used in the book, such a change refers to a short-term quantitative change or a shift in the economy as opposed to long-term structural transformation.

23 All FDI statistics are from The American Enterprise Institute and the Heritage Foundation, China Global Investment Tracker. Available at: http://www.heritage.org/research/projects/china-global-investment-tracker-interactive-map/china-global-investment-tracker-interactive-map.

24 These are Benin, Burkina Faso, Cape Verde, Ghana, Lesotho, Mali, Madagascar (later dropped), Mozambique, Namibia, Tanzania, The Gambia, and Senegal.

25 These are based on the World Bank's Governance indicators and the Doing Business Ranking as well as various other existing indices such as the World Heritage Foundation's Index of Economic Freedom. The initiative's eligibility assessment is based on composite indicators, consisting of control of corruption, voice and accountability, government effectiveness, rule of law, civil liberties, political freedom (measures of good governance); public spending on education and health as percentage of GDP, primary girls' education completion rate, and immunization rates for DPT and measles (measures of investing in people component); and inflation rate of lower than 15 percent, fiscal policy, trade policy, regulatory policy, days to start business and cost of starting business (used to measure economic freedom). Countries to qualify as "compact-eligible" should have values above the mean score on the composite index.

26 The Marshall Plan was a US four-year (1948–1951) aid plan conceived and advanced by US Secretary of State George C. Marshall in 1948 to rebuild war-devastated Western Europe (see Magid: 2012).

27 The Latin America-focused Alliance for Progress is the initiative of US President, John F. Kennedy, which was launched in 1961 for the period of 1961–1969 and designed to establish economic cooperation between the USA and Latin America (see Field: 2018).

28 These include schemes such as (a) the partnership agreements between EU and ACP; (b) the Everything But Arms (EBA) initiative of the EU in favour of the least developed countries – the majority of which are in Africa; (c) the Africa Growth and Opportunity Act (AGOA) and the Millennium Challenge Account of the USA; and (d) the Japanese Generalized System of Preference (GSP) for Africa's exports.

Bibliographical references

Acemoglu, D. (2007). *Introduction to Modern Economic Growth.* Department of Economics, Massachusetts Institute of Technology. Available at: https://www.theigc.org/wp-content/uploads/2016/06/acemoglu-2007.pdf

Altenburg, T. (2010). *Industrial Policy in Ethiopia.* German Development Institute, Bonn, Germany.

Africa Center for Economic Transformation-ACET. (2009). Looking East: China-Africa Engagements, Ghana Case Study, ACET, Accra, December 2009.

Bennet, A. (2012). Case Study Methods: Design, Use, and Comparative Advantages. Available at: https://minorthesis.files.wordpress.com/2012/12/andrew-bennet-case-study.pdf.

Brooke-Smith, R. (1987). The Scramble for Africa. In: *The Scramble for Africa: Documents and Debates*. Palgrave, London. https://doi.org/10.1007/978-1-349-08995-6_1.

Carmody, P. (2007). Competing Hegemons? Chinese versus American Geo-Economic Strategies in Africa. Iowa State University, Community and Regional Planning Publications. Available at: http://lib.dr.iastate.edu/communityplanning_pubs.

Collier, P. (2007). *The Bottom Billion: Why the Poorest Countries are Falling Behind and What Can Be done About It*. Oxford University Press, New York.

Collier, P., and Hoeffler, A. (2005). Resources Rents, Governance and Conflicts. *Journal of Conflict Resolution*, 49(4), 625–633.

Clark, C. (1957). *The Conditions of Economic Progress*. McMillan & Co., London.

CRS. (2006). Millennium Challenge Account: Implementation of a New US Foreign Aid Initiative, 2 June 2006. Congressional Research Service. The Library of Congress.

CRS. (2008). Comparing Global Influence: China's and US Diplomacy, Foreign Aid, Trade, and Investment in the Developing World. Congress Research Service Report. The Library of Congress.

Darga, A. (1998). A comparative Analysis of the Accumulation Process and Capital Mobilization in Mauritius, The United Republic of Tanzania and Zimbabwe. *African Development in A comparative Perspective*. UNCTAD, Studies No. 3.

Easterly, W. (2002). *The Elusive Quest for Growth: Economist's Adventures and Misadventures in the Tropics*, First MIT Paperback Edition. The MIT Press, Cambridge, MA.

Field, T. (2018). Alliance for Progress (1961–69). https://doi.org/10.1002/9781118885154.dipl0008.

Fisher, A. G. B. (1939). Primary, Secondary and Tertiary Production. *Economic Record*, 15(1), 24–38.

Fransman, M. (1998). The Relevance of East Asian Institutions Designed to Support Industrial and Technological Development in Southern African Countries. *African Development in A comparative Perspective*. UNCTAD, Studies No. 10.

Gunning, J., and Collier, P. (1999). Why has Africa Grown Slowly? *Journal of Economic Perspectives*, 13, 3–22. http://doi.org/10.1257/jep.13.3.3.

Hausman, R., and Rodrik, D. (2003). Economic Development as Self-Discovery. *Journal of Development Economics*, 72(2), 603–633.

Hettne, B. (1983). The Development of Development Theory. *Acta Sociologica*, 26(3/4), 247–266. https://www.jstor.org/stable/4194484.

Hepburn, C., O'Callaghan, B., Stern, N., Stiglitz, J., and Zenghelis, D. (2020). Will COVID-19 Fiscal Recovery Packages Accelerate or Retard Progress on Climate Change? Smith School Working Paper 20-02.

Hopkins, A. G. (1993). Blundering and Plundering: The Scramble for Africa Relieved. (Review Article). *Journal of African History*, 34, 489–494.

Krüger, J. J. (2008). Productivity and Structural Change: A Review of the Literature. *Journal of Economic Surveys*, 22(2), 330–363. https://ssrn.com/abstract=1105176; http://doi.org/10.1111/j.1467-6419.2007.00539.x.

Kuznets, S. (1966). *Modern Economic Growth: Rate, Structure and Spread*. Yale University Press, New Haven, CT.

Lancaster, C. (2007). *Foreign Aid: Diplomacy, Development, Domestic Politics*. University of Chicago Press, Chicago, IL.

Lin, J. Y. (2013). *New Structural Economics – A Framework to Re-Thinking Development and Policy*. The World Bank, Washington, DC.

Lin, J. Y., and Monga, C. (2014). The Evolving Paradigms of Structural Change. In *International Development: Ideas, Experience and Prospects*. Edited by B. Currie-Adler, R. Kanbur, D. Malone, and R. Medhora. Oxford University Press, New York, 277–294.

Lopes, C. (2016). Reinserting African Agency into Sino-African Relations. *Strategic Review for Southern Africa*, 38(1), 50–68.

Lumsdaine, D. (1993). *Moral Vision in International Politics: The Foreign aid Regime, 1949–1989*. Princeton University Press, Princeton, NJ.

Magid, J (2012). The Marshall Plan. *Advances in Historical Studies*, 1, 1–7. https://doi.org/10.4236/ahs.2012.11001.

Mbekeani, K. (2007). The role of Infrastructure in Determining Export Competitiveness. Framework Paper. Available at https://pdfs.semanticscholar.org/18c3/941e006fc1f3f60dce786854837bd99fc435.pdf?_ga=2.5002291.1652695529.1585833181-894806755.1563973926.

McMillan, M., and Rodrik, D. (2011). Globalization, Structural Change and Economic Growth. In *Making Globalization Socially Sustainable*. Edited by M. Bachetta, and M. Jansen. International Labour Organization, Geneva, 49–84.

Meredith, M. (2005). *The Fate of Africa: From the Hopes of Freedom to the Heart of Despair (A History of 50 Years of Independence)*. Published in the United States by Public Affairs.

Michalopoulos, S., and Papaioannou, E. (2011). The Long-Run Effects of the Scramble for Africa. *American Economic Review*, 106. http://doi.org/10.1257/aer.20131311.

Mkandawire, T. (1998). Thinking About Developmental States in Africa: African Development in a Comparative Perspective. UNCTAD, Studies No. 9.

Mkandawire, T. (2005a). Maladjusted African Economies and Globalization. *Africa Development*, 30(1), 1–33.

Mkandawire, T. (2015). Neopatrimonialism and the Political Economy of Economic Performance in Africa: Critical Reflection. *World Politics*, 67, 1–50.

Moorsom, T. L. (2010). The Zombies of Development Economics: Dambisa Moyo's "Dead Aid" and the Fictional African Entrepreneur. *Review of African Political Economy*, 37(125). Social Movement Struggles in Africa, September 2010, 361–371. https://www.jstor.org/stable/25767283.

Moyo, D. (2009). *Dead Aid: Why Aid is not Working and How There is a Better Way for Africa*. Douglas & McIntyre, Vancouver.

Myrdal, G. (1973). *Against the Stream: Critical Essay on Economics*. The Macmillan Press Ltd. London, U.K.

Naoroji, D. (1969). Cited in Hettne (1983). The Development of Development Theory. *Acta Sociologica*, 26(3/4),Saga Publication, 247–266.

Nordic Africa Institute. (2018). Africa's Mineral Economies: Breaking their Dependence on Mining. Policy Note No 6, Nordic Africa Institute (NAI), October 2018.

Nubler, I., and Ernst, C. (2013). Creating Productive Capacities, Employment and Capabilities for Development: The case of Infrastructure Investment. In *Beyond Macroeconomic Stability*. Edited by Islam et al. International Labour Organization, Palgrave Macmillan, London, 198–227.

Obiorah, N. (2008). *Rise and Rights in China-Africa Relations*. African Studies Programme, The Johns Hopkins University, School of Advanced International Studies, Washington, DC.

Ocampo, J. A., Rada, C., and Tayler, L. (2009). *Growth and Policy in Developing Countries: A Structuralist Approach.* Columbia University Press, New York.

OECD. (2019). *Development Aid at a Glance Statistics by Region: Africa 2019 Edition.* Organization for Economic Cooperation and Development. Available at: https://www.oecd.org/dac/financing-sustainable-development/

Oloruntoba, O. S. (2011). Paternity or Partnership EU-ACP Economic Partnership Agreement and Implications for Nigeria's Non-oil Sector. PAS Working Papers Number 21.

Osakwe, P. (2017). Enhancing the Impact of Chinese Development Finance for Sustainable Poverty Reduction in Africa. In *Foreign Capital Flows and Economic Development in Africa.* Edited by E. Wamboye, and E. A. Tiruneh. http://doi.org/10.1057/978-1-137-53496.5_4.

Ouma, S. (2012). The New Scramble for Africa. *Regional Studies: The Journal of the Regional Studies Association.* 46. http://doi.org/10.1080/00343404.2012.691237.

Owusu, Y. F. (2007). Post-9/11 U.S. Foreign Aid, the Millennium Challenge Account, and Africa: How Many Birds Can One Stone Kill? *Africa Today*, 54(1) (Fall, 2007), 3–26. https://www.jstor.org/stable/27666872.

OXFAM International. (2019). More than 52 Million People Across Africa Going Hungry as Weather Extremes Hit the Continent, November 2019. OXFAM International. Available at: https://www.oxfam.org/en/press-releases/more-52-million-people-across-africa-going-hungry-weather-extremes-hit-continent.

Oyeranti, A. O., Babatunde, M. A, Ogunkola, E. O., and Bankole, S. A. (2010). The Impact of China-Africa Investment Relations: A Case Study of Nigeria. The African Economic Research Consortium (AERC), Nairobi, Kenya, 28 February 2010. AERC Collaborative Research on China-Africa.

Pakenham, T. (1991). *The Scramble for Africa, 1876–1912.* Weidenfeld and Nicolson, London.

RAND Corporation. (2015). China's Expanding African Relations: Implications for U.S. National Security. Available at: www.rand.org.

Solow, R. M. (1956). A Contribution to the Theory of Economic Growth. *The Quarterly Journal of Economics*, 70(1), 65–94.

UNCTAD. (2002). *Least Developed Countries 2002 Report. Escaping Poverty Trap.* United Nations Publication, New York and Geneva.

UNCTAD. (2006). *The Least Developed Countries 2006 Report: Developing Productive Capacities in Least Developed Countries.* United Nations Publication, New York and Geneva.

UNCTAD. (2008a). *The Least Developed Countries 2008 Report: Growth, Poverty and Terms of Development Partnership.* United Nations Publication, New York and Geneva.

UNCTAD and UNIDO. (2011). *Economic Development in Africa 2011 Report: Fostering Industrialization Development in Africa in the New Global Environment.* United Nations, New York and Geneva.

UNCTAD. (2014). *World Investment Report 2014.* United Nations, New York and Geneva.

UNCTAD. (2020c). Investment Trends Monitor: Impact of the Coronavirus Outbreak on Foreign Direct Investment (FDI). Available at: https://unctad.org/en/PublicationsLibrary/diae_gitm34_coronavirus_8march2020.pdf.

UNCTADStat. (2019, 2020). Available at: https://unctadstat.unctad.org/EN/.

UNECA. (2011a). Minerals and Africa's Development: The International Study Group Report on Africa's Mineral Regimes, November 2011.

UNECA. (2020). *Covid-19 in Africa: Protecting Lives and Economies*. United Nations Economic Commission for Africa, Addis Ababa.

U.S. House of Representatives. (2007). The Millennium Challenge Corporation in Africa: Promise Versus Progress, 28 June 2007. Hearing Before the Subcommittee on Africa and Global Health, Committee on Foreign Affairs, House of Representatives, One Hundred Tenth Congress, First Session, 28 June 2007, Serial No. 110–82.

U.S. Geological Survey. (2014). Available at: https://www.usgs.gov/centers/nmic/mineral-commodity-summaries.

Vries, G. J. D., Timer, M. P., and Vries, K. D. (2013). Structural Transformation in Africa: Static Gains, Dynamic Losses. GGDC Working Papers, Vol.GD-136. University of Groningen, GGDC.

Wild, L. (2011). *Informing the Future of Japanese Official Development Assistance (ODA): Japanese ODA within an African Context*. The Oversees Development Institute, London.

World Bank. (1981). *Accelerated Development in Sub-Saharan Africa: An Agenda for Action*. Washington, DC, World Bank.

World Bank. (2000). *Can Africa Claim the 21st Century? April 2000*. The World Bank, Washington, DC.

World Bank. (2000/2001). *World Development Report 2000/2001. Attacking Poverty*. The World Bank, Oxford University Press., New York.

World Bank. (2007). *Challenges of African Growth: Opportunities, constraints, and Strategic Directions, 2007*. The World Bank., Washington, D.C.

World Bank. (2020a). For Sub-Saharan Africa, Coronavirus Crisis Calls for Policies for Greater Resilience, 9 April 2020. World Bank Group. Available at: https://www.worldbank.org/en/region/afr/publication/for-sub-saharan-africa-coronavirus-crisis-calls-for-policies-for-greater-resilience.

2 Why does Productive Transformation Matter for SSA?

2.1 Importance of Productive Capacities and Structural Transformation for SSA

The discussions in Chapter 1 show that productive capacities and structural transformation, irrespective of the factors driving them, are critically important for generating inclusive economic growth and accelerating development. While productive capacities are sine qua non for the fostering of structural transformation, the latter is equally vital for augmenting and sustaining productive capacities or capabilities in an economy. There are several further mutually reinforcing commonalities between the two concepts and processes that (i) their operationalization requires an abundance of productive resources such as labour in the subsistence (agricultural) sector and their movements towards the industrial (manufacturing) sector. Such shifts of labour and other factors of production across sectors gradually lead to production transformation, capital formation, and technological progress; (ii) the type and scale of productive capacities and the pace of structural transformation are dependent not only on the factors of production but also on policies, institutions, and growth acceleration processes; (iii) employment, especially in labour-intensive manufacturing, is key for absorbing excess labour from subsistence agriculture – the process which leads to better wages, capital accumulation, technological progress, and growth of output; (iv) country-specific conditions and resource endowments are key to build firm-level and/or industrial capabilities including social and institutional capabilities, which are important ingredients in the growth-facilitation processes; (v) knowledge and skills, technology, physical infrastructure (including electricity and Information and Communication Technology (ICT)), and the role of the state are key in kick-starting industrialization and structural transformation, especially in the early stages of development; and (vi) the nexus between trade and investment, including export diversification and competitiveness, particularly through manufacturing, is vital for developing productive capacities as a basis for economic growth and development. Despite the specifics and the particular attention given to each of these ingredients, one can observe two broad and competing paradigms towards fostering productive capacities and structural transformation (McCombie: 1983): the supply-oriented and the demand-oriented paradigms. Whereas the former articulates the role of factors of inputs (productive resources)

DOI: 10.4324/9781003295334-2

in limiting or facilitating the growth of output, the latter dwells on the demand factors. For the demand-oriented approach, capital accumulation is as much the result of output growth as the cause. Hence, capital accumulation has never been a limiting factor in economic growth (McCombie: 1983) and structural or production transformation.

The research and debate on labour productivity and other factors of production emphasize the crucial role of these in generating and sustaining economic growth and development. They particularly underscore the importance of productive resources in the subsistence (agriculture) sector that ought to be absorbed in the capitalist (industrial) sector to accelerate capital formation and technological progress. That is, country-specific conditions and endowments of natural resources are key to various productive capabilities – be they at firm level and/or industrial-scale capabilities, including social and institutional capabilities. The state can also play a proactive role in accelerating productive capacities, generating employment, building infrastructure, and kick-starting the process of industrialization. These are fundamental for growth and development processes, especially in the early stages of development, which free markets alone cannot provide. Among the many problems of the free market system which were widely prescribed to countries of SSA in the 1980s and 1990s are the series of general assumptions it made. These include assumptions such as that countries have comparative advantages and productive capacities to harness them; financial and monetary systems function well; and that they have institutions capable of guiding policies and strategies based on market signals (demand and supply) as well as rules of engagements (e.g. property rights) in place. Unfortunately, almost all of the countries in SSA where such assumptions do not hold true were pressured to embrace free market systems through multiple structural economic and institutional reform programmes: liberalization, stabilization, and privatization – which are designed to undercut the role of the State.

The interrelationships between productive capacities and structural transformation on the one hand and the role of the State in recalibrating production transformation on the other hand show that factors influencing economic growth and development trajectories vary and that the development process is long and complex. This is particularly the case when it comes to income convergence and technological catch-up between industrial economies and developing countries, such as those in Africa. How long, complex, and challenging a development process may be, there is consensus that the key for achieving inclusive growth and development is the fostering of productive capacities and structural transformation. The core in the notion of productive capacities is the embodiment of complex factors and diverse capabilities in the production and growth processes. These include technological capabilities; a vibrant and dynamic private sector; capable institutions and human resources to acquire, use, and disseminate technologies; a Developmental State which can recalibrate the development process by tapping opportunities and harnessing the potential of natural capital. These elements in combination will determine the speed, depth, extent, and scale of structural transformation in an economy. An important question is why productive capacities and structural transformation matter for SSA. There could be as many replies to this pertinent question as there are diverse schools of thought and perspectives. Building on existing research and analysis and drawing from recent development experiences and trajectories of countries such as Vietnam, the following five broad justifications in support of production transformation merit serious consideration.

First, productive capacities and structural transformation matter for achieving accelerated economic growth and development, which is conceptualized or defined differently in diverse theories and schools of thought. Despite the variation in conceptualization, socioeconomic development is a complex, gradual, and incremental creation of income and wealth with benefits to individuals and societies. It is the outcome of sustained economic growth, continued capital formation, higher productivity of the factors of production, and consistent production transformation. Development also means augmented overall investment in generating sustained and long-term economic growth that creates decent jobs, enhances prosperity for all, and consistently improves the quality of lives of citizens. Therefore, development is impacted, positively or negatively, by an interplay of a range of factors such as productive resources, technology, human capital, entrepreneurial capability, production linkages, and guiding institutions. These key elements collectively determine the quality and form of growth as well as sustain it for a long period for the satisfaction of the present generation without compromising the needs of future generations. Productive capacities (as argued in this book) are the causes and consequences of development in a virtuous circle where productive capacities lead to inclusive economic growth and development and vice versa.

Countries and economies that fostered the requisite productive capacities, such as those in East Asia, are the ones that transformed their economies and lifted up the living standards of their citizens in a relatively short period. These are also the countries that have been catching up or converging with traditional developed or industrialized economies in income, wellbeing, and technological advances. SSA's lack of socioeconomic progress and persistent vulnerability to various shocks is the outcome of weak productive capacities and a lack of deeper production transformation or structural economic transformation. As shown in Figure 2.1, while developed countries are in the higher-level equilibrium on the Productive Capacities Index (PCI)–Gross Domestic Product (GDP) distribution, countries of Africa (except Botswana and Mauritius) are locked in a low-level equilibrium trap (meaning a vicious circle of low productive capacities and low development outcomes). With a strong correlation coefficient (R = 0.87) almost all countries in SSA are on the bottom of the distribution. While high correlation does not indicate causality between the two, certainly higher productive capacities are positively correlated with higher GDP, with important policy implications for the operationalization of the productive capacities – structural transformation narratives, which are discussed in this book and recommendations contained in Chapter 9.

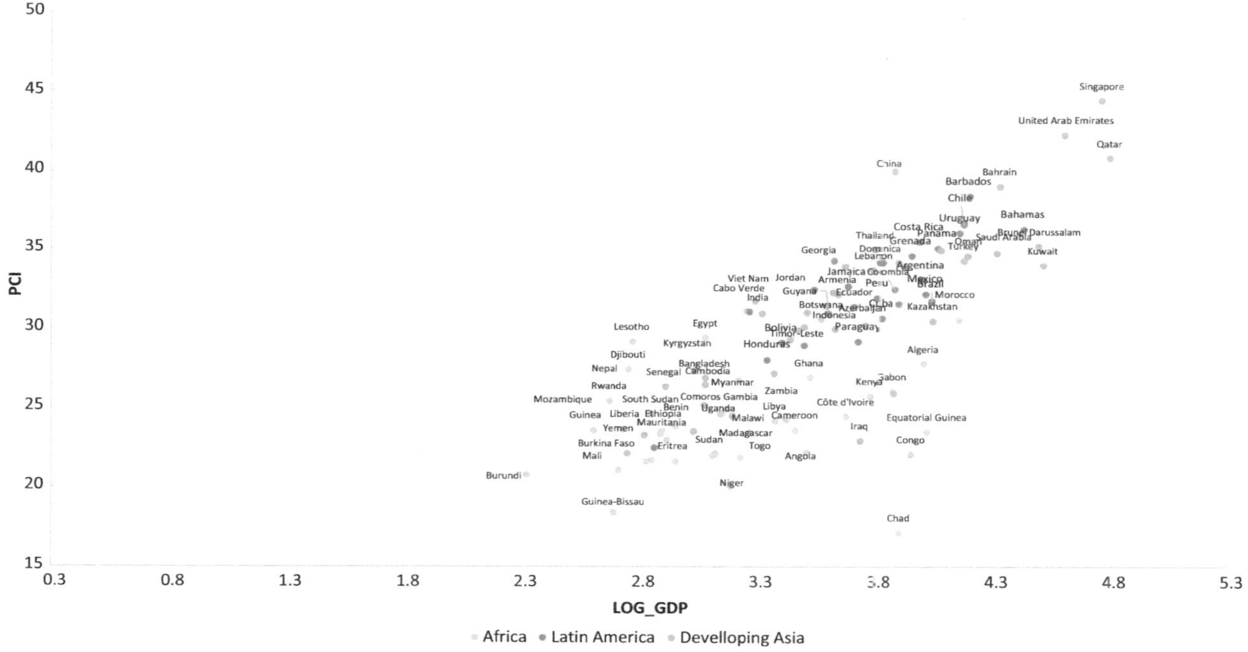

Figure 2.1 Correlation between PCI and log of GDP per capita (R = 0.87): Africa, Asia, and Latin America.

Source: Computed from the UNCTAD PCI and GDP dataset (2021).

Second, breaking overdependence on foreign aid requires the fostering of productive capacities and structural transformation. Limited and fragile economic growth leads nations to dependence on external financial, technical, or humanitarian assistance. In the poorest countries of the world, most of which are in SSA, aid dependency (measured as percentage of aid in GDP or total government expenditure) is the highest with little impact on economic growth and development. The growth performance of the most aid-dependent economies of SSA is the lowest when compared to economies that receive relatively smaller external aid in all its forms (Figure 1.1). In the absence of accountability and oversight mechanisms, aid exacerbates inequality instead of generating growth and narrowing gaps between the poor and the rich. In some countries where the overall governance, transparency, and management of aid resources have improved, this has not been complemented by sustained economic growth and improved absorptive capacities. Hence, the impact of aid on poverty reduction is short-lived. This is largely due to cyclical socioeconomic shocks that drag down more people into poverty than the number of poor lifted by aid. Debates on the development impact of aid are inconclusive. However, there has been a substantial body of literature that affirms that governments that increasingly depend on foreign aid to finance their expenditures (such as those in SSA) are less accountable to their citizens. Evidence shows that in such countries, aid has an undesired impact on institutional development and capability to address poverty and food insecurity (Moss et al.: 2005, Castel-Branco: 2008, Bishop and Hilhorst: 2010). Aid dependency and weak absorptive capacities can also undermine the policy-making capacities of recipient countries and shift priorities away from development towards political governance or social issues. The politics of development aid, stringent aid conditionality, and complex aid channels have undermined the development effectiveness of aid and marginalized institutional and policy-making capacities in recipient countries. While Asian countries such as South Korea have successfully tapped the development impact of foreign aid (perhaps with less conditionality, such as cooperating to halt the advances of socialism) in the same manner as post-WWII European countries did with the US Marshall Plan (see Chapters 1 and 5), the countries of SSA have miserably failed to do so. The role of Western aid agencies and trade policies pursued by developed countries has continuously marginalized the recipient countries of SSA in effective trade policy formulation, implementation, and industrialization (UNCTAD: 2006, Oya: 2006). Development aid has also become a business with a significant proportion of aid resources being allocated for the consultancy industry. For instance, according to the financial report of FY2021,[1] Price Waterhouse Coopers – known for its consultancy, audit, and quality-assurance services – recorded a total net revenue of USD 45.4 billion in 2021 – three times the amount it had generated in 2003. Out of the 2021 revenue, advisory services alone accounted for USD 17 billion. The annual net revenue of the firm, by far, exceeds the GDP of most countries of SSA. Foreign aid is also susceptible to changes in political or diplomatic relations between donors and recipient countries.[2] More troubling for recipient countries is an increasing importance donors attach to their aid agencies and non-governmental organizations (NGOs), particularly international ones in ensuring not only fungibility of aid resources but also in promoting accountability and transparency of development aid over African governments and institutions. This has created hidden and, at times, explosive relations, contentions, and frictions[3] between donors, recipients, and NGOs. There should be an understanding that while civil society entities can and will play an important role in contributing to development efforts of countries of SSA, they cannot replace or substitute legitimate national governments and institutions. The discussions of Vietnam's experience in Chapters 7 and 8 can provide a useful guide or starting points for cementing constructive relationships between African public institutions, local and international NGOs. Donors should avoid being seen as perpetuating aid dependency or using "aid-dependency trap diplomacy" in SSA. They should ensure mutual accountability, linking aid resources to national programmes or priorities and rebalancing development aid that goes to economic and social sectors. It is unfair to put all the blame on donor governments and their institutions for aid-dependency syndrome in SSA. Recipient governments also have crucial roles and responsibilities in making aid work for development, and more importantly, for building productive capacities so that they become self-sufficient.

Third, productive capacities and structural transformation are indispensable to ensure sustained growth, job creation, and poverty reduction. Economic growth in the countries of SSA remains weak with little or no impact on job creation and poverty reduction. Such persistent and systemic weakness of growth had to do with the form and quality of growth. Growth in SSA can be spectacular, as observed during the commodities boom of early 2000s, but it is short-lived. Commodity-driven growth patterns collapse with the downward trends of international commodity prices, with disastrous consequences for government revenues and their capacities to finance development projects or programmes. The key to address such adverse consequences of negative external shocks on economies and societies is through export diversification, value addition, and overall structural economic transformation. However, transformation remains elusive in SSA, even in countries that are known for their high-quality policies and institutions such as Botswana. In Botswana, despite high-quality successive policies of diversification (Economic Diversification Drive), the country's economy is structurally dominated by the mining sector, which, on average, has contributed to about 22 percent of total GDP over the recent decades. Diamonds are the dominant mineral of Botswana, and the revenues earned from their sale represent more than 90 percent of all mining activities. The export concentration index of Botswana remains one of the highest in the world with an average of above 90 percent during 2000–2018, which means that 90 percent of the country's export earnings is derived from one or two commodities (see Chapter 4). As with Botswana, the Zambian economy remains significantly dependent on the mining and export of copper, with ores and metals accounting for 71 percent of its exports in 2019, which has left the economy vulnerable to fluctuations in the copper price for most of its post-colonial history. The cause of the lack of diversification, value addition, and overall structural transformation in the economies of SSA is their weak or underdeveloped productive capacities. This notwithstanding, countries rich in the natural resources in the region such as Botswana, Angola, and others have huge potential to capture the natural resources rent in fostering economy-wide productive capacities. This includes tapping the potential in other sectors such as agriculture, agri-processing, and manufacturing where they have comparative advantages. It is equally important for these countries to re-balancing their incentive structures between foreign investment companies and the domestic private sector as well as strive to foster productive and business linkages between domestic and foreign firms. As shall be discussed in more detail in later chapters of the book, in several countries of SSA, current incentive structures are geared towards attracting foreign direct investment (FDI). Hence, they are grossly tilted in favour of foreign firms, undermining the growth, expansion, and competitiveness of their own domestic private sector, which remains largely informal, micro, or consisting of small and medium-sized enterprises.

Fourth, breaking the low- and middle-income traps cannot be achieved without developing productive capacities and kick-starting structural transformation. SSA's lag in multidimensional PCI is an indication of the weak productive capacities of the region, which is behind multiple depravations, growing inequality, and structural vulnerability to the vagaries of negative shocks. Asia's developing countries that made significant improvements in their productive capacities in recent years, but which were on more or less equal levels of income as SSA in the 1960s and 1970s, have managed to quickly break the low- and middle-income traps and moved to upper- and higher-income categories. On the contrary, the countries of SSA remain locked either in the low-income or in middle-income categories despite the fact that they possess greater endowments of natural resources than the Asian economies. Asian countries' advantages early in the transformation stages were only in their labour force or human capital (Chapters 7 and 8). As shown in Figures 2.2 and 2.3, for three decades (from 1987 to 2017) and considering 1987 as a base year, Asian countries quickly moved up the income ladder. For example, except India and Vietnam, most countries of Asia moved out of the lower-middle income category to upper income (two levels) in less than 20 years. It took the same number of years for India and Vietnam to move out from lower-middle income just to middle income (one level). These two countries are yet to break the second trap (from the middle to upper middle-income category) but they seem to be on course although it is difficult to tell when. While several factors can come into play, including the size of population and quality of economic growth, nevertheless, improved productive capacities and deeper structural transformation have played an important role in helping Asian economies to quickly break the low-income traps than many developing countries in the world (Figure 2.2).

In the case of countries of SSA (Figure 2.3), only very few countries such as Botswana have managed to reach upper middle-income category thanks to its diamonds, better institutions and income distributive policies. Most countries of the region are locked in the low-income trap. It has taken more than 25 years for Kenya, 20 years for Nigeria, and 17 years for Côte d'Ivoire to move from the

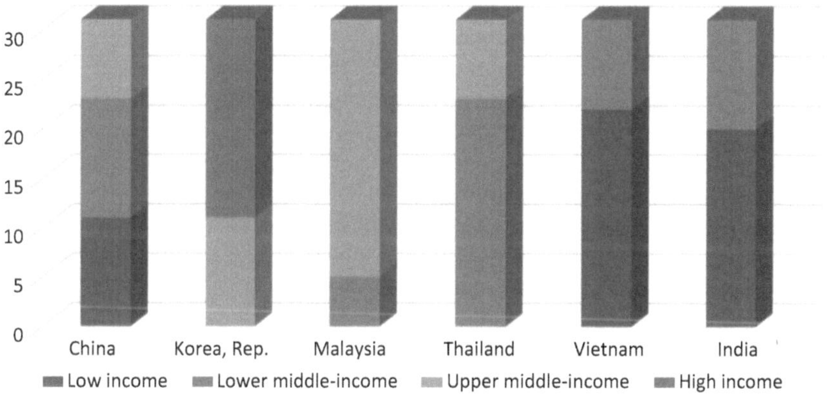

Figure 2.2 Breaking income traps: how long will it take? The case of selected Asian countries (1987–2017).

Source: Computed from the World Bank Classification by Income (2020).

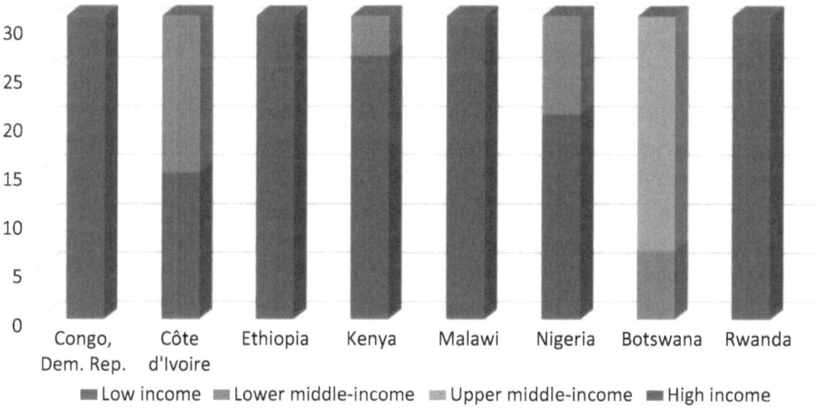

Figure 2.3 Breaking income traps: the case of selected African countries (1987–2017).

Source: Computed from the World Bank Classification by Income (2020).

low-income category to the lower middle-income category. The fear is that, if such trends continue, it may even take a much longer laps for these countries to break the middle-income trap and move to the upper middle-income category. Most countries of the region, including the Democratic Republic of Congo (DRC), Ethiopia, Malawi, or Rwanda have remained locked in a low-income trap for the last three decades. As is discussed in Chapters 3 and 4, the latter group of countries significantly lags behind the rest of the developing countries in fostering economy-wide productive capacities and kick-starting structural economic transformation.

Lastly, productive capacities matter for enhancing human capacities and improving overall wellbeing. Economic growth should be inclusive, which means that its benefits should be shared as equitably as possible among all citizens. This is because that inequality within and between nations not only impedes social and political stability but also weakens the productivity of the factors of production, entrepreneurship, productive linkages, and overall productive capacities. One way to make growth inclusive is to reduce the vulnerability of households and individuals not only through income or asset-building but also by making education and health accessible to citizens, particularly to the poor and most vulnerable sections. Building human capital is a vital ingredient in socioeconomic transformation – not only as a factor of production but also a propeller of total factor productivity in a given economy. This requires better-quality institutions and deliberate policies to improve access of citizens to education and health opportunities. Universal access to education and health is among important non-income indicators to test the degree of inclusivity of economic growth, although data[4] could be patchy and inconsistent across countries and over time. Measuring human capital by using indicators of income, education, and health is key to assessing the transformational and inclusive nature of economic growth. Such growth is qualitatively different from the quantity of growth and critically important in generating decent wages, income, and enhancing investment in vital social sectors (education and health) as well as infrastructure. Over the last couple of decades, African countries and their development partners have substantially increased expenditure on education and health in absolute terms and achieved significant progress, particularly in terms of universal access and coverage. However, as is discussed in Chapter 3, despite increased public expenditure on education and health, Africa's lag behind other developing regions in human capital formation is significant. In fact, the gap between Africa (notably SSA) and the rest of the developing regions in human capital has widened over the last nearly two decades, showing that a lot remains to be done in improving such an important area in SSA. Consequently, most countries in SSA (except Botswana, Mauritius, and Seychelles) find themselves in a low-level equilibrium on the distribution of the PCI and human development index (HDI) of the United Nations Development Programme[5] (Figure 2.4). That is, low productive capacities are associated with low human development outcomes and vice versa.

The congregation of countries of SSA in a low-level equilibrium on the PCI and HDI distribution will have several profound policy implications for Africa's policymakers and development partners, including China. First, an increase in public spending on education and health is still inadequate and urgent measures should be taken to further bolster the relative share of the two sectors as a percentage of each country's GDP or public expenditures. Opening opportunities and providing the necessary support to increase the participation of the private sector in education and health services, including through Public-Private Partnership (PPP) can help to bridge the investment gap. Second, the countries of SSA should also invest in technical skills in a manner consistent and commensurate with the fostering of productive capacities and structural transformation. In some countries of the region such as Botswana, the coverage of education and

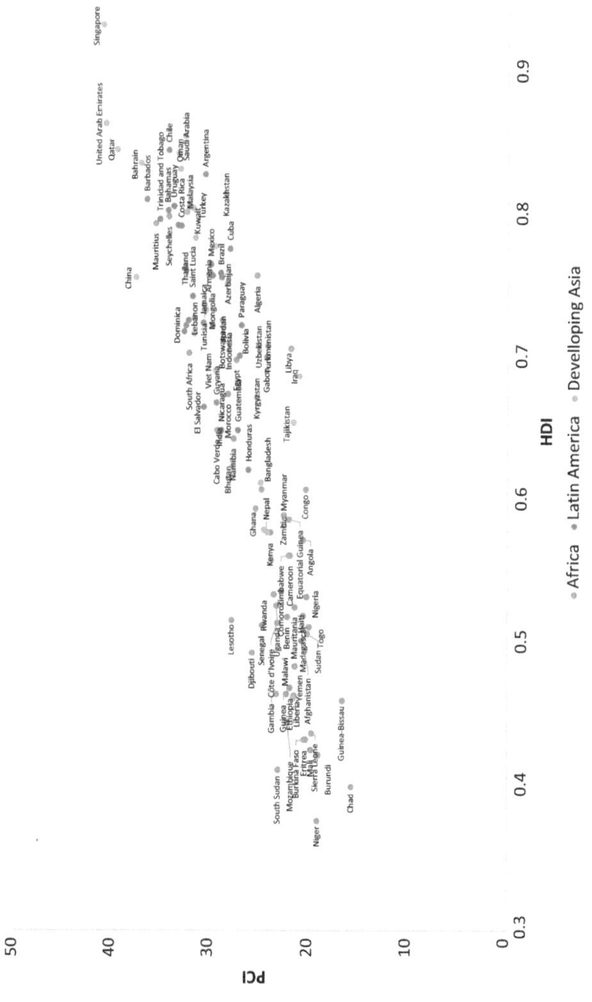

Figure 2.4 Correlation between PCI and HDI (R = 0.9).

Source: Computed from UNCTAD PCI and the HDI database of UNDP (2021).

health has improved tremendously, however, there is skill mismatch between the educated labour force and the requirements of the economy. While Botswana has produced highly educated labour force, still there is a paucity of mining engineers, surveyors, and technicians. Rwanda is another country that has boosted access to universal primary and secondary education and introduced a new curriculum that focuses on ICT, science, technology, engineering, and mathematics (STEM) – which, if fully implemented will be key to addressing the skills and knowledge gap existing in the country.

From the above discussions, building productive capacities and kick-starting the process of structural transformation are key for SSA to achieve inclusive growth, decent employment opportunities (with poverty reduction), breaking dependency on external aid and lower-income traps. However, currently, the level of productive capacities in the region is too low to have any impact on these key development outcomes. There is stark variation in comparative regional performances and the lag of SSA on key benchmarks and indicators of development. SSA remains locked in a situation of socioeconomic vulnerability, a low-income category, and overdependence on external aid. While these are the consequences of weak productive capacities and lack of structural transformation, they can also act as barriers for production transformation. The policy conclusion is that, if such weakness is not urgently addressed, the chance for SSA to escape poverty and relaunch inclusive and sustainable development will be very unlikely or difficult. Consequently, the vicious cycle of low productive capacities and low development outcomes that has characterized SSA for long in the past may continue in perpetuity into the future as well. In sum, the region will continue lagging behind the rest of the developing region in all measures of production transformation, capital accumulation, and wellbeing. The questions that must be carefully responded to are: will the Africa-China partnership help SSA to unlock itself from underdevelopment? How can SSA tap into opportunities associated with China's rise and its outstanding socioeconomic performance? The following section provides broad perspectives, arguments, and counterarguments to these and related questions.

2.2 Evolution of Africa-China Partnership

Debate on the Africa-China partnership is still sparse, inconclusive, or inadequate. This is due, partly, to the fact that the focus thus far has been on the need to understand the modus operandi of Chinese interests and engagement in Africa and the implications of this to global policymaking at large. On the other hand, there is excessive focus on the "quantitative" shift in Africa's trade, investment, and development finance relations away from the traditional North towards China. This aspect of the discourses ignores or overlooks the importance of examining qualitative shifts in Africa-China partnerships. This, in turn, has undermined opportunities to provide objective and evidence-based policy guidance and direction to make the growing relations impactful and beneficial to change Africa's weak socioeconomic performance. This notwithstanding, political, social, or ideological relationships between Africa and China are long-standing and have been increasing both in scale, scope, and intensity over the recent decades. Africa-China relations during the Cold War era were driven by Chinese interest to gain political influence on and strategic presence in the new states of Africa – most of which were emerging out of centuries of colonialism. This was in contrast to the interest of colonial powers whose primary objective was to strengthen the special relationships they had formed mostly with their former colonies. These ties between Africa and China have continued to expand as China emerges as a global player by becoming the trade and investment powerhouse in the developing South (see Ajakaiye: 2006, Cheru and Obi: 2010, Lin: 2012, Sun: 2014).

Politically, China seeks Africa's support for its "One China Policy"; ideologically, it finds Africa a fertile ground for replication of its growth and development model based on "self-imposed socialism" and the concept of post-socialist Developmental State (Bolesta: 2015) as a challenge to the prevalent and indeed dominant Washington Consensus. In the sphere of economic relations, China seeks to satisfy its growing demand for energy (oil), other raw materials, and market opportunities to fuel its own economic growth (Sun: 2014). Sun (2014) further argues that the principles[6] adopted by China in its economic and technical assistance to Africa were designed to simultaneously compete with "imperialists" (USA) and "revisionists" (USSR) alike and were aimed at advancing China's political and strategic interests on the continent and in the developing South. China's increasing economic ties with Africa as much as they raised hopes and expectations, also heightened suspicion, scepticism, and criticism. This is mainly because the increasing trade, finance, and investment relations between China and Africa will have ramifications for Africa's relations with the West and other emerging (economic) powers (Cheru and Obi: 2010).

From an optimistic perspective, Africa-China relations have created ample economic opportunities for African countries that have largely been long neglected by other investors and financiers. ACET report (2009) stresses that the growing ties between Africa and China signal the most significant shift in the continent's economic partnerships in recent history. Consequently, fragile and conflict-ridden states in Africa and in some cases neglected sectors such as agriculture, forestry, and infrastructure received renewed attention in the Africa-China relationship. The ACET report further argues that Chinese FDI has created new jobs in manufacturing and mining, while China actively supports training and research facilities in several African countries, which can serve as the bedrock for economic growth and transformation. In some corners,[7] Chinese engagements in Africa are also considered as remedial to the erroneous neoliberal socioeconomic prescriptions that seriously weakened state institutions and their capacities to formulate and implement policies and strategies – which in turn hampered the continent's progress towards fostering productive capacities and structural transformation.

Africa's political leaders are also equally optimistic about their countries' respective partnerships with China (Quartz Africa, 5 September 2018). Africa's political leaders[8] generally view the Africa-China partnership as deeply transformational and as based on mutual respect as on mutual interest. In sum, the

50 African heads of state and government, attending the 2018 FOCAC summit unequivocally expressed satisfaction with and strong conviction that their respective countries' relationships with China were mutually beneficial and supportive of their economic growth, socioeconomic transformation, and development. Furthermore, African leaders see that their countries prefer Chinese development partnership because China attaches no political conditionality or strings to its partnership. Overall, there is growing convergence among the proponents of the optimistic views (economic researchers, academics, and politicians alike) that a wide-ranging engagement of China in Africa's development can fuel the continent's progress towards fostering productive capacities and structural transformation as key for ensuring sustained economic growth and development. However, there is a divergence of views between African politicians (governments) and their civilian population on matters of Africa-China relationships. Some anecdotal evidence suggests that there is growing dissatisfaction among the civilian population in some African countries. Lopes (2016) states that, despite largely positive and growing economic and political ties between China and Africa, there was evidence of dissatisfaction in West Africa (particularly in Cameroon, Ghana, and Nigeria) regarding Chinese expatriates involved in local business. The dissatisfaction seems to have arisen in countries where Chinese entrepreneurs began to provide local consumer goods, competing and undermining local entrepreneurs that are technologically backward, inefficient, and financially weak.

Another aspect of the negative views of ordinary citizens of several African countries relates to an increasingly growing presence of Chinese migrants and/or expatriates in Africa, although there is no reliable and official data or statistics at least from the African countries. There is no doubt (at least intuitively) that relevant Chinese institutions, such as Ministry of Commerce, Foreign Affairs, and Immigration offices could have such data and statistical information, even though these have not yet been publicly available. The lack of official data raises speculation and forces analysts to rely on various estimates, which are not consistent, reliable, or comprehensive. Regarding Chinese migrants in Africa, estimates vary between 200,000 and 2 million (MPI Newsletter, 21 July 2021). While estimates (by the Chinese Academy of Social Sciences) put the figure at 1 million (see Wang: March 2014), another estimate (by the China Africa Research Initiative at Johns Hopkins University) indicates that in 2018 as many as 202,689 Chinese expatriates were working in Africa, largely in Chinese State-Owned Enterprises (SOEs), as private contractors or for firms operating on the African continent. These estimates mask the actual number of Chinese workers as they do not include those in family-owned or personal businesses, voluntary services, military, or disguised security personnel present in several African countries. Further studies conducted under the Africa-China project (Park: 2009, Oya and Schaefer: 2019) each provided different estimates of Chinese workers in Africa, respectively, between 580,000 and 800,000, and 200,000–240,000. All the estimates not only vary significantly in magnitude, but they are also low when compared to the presence of Chinese in other developed countries and given the long-standing relations between China and Africa. However, considering the scant employment opportunities available in SSA and given the unemployment challenge facing the countries of the region, close to hundreds of thousands of additional Chinese workers can be quite striking.

Regarding African migrants and/or expatriates in China, some studies reveal that the growing numbers of Africans are migrating to China seeking business opportunities or pursuing government scholarship opportunities, although there are no consistent official data and statistics. The Migration Policy Institute (MPI) estimates that more than 17,000 students from 50 African countries have been given Chinese Government Scholarships since the 1950s, more than 3,700 in 2006 alone. Although available data is inconsistent or incomplete, an estimated 500,000 African migrants lived in China in 2019 with tens of thousands living in major cities such as Guangzhou, Beijing, and Shanghai (MPI: 20 July 2021).[9] On balance, it can be said that there are more Chinese migrants and expatriates in Africa than African migrants and expatriates in China, despite huge disparities in terms of economic power and opportunities between the two.

Africa-China relations also raised serious criticism and pessimism in some parts of the world. Outside of the African continent, there are growing pessimistic, suspicious, or sceptical perspectives – predominantly in the USA and Europe. These are based on claims of unbalanced economic relations between China and Africa and the motivation behind it. In the USA, both in academic and public opinions, the growing economic ties between China and Africa (or the Chinese influence) are viewed as destructive to the long-standing ("hegemonistic") interest of the USA in Africa. China's role in Africa is also considered in the USA as undermining to the all-round efforts of the West in building a democratic political system and institutions in Africa (Schoeman: 2008). Recent hearings[10] (Meservey: 2018) of the various House Subcommittees and the Committee on Foreign Relations of the US Senate on Chinese influence in Africa and by the newly created US-China Security Review Commission[11] reinforce the long-standing position of the USA on increasing Africa-China ties as detrimental to improving governance and human rights situations in Africa. This emanates largely from the fact that Western nations (particularly the USA) attach political conditionality (such as governance, human rights, or democracy) to economic and trade-related assistance they extend to African countries. In sharp contrast to the West's political conditionality to development aid, market access, and technical assistance, the Chinese approach to partnership with Africa is based on non-interference in the domestic political and institutional arrangements of the African countries.

The concerns of Europeans on the growing influence of China in Africa – though similar to that of the USA – are much broader in scope, covering economic, political, and environmental aspects (Chari and Corbridge: 2008). According to Chari and Corbridge (2008), the EU views Chinese unfettered engagement in Africa as a form of political, economic, and environmental exploitation of the continent. China's aggressive pursuit of its global interest and influence, often in partnership with other emerging economies of the South, notably Brazil, India and, to some extent Russia, may undermine Europe's historical colonial relations and Western value systems in Africa (see also Schoeman: 2008). Economic and political ties between China and some states considered rogues by the West (such as Sudan and Zimbabwe) are particularly viewed as detrimental to the ongoing democratization processes of the African states. Woods (2008) argues that China's growing influence in Africa is marginalizing the role of established aid institutions such as the World Bank, regional development banks, and other donor agencies that place rigorous standards, principles, conditions, and terms on the use of development aid.

For the Europeans, China's growing involvement in the African continent may exacerbate and prolong Africa's various socioeconomic crises (Berger: 2007). Berger further concluded that China repeated European post-colonial strategies of asserting influence and shackling African countries into dependency. Dahoun and Raffinot (2012) also raised some concern about the growing indebtedness of some African countries despite the fact that most SSA countries have been benefiting from Multilateral Debt Relief Initiatives (MDRIs). Although there is a paucity of quantitative and qualitative data on Chinese loans to Africa, there is growing concern that the debt stock of several African countries has indeed been substantially increasing (Chiwanza: 2018). Accordingly, Angola, Cameroon, Congo, DRC, Ethiopia, Ghana, Kenya, Nigeria, Sudan, Tanzania and Zambia were the top ten countries of the region with substantial debt stock owed to China in 2018. These views are consistent with earlier arguments (Woods: 2008) that loans from emerging countries, largely from China to low-income countries, is exacerbating their indebtedness. Zambia with a debt to GDP ratio of more than 120 percent became the first country in SSA to default its debt owed to China in 2020- amid COVID-19. This led to the coinage of "Debt Trap Diplomacy" to describe the increasing Chinese loans to African countries and the growing indebtedness of several countries of the region.

In between the Africa-China optimism and pessimism lie (somewhat) realistic and pragmatic views or perspectives. Ayers (2012) dismisses the West's narrative of the new "Scramble for Africa" and mischaracterization of growing Africa-China economic ties as purely parochial, chauvinistic, and hypocritical. According to Ayers, such negative or pessimistic views are predicated on problematic, substantive, theoretical, and ontological assertions. In a similar discussion, Adem (2016) argues that despite unavoidable structural distortions, at least in the short run, China's increased involvement in Africa may be beneficial to both Africa and China in the long run. According to Adem, China would see Africa succeed so that China's interest in Africa's development is profound. Further arguments by Hanauer and Morris (2014) emphasize that Chinese engagement in Africa "defies conventional stereotypes and punchy negative news headlines" in the Western countries. According to the authors, China's support to Africa cuts across several areas (political, security, diplomacy, ideology, and economics), making China a major donor to the continent where the modus operandi of Chinese aid is misunderstood, misconceived, or misquoted in the press.

Breslin (2011) also offers a useful analysis on Chinese "exceptionalism"[12] and the challenge of replicating its development model or experience in Africa, in view of differences in local conditions, resource endowments, availability of capital, and institutional as well as human resource capabilities in formulating and implementing development policies. Moreover, the intensive rivalry among Western countries (particularly the USA) in Africa may be harmful to all parties with disastrous impacts on Africa's development prospects (Lei: 2020). Therefore, common ground must be found, particularly between the USA and China for a win-win outcome in Africa – with Africans being in the driving seat to choose their pressing priorities. This should include enhanced cooperation between the two global economic giants (not unhealthy competition) to relieve key binding constraints facing Africa by fostering market development, enhancing social capabilities (health and education), and building physical infrastructure (Lei: 2020).

Mkandawire (2005b) argues that Africans are willing partners of the Chinese, motivated by their "state-centric beliefs" that engaging with China is in their continental interest. He stressed, however, that:

> while it is clear that African States have found a new partner (China) for trade, investment and aid; and perhaps even political and diplomatic support to resist Western-initiated policies and interventions, it is also apparent that to accrue any sort of lasting benefits, African States must actively manage their relationships with China.[13]

Further discussions on the Africa-China partnership believe that without a vibrant and proactive African civil society, the benefits from such relations may not be fully realized. Obiorah (2008) particularly calls on African civil societies to hold accountable their respective political leaders and governments who may promote their selfish interests through Africa-China trade and investment ties at the expense of their societal and national interests. He further argues that Africa's civil society actors should mobilize themselves and initiate thoughts and actions on the strategic implications of China's increasing engagement with African countries to maximize benefits for Africa's growth, transformation, and development.

Some researchers hint to historical similarities between the Chinese path to growth and prosperity with that of Africa as critically important to shape the current, and further deepen future, Africa-China relations. Bolesta (2015) provides interesting insights into the Chinese "self-imposed socialism" and a history of protracted war of semi-colonialism of the 19th century. Bolesta also argues that a gradual shift in Chinese development experience from state-led heavy, chemical industries and rural development during the time of centralized planning towards light industry and dynamic enterprises during the time of market reforms could serve as a blueprint for several African countries. These were fundamental in shaping the concept of the Developmental State model in China, which several African countries have been attempting to incorporate into their forms of governance and institutional structures. An earlier Chinese development experience based on building light manufacturing (industry, especially military capabilities), agricultural expansion, and rural development can serve as a learning blueprint for several African countries. Lin and Wang (2014) argue that, beyond unlocking infrastructure bottlenecks in Africa through Chinese finance, China's path to development and structural transformation (historical and empirical evidence) can provide useful and practical lessons for Africa. They further stress that the dynamic growth in China and rising wages or the cost of labour may force Chinese firms to relocate outside of China, which can provide a great opportunity for developing countries such as those in Africa to jumpstart their industrialization and structural transformation processes.

Some other researchers also believe that China's substantial increase in trade, investment, and infrastructure finance to Africa may have relieved the latter from undue policy prescriptions and aid conditionality from the continent's traditional development partners (Sun: 2014). Unrelenting lectures by the donors about democracy, the rule of law, human rights, and environmental protection as conditional to their partnership may have contributed to an increasing interest of African countries to look more towards the "Global East" – shifting away from the "Global North". In a critical assessment of the public opinion in the West about China's engagement with failed states in Africa, Gu and Carty (2014) argued that China's relationship with Africa is a partnership and not mentoring, and that China's dealing with governance-related issues in Africa is based on and closely linked to its own development experience. They argue that Chinese presence in Africa is not for improving governance but to do business, emphasizing the reciprocal and transactional nature of Chinese business in Africa (Sun: 2014). More importantly, China argues that Western democracy (good governance, rule of law, transparency, and human rights) as their own norms and value systems which should not be imposed on other countries and cultures which are entirely incongruent with Western values and norms. For China, the Developmental State, with effective governance, capable institutions, and fiscal prudence capable of generating, managing, and accelerating economic growth and transformation is more conducive and necessary for African countries than pure Western democratic norms, values, systems, and standards. In fact, what the countries of SSA can learn from China is more its "effective Developmental State" than mere "state-led developmentalism". This is because most countries of SSA are not new to "state-led developmentalism" as their states and public institutions have been very much at the centre of economic governance, management, and key investors since the 1960s and 1970s (Meyns and Musamba: 2010).

However, unlike in China and several East Asian economies, African states, instead of leading their nations and citizens to prosperity, drifted into cronyism, state capture, clientelism, and overall rent-seeking behaviours (Meyns and Musamba: 2010). Moreover, global economic and trade environment has not been in favour of the aspirations of Africa's state-led developmentalism. The oil crisis of the 1970s, debt crisis of the 1980s, decades of external policy prescriptions (the 1980s and 1990s), global financial and economic crisis of the 2008–2009 as well as unfavourable global trade and financial policies have further accentuated the socioeconomic difficulty of SSA and incapacitated the state-led developmentalism in the region. This situation has brought the absolute necessity of fostering productive capacities and structural transformation to be placed at the centre of programmatic and forward-looking home-grown policies led by "knowledge, entrepreneurial capitalism and a new mindset but not through corrupt crony governments" (Moghalu: 2014).

From the political spectrum, as discussed in Ajakaiye (2006), several African political elites seem to be programmatic, which put an accent on the role of African states themselves in their relationship with China. According to these groups, as much as Western aid and partnerships have not transformed Africa over the years, nor will the new partnership with China or India put Africa on the path of sustained growth and development. Africans are the only ones to drive the continent's economic growth and transformation agenda. Therefore, they must be in the driving seat, and instead of Africa-China relations transforming the continent, the China-India twosome could lend assistance, to the transformation and development processes of the continent (*The China Monitor*: June 2006, Meidan: 2006). Thus, it is more pragmatic for Africa to focus on designing a suitable partnership arrangement aimed taking maximum advantage of the opportunities presented by the emergence of China on the world stage and ameliorating the adverse effects from such partnerships (Ajakaiye: 2006).

Whatever divergent views there can be, there is no denial that the Africa-China partnership is vast in history, scope, and magnitude. It is critically important to assess whether the partnership has led to foster productive capacities and structural transformation in Africa. How recent quantitative shifts in the Africa-China partnership have been viewed can provide useful insights. Ajakaiye (2006) stresses that China intends to enhance all-round cooperation with Africa notably in the fields of trade, investment, and development aid, which will drive Africa's economic growth and transformation efforts. Further work by Carmody (2007) shows that for the first time since the slave trade era, Africa's trade is being reoriented from the "Global North" to the "Global East". Consequently, Africa-China economic ties have gained importance not only in terms of their scope and magnitude but also the shift in the direction of such relations.

More strikingly, the last couple of decades have witnessed a fundamental shift in Africa-China economic relations: from an exclusive focus in the past on ideological, military, and geopolitical interests towards strong current economic ties. Such a paradigm shift puts the trade and investment interests of China and Africa as the "primary driver of the Africa-China relations" and reflects China's growing dominance in global trade and investment. With ever-increasing trade and investment ties between China and Africa, China is providing much-needed financial resources for infrastructure projects in Africa, and private loans to Africa's business, which, in turn, is providing much-needed liquidity to the sector, especially small and medium-sized enterprises (Foster et al.: 2009, Lopes: 2016). According to the authors, Chinese terms and conditions on loans have more grant components than those from traditional donors, with Chinese finance often going to large infrastructure projects such as hydroelectricity and railways. A more robust and very comprehensive analysis came from McKinsey & Company (2017), which argues that China has become the single largest economic partner of Africa in trade, investment, and aid, with Chinese firms bringing capital investment, technology, and managerial as well as technical know-how to the continent. According to the report, there is no other country that parallels China in terms of magnitude, depth, and breadth of engagements with Africa (see also Figures 1.3 and 1.4 in Chapter 1). The question is what is the implications of such unparalleled engagements of China in Africa to the region's productive capacities and structural transformation? Would the bulging trade, development finance, and investment ties between China and SSA (see Chapter 4) be any different from similar ties of the region with traditional development partners (EU, USA, and Japan) discussed in Chapter 5?

To respond to these and related questions and squarely situate the unfolding and unprecedented Africa-China relationship in relation to the region's productive capacities and structural transformation, Chapter 3 measures and benchmarks the two vital processes. Such an exercise is based on the conceptual underpinnings of productive capacities and structural economic transformation discussed in Chapter 1 and the UNCTAD PCI. The PCI consists of factors and drivers of production (such as natural and human capital; infrastructure including transport, ICT, and energy; institutions, structural change; and the private sector). These categories are key in fostering productive capacities and structural transformation. The discussions in Chapter 3 also help to understand the evolution of productive capacities in SSA and other developing regions for 2000–2018 – the period that has seen an astronomical increase in Africa-China trade, investment, and overall economic partnerships.

Notes

1 Available on: https://www.pwc.com/gx/en/about/global-annual-review-2021/financials.html.

2 On 23 December 2021, the USA announced the suspension of Ethiopia, Guinea, and Mali from the Growth and Opportunity Act (AGOA) as from 1 January 2022, for alleged human rights violations and failing to meet political conditions stipulated in AGOA (Ethiopia) and military coups (Guinea and Mali). The removal of these countries from AGOA will have serious consequences on export earnings of the three countries of SSA, particularly labour-intensive manufacturing such as textiles and apparel, leather and leather products.

3 According to humanitarian aid organizations, "the relief effort has been heavily politicized, as were prior aid operations in Ethiopia, where the central government has long controlled how humanitarian organizations work. Aid workers are accused of partiality and hammered with lies and vitriol from the government and its opponents, especially if they dare to speak out about the aid blockade and other aspects of the conflict". Available at: https://www.thenewhumanitarian.org/podcast/2021/11/10/politicisation-of-aid-in-Ethiopia-rethinking-humanitarianism.

4 For instance, data and statistical information on infant and maternal mortality particularly in Africa are not available for all countries and, when available, these are not complete or consistent overtime. Likewise, available indicators to measure access to education such as gross and net enrollment rates can be misleading because information on the quality of education is missing.

5 UNDP measures human development of nations by using composite indicators of life expectancy at birth, education (mean year of schooling and expected year of schooling) and Gross National Income per capita. Available at: http://hdr.undp.org/en/content/latest-human-development-index-ranking.

6 China adopted the Eight Principles of Economic and Technical Assistance to Africa following the 1963–1964 visit of Zhou Enlai, the first Premier of the People's Republic of China, to Africa centred on its long-standing policy of friendship with and non-interference in Africa's domestic affairs.

7 For instance, Oqubay and Lin argue that "China became Africa's most valuable partner in the post-1990 period at a time when prescriptions and structural adjustment reforms are coming to be seen as empty promises" (Oqubay and Lin: 2019, p. 3).

8 Paul Kagame, President of Rwanda, who was serving as the rotating president of the African Union at the time, in his remarks after meeting Chinese Premier Xi Jinping, visiting Kigali on 23 July 2018, stated that "China relates to Africa as an equal, and that the growing relationship between China and Africa is based on as much respects as mutual interests". He described the growing economic relations between China and Africa as "deeply transformational". See Africanews, 23 July 2018, Kenya, also available at http://www.africanews.com/2018/07/23/china-relates-to-africa-as-an-equal-paul-kagame/. Likewise, at the 2018 FOCAC summit, Cyril Ramaphosa, President of South Africa, addressing the gathering, rejected the "claims of Chinese colonization of Africa" and Mokgweetsi Masisi, President of Botswana, underlined that FOCAC was "unique in that it allowed African countries to come and forge stronger relations with the Asian Superpower – China".

9 For details, see: https://www.migrationpolicy.org/article/migration-trade-china-africa-traders-face-precarity.

10 Notable Hearings of the Senate include: The 4 June 2006 Hearing of the Committee on Foreign Relations (www.foreign.senate.gov); House Subcommittee on Africa, Global Health, and Human Rights, Remarks by David Shine of 29 March 2012.
(https://elliott.gwu.edu/sites/g/files/zaxdzs2141/f/downloads/news/shinn-china-role-influence-africa-032912.pdf); and Congressional Testimony before the House Subcommittee on Emerging Threats and Capabilities by Joshua Meservey (Heritage Foundation); and Hearings by the U.S.-China Economic and Security Review Commission (https://www.uscc.gov).

11 The Commission was created by the United States Congress in October 2000 with the legislative mandate to monitor, investigate, and submit to Congress an annual report on the national security implications of the bilateral trade and economic relationship between the United States and the People's Republic of China, and to provide recommendations, where appropriate, to Congress for legislative and administrative action (https://www.uscc.gov).

12 The phrase "Chinese exceptionalism" denotes promoting an alternative development experience (or model) which is in sharp contrast to the dominant global and economic order crafted, sponsored, and experimented by developed countries and their influential institutions, which is collectively called the "Washington Consensus".

13 Thandika, Mkandawire: From Maladjusted States to Democratic Developmental States in Africa, *Africa Development*, Vol. 30, Nos 1 & 2, 2005, pp. 1–33; Council for the Development of Social Science Research in Africa, 2005b.

Bibliographical references

Adem, S. (2016). Sino-Optimism in Africa. *African Studies Quarterly*, 16(3–4), 7–16.

Africa Center for Economic Transformation ACET. (2009). Looking East: China-Africa Engagements, Ghana Case Study, ACET, Accra, December 2009.

Ajakaiye, O. (2006). China and Africa: Opportunities and Challenges, African Economic Consortium, Scoping Studies Paper No. SSC_01.

Ayers, A. (2012). Beyond Myths, Lies and Stereotypes: The Political Economy of a 'New Scramble for Africa'. *New Political Economy*, 18, 1–31.

Berger, B. (2007). China Outwits the EU in Africa. Asia Times Online Ltd., www.asiatimes.com/IL13Ad01/html. Accessed on 04.01.2019.

Bishop, C., and Hilhorst, D. (2010). From Food Aid to Food Security: The Case of the Safety Net Policy in Ethiopia. *Journal of Modern African Studies*, 48(2), 181–202. https://doi.org/10.1017/S0022278X10000248.

Bolesta, A. (2015). *China and Post-Socialist Development*. Published by Bristol University Press, Bristol.

Breslin, S. (2011). The "China Model" and the Global Crisis: From Friedrich List to a Chinese Mode of Governance. *International Affairs*, 87(6), 1323–1343.

Carmody, P. (2007). Competing Hegemons? Chinese versus American Geo-Economic Strategies in Africa. Iowa State University, Community and Regional Planning Publications. Available at: http://lib.dr.iastate.edu/communityplanning_pubs.

Castel-Branco, C. N. (2008). Aid Dependency and Development: A Question of Ownership? A Critical View, Working Papers' Collection of the Institute of Social and Economic Studies (IESE), Mozambique.

Chari, S., and Corbridge, S., editors (2008). *The Development Reader*. Routledge, Abingdon, Oxon.

Cheru, F., and Obi, C., editors (2010). *The Rise of China and India in Africa*. Zed Books, London.

Chiwanza, T. (2018). The top Ten African Countries with the Largest Chinese Debt, 2 October 2018. The Africa Exponent. Online Outlet. Morogoro, Tanzania. https://www.africanexponent.com/post/9183-here-are-the-top-ten-countries-in-africa-bearing-the-largest-chinese-debt.

Dahoun, D., and Raffinot, M. (2012). Partenaires émergents : Quels enjeux pour la soutenabilité de la dette africaine ? Document De Travail (DT2012-14). Institut de recherche pour le développement, Dauphine Université Paris.

Foster, V., Butterfield, W., Chen, C., and Pushkan, N. (2009). Building Bridge: China's Growing Role in Infrastructure Financing in Sub Saharan Africa. The World Bank. Public Private Infrastructure Advisory Facility (PPIAF). Available at: https://openknowledge.worldbank.org/bitstream/handle/10986/2614/480910PUB0Buil101OFFICIAL0USE0ONLY1.pdf?sequence=1&isAllowed=y.

Gu, J., and Carty, A. (2014). China and African Development: Partnership not Mentoring. *Institute of Development Studies (IDS) Bulletin*, 45(4), 57–69.

Hanauer, L., and Morris, L. (2014). Chinese Engagement in Africa: Drivers, Reactions, and Implications for U.S. Rand National Research Institute. International Security and Defense Policy Center.

John Hopkins School of Advanced International Studies (SAIS). (2017). China-Africa Research Initiative. Loan Database, 2017. Available at: http://www.sais-cari.org/research-chinese-loans-to-africa.

Lei, W. (2020). China and the United States in Africa: Competition or Cooperation? World Century Publishing Corporation and Shanghai Institutes for International Studies. *China Quarterly of International Strategic Studies*, 6(1), 1–19. https://doi.org/10.1142/S2377740020500037.

Lin, J. Y. (2012). *New Structural Economics – A Framework to Re-Thinking Development and Policy*. The World Bank, Washington, DC.

Lin, J. Y., and Wang, Y. (2014). China-Africa Cooperation for Structural Transformation: Ideas, Opportunities, and Finance, WIDER Working Paper 2014/046, World Institute for Development and Economics Research.

Lopes, C. (2016). Reinserting African Agency into Sino-African Relations. *Strategic Review for Southern Africa*, 38(1), 50–68.

McCombie, J. (1983). Kaldor's Law in Retrospect. *Journal of Post-Keynesian Economics*, 5(3) Spring 1983, 414–430.

McKinsey &Company. (2017). Dance of the Lions and Dragons: How Africa and China Engage, and How Will the Partnership Evolve? June 2017.

Meidan, M. (2006). China's Africa Policy: Business Now, Politics Later. *Asian Perspective*, 30(4) Special Issue on "Rising China's Foreign Relations", 69–93. https://www.jstor.org/stable/42704565.

Meservey, J. (2018). Implications of China's Presence and Investment in Africa. Testimony before the Subcommittee on Emerging Threats and Capabilities. United States Senate, 12 December 2018. Heritage Foundation.

Meyns, P., and Musamba, C. (2010). *The Developmental State in Africa: Problems and Prospects*. Institute for Development and Peace, University of Duisburg-Essen.

Migration Policy Institute (MPI). (2021). As Migration and Trade Increase between China and Africa, Traders at Both Ends Often Face Precarity, 21 July 2021. Available at: https://www.migrationpolicy.org/article/migration-trade-china-africa-traders-face-precarity.

Mkandawire, T. (2005b). *From Maladjusted States to Democratic Developmental States in Africa*. Council for the Development of Social Science Research in Africa.

Moss, T., Pettersson, G., and Van de Walle, N. (2005). An Aid-Institutions Paradox? A Review Essay on Aid Dependency and State Building in Sub-Saharan Africa. The Mario Einaudi Center for International Studies, Paper No. 11-05. November 2005.

Moghalu, K. C. (2014). *Emerging Africa: How the Global Economy's 'Last Frontier' Can Prosper and Matter*, 2nd edition. Penguin, London.

Obiorah, N. (2008). *Rise and Rights in China-Africa Relations*. African Studies Programme. The Johns Hopkins University, School of Advanced International Studies, Washington, DC.

Oqubay, A., and Lin, J. Y. (2019). Introduction to China-Africa and Economic Transformation. In *China-Africa and Economic Transformation*. Edited by A. Oqubay and K. Ohno. Oxford University Press, Oxford, 1–18.

Oya, C. (2006). The Political Economy of Development Aid as Main Source of Foregn Finance for Poor African Countries: Loss of Policy Space and Possible Alternatives from East Asia. School of Oriental & African Studies, University of London.

Oya, C., and Schaefer, F. (2019). Chinese Firms and Employment Dynamics in Africa: A Comparative Analysis. IDCEA Research Synthesis Report, SOAS, University of London.

Park, Y. (2009). Chinese Migration in Africa, South African Institute of International Affairs, China-Africa Project. Available at https://www.saiia.org.za/wp-content/uploads/2013/06/saia_sop_24_park_20090218_en.pdf. Accessed on 31 March 2019, at 15:00 CET.

PriceWatersHouse Coopers. (2021). Financial Report. Global Annual Review 2021. Available at: https://www.pwc.com/gx/en/about/global-annual-review-2021/financials.html.

Schoeman, M. (2008). China and Africa: Whose Challenge and Whose Opportunity. *Journal of African Spectrum*, 43(3), 403–413. https://www.jstor.org/stable/40175257?read-now=1&seq=1#page_scan_tab_contents. Accessed on 04.01.2019.

Sun, Y. (2014). *Africa in China's Foreign Policy*. John L. Thornton China Center and Africa Growth Initiative, Brookings.

The China Monitor. (2006). World Economic Forum on Africa: Going for Growth and China's Role in the African Economy, June 2006. Available at: http://www0.sun.ac.za/ccs/wp-content/uploads/2009/04/ccs-china-monitor-june-06.pdf.

The Migration Policy Institute (MPI). (2021). As Migration and Trade Increase between China and Africa, Traders at Both Ends Often Face Precarity. *Newsletter*, 20 July 2021. Available at: https://www.migrationpolicy.org/article/migration-trade-china-africa-traders-face-precarity.

UNCTAD. (2006) *The Least Developed Countries 2006 Report, Developing Productive Capacities in Least Developed Countries*. United Nations Publication, New York and Geneva.

Wang, H. "Recent Trends in Migration between China and Other Developing Countries", a Presentation Made at the "South–South Migration: Partnering Strategically for Development", held in Geneva, Switzerland on 24 and 25 March 2014 in the framework of the International Dialogue on Migration (IDM). Available at https://www.iom.int/sites/g/files/tmzbdl486/files/migrated_files/What-We-Do/idm/workshops/South-South-Migration-2014/South-South-Migration-2014-Presentation-Huiyao-Wang.pdf.

Woods, N. (2008). Whose Aid? Whose Influence? China Emerging Donors and the Silent Revolution in Development Assistance. *International Affairs*, 84(6), 1205–1221. Available at: http://media.library.ku.edu.tr/reserve/resspring17/Intl532_ZOnis/13_required.pdf.

3 Mapping and Measuring Productive Capacities

SSA's Performance

The measurement and benchmark of productive capacities in this chapter are based on the conceptual definition provided by UNCTAD consisting of three pillars: *productive resources*, *entrepreneurial capabilities*, and *production linkages*. For analytical and measurement purposes, each of the three pillars is discussed and decomposed into components or categories in subsequent sections of this chapter. Along with the pillars and components, the chapter also introduces indicators used in the Productive Capacities Index (PCI) which is regarded as a tool to improve productive capacities-centred policy formulation and guide implementation.

The first pillar, *productive resources*, is the factors of production and consists of natural and human capital, financial capital, and physical capital, which are key in the production and supply of goods and services. Natural capital or resources, in turn, encompass agricultural land, water, marine and freshwater resources, forestry, mineral (metals), and energy resources, among others, which underpin economic activities. Human capital relates to the quantity and quality of human capital and therefore concerns issues of education (knowledge and skills), health, gender, demography, life expectancy, and the experience of the workforce in an economy. Financial capital refers to the availability, access, and cost of core financial resources to finance investments and the acquisition of technology, research and development (R&D), and innovation. Physical capital resources are capital stock (equipment and machinery) and physical infrastructure such as transport, energy (electricity), and telecommunications infrastructure.

The second pillar, *entrepreneurial capabilities*, concerns core competencies and the technological capabilities of firms and households that maximize business and production possibilities and produce ranges of goods and services efficiently and competitively. Core competencies refer to the ability to apply current skills, knowledge, and information on how to best transform existing productive resources into inputs and then into outputs. Technological capabilities deal with dynamic abilities to advance the core competencies and thereby increase productivity, competitiveness, and profitability. As such, they are the basis for the creativity, flexibility, and dynamism of an economy. They include expanding physical facilities (investment capabilities); upgrading products and processes (incremental innovation capabilities); developing new markets (strategic marketing

DOI: 10.4324/9781003295334-3

capabilities); benefiting from transfer of technology (linkage capabilities); and creating new technological capabilities.

The third pillar, production linkages, sometimes referred to as productive linkages, relates to (production, processing, business, information, and marketing linkages) which all together form interactions among enterprises through trade, production, investment, and technology flows. These flows can be among firms and farms, between domestic and foreign enterprises, and among economic sectors such as agriculture, industry, and services. Production linkages and flows between firms and enterprises have long been recognized as an important element for economic transformation and the competitiveness of countries. They enable firms and enterprises as well as economies to participate effectively in regional and global value chains, and production clusters. Thus, production linkages encompass different types of interactions that affect all types of enterprises – Small and Medium Sized Enterprises (SMEs), large firms, households, domestically owned, foreign-owned firms, and so on. Interactions and networks between buyers and sellers as well as intermediaries are key for channelling information and knowledge about the market, business structures, and the environment as well as management and knowledge systems. All these directly or indirectly influence or determine production and productivity at the firm level or across the economic sectors of an economy and lay the foundation for structural economic transformation.

The UNCTAD definition is not only broad in its articulation of the concept of productive capacities, but it is also multidimensional. Other institutions and development studies approach the concept from unidimensional perspectives or angles (such as trade, manufacturing, technology, human capital, or institutions)-driven processes. The advantage of using a multidimensional approach is that it encompasses a range of factors and their complex relationships that determine economic growth and development. Its main disadvantage, as discussed later in the chapter, relates to the systemic challenges it poses to precisely measure the degree and direction of influence of each of the elements.

The multidimensional aspect of the productive capacities is also valuable in that it helps to understand and address multiple development challenges simultaneously. Rather than being concerned with a single outcome (e.g., economic growth or poverty reduction), the building of productive capacities can have positive repercussions across a wide range of socioeconomic areas. For instance, they have direct impacts on supply-side constraints and unemployment which are key in facilitating or hindering economic growth and poverty reduction. Similarly, the building of productive capacities is integral to export diversification and structural transformation efforts – factors that are viewed as fundamental for long-term growth and development. Moreover, building productive capacities results in achieving broad development objectives such as breaking aid dependency or the low-middle-income traps, and enhancing the human and institutional capabilities necessary to advance economic growth and poverty reduction (Chapter 2).

In recognition of its wider policy implications, policymakers at national, regional, and global levels have taken the above-discussed conceptualization of productive capacities to heart (Chapter 1). However, the gap between the ambitions and their implementation (realization) is considerable. The main reasons behind such an increasing emphasis in development policy documents is the concerns about "jobless growth" and the mismatch between economic growth and poverty reduction in developing regions such as SSA.

The UNCTAD definition and conceptualization also builds on historical and empirical evidence from early adopters of productive capacities narratives as key for economic transformation. The pre-industrialization economic success of the USA provides useful clues on how nations can discover their comparative advantages, mobilize, and recalibrate their productive capacities to exploit such advantages in the development process. For instance, Alexander Hamilton – the founding father of the American economy – redesigned the US economy by gradually changing the structure of its comparative advantages. Hamilton's policy narrative is underpinned and inspired by the need to exploit comparative advantages through carefully sequenced policy measures and actions aimed at unlocking binding constraints. Protecting America's nascent industries from the highly advanced and more competitive British producers, through higher tariffs (Cohen and DeLong: 2016) was key in augmenting and sustaining America's productive edge and productivity gains. Agriculture – where America had comparative advantages over Britain and the imposition of high tariffs on goods imported (notably from Great Britain) played a pivotal role in providing labour (including through the slave trade) and intermediate goods to the flourishing infant industries of the USA.

The then US government also played a critical role in providing vital infrastructure, such as transcontinental railroads, which in turn gave rise to the development of entrepreneurship, commerce, and modern industries, such as steel and other complementary industries (Cohen and DeLong: 2016). Government intervention was based on Hamilton's arguments about the "shyness of capital", which requires the protection and facilitation of the state. America's continuous and unparalleled development of its productive capacities was the consequence of the combination of several factors: carefully designed and effectively implemented pragmatic economic policies aimed at exploiting the country's comparative advantages by unlocking binding constraints on the economy. These include effective protection of infant industries; investing in infrastructure; developing viable banking and financial sectors; incentivizing strategic industries that created jobs, built export competitiveness, and involved in R&D, as well as contributing to modernizing the US economy.

What we learn today from the economic history of one of the most successful economies in the world (the USA) is that development is predicated on a careful understanding of comparative advantages, effectively addressing binding constraints on growth (development) and a "Developmental State" (government) in fostering productive capacities. Hamilton's pragmatic and forward-looking economic policy formulation and implementation provided the basis for the emergence of complementary theories or approaches to development. Other historical or theoretical insights (List: 1841, Schumpeter: 1912/1934 and 1939, Lewis:

1954) focus on various drivers and determinants of productive capacities. These include entrepreneurial innovation, industrial locations and production linkages, technological sophistication and knowledge embodiment, or manufacturing value-added, which have enriched the discourse on transformational development based on building productive capacities and capabilities. In this context, further works worth highlighting include that of Hirschman (1958), which also addressed the linkages and economies of scale of the manufacturing sector on the one hand, and the spill-over effects from the sector. Accordingly, the shift of manufacturing value-added towards developing countries with scarce capital but abundant labour will be fundamental in accelerating economic growth, transformation, and development.

Rodrik (2004) offers the most recent insights into the industrialization-driven development processes with a focus on growth-acceleration mechanisms and the role of targeted industrial policies in promoting industrialization. Beyond targeted industrial policies or strategies, the types of industries (i.e., what and how to produce) matter and determine the extent of productive capacities of nations and the degree of structural economic transformation. In articulating what and how to produce, Hausmann et al. (2005), Hausmann and Klinger (2006), Hidalgo and Hausmann (2009), and Hidalgo et al. (2011) added a new dimension to the literature on growth through their industrialization (manufacturing)-based approaches and analysis of "product space". Their important contributions relate to examining or exploring export complexities (technological sophistication or knowledge embodiment of goods produced and exported) together with the importance of larger varieties (diversification) of goods produced in development. Their analysis is based on the role of natural endowments and competitive advantages in the process of diversification and value addition into export items, with technological sophistication and knowledge embodiments in exports. A similar work by Lin (2012) argues that countries should pursue a path of development that is based on the identification and exploitation of existing or revealed and latent comparative advantages. Yet, an elaborate work by Salazar-Xirinachs, Nubler, and Kozul-Right (2014) provided substantial evidence that, industrialization cannot occur in a vacuum. That is, market forces alone cannot guarantee industrialization, productive transformation, and structural change. Instead, the state – anchored in different institutional arrangements and mixes of policies – should and must play a proactive role in building markets, nurturing enterprises, encouraging technological upgrading, fostering learning process, accumulating capabilities, and unlocking constraints on infrastructure.

Several important policy lessons could be drawn from historical, theoretical, and empirical assessments of development experiences and within the "productive capacity–structural change" narratives: first, the notions of productive capacities and structural transformation involve enhancing total factor productivity and internally dynamic economic processes characterized by the reallocation of resources from traditional to modern sectors and from traditional to modern economic activities (including within a given sector). Second, structural transformation is not sporadic but consistent and incremental over time, involving a long period of capital accumulation (formation), technological progress, social capabilities, and innovation as key drivers of economic growth and development. Third, fostering productive capacities and structural transformation is not a short-term phenomenon but it is a long-term process that changes not only the units (or disaggregates) but also the composition of economic aggregates (Kruger: 2008). Fourth, productive capacities are key in accelerating the pace of structural transformation to impact not only the economy but also the wellbeing of citizens, with some sectors exhibiting faster long-term growth than others. Finally, industrialization or manufacturing is fundamental for ensuring sustained economic growth and sustainable development (UNCTAD: 2016a). These lessons are consistent with an argument posited in the preceding chapters that no nation has ever climbed the development ladder without industrialization and deeper structural transformation. They provide important insights into the measurement of economy-wide productive capacities and structural transformation in later sections of the chapter.

3.1 Mapping and Measuring Productive Capacities

Before delving into measuring productive capacities, it is important to map such capacities by further decomposing its main pillars into categories based on the conceptual definition discussed in previous chapters. The mapping of pillars and categories (components) of productive capacities provides coherent information on the interconnections between and among them, and the degree of influence of each of the factors determining economic growth and the development of nations. It also provides policy direction to expand the sources and catalyze enablers, drivers, and engines of growth and development. Figure 3.1 provides a galaxy of indicators, or "indicators map", in a conceptually consistent, logical, and meaningful way. This helps to realign the conceptual, definitional, and analytical narratives and historical evidence discussed earlier with the indicators.

As opposed to unidimensional indices (such as the Human Capital Index of the World Bank or the Human Development Index of UNDP – both of which measure human capital), the PCI mapping shows several key drivers of economic growth and development. Moreover, the indicators map also shows interconnectedness between the theoretical framework and the indicators on the one hand and between and among the indicators on the other. For instance, natural capital as captured through productive resources, requires better human capital (skilled and educated labour force, entrepreneurship), innovative firms, and technology to be fully harnessed for transformational development. A more interesting aspect of the mapping is that it further helps to see how each of the indicators identified are useful in measuring and benchmarking productive capacities and structural transformation in SSA and other developing regions.

The measurement of productive capacities is based on the indicators map shown in Figure 3.1. It provides hints on what drives growth and development and how productive capacities and structural transformation evolved in SSA in recent years (2000–2018). The period of statistical investigation (2000–2018) is particularly interesting as it denotes unprecedented increases in Africa-China

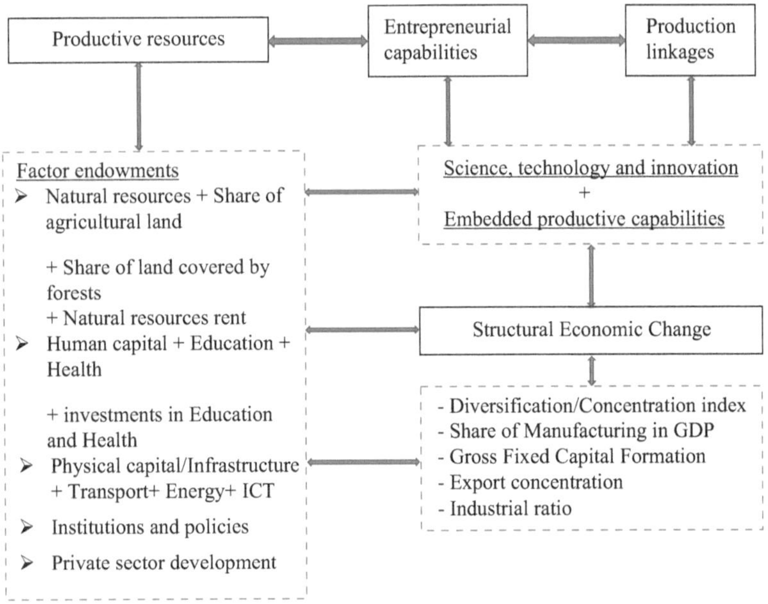

Figure 3.1 Map of key indicators of productive capacities and structural transformation.

trade, investment, and development finance ties. The outcome of statistical measurement also explains whether there is evidence of structural economic transformation in SSA, given the region's increasing economic relations with rising China. The analysis of the results is intended to inform policymakers and practitioners as well as researchers as to what are the levels and main drivers of productive capacities and structural economic transformation, if any, in SSA.

Measuring productive capacities is critically important, for at least three important reasons. First, to clearly assess or measure the impact of past development policies and strategies as well as international partnerships (such as Africa-China) on fostering such capacities and structural economic transformation. The indicators used in this chapter help policymakers and practitioners in measuring progress towards enhancing productive capacities and structural transformation as key to the realization of the objectives of domestic and global plans or visions, including Sustainable Development Goals (SDGs).[1] How can policies, institutions, and productive resources help generate growth that leads to sustainable and inclusive development in SSA? Second, to clearly identify areas of progress (and lack thereof) together with the main reasons for observed gaps and limitations. And, finally, it helps to articulate policy options and mobilize the necessary actions to effectively relieve binding constraints to development (as discussed in Chapter 9). Therefore, measuring productive capacities is essential to identify comparative advantages that help to kick-start the process of structural transformation. This is particularly important given the multidimensional nature of the indicators used or factors needed for productive transformation. It is equally important to note that not all countries have identical binding constraints or comparative advantages. Country heterogeneity (diversity) means that there is no "one-size-fits-all" approach in fostering productive capacities and structural transformation. Thus, country-specific policy recommendations and interventions need to be tailored to fit specific circumstances, not mere provision of generic prescriptions of policies and strategies (Crespi et al.: 2014). In this regard, the policy lessons and recommendations contained in Chapter 9 need to be redefined in country-specific initial conditions, comparative advantages, and key binding constraints.

Although valuable for policy formulation and implementation, measuring or benchmarking such complex concepts and processes is not easy or straightforward. This is partly due to data limitations (more so in SSA) and because of the vastness (multidimensionality) of the concepts themselves. Lack of accurate and reliable data in SSA is well known and is particularly conspicuous on matters related to structural economic transformation, productivity of resources, technology, or innovation. Vries et al. (2013) and many others in their respective statistical or quantitative analyses of economic development in Africa, argue that African statistics are often considered unreliable due to large measurement errors. This gave rise to what is regarded as "Africa's statistical tragedy" (Devarajan: 2013, Jerven: 2013). Even when data is available, it may not be consistent or complete over time. Moreover, the definition used for the collection and measurement of data and statistical information, may diverge from the ideal conceptual definition of productive capacities and structural transformation as discussed in the preceding chapters. Another challenge with data is the difficulty of clearly establishing causal relationships between the capacity to produce and transform economies on the one hand, and the indicator(s) used, on the other hand. The variables cannot respond to several relevant or systemic questions: what percentage of the change in productive capacities and structural transformation is due to changes in natural capital, human capital, or gross fixed capital formation? How can we decouple productive capacities and structural transformation in SSA resulting from domestic policy efforts from those that are due to engagements with China?

A further set of challenges relates to the dynamic nature of the indicators used and their inability to clearly explain the real causes or reasons behind the observed changes in time. How can changes in energy consumption per capita last year be captured in changes in the unit of production in subsequent years in an economy? How can we capture or measure the impact of spontaneous technological changes on identified indicators, production processes, and output growth? Further challenges relate to the concepts of productive capacities and structural transformation – which are vast (or all-inclusive) – making it difficult to select the best indicators and accurately measure them. For instance, is it the potential in natural capital (e.g., land for agriculture) or the actual use of land that should be considered central for building productive capacities and structural transformation? Are untapped mineral resources or those explored, processed, or traded that should be counted as productive capacities?

Data and measurement-related challenges as well as those related to conceptual issues, gave rise to consensus that precisely measuring and benchmarking productive capacities and structural transformation in SSA is complex or problematic. However, this does not diminish the necessity for measuring performance across a wide range of productive capacities' indicators. This is because productive capacity indicators together with related data and statistics are vital tools in assessing outcomes of policies. They are important policy tools to guide implementation and assist in comparing results between economies and charting future courses of action. UNCTAD's Global Productive Capacities Index uses carefully collected data from secondary sources[2] on key factors and determinants of productive capacities and structural transformation based on the indicator map. These are regrouped around three pillars and eight categories of productive capacities (Figure 3.2). Each of the categories uses specific and directly relevant indicators that can be quantified in terms of data and statistics.

With the view to facilitating the measurement and benchmarking efforts, the three pillars of productive capacities discussed earlier are realigned with specific categories and indicators or determinants used. Each of the pillars, categories, and indicators should not be viewed in isolation from one another. Rather, they

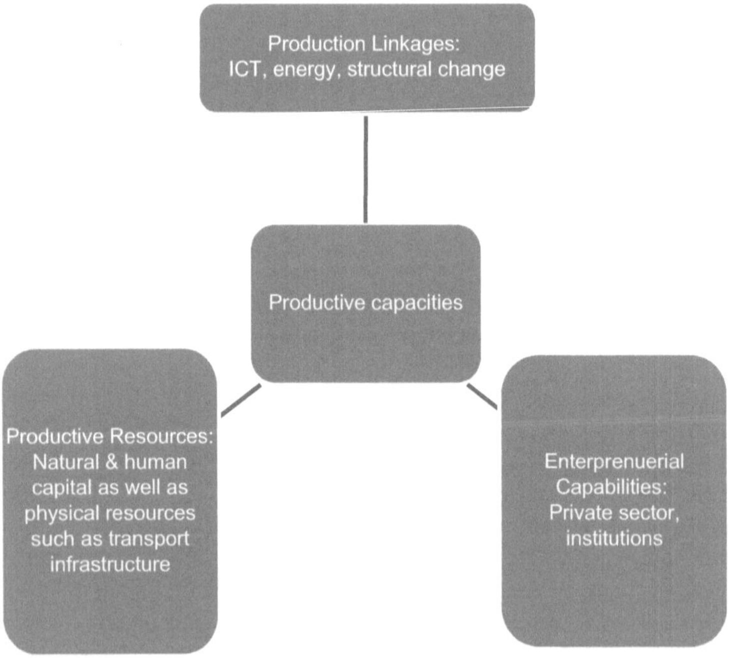

Figure 3.2 Core pillars and categories of productive capacities.

Source: Author's scheme. The eight categories used in measuring productive capacities under each of the three pillars are: natural capital, human capital, transport, energy, ICT, structural change, private sector, and institutions.

should be seen as systemic interconnectedness and linkages in virtuous circularity where a positive change in one will have concomitant positive changes in the other. That is, *productive resources* consist of key inputs (factors of production) in kick-starting the transformation process. However, this requires the right mix of policies, production technologies, energy (electricity), institutional capabilities, and a vibrant and dynamic private sector. Similarly, the demand for factors of production is a function of the demand for corresponding goods and services. Any factor of production (labour, land, capital, raw material, or intermediate goods) used in the processing of finished products provides a basis for productive transformation to meet industrial and human demand for end products or services. Countries that have successfully transformed their economies are those that have effectively harnessed their productive resources for growth and development by removing key binding constraints on economic development (Chapters 7 and 8). Such countries have also achieved a higher level of technological progress, income, and prosperity. Conversely, countries that are lagging behind in terms of productivity, socioeconomic transformation, and technological progress are those that have dismally failed to harness or misused their productive resources. The latter group of nations is unable to relieve key binding constraints to their development and are, therefore, stuck in the lowest echelon of the development ladder. In fact,

> economic performance [in poor countries] over the last 50 years has been held back by declining total factor productivity and, hence, there is an urgent need to set the conditions necessary to improve productivity to match the pace of better-performing countries.
>
> (Crespi et al.: 2014)

Entrepreneurial capabilities are determined or influenced by geographic (spatial) factors such as quality of infrastructure, labour force, financial services (Ghani et al.: 2014) as well as sociocultural, institutional, economic, and demographic factors. Entrepreneurial capabilities as a pillar of productive capacities also include a conducive environment for firms and enterprises to engage in innovation, technological learning, and upgrading as well as productivity growth. These capabilities refer to the overall competencies and competitive capabilities needed to induce economic change by fully harnessing existing natural endowments (productive resources). Such capabilities are key in relaxing systemic or binding constraints on business and unleashing overall comparative advantages, which a given economy possesses. Fully and effectively harnessing entrepreneurial capabilities requires capable institutions and policies conducive to private sector development – a micro- and macroeconomic environment for doing business, institutions that guide or facilitate technological learning and upgrading, including through targeted incentives that are key in unleashing entrepreneurial capabilities. These should also be realigned with the objectives of development policies as well as strategies for the production transformation. As firms learn new production methods and upgrade their innovation and technological capabilities, they can transform their productivity and enhance their international competitiveness.

Firms are also key to moving productive resources from low-skill and low-productivity activity or sectors to skill- and knowledge-intensive, sophisticated, and higher-productivity activities and sectors, which constitute structural transformation. The role of the state (and the public sector) in facilitating the building of entrepreneurial capabilities is substantial. Governments must lead the way through their proactive and facilitative policies and strategies as well as by providing targeted incentives to engage the private sector in production-transformation processes. In sum, entrepreneurial capabilities cover several hard or physical capital and soft skills such as knowledge within firms or industries, which in turn facilitate technological adaptation and foster innovation. As such, they are complex and multidimensional, which includes tangible and intangible assets as embedded in the production structure.

3.2 Where Does Sub-Saharan Africa Stand on the PCI?

The primary commodities-driven growth of the region has continued to be short-lived, unsustainable, and has fallen short of expectations in terms of sustainable growth and transformation. The growth trajectory of SSA and the conditions and factors influencing it are varied and complex (UNCTAD: 2017a). Reversing the declining socioeconomic trends in SSA and setting the region on the path to sustained and inclusive growth call for "new-generation domestic polices" and international partnerships, centred on the fostering of productive capacities and structural transformation. In this context, statistically measuring and benchmarking productive capacities help to frame a new development paradigm for SSA consistent with the kind of production transformation seen in the developed and newly emerging economies of East Asia, including latecomers such as Vietnam (discussed in Chapters 7 and 8). The measurement and benchmark also help to identify the most pervasive binding constraints to SSA's development and provide important insights into how to alleviate such constraints. This, in turn, helps nations to exploit their respective comparative advantages, including by mobilizing their actions and development resources (investments). For instance, how best can SSA fully harness expanding Africa-China trade, investment, and development finance ties for transformational development in SSA?

Category-specific data are used to compare SSA with the average performance of developing countries of Asia (excluding Japan and other advanced East Asian economies), Latin America, and China among the eight categories mentioned earlier in the chapter. This leads to the graphs (figures) discussed below with respect to specific categories. Along with the eight categories used in measuring productive capacities, SSA exceeded other developing regions only in one category: natural capital. As provided in the following sections, in all the remaining seven categories of productive capacities, SSA lags behind all the developing regions of the world, despite growing trade, investment, and development finance relations with development partners, including China.

3.2.1 Natural Capital

Four key indicators[3] are employed in measuring natural capital. As shown in Figure 3.3, the average score of SSA's natural capital is about 58 out of the maximum of 60 points on the scale. High natural capital indicates that SSA holds significant potential in natural capital for accelerated and transformational growth, if fully and effectively harnessed. That is, the sources of current and future growth performance of the region are directly associated with its high natural capital. When it comes to Africa-China trade, investment, and development finance ties, such an overdependence on natural resources in SSA has been the source of some speculation and pessimism, particularly in the West. This is because of a perception that the growing interest of China in Africa is driven more by its large appetite for natural (extractive) resources than the proclaimed solidarity or partnership with the continent. This should not be viewed as unique or specific only to Africa-China relations. The natural resources of SSA have always been magnets for the strategic, military, diplomatic, and economic interests of Western countries since the "partition of and scramble for Africa" in the 19th century.

Fully and effectively harnessing SSA's natural (extractive) resources for inclusive and sustainable economic growth and development proves to be complex and daunting. It primarily requires putting in place sound, transparent, and accountable economic management as well as the right development policies and strategies at the national level. These should be coupled with effective micro- and macroeconomic policies as well as regulatory and institutional frameworks. However, various studies and research efforts reveal that converting natural wealth into socioeconomic transformation is more challenging than is usually perceived. For instance, it seems too obvious to expect that resource endowments play a key role in fostering productive capacities and structural transformation. However, economies that have high degrees of dependence on natural capital for their economic activities are continuously characterized by low and vulnerable growth. Natural resources are more often the causes and

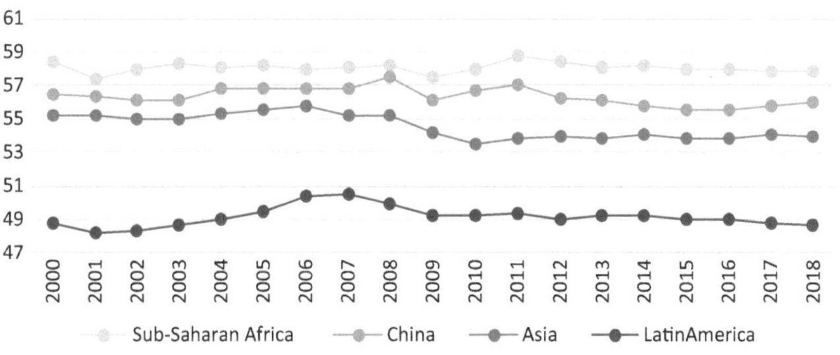

Figure 3.3 Natural capital component of productive capacities in SSA, Asia, Latin America, and China (2000–2018).

Source: UNCTAD global Productive Capacities Index (PCI).

consequences of capital flight than capital formation. Generally, economies with high natural capital such as those in SSA remain the locus of extreme poverty and known for micro- and macroeconomic instability and mismanagement of resources. They are particularly characterized by high levels of unemployment and low levels of total factor productivity (Venables: 2016, Golub et al.: 2011). The underlying reasons are many. Some are economic and technological, while others are political, institutional, or regulatory. Empirical evidence shows that technology and the capital-intensive nature of the extractive sector are not the best to generate jobs and distribute income. In the case of SSA, domestic financial and technological capacities are woefully inadequate to harness the natural resource wealth. This calls for the involvement of foreign firms and powerful companies. Dominant foreign firms and companies often crowd out domestic investment and suffocate local firms, rendering them uncompetitive. Evidence also suggests that, in some cases, powerful companies exacerbate rent-seeking behaviours among political elites. Moreover, foreign firms take advantage of the low negotiating capacities of governments in poor countries in exploiting natural resources. In terms of trade, countries that rely heavily on the export of primary commodities are also vulnerable to volatilities and low international commodity prices, which instigate external economic shocks. External shocks affect not only government revenues but also household incomes, aggravating the vicious circle between natural wealth and poverty reduction efforts (UNCTAD: 2017a). A further problem often observed in countries with natural resource wealth is the appreciation of the domestic currency in relation to foreign currencies with negative consequences, particularly for the manufacturing sector.

Natural resources also lead to patronage and corruption (Venables: 2016) and quite often, especially in SSA, contribute to civil or armed conflicts and state failures (Collier: 2007, 2010). In the case of SSA, production linkages in natural capital (particularly in the mining sector) are also weak in high-value-added processes and strong at the exploration and low-value-added parts in the sector. A study of the gold value chain in Tanzania (Mjimba: 2011) argues that the volume of local contents is higher in the exploration subsector than in the production, processing, and finishing subsectors in the gold value chain, undercutting the potential socioeconomic gains of the country from its natural resource wealth. Fostering beneficial linkages and enhancing the local content at the high end of the value chains require sound private and public sector policies (Mjimba: 2011). In theory and empirics, production linkages also go beyond a given geographical territory and include international trade, investment, and technology flows. For instance, venture capital is key to transferring technologies, new ideas, and production techniques, especially to firms and enterprises in developing countries. These, collectively, can have powerful positive impacts on firms and enterprises that lack funds and technologies but have high capacity to grow and transform economies. Despite systemic problems and challenges encountered by countries with ample natural resource wealth, the development experiences of countries such as Botswana, Chile, and Indonesia indicate that natural resource rents have indeed propelled socioeconomic transformation (UNCTAD: 2008b). Moreover,

Vietnam's socioeconomic performance provides fresh evidence as to how policies and institutions, including the targeted and facilitative support of governments, help to harness natural capital to build productive capacities with structural transformation (Chapters 7 and 8).

Figure 3.3 clearly indicates the high level of natural capital in SSA in comparison with developing regions of Asia and Latin America as well as China during 2000–2018. The vertical axis shows the mean of the aggregated and weighted values of the indicators used to measure natural capital category of productive capacities. Regions with a relatively lower natural capital component of productive capacities, particularly those in Asia, have radically transformed their socioeconomic transformation in a short period of time.

The results confirm three fundamental facts, namely: (i) SSA's economies continue to be hugely driven by natural capital and, hence, are vulnerable to various shocks; and (ii) natural resources have played a central role in attracting growing interest from development partners such as China. These resources also cause inevitable competition between major global players, poised to gain political and economic influence on the African continent; and (iii) the region holds significant potential for transformational development if it puts in place the right mix of economic policies, regulatory, governance, and overall institutional framework for effectively harnessing such a potential.

3.2.2 *Human Capital*

The discussions in previous chapters accord a central place to human capital as the basis for transformational development. Conceptually, human capital in an economy represents the overall human productive force or labour, including health, education, skills, expertise, knowledge, experience, social, or entrepreneurial capabilities of the population. The World Bank Group's Human Capital Project reveals that human capital looms largest in a country's wealth and is a primary driver of economic growth. The World Bank measures human capital in an economy through health, education, and nutrition. The United Nations Development Programme (UNDP) has a more comprehensive and widely known index: the Human Development Index (HDI). This measures the overall human development of nations by using a composite index consisting of life expectancy, education, and per capita income indicators. Except for the number of indicators used and areas of emphasis, statistical measurements employed by different institutions are not qualitatively different from one another. Nor are the methodological approaches or the outcomes (results) of the measurements. Overall, human capital or other development indicators of SSA show that the region significantly lags behind the rest of the developing regions, although there are modest signs of progress in recent years. Without adequate human capital formation, it will be impossible for nations to foster economy-wide productive capacities and transform their economies. Sustaining productivity, innovation, and seeking solutions to binding constraints on socioeconomic development requires educated, skilled, healthy, and productive labour force.

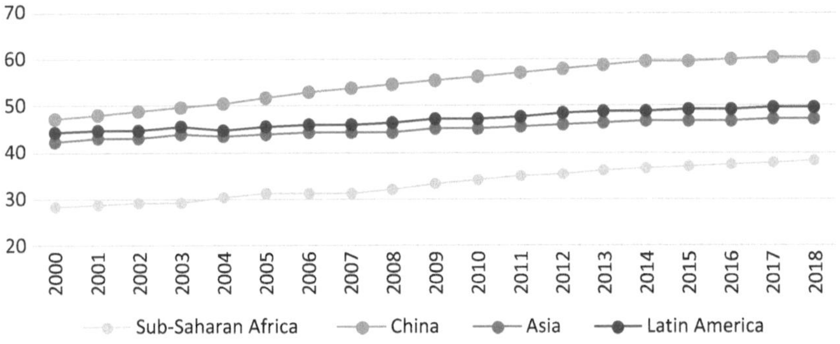

Figure 3.4 Human capital category of productive capacities in SSA, Asia, Latin America, and China (2000–2018).

Source: UNCTAD global Productive Capacities Index (PCI)

The indicators used in the PCI[4] under the human capital category consists of health, education, R&D and share of public expenditure in education and health, and gender aspects. The human capital component of productive capacities in SSA is, by far, the lowest when compared to the developing regions of Asia and Latin America as well as China. China's human capital is diverging away from the average level of other developing countries. This trend indicates fundamental transformation that has been occurring in China for the last couple of decades. Chinese performance in accelerating its human capital formation shows an increasing convergence with the developed world (UNCTAD: 2020a). While the developing regions of Asia and Latin America are also converging with one another and approaching the level attained by China in human capital, this is a particular area where SSA's progress has shown no significant improvement over the last 18 years (Figure 3.4). The growth and development experiences of successful East Asian economies, apart from Vietnam and a few others (Chapters 7 and 8), reveal that these economies do not possess as much natural capital as SSA. The core comparative advantages of Asian economies are in labour or human capital. They have successfully augmented the skills and productivity of such capital, built the overall social capabilities of individuals and societies (including institutions) as key for their production transformation, sustained growth, and development. On a composite index of the human capital category, the performance of SSA is significantly lagging behind the developing regions of Asia and Latin America, though slightly improving over time. Asia's transformation has been realized or led by the fostering of human capital in which the region has comparative advantages. This has helped countries such as Vietnam to kick-start labour-intensive manufacturing and gradually move into producing and exporting technology and knowledge-intensive industrial goods and services.

3.2.3 *Transport Infrastructure*

Transportation as a service and transport infrastructure as investment are key to productivity of resources, economic growth, competitiveness, and overall development of nations. However, such a relationship is complex and as such less well understood by policymakers. Transport infrastructure is fundamental for structural economic transformation through "public infrastructure formation" or public "infrastructure accumulation" as argued by Sebastian and Steinbuks (2017). Similarly, the Economic Commission for Africa emphasizes that economic infrastructure (roads, ports, energy, ICT) is a requisite for industrialization and structural transformation in Africa (UNECA: 2017). The International Trade Center (ITC: 2012), estimates that by investing in trade-related logistics and transport infrastructure, "SSA can increase its exports by 51 percent along with a GDP gain of USD 20 billion per year by 2025".

The relationship between transport and key economic variables such as productive capacities, structural transformation, competitiveness, economic growth, and development would need to be captured in the measurement exercise. Some institutions argue that the best economic indicators (e.g., Gross Domestic Product (GDP) or income) can provide proxy variables to measure transport infrastructure. This is because high-quality and efficient transport infrastructure, affordability, and the availability of competitive transport services are highly correlated with higher economic development and overall societal wellbeing (Rodrigue et al.: 2017). However, given the complex link between transport services and the production (manufacturing) sector, the dichotomy between transportation services and transport infrastructure and the diversity of indicators used to measures these aspects of transport vary from those captured by the economic indicators. Is it the quality of transport services, reliability, or the efficiency of auxiliary services such as the financial sector that play the most important or vital role in growth and transformation? Is it the cost and affordability of transport services delivery, or the quality and capacity of transport infrastructure, which best correspond to productive capacities and structural economic transformation, and enhance the creation of wealth in nations?

Furthermore, the diversity of countries (geographical and population size, location, and the varied priorities of governments) adds to the complexity in measuring and benchmarking the transport category of productive capacities. Small island developing states (SIDS), by virtue of their small landmass, have fewer transport networks but much higher density. The same applies to inland countries with smaller geographical size. Geographically, larger countries, although they may have a high number of (road or rail) networks, can still have lower density per square kilometre. Similarly, SSA's countries also vary significantly in population size, ranging from the least populous (Seychelles: 97,000 in 2018) to the most populous (Nigeria: 196 million in 2018). The size of population is very important in measuring the accessibility of transport networks and services as well as in measuring density per 100 or 1,000 people. Diversity across SSA also exists in government policies and strategies, which create further challenges when comparing and benchmarking the countries of SSA based on their transport infrastructure. Some governments prioritize road networks over rail networks, or they may not have the financial capabilities to build capital- or technology-intensive infrastructure such as rail or air connectivity. Sometimes, the objectives of prioritizing transport infrastructure may vary from country to country. In some countries, the objective of government policies may focus on how best to facilitate the flow of goods and services across regions or sectors of the economy through export-oriented strategies. In others, they may favour industrial location, mining, or manufacturing by creating transport connectivity between production sites and areas where productive resources are located (to facilitate forward and backward sectoral linkages).

The complex set of factors (indicators) involved when measuring transport infrastructure, the diversity of countries, and variations in the objectives of policies and strategies, make a given index unnecessarily burdensome. Complex indices pose enormous challenges to interpret and operationalize it through policies or institutions. Therefore, any operationally meaningful index should be simple, direct, and easy to make full use of in policy formulation and implementation processes as well as in tracking and measuring outcomes of such policies.

With a view to making the index easy but also realistic to interpret in a policy context and given the lack of comprehensive data on transport (e.g., percentage of paved roads just to measure the quality of roads across SSA), the focus in the UNCTAD PCI is on four important transport indicators.[5]

Figure 3.5 shows the level of transport infrastructure and its evolution in SSA as compared to the developing countries of Asia and Latin America as well as China during the 2000–2018 period. Interestingly, the score for China was as equal as the average of developing Asia and slightly above the rest of the developing regions in 2000. This reflects the greater importance in China of the weight of population, the density of some key transport infrastructure and the country's geographical size than the low level of transport infrastructure per se. However, the extraordinary progress made by China, particularly after 2005, shows how the transport component of productive capacities evolved in the country in a relatively short period of time. This reflects an increased investment[6] and modernization of the transport component in China. It also indicates the dynamism observed in the overall economic transformation of China that also propelled

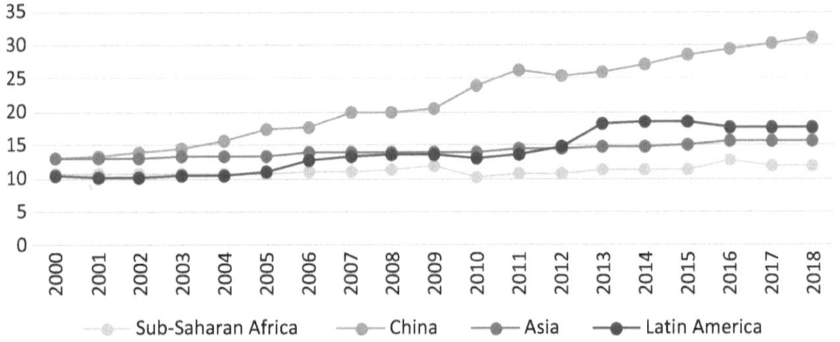

Figure 3.5 Transport category of productive capacities in SSA, Asia, Latin America, and China (2000–2018).

Source: UNCTAD global Productive Capacities Index (PCI).

other sectors such as the transport component to grow. The change observed in China is simply remarkable.

Statistically, as Figure 3.5 demonstrates, all the country groups have improved their transport components during the 2000–2018 period, although the degree of improvement varies across regional groupings. Latin America has also seen substantial improvement when compared to the Asian developing countries and SSA in recent years. Contrary to other developing regions, improvement in the transport component in SSA is very modest. The said lag in SSA is despite the increasing public investment (including grants, credits, and loans from China) in the transport sector. Poor or weak infrastructure often acts as constraint to development and vice versa. While the low level of the transport component in SSA reflects the overall underdevelopment of the region, its weak growth and lack of development also affects the capacity to invest in modern infrastructure. For instance, the poor level of transport infrastructure in SSA undermines the region's participation in regional and global production and supply networks. It also weakens export competitiveness, investment decisions, and the capacity to attract and benefit from private investments (domestic and foreign), thus undermining prospects for structural transformation.

3.2.4 *Energy (Electricity)*

The positive role of energy (electricity) in the production of goods and delivery of services has long been recognized. Energy is also vital for improving efficiency, productivity, and competitiveness as well as for generating economic growth. Countries that have achieved a higher level of economic growth and development also have reliable, affordable, and more efficient energy supplies than countries at a lower level on the development ladder. The World Economic Forum (WEF: 2012) argues that steady and reliable energy supplies are crucial to economic growth and transformation in developing countries. Accordingly, approximately 19 percent of the final energy consumption is in the form of electricity (WEF: 2012, 2018). Further work on the role of power (energy) in Chinese economic growth and transformation reveals that the combination of the three sources of energy (coal, oil, and renewable energy) are the main drivers of the impressive socioeconomic performance of China during the last several decades (Bloch et al: 2015). Other studies place emphasis on renewable energy as the driver of economic growth both in developed and developing countries. Building on data from 20 developed and developing countries for the period of 1995–2016, Singh et al. (2019) provide evidence that renewable energy production is closely associated with a positive and statistically significant impact on economic growth both in developed and developing countries. In developed economies, such as industrialized countries of the Organisation for Economic Cooperation and Development (OECD), Salim et al. (2014) also argue that there is a two-way relationship, particularly in the long run, that links energy consumption (both green and conventional) with industrial production and GDP growth.

At the enterprise level, firms that enjoy a reliable energy supply are more competitive, productive, efficient, and dynamic than firms that have little, costly, or intermittent energy supplies. The most recent World Enterprise Survey of the World Bank (see Chapter 6) indicates that bad or otherwise insufficient access, availability, and affordability of energy (reliable electricity) is among the most important factors undermining firms' competitiveness in developing countries, notably in Africa. Moreover, SSA's economic vulnerability is directly linked to the production and export of energy (fossil fuels). Volatility and changes in the international prices of fossil fuels are behind the causes of external economic shocks undermining SSA's socioeconomic performance and lack of structural transformation.

Overall, there is a positive role for energy for enhancing production, productivity, export competitiveness, and economic growth, both at micro- and macroeconomic levels. However, economists are divided on the causal relationship between energy consumption (input) and economic growth and the direction of such a relationship. For instance, Kraft and Kraft (1978) argue that there is a unidirectional causal relationship between the energy input (consumption) and GDP of the USA. However, subsequent works by Akarca and Long (1980) and Yu and Jin (1992) did not find any causal relationship between energy use and economic growth. Further work on the subject (Gosh: 2002, Stern and Cleveland: 2004) argues that there is a unidirectional relationship between energy and economic growth although there is no equilibrium relationship to speak of statistically or econometrically. For Asghar (2008), the causal relationship between energy consumption and GDP depends on the characteristics of a given economy (agriculture-, services-, or manufacturing-driven), and the source of energy used (coal, gas, or total energy consumption) in the production of outputs and delivery of services.

The importance of energy in sub-Saharan African economies is significant as more than ten countries in the region are classified as producers and exporters of fossil fuels. Nigeria, Angola, and Equatorial Guinea top the list in SSA and occupy important places among global oil and gas producing and exporting nations. Some studies (BP: 2011, UNECA: 2011b) argue that Africa as a whole, holds nearly 10 percent, 8 percent, and 4 percent, respectively, of the world's proven reserves in crude oil, natural gas, and coal. According to the International Energy Agency, these together account for about 50 percent of the total primary energy supply (TPES) and one third of energy consumption in SSA (IEA: 2011b).

SSA's share in world reserves is 6.52 percent of oil, 4.26 percent of natural gas, and 0.7 percent of coal (excluding South Africa, which is among the top ten producers of coal in the world). These correspond to 65.2 percent, 53.3 percent, and 17 percent, respectively, in the oil, natural gas, and coal reserves of the African region. However, the actual production level of SSA was 3.19 percent, 3.8 percent, and 0.2 percent, respectively, in 2014 (SOGA: 2019). Energy is also a major source of export revenue for several SSA countries. Extractive resources (oil and natural gas) account for 93 percent of Angola's (UNCTADStat: 2019) and 94.1 percent of Nigeria's export earnings in 2018 (WTEx: 2020). Several countries in SSA also hold huge potential in hydroelectricity although the scale and intensity of this source of energy in the "African energy mix" still has a long way to go. (The potential of SSA in hydroelectricity is estimated at about 16 percent of total energy generation and more than 50 percent of electricity consumed in several countries in the region (UNIDO: 2009, IEA: 2011a).) However, only 7 percent of the existing hydropotential in the subcontinent is utilized (World Energy Council – WEC: 2010).

Despite SSA's huge potential in total energy resources, the role of energy (power) in industrialization, structural economic transformation, and fostering the productive capacities of the region is insignificant and the lowest of all the developing regions (see Figure 3.6). Measured by key indicators,[7] SSA did not shown any improvements during 2000–2018. Developing Asia and China have outperformed the rest of the developing world. How countries such as Vietnam have harnessed energy (electricity) for transforming economic social sector outcomes such as health, education, and job creation, including in rural areas, can serve as a useful guide for countries of SSA (Chapters 7 and 8). SSA's score on the scale has remained disappointingly low and constant throughout the period examined. Overall, as can be seen from Figure 3.6, the Asian continent and China have shown a consistently higher level of energy (electricity) use in productive capacities. This shows China's phenomenal transformation in recent years and Asia's dominant role in the production and export of manufacturing. Until 2003 China's performance had been lower than or equal to that of the Asian developing countries (excluding China itself). However, after 2004, China has consistently exceeded one of the top performing regions in the energy category of productive capacities. Latin America has also performed consistently and significantly higher than SSA, although it has been outperformed by the Asian developing countries and China.

The low or woefully inadequate level of the energy (power) component of productive capacities in SSA means that: (i) with such a low level of energy

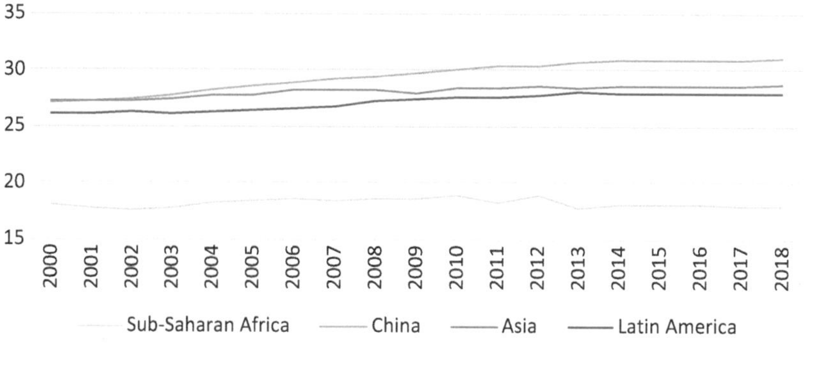

Figure 3.6 Energy category of productive capacities in SSA, Asia, Latin America, and China (2000–2018).

Source: UNCTAD global Productive Capacities Index (PCI).

(electricity) use in productive capacities, it will be extremely difficult for countries in SSA to quickly foster higher levels of productivity and structural economic transformation; (ii) the increasing level of trade and economic engagement of SSA with China has brought little or no change in the energy component of productive capacities of the region. This trend is despite the increased engagement of China in SSA's energy infrastructure. Also, in SSA, energy has not been used in large quantities for productive purposes. Therefore, the huge energy potential of the region has not contributed to building productive capacities or economic transformation (e.g. manufacturing); (iii) energy resources are still disproportionately geared towards exports without value addition and value retention in the economies of SSA as exports of crude oil dominate the export structure of major suppliers such as Angola, Equatorial Guinea, and Nigeria; (iv) the weak and low energy intensity of SSA economies means that entrepreneurship, competitiveness, and productivity of key sectors in the region are negatively affected; (v) the cost electricity in several countries of SSA remains high and varies widely, ranging from USD 24.40 per megawatt of electricity in Ethiopia (least expensive) to USD 490 in Liberia (most expensive) in 2016, which makes economies of the region internationally uncompetitive and unattractive for FDI firms and domestic private sector development; and (vi) with increasing pressure to reduce greenhouse gas emissions and to find environment-friendly alternative energy sources, the continued overdependence of several SSA countries on the export of fossil fuel can have serious repercussions on the overall socioeconomic performance of the region in the future.

3.2.5 *Structural Change*

As indicated earlier, in theory, structural change refers to short-term quantitative change in an economy. However, it can also show the type of structural transformation – the wrong or the right type (Chapter 8), depending on the degree, extent, and depth of changes observed. Structural change, when not accompanied with qualitative and transformative changes (e.g., change in the composition of GDP without fundamental internally dynamic transformation), signals the wrong type of transformation. Whereas, the right type of structural transformation occurs when internally dynamic and long-term qualitative changes are observed in a given economy (e.g., technological sophistication of exports or sustained qualitative change in the composition of GDP). As discussed in previous chapters, without productive capacities, kick-starting transformation and ensuring inclusive, equitable, and sustainable economic growth and development can be daunting. In the countries of SSA, commodity-driven growth failed to trickle down and has not created quality jobs or contributed to poverty reduction. Nor has it led to an increase in aggregate income, capital accumulation, or capital formation for production transformation. Despite structural change or change in the composition of GDP (a shift from subsistence agriculture to low-skill, low value-added services sectors), structural or long-term transformation (as defined in Chapter 2), remains weak or non-existent in SSA (Figure 3.7). What is observed in SSA is the wrong type of structural transformation.

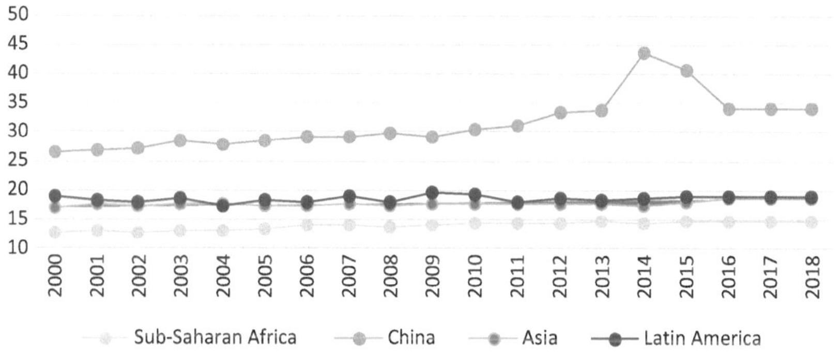

Figure 3.7 Structural change category of productive capacities in SSA, Asia, Latin America, and China (2000–2018).

Source: UNCTAD global Productive Capacities Index (PCI).

In measuring structural change, the indicators[8] used to compare SSA with other developing regions on the levels of structural change serve as a prelude to structural transformation or lack thereof. Along with individual indicators, SSA countries measure high on merchandise export concentration and diversification indices, both of which are negatively related to productive capacities and structural economic transformation. Higher export concentration and diversification indices show poor productive capacities, lack of transformation in the export sector, and the overdependence of SSA on exports of a handful of primary commodities. This is discussed in greater detail in Chapter 4, which is devoted to analyzing the role in and implication of the PCI for Africa-China economic ties when it comes to fostering productive capacities and structural transformation in SSA.

On a composite index consisting of the above-mentioned indicators of structural change, the performance of SSA is dismally low and inadequate when compared to other developing regions (Asia, Latin America, and China). China has demonstrated a rapid pace and higher level of structural change, converging with traditional developed or industrialized economies (UNCTAD: 2020b). The "hump" in 2013–2015 of China's structural change was the result of the continued intensification of manufacturing exports and the increasing technological sophistication of exports that exacts improved global demand for the country's such exports worldwide. Developing regions (Asia and Latin America) have also improved the level and degree of structural change as an indication of the region's economic transformation. However, the pace and level of transformation in the two regions has moderately decelerated during and after the 2008–2009 global economic and financial crises. The impact of these crises was also observed in all the regions and China itself. The 2015–2016 decline in China's scores reflect the slow growth in GDP and trade observed in the country, due largely to sluggish global demand for Chinese exports (WTO: 2016). Still, the level attained by China is remarkable and an indication of fundamental changes occurring in the country's economy. Contrary to other developing regions and China, the level of structural change in SSA is very low, although there is a moderate upward trend during the 2000–2018 period. While there are some positive (but weak) signs of structural change in SSA, it is not enough to make a dent on the poor and sluggish socioeconomic performance of the region. The change is too little or insignificant and does not allow the countries of the region to kick-start the process of fostering productive capacities and accelerating structural economic transformation. As with the other key components of productive capacities, the subregion is lagging behind the rest of the developing regions on structural change component. For SSA to converge with the other developing regions and to make progress in its socioeconomic transformation, the region should intensify economic diversification, including producing high-value and technologically sophisticated export items and a knowledge-intensive services.

3.2.6 *Information and Communications Technology (ICT)*

Understanding the role of technology, innovation, and technological progress in economic growth and development has been central to theories[9] of economic growth and development. Rapid changes in production and consumption structures are inevitable, given the differential impact of technological innovation on factor productivity and productive sectors of a given economy. Acemoglu (2007) provides comprehensive empirical and quantitative analysis on the subject and argues that the difference in income and development between nations is explained by investment in physical capital, human capital, and technological differences. Without technological upgrading and learning (through technology transfers, dissemination, and industrial and technology policies), public investment-led approaches alone will not lead to structural economic transformation – i.e., the production of high-value, high-quality, and more sophisticated products (Tesfachew: 2019). Further work on technology for development focuses on technological catch-up and convergence with developed countries (Abramovitz: 1986).

The advent of Information and Communication Technology (ICT) as well as exports of ICT services, now rapidly growing, has been the key driver of growth and an enabler of the transformation process (UNCTAD: 2017b). This trend has and will have profound implications for business, jobs creation, and achieving Sustainable Development Goals (SDGs), including specific goals and targets on poverty reduction and elimination of extreme poverty by 2030. Available evidence suggests that ICT is transforming not only the production and productivity landscapes of economies, but also the distribution and consumption patterns as well as the way individuals and societies live. However, the benefits of ICT have not yet been equally distributed across nations, regions, and firms. The digital economy (i.e., ICT, e-commerce, and other digital applications) not only creating new opportunities for trade and development but also digital divide between and within nations. These are being leveraged to promote entrepreneurship, productive activities, decent job creation, creativity, and technological innovation (UNCTAD: 2017b).

Sectors which are traditionally considered as backward such as agriculture are also getting the benefits of ICT in terms of accelerating the integration of the sector to markets and consumers. This includes improving on-farm and off-farm jobs, incomes, and businesses, facilitating the flow of market information, and enhancing forward and backward linkages. Such linkages are not confined only to the agriculture and industrial sectors. They also include the service sector such as hotels, transport, and distribution services. The report by the International Institute for Environment and Development (IIED: 2012) based on estimates provided by Vodafone and Accenture (2011), argues that more than other ICT drivers, mobile telephone subscriptions are revolutionizing the agriculture sector. The report estimates that this trend is expected to increase agricultural income by about USD 138 billion across several nations, including many developing countries in coming years. However, SSA continues to be a marginal player in embracing ICT for production transformation.

To measure the level of ICT in SSA and other developing regions and China (Figure 3.8), several important indicators[10] are used. The indicators used to measure this category provide some clues about the overall technological environment. Other useful indicators such as investments, capital, and technological acquisition, which can be used to measure the processes of technological capability-building, are not included in the assessment of this category of productive capacities because gross fixed capital formation (GFCF) has already been captured in structural change component.

China's outstanding performance in this category reflects the country's overall progress in building technological capabilities, notably in ICT. Latin America and developing regions of Asia have also made significant progress, increasingly converging with China. The modest improvement of SSA on ICT is better than the region's other categories such as transport, energy, human capital, and structural change. However, a closer examination of the evolving footprint of ICT shows that while China and other developing regions have made substantial progress on almost all the indicators used, SSA's progress is driven largely by mobile phone subscriptions. SSA significantly lags behind the rest of the developing world particularly in broadband internet use and access as well as in digitalization,

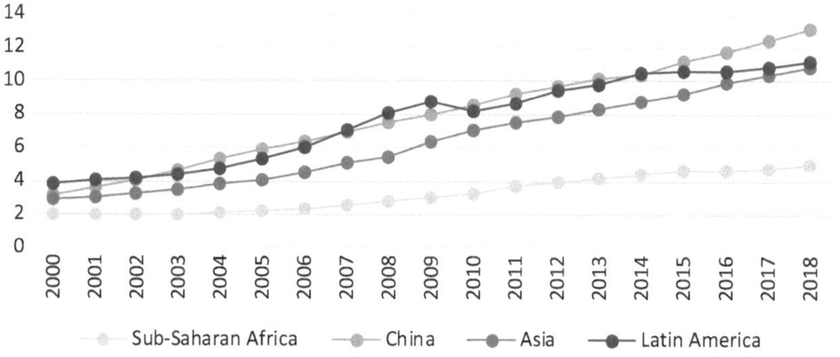

Figure 3.8 ICT category of productive capacities in SSA, Asia, Latin America, and China (2000–2018).

Source: UNCTAD global Productive Capacities Index (PCI).

trademark applications and patent registrations. While Asia, including Vietnam has become a producer and exporter of technology components, computer parts, communication equipment, digital applications, hardware, and software (see Chapters 7 and 8), SSA is significantly lagging behind the rest of the developing regions in technological progress and catch-up.

3.2.7 *Private Sector Development*

The private sector is an engine of productivity growth, competitiveness, employment creation and upgrading production processes. The sector is vital to foster social capabilities, entrepreneurship, and enhance investment and capital formation as well as the production of goods and the delivery of services. However, the sector cannot deliver all these on its own. It needs facilitative and conducive policy frameworks, functioning institutions, and support services from the public sector. If the public and private sectors do not work together towards economic transformation and development, attaining sustained economic growth and development will not be realized. A vibrant and dynamic private sector is necessary to make government policies and strategies more responsive to outcomes, or to become result oriented. Domestic policy reforms, be they in agriculture, manufacturing, or the service sectors, will not be fully implemented and achieve the desired outcomes without a vibrant and dynamic private sector. Overall, the private sector should be viewed as a powerful actor in the development process. It is key to harnessing the potential of the human capital and natural resources of countries for transformational development and technological progress.

The sector is also key to job creation, economic diversification, value addition, and overall structural economic transformation. These can be achieved via trade, investment, and technology flows as well as by joining production networks and fostering production linkages and business networks. That is, the private sector is vital in facilitating the participation of economies in national, regional, and global value chains. The sector is particularly instrumental in facilitating production linkages, innovation, business interactions, and production clusters not only between firms but also across the various economic sectors (through enhanced forward and backward interactions).

In SSA, the role of the private sector is very weak, despite improvements in policy and institutional frameworks that are believed to be supportive and facilitative of private initiatives. To illustrate gaps between improved policies and institutional environments and the results achieved in SSA, it is instructive to examine the case of countries which put in place the right mix of policies and institutions with the aim of fostering the private sector-led economy. Rwanda is one of the countries in SSA that has put in place several interesting strategies[11] and modern institutions[12] to enhance the role of the private sector and accelerate the fostering of productive capacities and structural economic transformation. The policies and strategies, as well as the institutional and legal frameworks of the Government of Rwanda, are clear indications of its strong commitment to foster private sector-led economy and accelerate the transformational development of the country, whose stated ambition is to become an upper middle-income and high-income country, respectively, by 2030 and 2050 (Ministry of Finance and Economic Planning of Rwanda: 2019).

However, the development challenges still facing the country are many, the private sector is weak and the task of significantly transforming the economy remains daunting. For instance, the above-mentioned proactive government policies and improved institutional and regulatory frameworks are in place, with the aim of fostering productive capacities and structural transformation as well as creating a dynamic and competitive private sector. However, the gaps and limitations related to the full operationalization of such policies left the private sector's contribution very small and the prospects of accelerated structural economic transformation narrow.

The Rwandan private sector also suffers from increasing informality and fragmentation. According to the latest Integrated Households Living Conditions Survey, more than 98 percent of the country's enterprises are regarded as micro, small, and medium-sized and more than 90 percent informal (NISR: 2017). The Government of Rwanda has been undertaking several policy and incentive-related initiatives aimed at building entrepreneurial capabilities. These include the provision of business development advisory services, support to access financial services, and the provision of targeted support through enterprise coaching. However, the weakness in the role and contribution of the private sector is beyond policies and institutions. Such poor performances are due to systemic constraints, which undermine the growth and expansion of the country's economy (Rwirahira: 2020). For instance, the cost[13] of access to finance undermines the availability of loans and credits to the private sector as well as lack of linkages[14] between domestic and foreign firms, undermining competitiveness, growth, and expansion of the role of the private sector in the economy of Rwanda. Consequently, there are no visible forward and backward sectoral linkages either, as foreign firms import 100 percent of their intermediate inputs and semi-finished products from abroad, principally from China in the case of textiles. Foreign firms use Rwanda only for cutting and trimming textiles (clothing) and for taking advantage of the market access offered to the country by the EU, the USA, and other developed and developing country markets. There are no economy-wide production linkages, transfer of skills, and knowhow, with little or no value retention within the domestic economy.

This notwithstanding, and given the history of the country, the progress achieved by Rwanda thus far in terms of addressing extreme poverty and establishing institutional and legal frameworks is remarkable. This includes the formulation and implementation of top-quality trade and development policies and strategies. However, the degree and extent of structural transformation is narrow, and the private sector remains weak. Rwanda's limited success in fostering productive capacities and structural economic transformation put into question the relevance of long-held premises of orthodox policy prescriptions from donors and multilateral financial institutions that creating conducive macroeconomic, regulatory, and institutional frameworks is a panacea for all socioeconomic woes.

The case of Rwanda also suggests that there is a need for the governments of SSA to go beyond the current preoccupation with poverty reduction objectives. This should include realigning or matching the ambitions of development visions, plans, and policies with financial and technical resources as well as institutional capacities. While the formulation of policies in Rwanda has significantly improved, gaps and limitations in the implementation of such high-quality policies are all too apparent. In some cases, there is a mismatch between available financial resources and policy ambitions as the country still heavily depends on Official Development Assistance (ODA) for financing its development priorities and objectives. The Government of Rwanda also needs to urgently revise its incentive schemes for the private sector, realigning such schemes with its transformational development and targeting them to domestic firms that generate jobs, and add value to the commodities sector. Incentives should particularly favour firms that are dynamic, able to learn, and innovate.

The case of Rwanda is not unique in SSA. It reflects the actual situation of several countries in SSA. According to Gebreeyesus (2019), in Ethiopia, the activities of the private sector are confined to the domestic service sector (not productive sectors such as manufacturing) and market where returns are relatively high and quick. In some other countries such as Botswana or Namibia, macroeconomic and institutional fundamentals are fine for the growth of the private sector, with states playing an indispensable role not only in formulating policies and providing incentives to firms, but also leading investments in key sectors. However, the private sector's contribution to economic growth and structural transformation in the two countries is very weak as it generates only one in five jobs. This may be related to the rigidity of the two economies, which are driven by technology- and capital-intensive extractive sectors. Africa's private sector development has also been adversely impacted by public indebtedness which constrained the countries' capacity to invest, diversify, and develop. This has constrained not only the fiscal space of Africa's governments but also the private sector because that governments are obliged to raise taxes in a bid to narrow their respective fiscal deficits and fulfil debt repayment obligations. The nexus between the mounting public debt of African countries and the insignificant role of their private sector has been among the subjects less debated between creditor and debtor nations.

Several indicators[15] are used in assessing private sector category (component) of the Productive Capacities Index (PCI) shown in Figure 3.9. Most of these indicators assess constraining factors bearing on the expansion of the private sector. Institutional indicators (as part of the overall macroeconomic framework) that are relevant to this issue are not included in this component or category of productive capacities. This is simply because institutional indicators are regarded as a category of their own – an important one for fostering productive capacities in the entire economy (see the section on institutions below).

As can be seen from Figure 3.9, the results on this component show significant variation between China's performance and the average scores of other developing countries during 2000–2018. This, in turn, indicates an increasingly important role of the private sector in the country's economy. Latin American and Asian private sectors have also maintained a relatively similar pattern and profile.

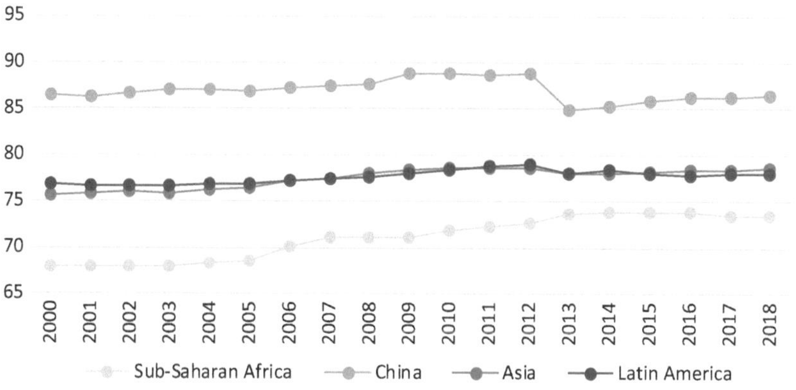

Figure 3.9 Private sector category of productive capacities in SSA, Asia, Latin America, and China (2000–2018).

Source: UNCTAD global Productive Capacities Index (PCI).

The somewhat lower level of the private sector component in Asia is the result of the high cost of exporting a container in the landlocked countries of the region (14 out of 32 such countries are in Asia). Asia also shows weakness in enforcing contracts and delays in starting a business, notably in the former republics of the Soviet Union (USSR) such as Kazakhstan, Uzbekistan, Turkmenistan, and so on. Not surprisingly, on all the indicators of the private sector component, SSA's performance is the weakest of all the developing regions. This confirms, once again, the weak and low contribution of the private sector in its economies. However, there has been an improvement in the index for SSA over the period covered by the measurement exercise. This modest improvement is an indication that some policy reforms implemented by SSA countries are beginning to bear fruit, although such is not enough to build productive capacities and transform the economies of the region. The policy implications of a low private sector score in SSA should be seen as an opportunity to address systemic challenges and structural problems that go beyond policy issues. It takes more than policies and strategies to enhance the role of the private sector in economic development in SSA. Besides putting in place coherent and consistent micro and macroeconomic policies and strategies, building institutions, providing key infrastructure such as electricity, improving access to finance, and designing an effective incentive structure are critically important for the development of the private sector in Africa.

3.2.8 *Institutions*[16]

The role of institutions in economic development had long been ignored by mainstream or orthodox economic theories, whose exclusive focus has been on endogenous variables such as total factor productivity and accumulation. Ronald Coase, who is regarded as the father of institutional economics through his seminal work "The Nature of the Firm" (1937), views this lack of interest in mainstream economics in institutions as the result of their excessive obsession with abstract economic concepts that fail to capture or understand the real world (Coase: 1998). Such omissions and errors are responsible for the absence, to date, of a dedicated theory or theoretical framework on institutions and their role in economic growth and development. Nevertheless, there has been a substantial body of literature on institutions and their role in economic development, which led to the advent of institutional economics (Coase: 1998, Williamson: 2000). Notwithstanding this, there is a "vast amount of unfinished business, refinements, new applications, extensions and good ideas" needed to develop a stand-alone theory of institutions and the part they play in the economy (Williamson: 2000).

Despite the lack of an overarching theoretical framework, there is growing understanding or convergence in the important role of institutions in economic development. Acemoglu et al. (2005) argue that economic institutions define and determine the incentives of and constraints on economic actors, and shape economic outcomes and, as such, differences in economic institutions are fundamental causes of cross-country differences in prosperity (Acemoglu et al. 2005). Besides economic institutions (formal and informal constraints), state institutions or public bureaucracies are central in formulating and implementing development policies and strategies. These include transparent and accountable governance; law enforcement mechanisms, agencies, and institutions; legal systems that promote equality and curb corruption; and political regimes that promote voice and accountability in public administration (World Bank: 2000/2001). All these are critically important in creating microeconomic, macroeconomic, and stable economic governance. These important aspects of institutional environments are often forgotten even in a traditional analysis of institutions, focusing more on resource allocation and efficiency gains than on creating conducive, facilitative, and functioning institutional frameworks or environments. Such a focus on efficiency in resource allocation contrasts with arguments in favour of vibrant and internally consistent state institutions such as those advanced by North (1991) and Evans and Heller (2018). Like Acemoglu, North (1991) argues that the role of institutions consists of creating order and reducing uncertainty, not only in the functioning of market forces but also in the daily operations and businesses of societies as they define "constraints and incentives by connecting the past with present and the future". Similarly, Evens and Heller (2018) emphasize the vital role of "capable and internally coherent bureaucracies in providing predictability" in rules and laws of engagement, administrative, and decision-making processes backed by public participation in the development process.

In most SSA countries, public or state institutions are far too weak to formulate and implement policies. In some countries the quality of policies has improved significantly in recent years, but implementation and outcome of the policies remain below expectations. This gap between policies and expected outcomes is largely because the goals are sometimes unnecessarily ambitious and are not realigned with the capacity of implementing institutions. Still, in most cases, institutions in SSA lack skilled labour, financial, and technical resources. At other times, the focus of policymakers has solely been on the quantity of political outcomes (e.g., quantity of growth) than the form, quality, inclusiveness, and sustainability of such growth. In fact, the quantity of growth is a highly politicized electoral issue in SSA – more so than in any other developing region. Excessive focus on achieving higher economic growth, ignoring inclusiveness and its distributional aspects, has been the rallying cry for political leaders in and out of office in most of SSA (see Chapter 1).

The types and scale of productive capacities and the pace of structural transformation are dependent on policies, institutions, and growth-acceleration processes. For instance, for industrialization, productive transformation, and structural change to occur, capable and proactive state institutions as well as the right mix of polices are necessary. These are key to building markets and nurturing enterprises, encouraging technological upgrading, fostering learning processes, accumulating capabilities, and unlocking constraints to infrastructure (for more detail on this, see Chapter 2, particularly the contributions of Salzar-Xirinaches et al: 2014).

Capturing institutions through a composite index is not straightforward. This is due to two important factors. The first one is the complex nature of institutions and the myriad of factors influencing them (Williamson: 2000). The second challenge relates to the limitations of data and an absence of direct indicators that precisely measure institutions and their environment. In the present discussions of the institutions category of productive capacities, several indicators[17] are used. The indicators have four important limitations: first, they are process-oriented and not outcome or output-oriented. This means that they do not tell us the periodic (yearly) outcome of a given policy implemented by institutions. Nor do they precisely indicate the causal relationship between institutions and economic growth. Notwithstanding this, empirical evidence demonstrates that countries with effective and high-quality institutions are also those which boast higher levels of economic growth and development. Secondly, the indicators are based on perceptions (subjective assessment) rather than actual outcomes or direct performance. Indicators on regulatory quality, government effectiveness, and the level of corruption are measured through perception-based indices. Third, the indicators used to measure the institutional category of productive capacities do not measure institutional strength or capacity to formulate and implement policies as well as achieve desired results. Nor do they help us to understand how decisions are made, how technical and financial resources are allocated and how these are realigned with the overall development objectives, goals, and targets contained in policies and strategies. Therefore, the indicators used in the measurement leave several questions unanswered. How do institutions contribute to the achievement of specific goals and targets contained in domestic or global policy documents? What level of financial and technical resources is made available to them? How do they (institutions) provide incentives to improve the delivery of services or curb cronyism or corruption? Finally, the indicators used do not indicate or measure the level or degree of policy coordination (or lack of it) among the various institutions. How are institutions coordinated and what coordination mechanisms exist in the countries and regions compared and benchmarked? Are coordination mechanisms, if any, participatory? How is the flow of information facilitated between and among institutions? These limitations or shortcomings are important and, as part of the "unfinished business" of developing a dedicated theory of institutions, as argued by Williamson (2000), the search for more direct and statistically measurable indicators should be vigorously pursued. Despite these limitations inherent in the indicators, lack of data, and statistical information, the indicators used are important in assessing the role of institutions in fostering productive capacities and structural economic transformation (Figure 3.10). In other words, lack of voice and accountability and prevalence of corruption are the causes and consequences of weak institutions. These undermine the economic growth, inclusiveness, or distributional impacts of such growth, thus maximizing the risk of social and political instabilities and eventually leading to the situation of failed states. Therefore, the results of the measurement should be taken seriously.

As can be observed in Figure 3.10, the Latin American region has performed consistently higher than developing Asia, China, and SSA during the period considered. However, all the regions have shown, in varying degrees, modest improvements in their institutional score over the last nearly two decades apart from Latin America. Unlike SSA, the rest of the developing regions and China have shown some level of convergence. China's performance was accelerating during 2000–2018. In 2001 (the lowest reference year for all the regions and China), the mean value for Latin America was 50, for developing Asia 46.4, for China 43.5, and 38.8 for SSA. Seventeen years later (in 2018), the respective mean values were about 52, 47, 46, and 39. Such slow rates of change for all the countries compared underline the fact that institutional changes are not automatic but are slow or incremental which require consistent and long-term efforts. As with other categories discussed earlier, the performance of SSA in institutions is low and weak throughout the period compared. The low score of the region is the result of several factors such as lack of financial, human, and technical resources; protracted conflicts and interethnic tensions; authoritative governance and mismanagement of rents from natural resource, including corruption, kleptocracy, nepotism, and cronyism.

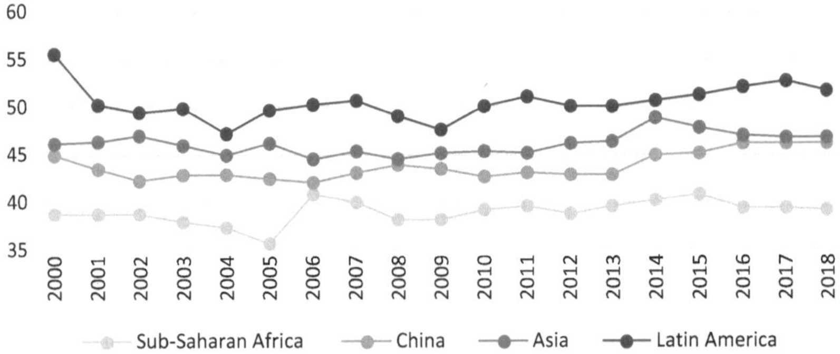

Figure 3.10 Institutions category of productive capacities in SSA, Asia, Latin America, and China (2000–2018).

Source: UNCTAD global Productive Capacities Index (PCI).

3.2.9 Productive Capacities Index (PCI) in Comparison

The components (categories) of productive capacities discussed above should not be viewed in isolation from one another. Each of the categories is essential for production transformation in any economy – developed or developing. Each of them is also interconnected and improvements in one lead to improvements in the rest of the categories. For instance, if natural capital is sustainably harnessed and rents are judiciously captured in human capital formation, this leads to improvements in institutions, private sector development, and better absorption and utilization of ICT in enhancing productivity and structural transformation. Likewise, better investment in energy including clean energy sources, will enhance the competitive edge of the private sector and application of ICT in knowledge and capital formation. Each category therefore leads to productive capacities, and as hinted earlier, productive capacities and structural transformation go hand in hand. Without the requisite domestic productive capacities and structural transformation, it will be difficult or impossible for developing countries such as those in SSA to relax binding constraints to their development. Moreover, exploiting comparative advantages, building international (export) competitiveness, and addressing overall socioeconomic vulnerabilities require fostering productive capacities and structural transformation. The continued socioeconomic vulnerabilities and fragilities inherent in SSA are the causes and consequences of weak productive capacities and the absence of structural economic transformation. These challenges have made convergence of income levels and technological catch-up between SSA and the rest of the world difficult. This, in turn, has undermined efforts aimed at closing the growing development gap between these countries and industrialized economies (McMillan et al.: 2017). By using the mean values of each of the eight categories and applying standard statistical aggregation and weighting methods developed by UNCTAD (UNCTAD: 2020d), a composite index – Productive Capacities Index (PCI) – is developed to measures the overall productive capacities of SSA and other developing regions for the 2000–2018 period (Figure 3.11).

China's performance is unsurprisingly outstanding. This impressive performance on overall PCI explains the country's unprecedented socioeconomic progress which is increasingly converging with industrialized economies. Latin America and developing Asia are also following in the footsteps of China in the composite PCI. The index for SSA has also shown modest improvement. However, the region has been consistently lagging behind the developing regions and China throughout the years observed. Even the improvements observed in SSA are largely driven by the natural capital component. Statistically, this slightly diminishes the PCI for other regions and proportionately increases that of SSA's scores. When the natural component is removed from the scale, SSA's PCI has shown little or no improvement over the years considered.

The conclusion from the above comparison of levels and conditions of productive capacities and of the degree of structural change is that SSA remains the weakest of all the developing regions, despite its increased trade, investment, and development finance ties with China. Likewise, the flow of ODA, investments, and increased market access provided for SSA by traditional development partners have

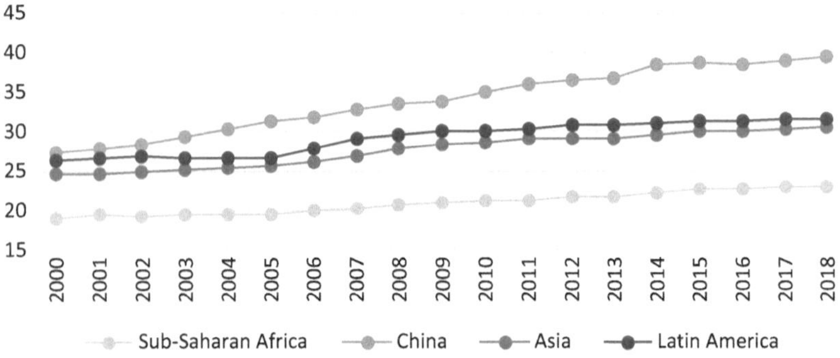

Figure 3.11 Composite Productive Capacities Index (PCI) in SSA, Asia, Latin America, and China (2000–2018).

Source: UNCTAD global Productive Capacities Index (PCI).

not altered the region's core growth-facilitating fundamentals: weak productive capacities and lack of structural economic transformation. For SSA, improving the level of productive capacities and reaching those of Asia and Latin America would have made the sub-region's socioeconomic performance comparable to the two developing regions. The question is: what are the implications of such low levels and conditions of SSA's productive capacities for Africa-China expanding trade, development finance, and investment relations? Chapter 4 analyzes these implications by providing further evidence and key statistical indicators or benchmarks.

Notes

1 Sustainable Development Goals (SDGs) are the goals and targets of the United Nations adopted by the heads of state and government of the member states of the United Nations in 2015 as successors to the previous Millennium Development Goals (MDGs) implemented during 2000–2015 period – with mixed outcomes (for details, see https://www.un.org/sustainabledevelopment/sustainable-development-goals/).

2 Data sources used in the construction of the PCI include diverse sources such as the World Development Open Data, World Bank Development Indicators, World Enterprise Survey (World Bank), Doing Business Raking (World Bank), Energy For All, UNCTADstat, UNIDOstat, Comtrade, ITU, WIPO Innovation Index, and OECD data, among others.

3 These include (i) percentage of total agricultural land in total land area; (ii) share of total arable land in total land area or share of land covered by forests; (iii) natural resources rent as percentage of GDP; and (iv) total extractive material in kilograms/USD. The fourth and last indicator is the sum of extraction of fossil fuels, industrial minerals (such as copper, iron, and aluminium) in a year.

4 These include life expectancy as a proxy for sustained contribution of societies to productive capacities; average years of schooling as a proxy for the duration and expected years of education; R&D expenditure as share of GDP; number of researchers per million people and the respective GDP shares of government expenditure on education and health.

5 These include two indicators in air transport (such as registered carrier departures worldwide per 100 people, and freight in million t/km), one in road transport (in km of roads/100 km^2 of land) and one more in rail infrastructure (total km rail lines per capita). Investments (public and private) or share of investment going to the transport infrastructure or services could have been used as an additional indicator to measure the level of transport infrastructure in SSA. However, comprehensive and consistent data is hard to find.

6 Gross Fixed Capital Formation (GFCF) as a proxy for net investments (public and private) is used in another more relevant component, it is not used in the transport component to avoid double counting of indicators.

7 These include percentage of people with access to electricity, transmission, and distribution losses as percentage of total primary energy supply, total primary energy supply per capita, total energy consumption per capita; and share of renewable energy in total energy consumption.

8 These include indicators such as the Merchandise Export Concentration Index (MECI), the Merchandise Export Diversification Index (MEDI), the value and ranking of the Economic Complexity Index, the Industrial Ratio (i.e., the average share of industry and services in GDP), and the Gross Fixed Capital Formation as a percentage of GDP. The Economic Complexity Index (EIC) used here is the one developed by Hausmann, Hidalgo, and their collaborators. Available at: http: //atlas.cid.harvard.edu.

9 Kuznets (1971, 1973), Syrquin (2007), Kruger (2008), and McMillan et al. (2017) underscored the importance of various aspects of technology in production and structural transformation processes.

10 These include fixed broadband subscriptions (per 100 people), mobile cellular subscriptions (per 100 people), telephone lines (per 100 people), secure internet servers (per 1 million people), and internet users (per 100 people).

11 According to a report by the Ministry of Trade and Industry of Rwanda (2019), the key national strategies of Rwanda include the National Strategy for Transformation (NST) which runs through 2018–2024, Private Sector Development and Strategy for Youth Employment (PSDSYE), National Export Strategies I & II, National Science, Technology, and Innovation and an education system focusing on them are some of the notable strategies of the country.

12 Rwanda has established dynamic and vibrant institutions and facilities such as the Rwanda Industrial Parks (IPs), Special Economic Zones (SEZs), Rwanda Development Board (RDB), Rwanda Standards Board (RSB), National Commission for Science and Technology (NCST), Labour Market Information System Agency (LMISA), Rwanda Information Society Agency (RISA), National Industrial Research, and Development Authority (NIRDA).

13 The cost of finance for the private sector in Rwanda is one of the highest in SSA with current lending rates from domestic banks to the sector are in the range of 17–21 percent against 6.5 percent in Ethiopia, about 7 per cent in Botswana, and 6 per cent in Mauritius.

14 Rwanda's private sector remains weak: 80 percent of the firms in the textile and apparel processing hub of the Kigali SEZs were foreign (largely Chinese). More disturbingly, 100 percent of the textile exports to developed county markets are from Chinese firms, while Rwanda's domestic private sector, which accounts for less than 20 percent in the hub, is predominantly confined to domestic markets with very few exports of textiles to regional markets.

15 These include export costs (USD per container), time to export (days), time required to enforce a contract (days), time required to start a business (days), trademark registration, application of patents, and domestic credit to the private sector (percent of GDP).

16 Throughout the book, based on the indicators used and empirical evidence, institutions are broadly understood to consist of state (or public administration) and non-state institutions as well as the rules of the game (formal and informal) which collectively

guide the formulation and implementation of policies and strategies; defining incentive structures to take advantage of opportunities with the aim of maximizing socioeconomic gains for societies, foster economy-wide productive capacities, facilitate structural economic transformation, and unlock binding constraints on development.

17 These relate to voice and accountability, political stability and the absence of violence/terrorism, government effectiveness (perception of quality of public services), regulatory quality, rule of law and control of corruption. These indicators in combination or in isolation are invariably used by several institutions including the World Bank (World Bank Governance Indicator), Transparency International (Corruption Perception Index), and several others.

Bibliographical references

Abramovitz, M. (1986). Catching Up, Forging Ahead and Falling Behind. *The Journal of Economic History*, 46(2) The Task of Economic History (June 1986), 385–406. https://www.jstor.org/stable/2122171.

Acemoglu, D. (2007). *Introduction to Modern Economic Growth*. Department of Economics, Massachusetts Institute of Technology, Cambridge, MA.

Acemoglu, D., Johnson, S., and Robinson, A. J. (2005). Institutions as a Fundamental Cause of Long-Run Growth. National Bureau of Economic Research (NBER), Working Paper 10481. Available at: http://www.nber.org/papers/w1048.

Akarca, A. T., and Long, T. V. (1980). On the Relationship between Energy and GNP: A Re-Examination. *Journal of Energy and Development*, 5, 326–331.

Asghar, Z. (2008). Energy-GDP Relationship: A Causal Analysis for Five Countries of Southeast Asia. *Applied Econometrics and International Development*, 8–1, 167–180.

Bloch, H., Rafiq, S., and Salim, R. (2015). Economic growth with coal, oil, and renewable energy consumption in China: Prospects for fuel substitution. *Economic Modelling*, 44(C), 104–115.

BP. (2011). *BP Statistical Review of World Energy*. Available at: http://www.bp.com/sectionbodycopy.do?categoryId=7500&contentId=7068481.

Coase, R. H. (1937). The Nature of the Firm. *Economica*, 4, 386–405.

Coase, R. H. (1998). The New Institutional Economics. *The American Economic Review*, 88(2) Papers and Proceedings of the Hundred and Tenth Annual Meeting of the American Economic Association (May 1998), 72–74.

Cohen, S., and DeLong, B. (2016). *Concrete Economics: The Hamilton Approach to Economic Growth and Policy*. Harvard Business Review Press (hardback).

Collier, P. (2007). *The Bottom Billion: Why the Poorest Countries are Falling Behind and What Can Be done About It*. Oxford University Press, New York.

Collier, P. (2010). *The Plundered Planet*. Oxford University Press, Oxford.

Crespi, G., Fernández-Arias, E., and Sein, E. (2014). *Rethinking Productive Development: Sound Policies and Institutions for Economic Transformation* (eds). Inter-American Development Bank (IDB). Palgrave Macmillan, New York.

Devarajan, S. (2013). Africa's Statistical Tragedy. *Review of Income and Wealth*, 59 (10 January). Available at: https://doi.org/10.1111/roiw.12013.

Evans, P., and Heller, P. (2018). The State and Development. WIDER Working Paper 2018/112. September 2018. United Nations University, UN-WIDER, ISSN 1798-7237. ISBN 978-92-9256-554-1.

Gebreeyesus, M. (2019). The Private Sector in Ethiopia's Transformation. In *The Oxford Handbook of the Ethiopian Economy*. Edited by F. Cheru, C. Cramer, and A. Oqubay. Oxford University Press, Oxford, 721–741.

Ghani, E., Kerr, R. W., and O'Connell, S. (2014). Spatial Determinants of Entrepreneurship in India. *Regional Studies*, 48(6), 1071–1089. https://doi.org/10.1080/00343404.2013.839869

Ghosh, S. (2002). Electricity Consumption and Economic Growth in India. *Energy Policy*, 30, 125–129.

Golub, S., Bernhardt, A., and Liu, M. (2011). Development and Trade Strategies for LDCs 2001–2010 and Looking Ahead. Unpublished background paper for UNCTAD in the run up to the Forth United Nations Conference on LDCs.

Hausmann, R., Hwang, J., and Rodrik, D. (2005). What You Export Matters. Working Paper 11905. National Bureau of Economic Research (NBR), December 2005. Available at: http://www.nber.org/papers/w11905.

Hausmann, R., and Klinger, B. (2006). Structural Transformation and Patterns of Comparative Advantage in the Product Space. Center for International Development Working Paper No. 128.

Hidalgo, C. A., and Hausmann, R. (2009). The Building Blocks of Economic Complexity. *Proceedings of the National Academy of Sciences of the United States of America (PNAS)*, 106(26), 10570–10575.

Hidalgo, C. A., Hausmann, R., Bustos, S., Coscia, M., Simoes, A., and Yıldırım, A. M. (2011). *The Atlas of Economic Complexity*. Puritan Press, Cambridge, MA.

Hirschman, A. O. (1958). *The Strategy of Economic Development*. New York: Norton.

International Energy Agency. (2011a). World Energy Outlook 2011. Available at: https://webstore.iea.org/download/summary/563?fileName=Arabic-WEO-2011-ES.pdf.

International Energy Agency. (2011b). Energy for All: Financing Access for the Poor. Special early excerpt of the World Energy Outlook 2011. Available at: https://webstore.iea.org/download/direct/2747.

International Institute for Environment and Development IIED. (2012). Information and Communication Technologies for Development. Available at: https://pubs.iied.org/pdfs/16510IIED.pdf.

International Trade Centre. (2012). Africa's Trade Potential: Export Opportunities in Growth Markets Geneva: ITC, 2012. Technical paper.

Jerven, M. (2013). *Poor Numbers: Howe We Are Misled by Africa's Development Statistics and What to Do About It*. Cornell University Press.

Kraft, J., and Kraft, A. (1978). Note and Comments: On the Relationship between Energy and GNP. *The Journal of Energy and Development*, 3, 401–403.

Kruger, J. (2008). Productivity and Structural Change: A Review of the Literature. *Journal of Economic Surveys*, 22(2), 330–363. Available at http://www.vwl.tuwien.ac.at/hanappi/AgeSo/rp/Kr%C3%BCger_2008.pdf. Accessed on 25 December 2018.

Kuznets, S. (1971). *Economic Growth of Nations: Total Output and Production Structure*. Harvard University Press, Cambridge, MA.

Kuznets, S. (1973). Modern Economic Growth: Findings and Reflections. *The American Economic Review*, 63(3), 247–258. Accessed 3 March 2019.

Lin, J. Y. (2012). *New Structural Economics – A Framework to Re-Thinking Development and Policy*. The World Bank, Washington, DC.

List, F. (1841). *The National System of Political Economy*. Frank Class, London.

Lewis, W. A. (1954). *Economic Development with Unlimited Supplies of Labour*. The Manchester School, May 1954.

McMillan, M., Rodrik, D., and Sepúlveda, C. (2017). Structural Change, Fundamentals, and Growth: A Framework and Case Studies. Policy Research Working Paper, No. 8041. World Bank, Washington, DC. ©World Bank. https://openknowledge.worldbank.org/handle/10986/26481.

Ministry of Finance and Economic Planning of Rwanda. (2019). *Draft Vision 2050 (blueprint), December 2019*. Government of Rwanda, Kigali.

Ministry of Trade and Industry of Rwanda. (2019). *Entrepreneurship Development Policy: Developing an Effective Entrepreneurship and MSME Ecosystem in Rwanda*. Ministry of Trade and Industry of Rwanda, Kigali.

Mjimba, V. (2011). *The Nature and Determinants of Linkages in Emerging Mineral Commodity Sectors: A Case Study of Gold Mining in Tanzania*. Center for Social Science Research, University of Cape Town, Cape Town, South Africa.

National Institute of Statistics of Rwanda-NISR. (2017). *Integrated Households Living Conditions Survey (EICV), 2016/17*. National Institute of Statistics of Rwanda, Kigali.

North, C. D. (1991). Institutions. *The Journal of Economic Perspectives*, 5(1) Winter 1991, 97–112. http://links.jstor.org/sici?sici=0895-309%28199124%295%3A1%3C97%3AI%3E2.0.CO%3B2-W.

Rodrik, D. (2004). Industrial Policy for the 21st Century. Faculty Research Working Paper Series, RWP04-047, November 2004.

Rodrigue, J.-P., Comtois, C., and Slack, B. (2017). *The Geography of Transport Systems*. New York, Tayler & Francis Ltd, Routledge, London.

Rwirahira, J. (2020). Enhancing Policy Coherence to Strengthen Rwanda's Productive Capacity. Report commissioned by UNCTAD and prepared for the Ministry of Trade and Industry of Rwanda. September 2020.

Salim, R. A., Hassan, K., and Shafiei, S. (2014). Renewable and Non-Renewable Energy Consumption and Economic Activities: Further Evidence from OECD Countries. *Energy Economics*, 44, 350–360.

Salzar-Xirinaches, J., Nubler, I., and Kozul-Wright, R. (2014). In Industrial Policy, Productive Transformation, and Jobs: Theory, History, and Practice (eds). International Labour Organization, Geneva, 1–38.

Schumpeter, J. A. (1912/1934). *The Theory of Economic Development: An Inquiry into Profits, Capital, Credit, Interest and the Business Cycle*. Galaxy Books, Oxford.

Schumpeter, J. A. (1939). *Business Cycles: A Theoretical, Historical, and Statistical Analysis of the Capitalist Process*. McGraw-Hill, London.

Sebastian, F., and Steinbuks, J. (2017). Public Infrastructure and Structural Transformation. Policy Research Working Paper 8285. Development Research Group. Environment and Energy Team. World Bank.

Singh, N., Nyuur, R., and Richmond, B. (2019). Renewable Energy Development as a Driver of Economic Growth: Evidence from Multivariate Panel Data Analysis. *Sustainability*, 11, 2418. https://doi.org/10.3390/su11082418.

SOGA. (2019). Overview of Oil and Gas in Sub Saharan Africa. South African Gas and Oil Alliance (SOGA). Available at: https://www.saoga.org.za/oil-gas-hubs/overview-oil-gas-sub-saharan-africa-region.

Stern, I. D., and Cleveland, J. C. (2004). *Energy and Economic Growth. Rensselaer Working Papers in Economics*. Department of Economics. Rensselaer Political Institute, Troy, New York.

Syrquin, M. (2007). Kuznets and Pasinetti on the study of structural transformation: Never the twain shall meet? International Center for Economic Research (ICER). Working Paper Series. Working Paper Number 46/2007.

Tesfachew, T. (2019). Technological Learning and Industrialization in Ethiopia. In *The Oxford Handbook of the Ethiopian Economy*. Edited by F. Cheru, C. Cramer, and A. Oqubay. Oxford University Press, Oxford, 721–741.

UNCTAD. (2008b). *Economic Development in Africa 2008 Report. Export Performance Following Trade Liberalization: Some Patterns and Policy Perspectives*. United Nations, New York and Geneva.

UNCTAD. (2016a). *Trade and Development Report*. United Nations Publication, New York and Geneva.

UNCTAD. (2017a). *Commodities and Development 2017 Report: Commodity Market*. Economic Growth and Development, United Nations, New York and Geneva.

UNCTAD. (2017b). *Information and Communication Technologies Report 2017: Digitalization, Trade and Development*. New York and Geneva.

UNCTADstat. (2019). Available at: https://unctadstat.unctad.org/EN/Index.html.

UNCTAD. (2020a). *Productive Capacities Index: Focus on Landlocked Developing Countries*. United Nations Publication Issued by the United Nations, Geneva.

UNCTAD. (2020b). *Building Capacity in Least Developing Countries to Fully Harness the Potential of Fisheries and Aquaculture*. Training Manual, United Nations, Geneva.

UNCTAD. (2020d). *UNCTAD Productive Capacities Index: Methodological Approach and Results*, United Nations, Geneva.

UNECA. (2011b). *Fossil Fuel in Africa in the Context of a Carbon Constrained Future*. United Nations Economic Commission for Africa Working Paper 12. Africa Climate Policy Council.

UNECA. (2017). *Promoting Infrastructure Development for Africa's Industrialization*. United Nations Economic Commission for Africa, Addis Ababa.

UNIDO. (2009). Scaling up Renewable Energy in Africa. 12th Ordinary Session of Heads of State and Governments of the African Union. Addis Ababa. Available at: http://www.uncclearn.org/sites/www.uncclearn.org/files/unido11.pdf.

Venables, A. J. (2016). Using Natural Resources for Development: Why Has it Proven So Difficult? *Journal of Economic Perspectives*, 30(1), 161–183.

Vodafone and Accenture. (2011). *Connected Agriculture: The Role of Mobile-phones in Driving Efficiency and Sustainability in the Food and Agriculture Value Chain*. Vodaphone Group PLC, Newbury and Accenture, London. Available at: www.vodafone.com/content/dam/vodafone/about/sustainability/2011/pdf/connected_agriculture.pdf.

Vries, G. J. D., Timer, M. P., and Vries, K. D. (2013). Structural Transformation in Africa: Static gains, dynamic losses. GGDC Working Papers, Vol.GD-136. University of Groningen, GGDC.

Williamson, O. E. (2000). The New Institutional Economics: Taking Stock, Looking Ahead. *Journal of Economic Literature*, 38(3), 595–613.

World Bank. (2000/2001). *World Development Report 2000/2001. Attacking Poverty*. The World Bank, Oxford University Press, New York.

World Economic Forum. (2012). *Energy for Economic Growth Energy Vision Update 2012*. World Economic Forum, Geneva, Switzerland.

World Economic Forum. (2018). Transformation of the Global Energy System. Report of the Global Future Council on Energy 2016–18, Geneva, Switzerland

World Energy Council (WEC). (2010). 2010 survey of energy resources. Available at: www.worldenergy.org/documents/ser_2010_report_1.pdf.

World Trade Organization-WTO. (2016). World Trade Statistical Review 2016. Available at: https://www.wto.org/english/res_e/statis_e/wts2016_e/WTO_Chapter_03_e.pdf.

World's Top Exports-WTEx. (2020). Rice Exports by Country. Available at: http://www.worldstopexports.com/rice-exports-country/.

Yu, E. S. H., and Jin, J. C. (1992). Cointegration Tests of Energy Consumption, Income, and Employment. *Resources and Energy*, 14, 259–266.

4 Implications of SSA's Low PCI for Africa-China Relations

The results of measurement and discussions in Chapter 3 clearly indicate where SSA stands in fostering productive capacities and structural economic transformation. It shows significant gaps and limitations in SSA's productive capacities, despite the region's increasing trade, development finance, and investment flows from China. The analysis confirms the narratives and arguments in the preceding chapters that SSA's socioeconomic vulnerabilities continue to be the causes and consequences of weak productive capacities and lack of structural economic transformation in the region. This chapter closely investigates further evidence and the implications of SSA's low productive capacities despite the region's increasing partnership with China in trade, investment, and finance.

SSA leads other developing regions in only one (natural capital) of the eight components of productive capacities. This reconfirms that the socioeconomic progress of the region is still driven by natural (extractive) resources, with heightened risks of vulnerabilities and uncertainties. It can also be argued that natural capital is the driving factor behind SSA's partnership with developed countries and China. However, if sustainably harnessed and effectively used, rents from natural resources are key to enhancing investment in productive capacities and initiating the process of structural transformation for inclusive growth and sustainable development. Revenues from extractive resources, especially during the period of a commodities boom, can finance public investment in physical and human capital formation (education and health), accelerate public investment in infrastructure (transport, energy, ICT), and raise productivity in other sectors. Doing so requires a range of functioning policies and strategies where microeconomic and macroeconomic, trade, industrial, institutions, infrastructural, and other sectoral policies are geared towards the fostering of productive capacities. It also needs strengthening government capacity to mobilize, manage, and effectively utilize revenues from natural resources endowments. The nexus between sound policies and vibrant institutions is particularly vital for countries to pursue policies for employment-rich growth to absorb the growing labour force and combat poverty and underdevelopment. Unfortunately, for most countries in SSA, natural capital has thus far entrenched their dependence on the export of primary commodities, further marginalizing them in international trade and the global economy. These, in turn, contribute to weak growth and the deepening of structural socioeconomic vulnerabilities

DOI: 10.4324/9781003295334-4

forming a vicious circle between weak productive capacities and underdevelopment. Subsequent discussions examine the growing Africa-China partnership and the contributions of this to production transformation in SSA.

4.1 SSA-China Trade Relations: Challenges and Prospects

There is increasing recognition of the role of trade (particularly international trade) as an engine of economic growth, poverty reduction, and sustainable development. Sustaining and broadening the role of trade in the development of developing countries depends on the productive and supply capacities of nations and the predictability of global trade policies and agreements. Provided that nations foster productive capacities and transform their economies and given that there are predictable and development-friendly trade policies, international trade can provide opportunities for firms and nations to acquire capital and technology. Trade also facilitates the exchange of market information, know-how, and other dynamic gains. Therefore, international trade is a key factor in enhancing productivity and competitiveness by fostering productive capacities and structural transformation. Developing countries that are well integrated into international markets have grown faster than developed countries (Ades and Glaeser: 1999, World Bank: 2000). And trade, particularly with richer countries, can speed up the process of technological learning and "catch-up" (Quah: 1997, 1999). However, gains from international trade are not automatic. Nor are they straightforward. The role of trade in economic growth, inclusiveness, and the sustainability of such growth rests on fostering productive capacities. Understanding the impact of trade on transformational development and the trading environment depends on complex sets of interactions among domestic and global trade policies, institutions, firms, history, geography, and overall initial conditions of nations.

Overall merchandise exports and imports between SSA and China have shown tremendous growth during the last two decades (see Figures 1.3 and 1.4). However, three fundamental challenges persist, which are the focus of the following sections of this chapter. These are: (i) heavy commodity dependency, high export concentration and lack of diversification of exports; (ii) SSA's weak manufacturing sector and inability to foster capital accumulation; and (iii) SSA's export market concentration and inabilities of these economies to "create trade" continue despite a shift in partnership from "West to East". The three challenges led only to trade diversion from West to East without "trade creation". These challenges will have implications to unlock binding constraints to SSA's trade, foster productive capacities in the region as well as enhance the role of Africa-China relations in the transformational growth of SSA.

4.1.1 *Commodity Dependence*

SSA's merchandise exports are known to historically suffer from commodity overdependence and export market concentration. The former refers to a phenomenon where a single or a few primary commodities generate a significant share of export revenues. The latter denotes a situation where a single or a handful export destinations dominate export markets. Both commodity dependence and market concentration make the economy of the region vulnerable to changes in global aggregate demand and international commodity prices as well as the conditions and requirements in export markets. According to the UNCTAD definition,[1] in 2019, there were 42 of the 49 countries in SSA that were categorized as commodity-dependent and by region, 89 percent of countries of SSA were commodity-dependent, compared to two thirds in the Middle East and North Africa, half in Latin America and the Caribbean, and half in East Asia and the Pacific (UNCTAD: 2019a).

In assessing the degree of export dependence of SSA, it is necessary to examine two important indices, which are directly relevant for Africa-China relations. These are the Merchandise Export Concentration Index (MECI)[2] and the Merchandise Export Diversification Index (MEDI). Other indicators such as the number of products exported by SSA over the years are discussed in Chapter 8 (in comparison with Vietnam). These two indices, which are widely used in economics and trade theories as well as in quantitative analyses, are discussed below.

The MECI estimates a country's reliance on a limited number or group of export items as its main source of foreign exchange. It tells us whether a large share of a country's exports (in value terms) is accounted for by a small number of commodities, or if its exports are well distributed among many products or product groups. The MECI also measures the degree to which a small number of products contribute to significant exports of a given country (in value terms) with normalized values between 0 and 1. A value closer or equal to 0 means that the export products of a given country are evenly or fairly represented in its total export basket or foreign exchange earnings (equal to 0 means perfect distribution). On the contrary, values closer to 1 mean exports are driven by one product or one group of products (equal to 1 means perfect concentration). Therefore, the lower the MECI value, the less vulnerable the export structure of a given country is to external shocks. And conversely, the higher the value, the higher the degree of exposure and vulnerability to external shocks. It can be conveniently said that the MECI can serve as an indirect but important measure of economic complexity, vulnerability, or resilience of exports.

Turning to SSA, while the volume and value of exports of the region have shown tremendous increase (particularly with China), there has been little or no change in the export concentration index of the region throughout the 2000–2017 period. The median value of MECI remained above 0.75 (Figure 4.1) for SSA, with an average value of 0.45. However, the median and mean values mask significant variations across countries and economies. For economies heavily dependent on the export of extractive resources, the MECI is, by far, the highest of all country groups or economies. In 2016, Angola (with 0.93), Botswana (0.89), Guinea-Bissau (0.88), and Nigeria (0.76) lead the group as countries with near "perfect" concentration. Other countries of the subregion such as Mauritius (0.20), Senegal (0.21), Kenya (0.24), and Togo (0.24) have relatively lower

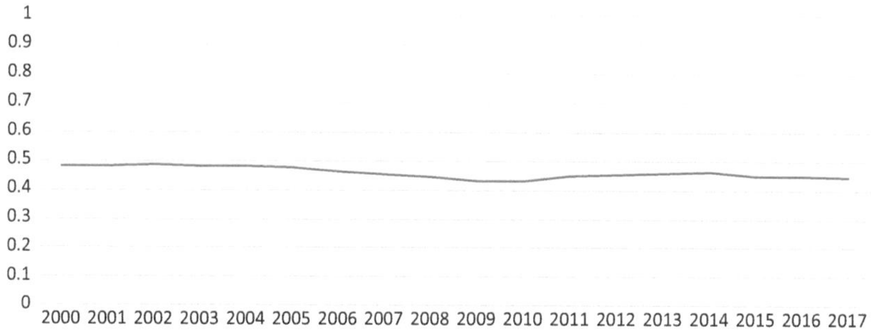

Figure 4.1 Mean Merchandise Export Concentration Index for SSA (MECI) (2000–2017).
Source: UNCTADStat (2018).

MECI scores, indicating that their export items are more varied and equally represented in their respective export baskets or earnings (for more country values see UNCTADstat: 2020).

SSA's higher average MECI will have important implications for Africa-China relations. It means that the heavy dependence of SSA on a single or a few primary products for exports is one of the most visible causes and consequences of their weak productive capacities and absence of structural transformation in the region. It also means that the increasing shift in trade towards China has not helped to improve the concentration challenges that the countries of SSA have been facing for decades. Nor has it created new trade opportunities in parallel with increasing Africa-China ties or growing partnerships. The high concentration index also goes against mercantilist (classical) trade theories, which advocate for export sophistication and specialization based on comparative advantages. What we see in the case of SSA is not a deliberate strategy for specialization (without technological or knowledge sophistication) in production, value addition, and exports. But it rather portrays specialization in low-skill and low value-added exports dictated by the abundance of natural resources, and increasing demand from importing countries for such resources. It also shows weak productive capacities and structural rigidity to transform the economies of SSA. The combination of these has left the trade pattern of SSA and its structure qualitatively unchanged or untransformed (see also Chapter 1, Figure 1.4) since the colonial and post-colonial era. Such a heavy dependence on primary commodities also means that the countries' trade and their integration patterns are heavily influenced by their natural resource endowments. This also hinders beneficial integration of the countries of SSA into the global economy, and further entrenches exploitative relationships between the region and its trade partners, including China. This, in turn, intensifies SSA's socioeconomic vulnerabilities and its continued marginalization in the global economy.

Another important indicator of a country's trade performance and qualitative change in exports is the MEDI, which is shown in Figure 4.2. The MEDI is used to understand whether the structure of export products of a given country or

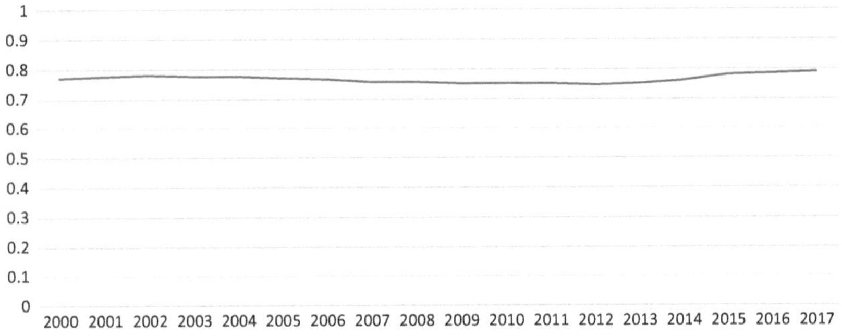

Figure 4.2 Mean Merchandise Export Diversification Index (MEDI) for SSA (2000–2017).
Source: UNCTADStat (2018).

group of countries differs from the structure of products of the world average. It is measured by the absolute deviation of a country's share from the average of the world export structure. Methodologically or statistically, it is the inverse of the Herfindahl-Hirschmann Export Concentration Index. In other words, the MECI is a mirror reflection of the MEDI. As with the MECI, the MEDI has weighted values between 0 and 1. The MEDI value of 0 means that there is no variation between the structure of trade of a given country or country group and the world export structure. Conversely, the value of 1 means that there is significant or absolute variation between a country's export structure and that of the world, meaning no diversification.

Export diversification is particularly important for developing countries such as those in SSA. It is key to minimize terms-of-trade shocks, growth collapse, and the socioeconomic consequences of such shocks. During the commodities boom period (2002–2007), SSA's commodity-dependent economies registered an impressive average growth rate of 7 percent or higher per year. Such growth performance was one of the highest to be observed in the region in several decades, although the socioeconomic impact of such a growth was little or marginal. The financial and economic crises of 2008–2009 revealed vulnerabilities inherent in the economies of the SSA as growth rates plummeted to below 4 percent during and after the crises. Similarly, since the decline of international oil prices by 40 percent between 2016 and 2019, Angola, and several oil-exporting countries of SSA have faced serious budgetary constraints. This has made it difficult to finance their respective mega-projects, most of which were planned during the period of oil price boom (above USD 140/barrel). Such volatility and abrupt changes in commodity prices have had serious socioeconomic repercussions, particularly on oil-exporting SSA's economies. On the other hand, countries with diversified export structures particularly those in Asia such as Vietnam (see Chapters 7 and 8) withstood the negative impacts of external economic shocks. That is, countries that have increased value-added, manufacturing, and sophisticated exports to their baskets have more resilient and dynamic economies. These economies have also registered higher job intensity of growth, stable exchange earnings, and accelerated structural transformation as discussed in Chapters 7 and 8. These countries are also the ones that have maximized or benefited from other dynamic gains from international trade such as new technologies, modern production methods, and increased innovation and discovery of new export products.

The average diversification index score for SSA has evolved in an unfavourable direction, reaching 0.8 in recent years – from 0.77 in the 2000s, which itself was higher than the average for other developing regions. This means that the region's export structure has not only deviated from the world export structure, but such a deviation has been on the rise since 2010. In a country-by-country examination (see UNCTADstat: 2020) most of the extractive resource-dependent economies of SSA have a higher export diversification index than the region's average. Botswana leads the group with a MEDI of 0.93 in 2016, followed by Nigeria and Zambia (0.86), Sierra Leone (0.85), and Ghana (0.82). The exception in this group is Angola, which despite its high MECI score saw its performance in terms of diversification has improved recently (Angola's 2016 MEDI value stood at 0.47). This means that, while Angola's export earnings are still heavily concentrated in one or a few products (usually oil and gas), it is making efforts to diversify its export structure. The recent addition of exports of diamonds, wood (timber), cement, and beverages (beer to neighbouring countries) in the country's export basket is captured by its MEDI. However, the diversification of the export structure has not changed or altered the export concentration index of the country, which is still largely driven by oil and gas.

Overall, the astronomical increase in exports (in both value and volume) of SSA with China has failed to alter both export concentration and diversification indices of the region. It also shows that economies in SSA could not create trade opportunities in parallel with fostering increasing partnership with the world's second largest economy and a leading source of foreign direct investment (FDI). This reflects very weak productive capabilities and lack of diversification, value addition, and overall structural transformation in SSA's economies.

4.1.2 Weak Manufacturing Sector and Lack of Capital Accumulation

Another important indicator of productive capacities and structural economic transformation is the percentage share of manufacturing value-added (MVA) in Gross Domestic Product (GDP). Usually, MVA is an estimate of net output of the manufacturing sector, calculated after adding up all the outputs and subtracting the intermediate inputs.[3] MVA can provide a useful insight into whether the manufacturing sector's contribution to GDP is growing as an indication of the right pathway to economic development. It is an important indicator of a country's industrial output or production, labour productivity, exports, and income growth. Figure 4.3 provides the trend of MVA in SSA at the aggregate level (not at industry level) for the 2000–2012 period. SSA's MVA is not only the lowest when compared with the average of the developing regions, but it has been consistently declining from 12 percent in 2000 to less than 11 percent in 2016. The average for North African countries is 17 percent (Anyanwu: 2018). According to the 2018

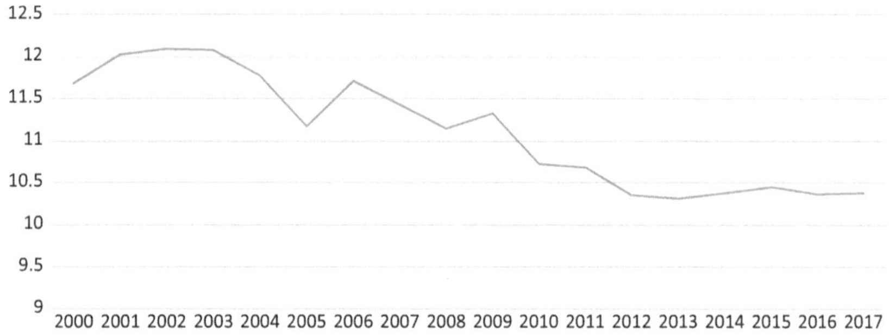

Figure 4.3 Average share of manufacturing value-added in GDP (percent) in SSA (2000–2017).

Source: UNCTADStat (2018).

World Industrial Development Report (UNIDO: 2018a, pp. 162), in 2016, Asia and the Pacific region accounted for nearly 50 percent of the global manufacturing output as a percentage of total global manufacturing value-added. The share of Europe in global manufacturing value-added was 25 percent, followed by North America (17 percent), Latin America (6 percent), and Africa (1.7 percent). For China, the manufacturing sector contributes a whopping 41 percent of the GDP (UNIDO: 2018a). The low and declining share of SSA's MVA and Africa's tiniest share in the global MVA shows that deindustrialization has continued unabated in Africa (notably in SSA). The low level of the MVA in SSA as shown in Figure 4.3 is perfectly in line with UNIDO's arguments and it is consistent with the conclusions of various researchers and academics. For instance, Lin and Xu (2019) described the declining share of MVA in SSA as "premature deindustrialization" – a phenomenon occurring when developing countries run out of industrialization steam sooner or at much lower levels of income, in comparison with early industrializers (Rodrik: 2016). Such a low and declining level of the percentage share of MVA in GDP is occurring against the increasing trade, investment, and development flows to the region from China. This trend is also a reflection of the low share of FDI, and development finance accorded to the industrial sector (see Table 4.3, Sectoral Distribution of Chinese loans in SSA during 2000–2017).

A country-by-country examination of the data shows that there is significant variation across SSA: Eswatini (with 32 percent) and Equatorial Guinea (24 percent) lead SSA, followed by Senegal (19 percent), Lesotho (16 percent), Benin (14 percent), and Mauritius (13 percent) in 2017. The lowest performing countries include South Sudan and Sierra Leone (2 percent each); Liberia and the Gambia (4 percent each), Eritrea, Ethiopia, Niger, Rwanda, and Tanzania (each with 6 percent).

As with the manufacturing value-added, on another important measure of economic wellbeing of nations, the Gross Fixed Capital Formation (GFCF),[4] Africa has a long way to go. Earlier chapters emphasized the importance of capital formation and accumulation in development. In fact, the difference in economic development across nations is the result of the difference in the levels of technological progress and capital accumulation (Wolff: 1993). Odili and Ede (2015) further emphasized the importance of estimates of capital formation in analyzing the results of productive activity in an economy. Such estimates help to understand the magnitude of and changes in the productive capacities of an economy over time. Beyond measuring overall economic activity and productive capacities, GFCF is a useful tool to understand changes in the value of economic assets as one of the determinants for successful business and investment decisions. An accurate indicator of capital formation is also important in policymaking processes by identifying the proportion of GDP that goes towards capital investments. GFCF is a useful policy tool to facilitate the intervention of governments in maximizing dynamic relationships between the stock market and the flow of long-term capital (investment) to finance long-term development needs. The trend in average GFCF in SSA, as shown in Figure 4.4, is inconsistent throughout 2000–2017. Interestingly, SSA's GFCF follows the commodity super cycle. During the 2000–2005 period, aided by better international prices of key exports, SSA registered relatively higher levels of GFCF, which then collapsed between 2006 and 2008 due to low commodity prices and the global financial and economic crises. It picked up again in the few years which followed the crises (2009–2012) – a period characterized by high oil prices. Since 2013, with dipping international oil and key commodities' prices, the GFCF plunged again to a low level in 2017.

In sum, Africa-China growing trade, investment, and development finance ties have not substantially contributed to capital accumulation or capital formation in SSA. This, once again, reflects the continued weakness in productive capacities and structural economic transformation of the region, which lead to vulnerability of these countries' socioeconomic performances. This in turn contributes to the sluggish performance of SSA, which lags behind the rest of the developing regions in productive capacities and socioeconomic development. Such a disappointing performance will have serious policy implications for the Africa-China current and future partnerships and offers direction as to what can be done to reverse the declining trend.

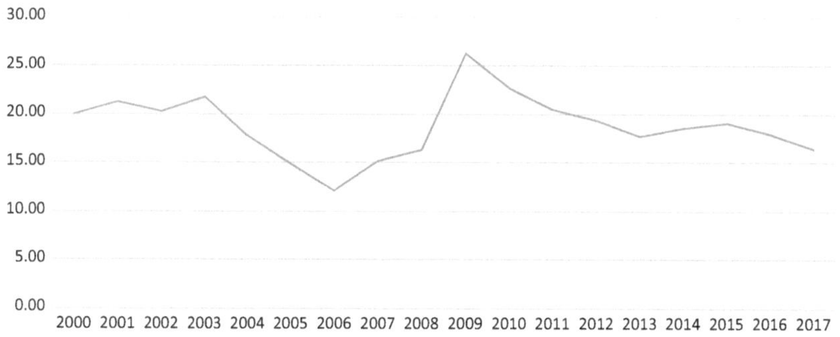

Figure 4.4 Average Gross Fixed Capital Formation (GFCF) in SSA (2000–2017).
Source: World Bank Data.

4.2 Africa-China Investment Relations

Investments (public and private) are key to fostering productive capacities and structural transformation of nations. China has become an important investor in SSA. For SSA where data is partially or fully available, Chinese FDI stock has geometrically increased over the years (see Table 4.1). Although the 2016 Chinese FDI stock in SSA accounts for less than 5 percent of Chinese FDI stock globally, and it is only about 4 percent of the GDP of the region, the increase over the last 15 years has been substantial for SSA, which is known for its significantly higher investment needs and enormous development finance gap. There are several other encouraging or positive sides to the Chinese FDI stock in SSA: first, it is not restricted to countries with natural (extractive) resources. In fact, it seems that, in addition to extractive resources, Chinese investment has increasingly been targeting countries with comparative advantages (outside of the extractive sectors). They have also begun to focus on countries with high growth performance. As can be seen from Table 4.1, countries that have commercially viable agricultural resources such as Ethiopia (oilseeds) and Zimbabwe (tobacco) have captured a relatively sizable share of Chinese FDI stocks in 2016. Moreover, Mauritius, which is not among countries dependent on extractive resources, captures an important share of Chinese FDI. In fact, every country in SSA for which data is available has received Chinese FDI of sizable proportions relative to its respective domestic investments or GDP.

However, in recent years, Chinese FDI has been increasingly skewed more towards countries with extractive resources. Excluding South Africa which has 36.8 percent of Chinese FDI stock, Nigeria accounted for 22.3 percent in 2016. Other than Nigeria, in the same year, there is no other extractive resource-dependent economy that captured more than 10 percent of total Chinese FDI stocks. Countries with a comparatively equal share (but lower than Nigeria and South Africa) of Chinese FDI include Angola (7 percent,) DRC (5 percent), Ghana (7 percent), and Mozambique (8.5 percent). All these countries are extractive resource driven. Moreover, within countries, Chinese FDI still favours the extractive sectors, as seen in Angola, Equatorial Guinea, and Nigeria in particular.

On a more positive note, during the period investigated (2001–2016) for the countries of SSA for which investment data is available, the stock of Chinese investment has not been as important in extractive sectors as it used to be. The distribution of FDI stock has covered a large number of economies that are not known for their mineral resources. This trend is in sharp contrast with what has been portrayed in most Western media that Chinese interest in Africa is solely driven by its appetite for natural resources. Therefore, first, claims and blames that Chinese investment primarily targets Africa's extractive sectors are overly exaggerated at best or misplaced at worst. Secondly, within countries that are not rich in commercially viable mineral resources the stock of Chinese FDI is more diversified across sectors. In Ethiopia, agriculture (oilseed) and manufacturing sectors (textiles, leather, and leather products) and infrastructure (road

Table 4.1 Stock of Chinese Investment in SSA in USD Thousands (2001–2016)

Country	*2001*	*2005*	*2010*	*2015*	*2016*	*Percent Share in 2016*
Angola	10,122.63	16,336.50	32,457.88	32,311.63	29,184.14	6.91
Benin	173.82	284.33	604.11	1,631.78	1,705.43	0.40
Botswana	1,388.49	1,664.06	3,350.64	5,018.24	5,041.75	1.19
Burkina Faso	15.91	75.36	353.85	1,744.96	2,061.49	0.48
Burundi	46.79	47.41	13.34	251.99	241.38	0.05
Cape Verde	204.53	360.05	1,251.59	1,571.56	1,623.72	0.38
Cameroon	989.89	2,248.03	3,099.01	5,137.61	5,602.31	1.32
Central African Republic	109.48	198.28	510.61	626.00	633.25	0.15
Chad	1,035.74	3,039.98	3,593.94	4,859.73	5,104.22	1.20
Comoros	21.79	24.25	59.51	106.86	110.42	0.02
Congo	1,969.83	3,006.42	9,260.89	15,236.55	16,847.07	3.99
Côte d'Ivoire	2,620.40	4,511.74	6,978.23	7,381.01	7,696.74	1.82
Dem. Rep. of the Congo	719.58	1,974.06	9,368.13	19,982.10	21,186.81	5.01
Djibouti	43.42	158.73	878.47	1,629.48	1,789.47	0.42
Equatorial Guinea	2,000.73	4,123.96	9,412.55	13,356.87	13,410.83	3.17
Eritrea	349.54	422.84	666.42	886.47	938.78	0.22
Eswatini	353.05	786.15	926.72	520.92	867.68	0.20
Ethiopia	1,290.54	2,820.75	4,206.28	10,936.80	14,925.75	3.53
Gabon	NA	362.62	3,286.97	6,750.30	7,991.28	1.89
The Gambia	220.93	372.45	322.76	399.33	359.89	0.08
Ghana	1,643.36	2,144.55	10,079.69	25,397.40	29,882.30	7.07
Guinea	264.99	580.69	486.10	2,140.09	3,737.43	0.88
Guinea-Bissau	38.41	5.92	62.54	134.18	152.77	0.03
Kenya	937.02	1,113.65	5,448.71	10,838.85	11,520.17	2.72
Lesotho	357.77	192.89	928.60	571.92	590.57	0.13
Liberia	3254.86	3,788.04	10,205.57	7,879.70	8,332.88	1.97
Madagascar	142.58	250.29	4,382.60	5,619.14	5,882.42	1.39
Malawi	381.22	553.16	962.81	713.67	1,083.18	0.25

(Continued)

Table 4.1 Continued

Country	*2001*	*2005*	*2010*	*2015*	*2016*	*Percent Share in 2016*
Mali	210.43	871.59	1,963.59	3,013.53	3,257.22	0.77
Mauritania	222.74	1,608.01	2,372.22	6,478.35	6,749.55	1.59
Mauritius	657.83	804.74	4,658.35	4,363.85	4,616.53	1.09
Mozambique	1,504.63	2,578.12	4,331.34	29,273.66	35,714.18	8.45
Namibia	715.01	2,453.44	3,595.48	5,095.02	6,120.85	1.44
Niger	61.46	99.96	2,251.20	5,165.37	5,288.16	1.25
Nigeria	25,063.81	26,345.00	60,326.67	89,735.40	94,184.14	22.30
Rwanda	57.00	77.27	422.08	1401.80	1680.30	0.39
Sao Tome and Principe	14.44	40.64	259.84	409.51	430.28	0.10
Senegal	194.25	358.22	1,699.34	3,431.08	3,771.92	0.89
Seychelles	579.95	809.35	1,700.83	2,761.78	2,917.02	0.69
Sierra Leone	293.80	299.88	482.20	1,042.11	843.23	0.19
Somalia	3.69	22.19	566.19	1,597.52	1,931.52	0.45
South Africa	34,695.42	96,693.28	179,564.80	126,755.50	135,453.50	32.00
South Sudan	NA	NA	NA	NA	NA	0.00
Togo	141.09	234.72	565.48	1,568.39	1,474.45	0.34
Uganda	958.59	2,024.36	5,575.23	10,567.14	11,192.84	2.65
Tanzania	2,867.20	4,438.80	9,712.00	17,805.10	18,669.10	4.42
Zambia	4,037.70	5,409.00	7,432.50	16,488.17	18,855.10	4.46
Zimbabwe	1,241.85	1,383.05	1,814.45	3,966.75	4,338.56	1.02
SSA	104,422.90	198,359.00	413,704.10	517,126.90	557,616.40	75.70
SSA without South Africa	69,727.46	101,665.70	234,139.30	390,371.40	422,162.90	

Source: UNCTADStat (author's calculation).

and railways) captured the lion's share of Chinese FDI. In Zimbabwe (tobacco), Mauritius (transport infrastructure), Rwanda (textiles and clothing), Uganda (hydropower), Kenya (road and railways), and Sudan (thermal energy) are key areas with dominant Chinese FDI stock. In many other countries of SSA, physical infrastructure projects (seaports, airports, roads, and railways) have attracted more Chinese investments outside of the extractive sectors. Third, Chinese investments in SSA have few or no political strings attached and hence countries that have traditionally been labelled as hostile to Western liberal democracies (e.g., Zimbabwe, Sudan) or countries that have prolonged political instability such as DRC continue to attract the interest of China as an investment source. Lastly, although there is no accurate data on the sectoral distribution of Chinese investment, there has been a consistent increase, particularly in the infrastructure, power, and manufacturing sectors over the recent years (for details on the distribution of Chinese FDI in SSA, see Table 4.1).

Notwithstanding an increasing trend of Chinese FDI stock in terms of country and sectoral distribution, the performance of SSA on infrastructure, including energy (electricity) and ICT categories of productive capacities remained the weakest and the lowest of all the developing regions. The analysis in Chapter 3 shows that the productive capacities of SSA have shown little or no improvements in these categories irrespective of increasing Africa-China economic ties. In the three categories measured (transport, energy, and ICT), SSA significantly lags behind Asia, Latin America, and China itself. The lack of significant impact of Chinese investment on these key aspects of productive capacities can be due to four important factors. First, the Chinese FDI stock is still too low to have significant positive impacts on productive capacities, especially on transport when compared to the region's needs and gaps in financing physical infrastructure. According to the African Development Bank (Africa Economic Outlook: 2018), the African infrastructure need is estimated at the range of USD 130–170 billion a year with an investment gap of estimated at about USD 68–108 billion. It is equally important to underline that the problem of poor infrastructure in SSA is not only the result of lack of investment capital in the sector. Rather it is also the outcome of misguided policies, poor quality management, and a weak culture of timely maintenance. African governments, their traditional donors, and China need to enhance their collaboration to address the huge gap in infrastructure financing, and to tackle policy-related distortions and limitations. The overall low level of the productive capacities index (PCI) of SSA in relation to other developing regions and China in the three crucially important categories (transport, ICT, and energy) is the reflection of huge financing needs and investment gaps facing the region. Second, the investment/GDP ratio for SSA countries, though improving over the years, has remained low (on average only 20 percent of GDP per annum between 2010 and 2017 invested in SSA). However, the share in some countries has significantly improved over time (Ethiopia, Rwanda, and Zambia). When compared to China and other East Asian countries, which invest on average 44 percent and 40.5 percent, respectively, the investment GDP ratio of SSA is very low (World Bank Open Data: 2019). Consequently, the GFCF of Africa (Figure 4.4), which is used to assess the impact of investments (domestic and foreign) has been volatile, low, and declining over time. Moreover, with the view to maximize the development potential of FDI in Africa by easing Africa's well-known deficit in infrastructure, finance, several countries of SSA have built industrial parks, special economic zones, and /or export processing zones[5] at a high cost to their respective economies, often from external borrowing (largely from China). In Ethiopia, Kenya, and Rwanda leading investors and exporters in these government-built facilities are Chinese firms, predominantly State Owned Enterprises (SOEs). In Ethiopia, 100 percent of those occupying some of the industrial parks such as Bole Lemi (on the outskirts of the capital, Addis Ababa) are foreign firms, which exclusively produce for export and benefit from government incentives. In Rwanda, 90 percent are foreign firms which dominate the country's industrial parks or special economic zones such as the Kigali Special Economic Zone (SEZ), but these account for 100 per cent of the country's manufacturing exports from the SEZ. The situation in most countries of SSA is not any different from the case of Ethiopia and Rwanda except Mauritius and South Africa and to some extent in Kenya that small number of foreign firms outsource raw materials and some production inputs from local sources especially in the agri-processing sector. In terms of ownership, Kenya is better than most countries of SSA because the share of foreign and domestic firms is more or less equal (40 percent firms are foreign owned, 40 percent locally and 20 percent in join-ventures), except the foreign firms largely dominate in value-added activities and exports. Overall, there are few or no linkages between foreign and domestic firms or between these and the domestic economy as most of the foreign firms import raw materials and intermediate input from FDI home countries, predominantly from China. Such a situation undermined long-term development objectives such as industrialization, productive capacities, and structural economic transformation as key for generating inclusive economic growth and sustainable development.

Third, productive capacities by their nature are transgenerational and cannot be significantly enhanced in a relatively short period of time. Fostering productive capacities and structural economic transformation requires consistent, yet incremental improvements in all the categories identified. Therefore, the investments made in the current decade or so can have more ripple or multiplier effects on such capacities only in the longer term. This means that the investment stocks of China in SSA that have continued to increase in recent years can only have visible impacts several years down the road, provided that the positive trend continues. The precise impact will be known only in the future. Finally, African countries need to build their regulatory and institutional capacities to maximize the positive impact of Chinese investment. This should include, among other things, efforts to monitor the timely execution of capital projects and improving the quality of infrastructure projects so that the region's return on infrastructure investment could be substantial and long lasting, with visible impact on its productive capacities and structural transformation.

4.3 China's Credits, Grants, and Concessional Loans to SSA

According to the Development Assistance Committee (DAC) of the Organisation for Economic Cooperation and Development (OECD), Official Development

Assistance (ODA) denotes flows of development aid provided by official agencies, including state and local governments or by their executive agencies to promote economic development and welfare in developing countries. The DAC also specifies that ODA is concessional in character, which should convey a grant element of at least 25 percent calculated at a discount of 10 percent.

China still is considered as a developing country by multilateral organizations, including the World Trade Organization. Therefore, as a matter of principle, it does not provide ODA, which is traditionally in the confines of bilateral donors (developed or industrialized economies). This means that, as indicated in Chapter 1, China does not participate in the OECD's Creditor Reporting System. Hence, Chinese creditor institutions, including financial firms or contractors, do not publish official data on financing agreements, credits, and loans they have extended to countries of SSA.

However, it appears that China applies some of the OECD principles in the allocation of its development finance (loans, grants, and credits) to SSA. Projects that are considered as development-oriented have a 25 percent grant component in Chinese government financial flows (development finance) to Africa. This includes direct financing of development- or infrastructure-related projects, scholarships, and other technical assistance. Conversely, projects that do not primarily focus on development cannot benefit from Chinese concessional loans. Similarly, for countries that are not eligible for traditional ODA (because of their income levels), Chinese development finance can be extended at lending (commercial) rates, but it cannot be concessional. The non-concessional loan category includes projects that are primarily commercial or representational such as export credits, funding trade fairs, commercial attachés, which are collectively considered as Other Official Flows (OOF). These approaches by China in the allocation of its development finance to SSA are aligned, to some extent, with DAC directives. Some statistical sources also categorize part of Chinese allocation as "Vague Official Finance" (VOF). This category of flows captures officially financed projects where there was not enough information about the project's concessionality level (or intent) to make a clear ODA or OOF determination.

Another aspect of the similarity between Chinese and OECD development resource flows is the diversity of institutions through which loans and grants are channelled. In the case of China, Exim Bank of China, Chinese commercial banks, Ministry of Commerce (MoFCom), and recently the Chinese Development Bank (CBD) are the main channels through which grants, credits, and loans have been distributed or allocated to the countries of SSA. During 2000–2017, 59.7 percent of the total Chinese development finance was provided to SSA through Exim Bank, 18.2 percent via the Chinese Development Bank, and 22.1 percent was through Chinese commercial banks and Chinese contractors (see Figure 4.5 and Table 4.2).

Despite similarities in the modalities and channels of development finance between the OECD and China, there is hardly any consistent, reliable, and official data and statistics on Chinese development finance in SSA. Different sources report different data and statistical information on Chinese development finance to Africa. The absence of official data on Chinese development finance or loans

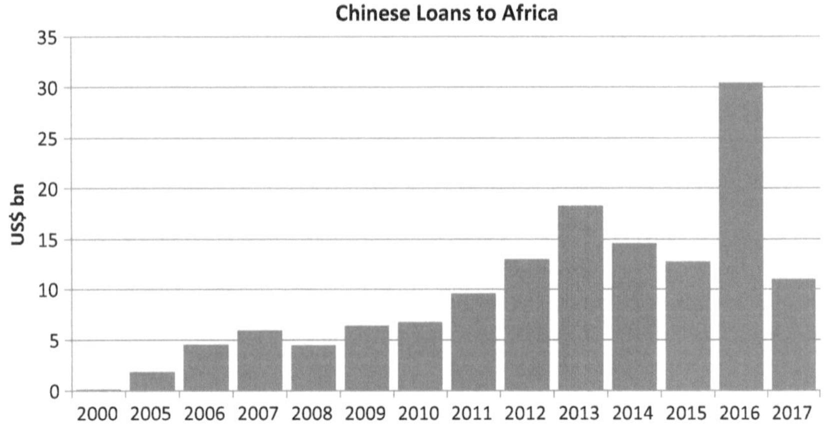

Figure 4.5 Chinese development finance to SSA by financier in USD millions (2000–2017).
Sources: Johns Hopkins SAIS China Africa Research Initiative (2017).

Table 4.2 Annual Chinese Development Finance to SSA, by Lender in USD Millions (2000–2017)

Year	*Exim Bank*	*CDB*	*Other Chinese**	*Sum*
2000	52	0	68	121
2001	20	0	242	262
2002	157	0	517	674
2003	1,063	0	557	1,620
2004	542	0	421	962
2005	1,563	0	269	1,831
2006	2,554	0	1,948	4,502
2007	5,891	17	37	5,945
2008	3,397	50	469	3,916
2009	5,022	0	1,360	6,382
2010	3,034	22	3,041	6,097
2011	6,665	2,783	474	9,922
2012	7,168	1,801	1,303	10,273
2013	9,445	4,280	2,986	16,711
2014	8,025	2,446	2,975	13,446
2015	8,454	898	2,413	11,764
2016	18,098	5,517	6,700	30,315
2017	6,392	1,948	2,366	10,706
Sum	87,542	19,762	28,147	135,450

Sources: Johns Hopkins SAIS China Africa Research Initiative.

*Includes commercial Chinese banks and Chinese contractors.

has contributed to growing suspicion (particularly in developed countries) on the motivation of the robust Chinese presence in and engagement with Africa.

The total loan disbursement from three main Chinese sources to Africa has increased substantially. Between 2000 and 2017, the sum of Chinese loans reached USD 143 billion of which the combined share of SSA was nearly USD

135 billion (94.4 percent) during the same period (Table 4.2). The annual disbursement from the three main channels has increased from USD 120 million in 2000 to USD 30.3 billion in 2016 before it dived to USD 10.7 billion in 2017. Regarding the country concentration of development finance, interestingly, it seems as if China has quickly addressed the constant blame or criticism, it has been facing that its economic relations exclusively focus on a handful of extractive resource-rich countries in SSA. In 2006, the total Chinese loan disbursement to SSA was about USD 6 billion, of which the top five recipients (Angola, Congo, Equatorial Guinea, Ethiopia, and Sudan) received USD 5.7 billion (95 percent). Except for Ethiopia, the four top recipients were oil and gas exporters in the same year. However, since 2014 ODA-like flows are almost evenly distributed across countries of SSA. The values indicated in Table 4.2 should not be taken as the current level of indebtedness of SSA countries as variation is apt to occur between the current level of debt and the loan, simply because countries have begun loan repayment schedules, including (where applicable) interest payments. Another important dimension of Chinese loans to eligible countries of SSA is its sectoral distribution. The share of agriculture and industry, which are two important sectors for fostering productive capacities and structural transformation received 1.6 percent and 2.7 percent, respectively, during the 2000–2016 period. The shares of the education and health sectors which are equally important to enhance the human capital component of productive capacities were 0.8 percent and 0.7 percent, respectively, during the same period. Similarly, the share of government, water, and other social sectors each account for 3.4 percent, 4 percent, 3.6 percent, respectively. These and other non-economic sectors all together account for 23.9 percent (see Figure 4.6). The three economic sectors whose respective shares were substantial during the 2000–2016 period include mining (15.4 percent), power (24.1 percent), and transport (30.6 percent) (Table 4.3).

The sectoral distribution of Chinese loans indicates that almost all the sectors received allocations, albeit in varying proportions. The low share of the agricultural and industrial sectors can be a matter of policy concern which should be addressed in subsequent arrangements. The two sectors hold significant potential for fostering productive capacities and structural transformation for inclusive and sustainable growth in the region. On the other hand, the low shares of the social sectors, especially the education and health sectors, may not have significant negative impact on their financing. This is because these sectors have been receiving significant amounts of aid from traditional donors and increased budget allocations from domestic public sources during the era of the Millennium Development Goals (MDGs). These situations have often been criticized for putting too much emphasis on social sectors at the expense of productive or economic sectors such as agriculture and industry. The relatively higher share of the mining sector (15.4 percent) shows an increasing importance of the sector in driving SSA economies and the undiminishing level of interest of creditors, including China, in the sectors.

An encouraging trend of Chinese loan disbursement to SSA is its heavy emphasis on transport (30.6 percent), communications (6 percent), and power or

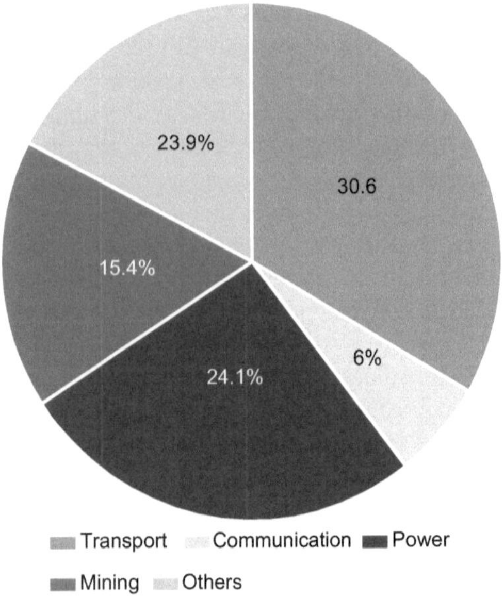

Figure 4.6 Percentage share of main sectors in total Chinese loans to SSA (2000–2016).
Source: Johns Hopkins SAIS China Africa Research Initiative (2017).

Table 4.3 Distribution of Chinese Loans across Sectors of SSA in USD Millions (2000–2016)

Main Sectors	*2000*	*2005*	*2010*	*2015*	*2016*	*Yearly Sum in Millions of USD*	*Percentage Share*
Education	0	187	0	254	50	1,056	0.84
Health	10	226	49	0	136	941	0.75
Water	18	194	24	649	1,107	4,974	3.98
Government	0	83	999	0	681	4,266	3.41
Other social	2	20	2,770	210	37	4,313	3.45
Transport	0	472	700	4,590	8,103	38,171	30.57
Communication	0	133	187	236	202	6,967	5.58
Power	26	284	1,055	4,510	7,302	30,118	24.12
Banking	0	0	0	200	0	200	0.16
Business	2	0	0	143	700	890	0.71
Agriculture	0	147	42	0	0	1,959	1.56
Industry	42	37	160	700	170	3,427	2.74
Mining	0	0	0	0	10,000	19,187	15.36
Trade	0	0	26	0	0	294	0.23
Environment	0	0	0	0	38	38	0.03
Multisector	7	0	0	2	650	3,854	3.08
Budget	0	0	0	0	1,000	1,004	0.80
Food	0	0	6	0	0	46	0.03
Other commodities	0	0	0	96	0	358	0.28
Unallocated	12	49	79	173	231	2,785	2.23

Sources: Johns Hopkins SAIS China Africa Research Initiative, 2017.

energy (24.1 percent). These are sectors with a multiplier effect but often remain underfunded either from domestic or external sources, and hence, they are among the key binding constraints to the economic performance of the countries of the region. However, this increased emphasis of Chinese loan disbursement has done little to contribute to efforts aimed at fostering productive capacities and accelerating structural transformation of the countries of SSA. As with the increased Chinese investment in infrastructure, notably transport, ICT, and energy, there has been an increased disbursement of its loans to these sectors. However, SSA has been significantly lagging behind the rest of the developing regions, particularly in the three areas of emphasis. This means that beyond the loans and increased investments from China, a fundamental change is urgently needed not only in terms of finance from traditional bilateral and multilateral donors but also in strategic changes in the priorities of policies of national governments in support of sectors with multiplier effects. These should include multilateral and regional financial institutions, emerging economies including China itself, and the governments of the countries themselves, to effectively address the huge gap in infrastructure financing in SSA.

Another area that requires full understanding of the implications of increasing loans from China is the possibility of debt build-up in the debtor nations. There is huge potential for Chinese loans to lead to external indebtedness of countries of SSA. Most countries in SSA are not only under the category of low income, most of them are also heavily indebted poor countries (HIPCs). Therefore, they have been benefiting from debt relief initiatives. Those countries that are not HIPCs also benefit, on a case-by-case basis, through Multilateral Debt Reduction Initiatives. The external debt burden of most of SSA's economies have significantly declined between 2001 and 2010 (Table 4.4) largely due to the robust debt relief initiatives undertaken by major creditor nations and financial institutions, particularly in the context of MDGs and Poverty Reduction Strategy Papers (PRSPs).

However, in recent years, several SSA countries have seen their Chinese loans increasing with a corresponding increase in their external indebtedness. There is no indication or information as to whether China applies standard or existing debt relief initiatives such as the HIPC and/or Multilateral Debt Reduction Initiative

Table 4.4 External Debt-GNI Ratio of Selected SSA Countries, 2001–2017

Country Name	*2001*	*2005*	*2010*	*2015*	*2016*	*2017*
Angola	119.00	50.50	22.76	28.94	39.26	31.58
Congo	244.98	156.07	26.70	47.96	51.94	56.12
Ethiopia	70.24	49.94	24.42	32.74	32.70	33.17
Ghana	131.76	69.18	28.79	56.24	51.18	48.12
Nigeria	78.46	26.04	4.42	6.17	7.86	11.04
Sudan	122.07	71.51	36.89	24.25	24.38	20.25
Zambia	157.51	70.91	23.19	56.49	75.76	65.22
Zimbabwe	56.68	81.10	75.81	61.00	59.57	59.07

Source: World Bank Open Data, author's calculation.

(MDRI). As can be seen from Figure 4.7 and Table 4.4, the eight countries of SSA which have been among the top recipients of Chinese loans, have seen their external debt to Gross National Income (GNI) ratio skyrocket in recent years, except Sudan. Zambia's indebtedness as measured by the debt-GNI ratio increased at an alarming rate from about 23 percent in 2010 to more than 70 percent in 2016 and to 120 percent of debt-GDP ratio in 2020 (latest available data). Zambia is currently under the situation of debt distress and default. Similarly, Congo and Ghana also saw their external indebtedness more than double – for Congo from 26 percent in 2010 to 56 percent in 2017 and for Ghana from 28 percent in 2010 to nearly 56 percent in 2015 before it moderately declined to 48 percent in 2017. Zimbabwe's indebtedness has only shown a moderate decline (from about 78 percent in 2010 to 60 percent in 2017) which is still among the highest in the region. The remaining top recipients of Chinese loans (Angola, Ethiopia, and Nigeria) also saw sharp increases in their external indebtedness during the same period. This situation has led to a growing characterization particularly in Western media and think-tanks that China applies "Debt-trap Diplomacy"[6] in Africa.

The increased debt burden of SSA countries means that they can face rising debt repayment obligations at the expense of investing in their future, thus undermining their socioeconomic performance. It will also frustrate all efforts aimed at boosting public investment and fostering capital accumulation for productive capacities and structural economic transformation in the region. Increased debt servicing obligations also mean that government revenues will shift away from domestic savings and investments in infrastructure, energy, or ICT towards debt repayments. Debt repayment schedules can also undermine the ability of governments to run essential services such as education, health, and other key

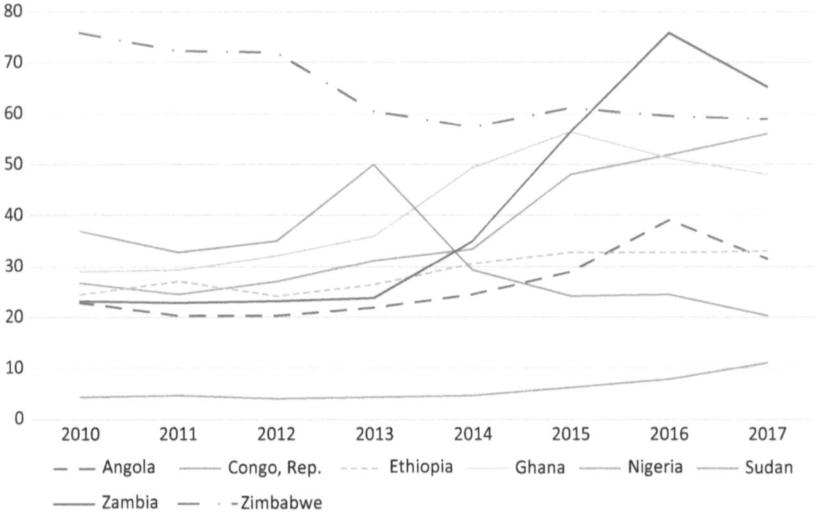

Figure 4.7 External debt-GNI ratio for selected countries of SSA (2010–2017).

Source: World Bank Open Data, author's calculation.

obligations such as the maintenance of law and order or paying salaries for public servants. In other words, an external debt burden can frustrate domestic policy formulation and implementation as well as the ownership capabilities of governments and the effectiveness of their institutions. Therefore, it is important for governments of debtor countries and creditor nations alike, including China, to pay particular attention to avoiding potential build-ups of external debt of the economies of SSA. Otherwise, the recurrence of the debt crisis of the 1980s, with all its disastrous impacts, could be imminent.

The key messages from Chapters 3 and 4 are: (i) there have been modest and incremental improvements in the composite PCI of SSA but these are not enough to have visible impact on generating inclusive and sustainable growth. In fact, SSA has been lagging behind the rest of the developing regions of the world in all measures of the productive capacities except in natural capital. The gap is particularly large in areas such as transport, human capital, structural transformation, energy, institutions, and ICT. Weak productive capacities, and the absence of structural economic transformation in SSA, means that its socioeconomic vulnerability will continue, leading to a further marginalization of the region in the global economy. (ii) Trade, investment, and the overall economic ties of SSA with China have reached an unprecedentedly high level, although there are no qualitative changes in the structure and composition of export products. (iii) The quantity and distribution of Chinese investment stock and development finance, including concessional loans across countries and economic sectors have improved over the years. However, these increases have not yet resulted in any clearly discernible qualitative impact on the socioeconomic landscape of SSA. The region has not been able to foster productive capacities and structural transformation. In fact, SSA has seen deindustrialization, continued heavy commodity concentration, and erratic GFCF. The formation of human capital, the infrastructure sector including energy (power), ICT, institutions, and structural change are areas that are significantly lagging behind the rest of the developing regions. This means that the growing Africa-China ties are not enough to close the huge investment finance gap of SSA in these areas. Moreover, building productive capacities cannot be realized in a short time span and requires more time to materialize. (vi) A holistic approach is required to further enhance the impact of the growing Africa-China trade, investment, and economic ties on fostering productive capacities and structural economic transformation of the region. For instance, trade policies, if not accompanied by institutional capacities to meet market requirements such as health and quality standards, do not lead to trade expansion, especially for countries that have comparative advantages in agri-food, horticulture, fisheries, meat, and related products. Products for which several SSA countries have natural or comparative advantages find it difficult to penetrate important marketplaces. Relieving binding constraints to trade and diversification with a view to maximizing existing market opportunities also requires specific and targeted investments in the areas where SSA holds comparative advantages in line with Vietnam's experience elaborated in Chapters 7 and 8.

Notes

1 UNCTAD defines an economy as commodity-dependent when the percentage share of commodities in total export earnings equals or exceeds 60 percent (UNCTAD: 2016).

2 Merchandise Export or Product Concentration Index is calculated by using the Herfindahl-Hirschmann Concentration Index (methodological details are available at: www.unctad.org, and https://datacatalog.worldbank.org/export-product-diversification-index.

3 For more details on methodology and definition, see https://unstats.un.org, UNCTADstat (at www.unctad.org), https//stat.unido.org, or World Bank data at https://data.worldbank.org.

4 GFCF refers to the difference between total investment and disposal (depreciation) of assets and serves as indicator of the capability of economies to foster productive transformation. It is multi-dimensional indicator, consisting of tangible and intangible assets (such as goodwill), produced and non-produced assets, as well as improvements in fixed assets (e.g., upgrading land or investing in other natural resources), contracts, inventories *minus* disposals of values in constant or current prices (OECD: 2020).

5 Africa does not seem to have learned from its own experiences of the 1970s and 1980s when such facilities grossly failed to attract Foreign Direct Investment (FDI) and help the countries of the region to grow and develop. With evidence gathered from the field in the context of the research for this book, it is difficult to substantiate the renewed optimism held by African governments regarding Chinese-led investment in the newly built facilities which focus on creating short-term employment for small proportion of unskilled and semiskilled workers and generating much needed foreign exchange, both of which can be regarded as short-term objectives as opposed to long-term development objectives.

6 Western media and think tanks often accuse China's increasing loan and credit to African countries as a predatory system designed to ensnare countries into a strait-jacket of debt servitude and that, despite explicit political conditionality, there is certainly "no free lunch", and such arrangements pose a threat to the sovereignty of vulnerable countries of SSA.

Bibliographical references

Ades, A., and Glaeser, E. (1999). Evidence on Growth, Increasing Returns and the Size of the Market. *Quarterly Journal of Economics*, 114(3): 1025–1046.

African Economic Outlook. (2018). Africa's Infrastructure: Great Potential but Little Impact on Inclusive Growth. Chapter 3. https://www.afdb.org/fileadmin/uploads/afdb/Documents/Publications/2018AEO/African_Economic_Outlook_2018_-_EN_Chapter3.pdf.

Anyanwu, J. C.(2018). Does Human Capital Matter in Manufacturing Value Added Development in Africa? *Asian Journal of Economic Modelling*, 6(3), 294–316.

Lin, J. Y., and Xu, J. (2019). China's Light Manufacturing and Africa's Industrialization. In A. Oqubay and J. Yifu Lin (Eds.), *China-Africa and An Economic Transformation, Chapter 13* (pp. 265–281). Oxford University Press, Oxford.

OECD. (2020). Investment (GFCF) (indicator). https://doi.org/10.1787/b6793677-en. (Accessed on 25 October 2020).

Odili, O., and Ede, U. P. (2015). Evidence on the Dynamic Relationship between Stock Market Share Index and Gross Fixed Capital Formation in Nigeria. *ISOR Journal of Business and Management*, 17(I) January 2015, 85–94.

Quah, D. (1997). Empirics of Growth and Distribution: Stratification, Polarization and Convergence Club. Centre for Economic Performance Discussion Paper 324. London School of Economics and Political Science.

Quah, D. (1999). 6 x 10^9: Some Dynamics of Global Inequality and Growth. Background Paper for World Development Report 2000/2001. London School of Economics and Political Science. Suntory and Toyota International Centers for Economics and Related Disciplines and World Bank, Washington, DC.

Rodrik, D. (2016). Premature deindustrialization. *Journal of Economic Growth*, 21(1), 1–33.

UNCTAD. (2019a). *Commodities and Development 2017 Report: The State of Commodity Dependence 2019*. United Nations Publication, New York and Geneva.

UNCTADStat. (2018, 2019 and 2020). https://unctadstat.unctad.org/EN/

UNIDO. (2018a). Industrial Development Report 2018. Demand for Manufacturing: Driving Inclusive and Sustainable Industrial Development, United Nations Industrial Development Organization, Chapter 7, 162.

Wolff, N. E. (1993). Capital Formation and Productivity Convergence Over the Long Term. *The American Economic Review*, 81(3) June 1991, 565–579. https://www.jstor.org/stable/2006519.

World Bank. (2000). *Can Africa Claim the 21st Century? April 2000*. The World Bank, Washington, DC.

World Bank Data. (2019). *World Bank Open Data*. https://data.worldbank.org/.

5 SSA's Partnerships with EU, USA, and Japan in Comparison with China

The discussions in this chapter build on the key conclusions in Chapters 3 and 4 that the level of productive capacities in SSA lags behind that of other developing regions and that the increasing Africa-China partnership has made little difference in enhancing the productive capacities of SSA. Moreover, modest improvements in SSA's productive capacities brought about by an increased partnership with China could not help to bridge the widening gap between SSA and the rest of the developing regions.

The countries of SSA have been accorded Official Development Assistance (ODA), preferential market access, and facilitated investment relations with the three major global economic powerhouses (the EU, the USA, and Japan) for decades. In recent years, however, there has been a shift in Africa's relations away from these economies towards China and (to some extent) India. Contemporary relations between the EU and SSA are rooted in historical, political, and strategic partnership between the two. While the colonial legacy played an important part in cementing the partnership, the relations between the EU and SSA are characterized by the confluences of trade and investment flows as well as broader economic cooperation and strategic partnerships. These have been formalized through various frameworks and agreements such as the Lomé Convention,[1] the Cotonou Agreement, and the Economic Partnership Agreement (EPA) as well as various market access initiatives in support of SSA's trade.

The EU and Africa have also established a formal mechanism for political dialogue on the "EU-Africa Partnership and Joint Strategy". The latter's declared objective is to bring the two partners closer by enhancing trade, investment, and economic cooperation. The two parties, despite apparent asymmetries in economic and negotiating powers, also commit themselves to working together on several common global political, environmental, and social issues. These include areas such as peace and security, sustainable development (including SDGs), democracy, solidarity, human dignity, and migration. Currently, the EU and members of the Africa, Caribbean, and Pacific (ACP), which include all the countries of SSA, are negotiating a successor to the Cotonou Agreement called EU-ACP Economic Partnership Agreement (Schmieg: 2019). The EU-ACP agreement is a long-term arrangement which defines formal relationships between the member countries of ACP and their former colonial powers.

DOI: 10.4324/9781003295334-5

SSA has also developed broad partnerships with the US. With the aim of boosting Africa's exports and facilitating investment flows, the US grants market access opportunities to several countries of SSA through the Africa Growth and Opportunities Act (AGOA) – a non-reciprocal trade preference programme granted by the USA to 39[2] countries of SSA. Despite increasing US strategic interests in Africa and its market access initiatives, the role of the USA in SSA's trade and investment has been on a continuous decline over the years. The share of SSA's exports to the USA has continuously deteriorated (Figures 5.3 and 5.4) during the years examined. In 2015, over 40 percent of US exports were destined for only two countries in SSA: South Africa and Nigeria (US International Trade Commission – USIT: 2018). Similarly, between 2010 and 2017, the US foreign direct investment (FDI) stock in SSA plummeted, while annual FDI flows are heavily concentrated in only three countries: Mauritius, South Africa, and Nigeria (USIT, 2018). The USIT also reported that, between 2001 and 2013, 90 percent of US trade with SSA was in crude oil, although, in recent years, imports of cocoa, confectionery, and apparel have emerged as among the fast-growing import items from SSA. The sluggish trend in trade and capital flows has relegated US-African relations to a bare minimum, with the USA trailing far behind the EU, China, and India.[3] Regarding ODA flows to SSA, the contribution of USA is the second largest, following the EU's. The US Millennium Challenge Account (MCA) has further augmented US financial assistance to developing countries by almost 50 percent (Owusu: 2007). The initiative targets 24 low and middle-income developing countries, includes 12 from SSA as recipients of MCA resources (Chapter 1). The USA has also pledged additional USD 15 billion to combat HIV/AIDS in Africa and the Caribbean region. Consequently, the USA has become the largest single donor (in absolute terms) for several countries of SSA, particularly in social sectors (health, education, security, or the fight against international terrorism). However, due to this increasing orientation towards the social sector, the share of US development aid that goes to key productive sectors such as infrastructure (transport and communications) and industry or agriculture in recipient countries, has declined during the years examined (Figure 5.11). Even within the social sector, the effectiveness of US financial aid and its impact on economic growth and development have been seriously undermined by a complex set of eligibility criteria, which focused more on political outcomes and process than on generating inclusive and sustainable growth in recipient countries. While the MCA can be regarded as the largest US initiative in support of poor and vulnerable nations since the 1940s and 1960s, it suffers from a series of systemic problems and challenges, discussed in Chapter 1.

Japan has also emerged as the key development partner of SSA since the 1970s, although its contributions have been dwarfed by bigger global players such as the EU, the USA, and recently China. Relations between Japan and SSA were rooted in technical assistance, diplomatic relations, and sharing its development experience with SSA. Since the 1990s, Japan has indeed become one of the top providers of ODA to several African countries (Cornelissen: 2012). This development has also led to the formation of Tokyo International Conference for African Development (TICAD) in 1993. An interesting aspect of Japanese engagement in support of SSA is its sectoral approach with a focus on food security, regional infrastructure development, and improving access to safe water (TICAD IV). Japan has been associated with efforts to boost agricultural productivity in Africa, which also led to the creation of the Coalition for African Rice Development (Cornelissen: 2012). In addition, Japan has been helping several countries of SSA in enhancing Public-Private Partnerships (PPP) to foster trade, investment, and private sector development. Boosting agricultural productivity, enhancing regional infrastructure, and improving access to safe drinking water, were among the priority areas identified at TICAD IV held in 2008. In recent years, Japan has also joined hands with India in designing a "New Joint Strategic Vision" document with the declared aim of fostering industrialization and industrial networks between Asia and Africa (Panda: 2017). This India-Japan coalition on an "Asia-Africa Growth Corridor" had at least three implicit objectives: (i) to counter the growing and an unprecedented economic and political influence of China in Africa and Asia, including through China's Road and Belt Initiative (RBI); (ii) to look for "new pastures" (Alam and Gupta: 2011) to meet their consistently growing demand for raw materials, of which Africa can be a permanent supplier; and (iii) to expand and protect their trade, economic, and strategic interests in both Asia and Africa.

The following sections closely examine trade, investment, and development finance partnerships of SSA with the EU, the USA, and Japan in comparison with China, and India. This is examined in relation to the overall (global) performance of SSA in trade, investment, and aid flows. In so doing, the chapter reflects on whether such relationships have contributed to fostering structural transformation in SSA.

5.1 SSA's Performance in International Trade

As discussed in the preceding chapters, for several decades, the countries of SSA have undertaken a wide range of policy and institutional reforms, largely prescribed by Washington-based institutions and the World Trade Organization (WTO). Further reforms have also been implemented in SSA through unilateral measures or via bilateral, regional, and intra-regional initiatives (e.g., through the EPA of the European Union, AGOA of the USA, and commitments, more recently, through the Africa Continental Free Trade Area – ACFTA). Cardinal to these reforms were economic stabilization, privatization, and liberalization programmes, including the removal of distortions in trade and investment as well as private sector development. The declared objectives of the reforms were to enhance SSA's economic growth, generate employment, enhance the role of trade and investment in development, facilitate access to technology, and capital accumulation with substantial impact on poverty reduction. The goals of the reforms and adjustment efforts were also to gradually diminish the role of the state, while enhancing that of the market and the private sector in resource allocation, production, and distribution of economic gains, if any.

All the efforts to implement prescribed reforms have failed to deliver intended results. Where modest success has been observed, it is in the mining sector where reforms have led to improved investment governance in the sector, contributed to allocative efficiency in the use of revenues from the extractive sector and the environmental sustainability of mining operations (Nordic Africa Initiative: 2018). For instance, reforms combined with aid or debt-relief initiatives by donors have led to deregulation and privatization of the mining sector, which, in turn, have contributed to relative improvements in resource governance in some countries of SSA such as Botswana and Ghana. These improvements, buoyed by increased global demand, have generated profits and heightened competition among multinational companies and major investment home countries. These have contributed to improved FDI flows to the extractive sectors of the region. Unfortunately, these developments have not been accompanied by substantial impact on job creation, income distribution, and more importantly, poverty reduction and structural economic transformation in SSA. Available evidence shows that externally prescribed policies and strategies, as well as multilateral and regional trade rules which countries of SSA have accepted to implement, have severely "constrained their abilities to effectively use the full range of instruments that were exploited by industrialized and newly industrializing economies in their respective early stages of industrialization and processes of structural economic transformation" (UNECA: 2011a).

Moreover, preferential market access and increasing trade and investment partnerships of SSA countries with major developed countries have not altered the trade structure, share, and deteriorating terms of trade of the former. SSA's share in global merchandise and services trade (particularly exports) has remained negligible and precipitously declining over the years. The dependence of the countries of SSA on exports of primary commodities has also increased instead of decreasing. Likewise, manufacturing value-added as a percentage of GDP has continued to plunge over the years (Chapter 4). The continued trade imbalance which SSA sustains is the outcome of the confluences of trade reforms which increased imports more proportionately than exports and aggravated structural supply and demand side impediments. Supply and demand side challenges include weak productive and supply capacities; lack of export diversification (value addition) and continued dependence of the region on the export of primary commodities whose international prices are low, unpredictable, and volatile. These trends are against SSA's imports of light manufactures and value-added products whose international prices are constant or increasing, which lead to SSA's declining terms of trade; and paucity of investment to unlock structural bottlenecks such as poor infrastructure, etc.

The emergence China and India as new powerhouses brought added dynamism to SSA's trade, with new opportunities. This has not resulted in trade creation or expansion for SSA, unfortunately. What can be observed from available data is trade diversion or a shift in the direction of trade of SSA from West to East, with no change in the structure, composition, and form of exports. Besides well-documented structural impediments to development, failed policy reforms have further undermined SSA's economic viability, recovery, and development. Indeed, the reform programmes prescribed by International Financial Institutions (IFIs) have failed dismally, particularly in low-income countries such as those in SSA (Shafaeddin: 2005, Kassim: 2016). Despite the reforms, low-income countries have consistently experienced slow growth in exports, a declining share of manufacturing value-added or "premature deindustrialization",[4] loss of tax revenues, and increased exploitation of natural resources with persistent commoditization of SSA's exports. Only a small number of East Asian economies have managed to accelerate economic growth in the last couple of decades. This is primarily because the East Asian economies have built and expanded their productive capacities and upgraded their production structures. Contrary to this small group of successful countries, most low-income countries in Africa and Latin America have seen increasing poverty trends, lack of investment, and transfers of technology. Consequently, SSA has experienced declining manufacturing value-added in GDP, low levels of capital accumulation, and low and volatile fixed capital formation as discussed in Chapter 4.

In the area of international trade, the poor outcome of adjustment programmes observed in SSA is against an unprecedented growth in world trade. The global trade in goods and services has evolved significantly over the years, not only in volume but also in value, type, structure, and composition. In 2017, the total value of WTO members' trade in merchandise and commercial services reached USD 17.43 trillion and USD 5.19 trillion, respectively, with merchandise trade growing by 4.7 percent whereas services trade grew by 8 percent (WTO: 2018). Developing countries accounted for 40 percent of merchandise trade and 34 percent of commercial services trade (in value) in the same year. Africa's services trade was heavily concentrated on tourism and travel which grew by about 25 percent. However, the share of Africa in high-skill services sectors such as ICT services, banking and insurance, and services related to manufacturing and Intellectual Property (IP) remains negligible. Overall, Africa's contribution to the global services trade has shrunk from about 2.6 percent in 1980 to 2.03 percent in 2013 and further to 1.85 in 2016 (Table 5.1) before slightly bouncing back to about 1.97 percent in 2018. The corresponding share for SSA (without South Africa) has deteriorated from about 1.53 percent in 1980 to 0.82 percent in 2013 before slightly picking up to 0.88 percent in 2018. Apart from 1980, the total share of SSA in total worldwide services trade has remained below 1 percent.

Overall, while developing regions of the world (excluding China) had a share of 25.2 percent in global service trade in 2018, the share of Africa was about 2.01 percent and that of SSA 0.88 percent in the same year. Unlike the service trade, a closer examination of growth in global merchandise trade paints a mixed picture. Undoubtedly, the trend in merchandise exports follows the global boom–bust cycle. The overall growth rates in merchandise exports remained positive between 1981 and 2014 (Figure 5.1).

Bouncing back from the collapse of world merchandise exports during the 2008–2009 global economic crises, the growth rate reached its maximum in 2010–2014 before diving back into negative territory in 2015–2016. The fall in

Table 5.1 Sahres of Different Economic Groups in Total World Trade in Services (Exports and Imports), 1980–2018

MEASURE				*Percentage of total world*	PARTNER	*World*	FLOW	*Exports*	CATEGORY	*Services*							
YEAR	*1980*	*1990*	*2000*	*2005*	*2006*	*2007*	*2008*	*2009*	*2010*	*2011*	*2012*	*2013*	*2014*	*2015*	*2016*	*2017*	*2018*
ECONOMY																	
Developing economies excluding China	18.02	17.38	21.13	20.13	20.59	20.73	21.31	21.67	23.46	23.63	24.90	24.92	25.13	25.56	25.35	25.41	25.48
Developing Economies: Africa	2.61	2.22	2.22	2.29	2.29	2.26	2.28	2.35	2.39	2.18	2.24	2.03	2.01	2.01	1.85	1.97	1.97
Developing economies: America	4.79	3.80	4.05	3.48	3.40	3.25	3.27	3.33	3.42	3.44	3.59	3.49	3.42	3.49	3.50	3.44	3.24
Developing economies: Asia	10.27	11.58	16.82	17.15	17.88	18.83	19.65	19.82	22.03	22.40	23.36	23.53	23.79	24.34	24.02	24.03	24.63
China	……	0.70	1.99	2.92	3.09	3.72	4.01	3.93	4.49	4.50	4.38	4.23	4.18	4.37	4.12	4.12	4.45
Sub-Saharan Africa excluding South Africa	1.53	0.96	0.75	0.77	0.71	0.69	0.71	0.75	0.77	0.81	0.83	0.82	0.77	0.86	0.84	0.87	0.87
Developed economies	78.97	79.90	75.54	76.94	76.30	75.53	74.67	74.39	72.04	71.86	70.70	70.83	70.68	70.06	70.52	70.45	70.05

Source: UNCTADstat 2019 (Author's calculation)

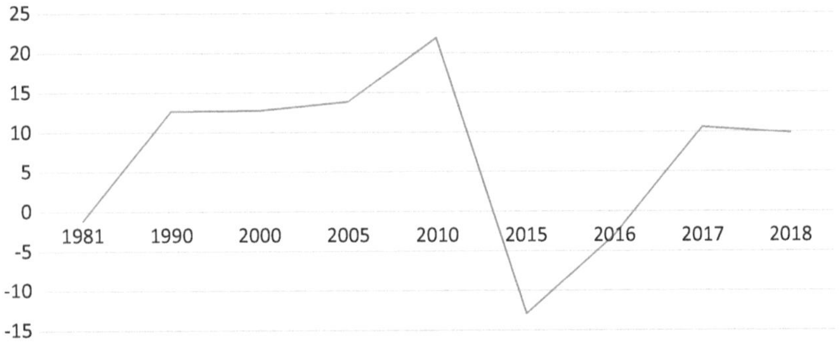

Figure 5.1 Growth rates of global merchandise trade: 1981–2018.
Source: UNCTADstat (2019).

growth rates during 2015–2016 was spectacular, despite an increase in the volume of merchandise exports during the two years. The combination of low export prices, sluggish global demand, and relative appreciation of the US dollar vis-à-vis major global currencies are responsible for the decrease in growth of the world merchandise trade. Almost all the regions were affected by the fall in the growth of merchandise trade, although the value of trade tumbled the most in commodity exporting regions. For SSA, "export earnings have declined by an average of about 20 percent per year since 2010, by 30 percent in 2015 and an additional 10 percent in 2016" (UNCTAD: 2017c, pp. 2–3). During subsequent years (2017–2018), global merchandise trade has moderately recovered (although still lower than the level in 2014). The recovery was largely driven by fuel exports, which increased by about 28 percent in 2015–2016. The impact of the current global health crisis (COVID-19) on international trade is expected to be significant, especially for SSA. Notwithstanding intertemporal contraction, the value of the global merchandise trade has shown an unprecedented growth in the last six decades – from USD 130.3 billion in 1960 to USD 6.5 trillion in 2000 and USD 19.5 trillion in 2018. This phenomenal growth, over the 1960–2018 period, represents a 1,500-fold increase (Table 5.2).

In 2017, the value of the world merchandise trade increased by 11 percent – the largest increase since 2011 (WTO: 2018). The recent growth is mainly driven by fuel exports, which increased by 28 percent followed by increases in manufactured exports by 9 percent, and agricultural exports 8 percent in 2018. As Table 5.2 depicts, the share of developing countries (excluding China) in world merchandise trade has increased from 22.6 percent in 1960 to 28.1 percent in 2000, and to 31.8 percent in 2018. China's share has shown an amazing performance, increasing from a little less than 2 percent in 1960 to 3.8 percent in 2000 and to 12.8 percent in 2018. Developing Asia, aided by China's impressive performance, has maintained a significantly higher and increasing share in total world merchandise trade, which increased from 11 percent in 1960 to 23.8 percent in 2000 and 36.5 percent in 2018. Within the developing economies,

Table 5.2 World Merchandise Trade in Value: Trends and Shares at US Current Prices in Millions (1960–2018)

Column1	*Column2*	*Column3*	*Column4*	*Column5*	*Column6*	*Column7*	*Column8*	*Column9*	*Column10*	*Column11*
YEAR	*1960*	*1970*	*1980*	*1990*	*2000*	*2010*	*2015*	*2016*	*2017*	*2018*
ECONOMY										
China	2571.28	2307.25	18099.30	62091.00	249203.00	1577754.00	2273468.00	2097632.00	2263346.00	2487045.00
Share in world trade (%)	1.97428	0.72	0.88	1.77	3.86	10.31	13.75	13.08	12.76	12.76
Sub-Saharan Africa	5708.85	11032.18	77335.67	68020.63	92783.16	343670.74	281478.22	251723.92	298604.77	340864.11
Share in world trade (%)	4.38	3.46	3.77	1.94	1.43	2.24	1.70	1.57	1.68	1.75
Africa	7335.35	16128.82	121377.95	104877.03	147904.53	521435.01	388463.96	356168.08	421415.27	478717.31
Share in world trade (%)	5.63	5.06	5.92	3.00	2.29	3.40	2.34	2.22	2.37	2.45
Latin America and the Caribbean	9731.24	17305.66	111502.95	145622.30	367998.30	891609.18	923048.23	888708.68	996300.02	1085796.33
Share in wolrd world trade (%)	7.47	5.43	5.43	4.16	5.70	5.82	5.58	5.54	5.61	5.57
Developing economies: Asia	14760.48	26803.96	373191.21	589790.08	1538457.50	5016321.70	6074722.10	5780941.20	6435301.32	7107171.16
Share in world trade (%)	11.33	8.42	18.20	16.87	23.84	32.78	36.74	36.05	36.29	36.49
Asia	19031.80	46900.16	509169.71	889450.08	2066951.00	5954790	6851223.50	6558401.20	7284328.05	8015380.64

(Continued)

Table 5.2 Continued

Column1	*Column2*	*Column3*	*Column4*	*Column5*	*Column6*	*Column7*	*Column8*	*Column9*	*Column10*	*Column11*
YEAR	*1960*	*1970*	*1980*	*1990*	*2000*	*2010*	*2015*	*2016*	*2017*	*2018*
Share in world trade (%)	14.61	14.74	24.83	25.44	32.03	38.91	41.44	40.90	41.07	41.15
Developing economies excluding China	29441.00	58517.80	590223.42	780976.53	1810329.20	4860690.10	5124521.10	4939952.20	5603509.13	6198693.83
Share in world trade (%)	22.60	18.39	28.78	22.34	28.05	31.76	30.99	30.81	31.59	31.82
Developing economies	32012.28	60825.05	608322.72	843067.53	2059532.20	6438444.10	7397989.10	7037584.20	7866855.13	8685738.83
Share in world trade (%)	24.57	19.11	29.67	24.11	31.91	42.07	44.75	43.89	44.36	44.59
Developed economies	92047.06	242848.94	1356328.90	2534229.90	4243212.40	8254559.80	8612098.40	8550734.10	9315920.38	10113281.50
Share in world trade (%)	70.67	76.33	66.15	72.49	65.76	53.94	52.09	53.33	52.53	51.92
World	130238.45	318152.89	2050129.20	3495675.40	6452317.90	15302149	16531558	16031517	17732796	19476195.70

Source: UNCTADstat (2019).

the combined average share of Latin America and the Caribbean has slightly dropped from 7.5 percent in 1960 to 5.7 percent and 5.5 percent in 2000 and 2018, respectively.

Unfortunately, the African region, with a total population of 1.225 billion in 2016 (about 17 percent of the world's population), accounts for only 2.2 percent of the world's merchandise trade in the same year. Africa's trade performance has been one of the most disappointing, even in comparison with the rest of the developing world. The region's share declined continuously, although the absolute value and volume of its trade has increased over the years. Africa's share in 1960 was about 5.6 percent, dived to 2.3 in 2000, before it slightly bounced back to 2.46 percent in 2018. The share of SSA (with an estimated population of 1.1 billion in 2018) mimics the trend in the share of the African region, but it collapsed much faster and deeper than the share of the continent in the global merchandise trade. The share of SSA declined from 4.4 percent in 1960 to 1.4 percent in 2000 before a marginal reversal to 1.75 percent in 2018 (Table 5.2).

The continuous decline in SSA's share in global merchandise trade was despite its increasing partnership with China, wide-ranging policy and institutional reforms, and favourable preferential market access[5] conditions granted to it by major trading partners (EU, Japan, USA). Preferential market access initiatives were designed to facilitate trade and investment flows, with the ultimate objective of expanding Africa's trade, accelerating economic growth, boosting job creation and income with substantial poverty reduction. After decades of operationalizing multiple initiatives, none of the intended objectives have been attained to date. The export share of SSA has continued to deteriorate over time, export concentration has increased instead of decreasing; unemployment and poverty reduction remain persistent challenges facing SSA. Consequently, the commodity-led growth model characterized by weak productive capacities and a lack of structural economic transformation plagued trade and the overall socioeconomic performance in SSA. This shows that policy reforms and preferential market access grants alone are not sufficient to improve SSA's trade and economic performance if not accompanied by the fostering of productive capacities and structural economic transformation. In sum, Africa's poor socioeconomic performance, including its declining share in world exports, is the cause and consequence of the region's weak productive capacities and lack of transformation. The sluggish performance of the countries of SSA is manifested in its declining share in world trade, increased commoditization of exports, continuously shrinking manufacturing value-added, and premature deindustrialization.

SSA also consists of several countries whose degree of dependence on exports of a handful primary commodities has increased over the years as measured by their export concentration. For selected countries in SSA, the Merchandise Export Concentration Index has increased except for Equatorial Guinea, Gabon, and (moderately) Nigeria (Figure 5.2). Angola leads the group with its index increasing from about 0.88 in 2001 to 0.95 in 2012–2018, followed by Guinea Bissau and Botswana. The shockingly upward trend is that of Zambia, whose

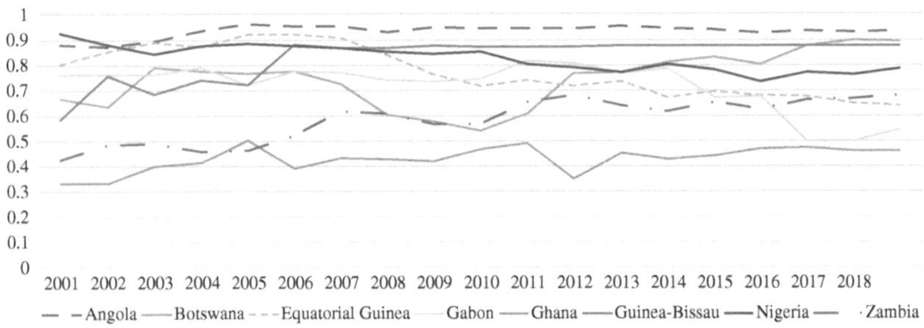

Figure 5.2 Merchandise Export Concentration Index (MECI) in selected oil and mineral-exporting SSA countries, 2001–2018.

Source: UNCTADStat (2019).

concentration index has skyrocketed from 0.43 in 2001 to 0.68 in 2018 (an increase of about 60 percent).

Besides product concentration, Africa's – not least SSA's – markets (export destinations) are also heavily concentrated. Whereas three major countries or regions (EU, USA, Japan) long dominated the scene, China and India have recently absorbed the lion's share of the region's trade. Africa also trades least among countries of its own region. Intra-African exports are the lowest of all intra-regional exports when compared to Europe, Asia, and Latin America, which, during the same period, were 68.1 percent, 59.4 percent, 55 percent, respectively (UNCTAD: 2019b). However, there still is hope for the continent as intra-African exports increased from about 10 percent in 2010–2015 to 16.6 percent in 2017 (UNCTAD: 2019b). Total intra-African trade (imports plus exports) remains marginal (2 percent) in 2015–2017, showing that the region still trades less with itself than with other continents. This meagre percentage is expected to improve as the continent embarks on the most ambitious African Continental Free Trade Area (AfCFTA), provided that major stumbling blocks and key binding constraints (such as weak productive capacities and the absence of structural economic transformation) are effectively addressed.

5.1.2 SSA and Its Main Development and Trade Partners

The developed economies of Europe remain the largest development and trading partners of SSA although their combined relative share in the region's exports and imports has declined, respectively, from about 75 percent and 67 percent in 2000 to about 44 percent and 40 percent in 2018 (Figures 5.3 and 5.4). The largest decline in the share of exports and imports during the 2000–2018 period was observed in the case of the USA. SSA's exports to the USA dived from 22 percent in 2000 to about 5.5 percent in 2018, while imports of SSA from the USA have declined from about 7.8 percent in 2000 to 4.6 percent in 2018. The precipitously declining share of SSA's exports to the USA is despite improved market access offers granted to several countries of the region through the US AGOA.

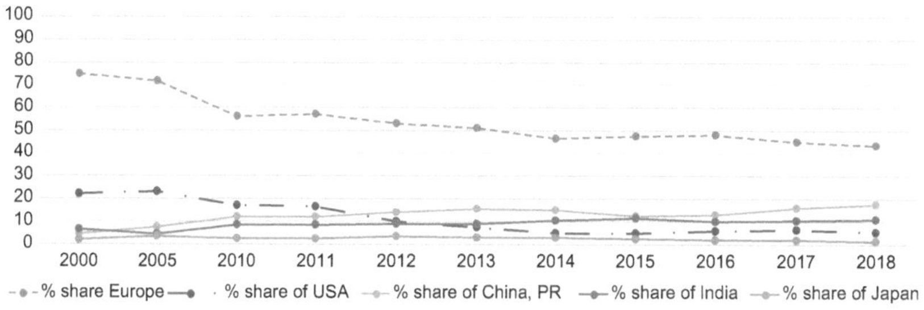

Figure 5.3 Top destinations of SSA's exports, FOB (percent of total exports in value) (2000–2018).

Source: IMF, Direction of Trade Statistics (DOTS) (2019).

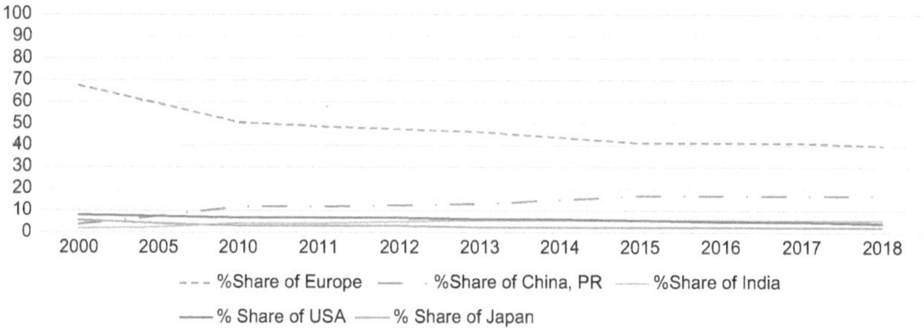

Figure 5.4 SSA's imports from key partners: percentage share in total value of imports, CIF (2000–2018).

Source: IMF, Direction of Trade Statistics (DOTS) (2019).

The shares of SSA's exports to and imports from Japan remain relatively small over the period under examination (Figure 5.3). The values oscillate between 1.8 percent and 2 percent for exports during 2000–2018. Similarly, SSA's imports from Japan have gone down from about 5 percent in 2000 to less than 2 percent in 2018. By contrast, China and India have consistently and substantially increased their respective shares of exports to and imports from SSA during the 2000–2018 period. China's share in SSA's total exports has increased from less than 3 percent in 2000 to about 17.5 percent in 2018, while its share in combined SSA imports has increased from about 5 percent in 2000 to 16.8 percent in 2018. Likewise, India's share in SSA's total exports has jumped from 6.6 percent in 2000 to 11.23 percent in 2018, whereas SSA's imports from India have also increased from 1.9 percent in 2000 to about 5 percent in 2018 (Figure 5.3). Therefore, China and India have emerged as the second and third top trading partners for SSA following the developed economies of Europe. The USA and Japan have increasingly lost ground to China and India and become marginal players when it comes to trading with SSA. A further important feature of SSA trade has been that the region's export within itself has continued to increase from less than 10 percent in 2000 to about 16.6 percent in 2017, although intra-African trade (export and import) is still, by far, lower than intra-European, intra-American, and intra-Asian trade (UNCTAD: 2019b).

The rising share of China and India in SSA's exports and imports indicates the growing importance of the two largest developing economies. Both countries have become important global economic powerhouses in their respective stance in the global economy in recent years, offering increased opportunities for SSA's trade and development. China and India have, in a way, become leading trade partners for the commodity-driven economies of SSA in the face of sluggish global demand for primary commodities. As critically important as this role of the two economies can be, the nature of the trade has entrenched the commoditization of SSA's trade and economies. SSA's exports, particularly to China, largely consist of primary commodities – oil- and mineral-based commodities (Figures 1.3 and 1.4). For instance, in 2018, nearly 97 percent of SSA's total exports to China were in primary commodities. Currently, SSA is also the second largest oil supplier to China, after the Middle East, with more than 21.5 percent (average) between 2010 and 2016 (Obi: 2019). The excessive dependence of SSA on exports of primary commodities and oil has continued with the emergence of China and India as its important trade partners. The increasing trade ties with China (also India) have further entrenched the region's dependence on exports of unprocessed commodities. This has compounded the challenges of diversification, value addition, and overall structural economic transformation in SSA, although both nations offered huge trade opportunities to the region – for exports and imports alike.

5.1.3 *Trade Balance and Share in GDP and Imports of SSA*

The trade balance is the largest single source of changes in the current account[6] balance of SSA, and hence the balance of payments. Therefore, the focus in this section is exclusively on the trade balance (not current account balance). Moreover, the trade balance has a direct relevance to productive capacities and economic transformation as it directly or indirectly influences endogenous factors (such as exchange rates, labour productivity, savings rates, or goods produced and exported, etc.) in an economy. Therefore, it bears more directly on the core issues raised and discussed in this book – productive capacities and structural transformation – than on the current account balance or the overall balance of payments of nations.

A negative (deficit) or positive (surplus) trade balance has always been controversial not only within mainstream economics but also in political discourses. Generally, nations and their policies have always strived to attain positive trade balances on the assumption that a surplus in trade balance is good (or deficit is bad) for the economy. Such a perception is in line with the conventional wisdom of mercantilists, that gains from international trade (surplus) depend on more exports and fewer imports. These views are behind protectionist policies that governments often put in place to encourage (more) exports while curbing imports to achieve prosperity and economic wellbeing. The conventional wisdom and mercantilist assertions regarding trade balances are in stark contrast with prevalent views in mainstream economics. The latter regards a trade deficit as the inevitable consequence of a country's performance and should not be a cause for concern (Gould et al.: 1996). Such variation in views is also manifest in classical trade theories, which regard consistent trade surpluses as the cause for macroeconomic instability in an economy. This is because excess international reserves from trade surpluses can increase hoarding or lead to inflation. Gould's assertions regarding the macroeconomic impact of trade surpluses may be valid for the circumstances of developed countries. However, in the case of developing countries such as those in SSA, trade surplus may help to acquire capital and technology (imports), finance infrastructure, and foster industrialization and economy-wide productive capacities and structural economic transformation, without resorting to borrowing.

In trade policy contexts, a negative trade balance has been the single most important cause of the simmering trade wars between the US administration and China, between the USA, Canada, and Mexico, and intermittently between the USA and the EU. A more worrying trend is the withdrawal of the Trump administration from one of the largest regional trading blocs – the Trans-Pacific Partnership Free Trade Agreement (TPP), on 30 January 2017 (Chow et al.: 2018). The withdrawal was based on the perception that the TPP agreement was unfair to the USA. The most troubling feature of this trend is that the decision to withdraw was the result of the new or emerging "economic nationalism" and protectionist tendencies of the previous US administration, in line with the "Make America Great Again" slogan or "America First" economic agenda (Chow et al.: 2018).

Within the contemporary mainstream economics profession, there are divergent views as far as negative trade balances (deficits) are concerned. Some argue that a terms-of-trade deterioration (i.e., the rise of import prices relative to prices of exports) is apt to improve a country's trade balance, provided that the sum of a country's price elasticity of demand for exports and imports is greater than 1 in absolute value (Hamoni: 2008). Okoro (2013), based on Nigeria's experience, asserts that a surplus trade balance is key to reducing overall fiscal deficits, whereas a continuously negative trade balance leads to fiscal deficit in public expenditure financing. Osakwe and Verick (2007) argue that, given the low levels of investment and economic growth in the countries of SSA, maintaining trade deficits is not beneficial over the long run. Contrary to these views Lawrence (2018), provides a detailed account of why the focus on trade deficits is misleading and counterproductive as countries, generally, benefit both from importing and exporting to raise the standards of living of their citizens. According to the author, trade policies and trade agreements should focus more on reducing trade and investment distortions than on reducing trade imbalances through protectionist or nationalistic measures.

Notwithstanding these divergent views, there is consensus that a negative trade balance is not desirable if it is systemic, persistent, and the outcome of poor economic policies and strategies, as is the case in SSA. For commodity-dependent economies of SSA, a negative trade balance exacerbates economic woes. This is because persistent and profound trade deficits could weaken domestic industries, enhance capital flight, undermine job creation, and above all increase indebtedness. Systematic or persistent negative trade balances mean that exports are unable to finance imports. Hence, countries accumulate external debts or liabilities as they seek to finance their deficits through foreign credit (loans), development aid, FDI, international reserves, and other forms of capital flows such as remittances, royalties, and taxes on foreign investments. Figure 5.5 shows SSA's trade balance in goods and services in millions of US dollars for the 2005–2017 period. Apart from the commodities boom period (2002–2006), the region's trade balance has not only been in deficit, but the magnitude of the deficit has been continuously increasing. This has continued and deepened particularly since the global financial and economic crises of 2008–2009. Such a steep fall in the trade balance of SSA shows vulnerabilities and systemic challenges inherent in the region's economy – weak productive capacities and lack of structural economic transformation. The 2014–2016 period has been the worst for the region's trade balance as the deficit hit about USD 120 billion in 2015, although it has moderately eased since then.

Figure 5.6 shows that the share of the trade balance in GDP has gone down from the highest level of about 50 percent in 2006 to the lowest level

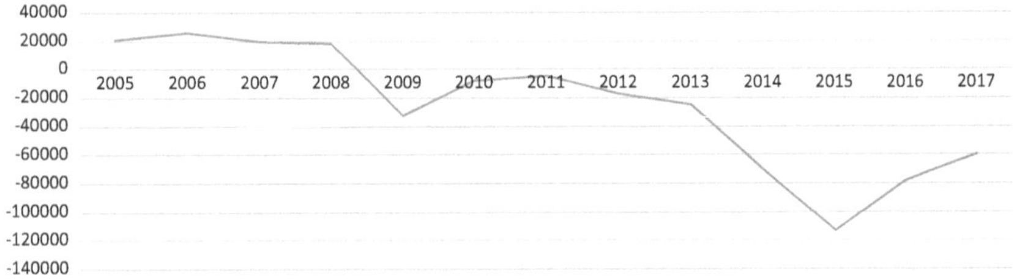

Figure 5.5 SSA's trade balance of goods and services at current prices in USD millions (2005–2017).

Source: UNCTADStat (2019).

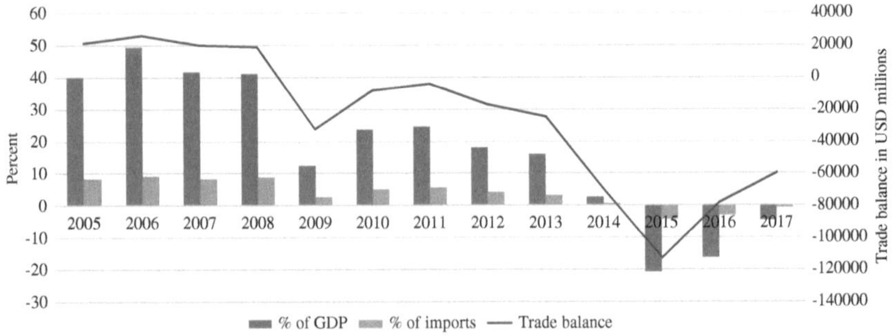

Figure 5.6 SSA's total trade balance (goods and services) at current prices in USD millions and as percentage of imports and GDP: 2005–2017.

Source: UNCTADStat (2019).

(–20 percent) in 2015. Likewise, the share of trade balance in the total exports of the region has collapsed from about 9 percent in 2006 to 5 percent in 2010 and – 7 percent in 2015 (Figure 5.6), which is the lowest level in decades. The relatively low shares of trade balance in GDP and imports indicates the different trends in exports and imports performance, where the values of imports consistently exceed the values of exports. In other words, the countries of SSA spend more on imports than they earn from exports, which is also the cause and consequence of these countries' current account imbalances. Such a persistent and increasing trade imbalance in the region affects the real exchange rates in the countries, further distorting the allocation of resources (labour and capital). Trade balances have become more sensitive to real exchange rates, despite the view that the advent of regional and global value chains has significantly reduced such sensitivities (Kharroubi: 2011). Countries should address their trade problems by boosting their exports and improving trade balance to reduce sensitivities in real exchange rates, capital flight, and job losses.

The negative trade balance of SSA is the result of the lag in exports behind imports, which is due to several factors: first, the lack of capacity to exploit existing (revealed) or latent comparative and competitive advantages in the production and exports of goods and services. Although the assumption behind the theory of international trade is that every nation would have a given comparative advantage over the other, in most cases, the variation in the nature of the binding constraints and inability to relieve them can undermine efforts to exploit a given comparative advantage. Second, the consistently increasing, or higher relative prices of goods and services imported vis-à-vis the low and falling prices of exports of goods and services is one more factor behind trade deficits. Such is the situation in the countries of SSA, which are dependent on the production and export of raw materials (commodities) and low-skill services and import of manufactured goods. This translates into commodity-driven growth, lack of diversification (value addition), poor technological sophistication of exports, and absence of overall structural transformation in the economies. This also leads to the continuous deterioration of the terms of trade as the relative price of imports continues to outweigh that of exports. Third, the "income export paradox" which occurs when countries discover quick or "windfall" profits (e.g., through the exploitation of natural oil or other mineral reserves), penalizing a country's overall economy, can also lead to a trade deficit. Such a paradox is usually referred to as "Dutch Disease" in economics, which is the phenomenon in most oil- and mineral- exporting countries of SSA. SSA's manufacturing is the sector most sensitive to the Dutch Disease condition. This is because of its underlying or systemic weakness in production and productivity as well as the low competitive edge inherent in the sector, particularly in relation to relatively cheaper imports.

Fourth, an increase in domestic income generates more demand for imports due to variations in domestic supply responses – one further factor behind trade deficits. The lack of capacity of firms and industries to produce goods and services in response to an increase in domestic income (and demand) leads to dependency on imports. Fifth is the decline in the relative costs of production of a given product or item and the proportionate fall in the price of foreign products relative to domestic products. Sixth, bad monetary, fiscal, or trade policies, which hamper exports but facilitate imports are also among the main reasons behind trade deficits. As indicated in the preceding sections of this chapter, trade liberalization and other economic policy reforms pursued, particularly by countries of SSA, could not stimulate exports. Instead, they facilitate more imports and became causes and consequences of trade deficits of the countries of SSA. Finally, economic shocks, crises, and emergencies which may hamper domestic production and productivity can compel nations to import more than they export. Running a trade balance deficit is not a problem only for the countries of SSA or developing countries for that matter. Developed nations also incur trade deficits in different periods and for a variety of reasons. In the 1980s, the United Kingdom had a chronic trade deficit. Similarly, Germany, Spain, and the UK had a current account deficit of 1 percent of their respective GDPs, while the figure for the USA was double that ratio (UNCTAD: 1996). Similarly, at the regional level, Latin American countries incurred persistent trade deficits in 1991–1994 due mainly to trade liberalization, and such trade deficits have also continued to increase due to their substantial increase in imports of capital goods and intermediate raw materials (UNCTAD: 1996).

However, the impact on and duration of trade deficits in developed and developing countries is not the same. It can have dire socioeconomic consequences on the latter group of countries, especially when it is structural, cyclical, or worsening over time. Contrary to this view, Gould et al. (1996) and Lawrence (2018) argue that trade deficit is not a good measure of how well a given country or economy is doing, and that a deficit can also enhance societal welfare, especially in the short run, by stabilizing consumer prices. A joint paper by the IMF, the World Bank, and the WTO (2010), further argues that inward-looking policies (like import substitution strategies), or other policies that curb imports with the aim of reducing trade deficits, are not preferred paths to accelerated growth and development. The paper argues that open markets offer more opportunity and higher standards of living than closed economies, and that East Asian economies which have created more opportunities and substantially higher levels of standards of living for their respective citizens, are those that have open trade and investment regimes. The World Bank in its earlier assessment (World Bank: 1993) emphasized that export expansion (over imports) has been beneficial for both developed and developing countries as it helps "to generate capacity utilization, increase scale economies, bring about technological progress, relax current account deficits and increase total factor productivity" (World Bank: 1993). These earlier assessments of the World Bank are in apparent contradiction with its subsequent views as far as trade deficits are concerned.

The profound and prolonged (or worsening) trade deficits seen in SSA are indeed bad for these economies. Such a situation can weaken domestic industries, entrench abject poverty, enhance capital flight, decrease employment opportunities, and more importantly exacerbate the countries' indebtedness and socioeconomic vulnerabilities while undermining the overall attractiveness of their economies. In short, profound, prolonged, and persistently increasing trade balance deficits entrench the structural problems of the economies of SSA. The persistently worsening terms of trade and trade deficits of SSA are indications that domestic policy reforms and improved market access offers granted to it by development partners, have failed to improve the export capabilities of these countries. In the absence of robust productive and supply capacities, preferential market access alone cannot help SSA's economies to take advantage of trade opportunities. The irony of market access is that it does not mean market entry. The latter involves meeting a series of market demands and consumer preferences, including complex sets of sanitary and phytosanitary as well as other technical standards – private and public alike. Cumbersome market entry requirements nullify preferential market access granted to SSA's economies by their traditional and emerging trade and development partners. A Kenyan agri-processing firm located in the Export Processing Zone near Nairobi managed to export to the EU markets after successfully meeting a series of safety and quality standards as well as social and environmental requirements of the markets. However, the firm is still unable to supply directly to high-end markets such as hotels and supermarkets which offer premium prices. This is because that such lucrative markets require meeting private standards that are much higher and cumbersome to meet by smaller producers than public standards. Although most countries of SSA enjoy preferential market access to the EU, market entry remains one of the most pervasive obstacles due to increasingly complex non-tariff barriers (NTBs) to trade, facing exporters of the region.

Moreover, domestic trade liberalization policies pursued by SSA (often prescribed from outside) have also contributed to expanding and deepening the region's trade deficits by substantially increasing imports over exports. The Asian experience discussed in Chapter 7 reveals that markets (market-driven reforms) alone have played little or no role in the countries' productive transformation and continued improvement in the living standards of their population. Instead, the functioning of market forces has been guided by capable states (with both market and state institutions functioning in harmony) facilitating economic growth and development. In these economies, the role of the state has been beyond correcting market failures but included strategic state-led interventions. These include (but are not limited to) putting in place effective import controls, providing targeted subsidies for domestic firms and industries and rationalizing foreign currency allocations. Asian Developmental States such as Vietnam have also pursued aggressive state-led interventions in technology policies, restricting foreign investment and company ownerships, enhancing state-led investments in R&D and related capabilities, and building vibrant and a competitive domestic enterprises sector – all of which are key to fostering productive transformation as foundational for generating and sustaining inclusive economic growth and development. Selective but targeted state-led interventions in the economy have been behind East Asia's socioeconomic transformation, whereas in SSA the role of the state has been further weakened by externally imposed market-led reforms and policy prescriptions.

In sum, despite wide-ranging policy reforms and favourable market access conditions, the structure, composition, and form of trade characterizing SSA are not conducive to foster productive capacities and structural economic transformation. Systemic and persistent negative trade balances, heavy dependence on commodity exports, and a commodity-driven growth model pursued by countries of SSA are symptomatic of weak productive capacities and lack of structural economic transformation. This phenomenon, in turn, entrenches the vicious circle of commodity dependency, underdevelopment, and generalized poverty in the countries concerned. Therefore, the key binding constraints on SSA's economic growth and development that undermine the region's capacities to exploit its comparative advantage in natural capital are weak productive capacities and lack of structural economic transformation. This means that comparative advantages alone are not enough to help SSA to expand trade, generate investment capital, and relieve key binding constraints. This calls for new-generation policies and strategies centred on fostering productive capacities and structural economic transformation as "business-as-usual approaches" are no longer viable for transformational growth of SSA. The suggested content and approaches of new-generation policies – domestic and international – are discussed in the last chapter (Chapter 9), drawing on the development experiences of Vietnam.

5.2 SSA's Partnerships and Investment Flows

From the foregoing discussions, the nature and form of trade policies that SSA countries have been pursing have led them to liquidity problems. This undermined the capacity of countries to finance productive capacities and structural transformation. In the absence of domestic resources to finance much needed productive capacities and structural transformation, the critical importance of external sources of financing cannot be overemphasized. There is consensus, therefore, that fostering productive capacities and structural transformation cannot be realized in a vacuum. Such a daunting task not only needs a huge influx of finance and capital including FDI, but also the right mix of capital and technology flows, with balanced allocation between the social and productive (economic) sectors.

UNCTAD (2016a) argues that adequate investment financing of priority sectors is essential for fostering structural transformation, achieving rapid productivity growth, creating decent jobs, and generating higher income. In such processes, domestic and foreign investments play a critically important role. FDI accounts for 39 percent of development finance in developing countries (UNCTAD: 2018). Likewise, the Asian Development Bank (ADB: 2017) stresses the critical role of the growth of investment in fixed capital formation, economic growth, industrial expansion, and improvements (or increases) in sectoral productivity as well as profitability of firms in China (ADB: 2017). Furthermore, an increase in investment rates is responsible for an increase in the size of the industrial sector, share of the industrial value-added and that of the manufacturing sector in newly industrializing economies of Asia such as South Korea, Malaysia, and Thailand (Garcia-Santana et al.:2016).

In recognition of the important role of investment (domestic and foreign), the countries of SSA have opted for open investment regimes. They made consistent efforts to remove distortions, biases, and impediments to investments; to enhance the role of the domestic private sector; and diversify sources of development finance and build overall competitiveness. They created institutions and "one-stop" investment facilitation centres to reduce red tape and bureaucracy (administrative processes) to investors. The countries of SSA have also signed several bilateral, subregional and regional investment agreements and treaties to attract and benefit from FDI – whether market-seeking (horizontal), resource-seeking (vertical), or efficiency-seeking foreign capital. Despite these domestic efforts and international support mechanisms, the performance of SSA in attracting and benefiting from foreign capital is disappointing (Michalowski: 2012). Although FDI flows have increased over the last couple of decades (relative to the countries' GDP), they spread unevenly across the countries of SSA and between sectors, showing a high degree of concentration in a few countries and extractive sectors. Extractive sectors are capital-intensive, have less propensity to create jobs and distribute wealth. They are known for their structural rigidity, with weak backward and forward sectoral linkages particularly in weaker economies such as those in SSA, higher leakages, and limited spill-over effects (Michalowski: 2012). Chen et al. (2015) argue that SSA has lagged behind in industrialization, which has mainly related to the challenges facing the countries in attracting sufficient manufacturing FDI. Although there are not internationally comparable and consistent data on determinants of FDI in SSA and its sectoral distribution, the authors provided indicative data that between 2011 and 2014, only 28 percent of the EU's, 12 percent the USA's, 19 percent India's, and 5 percent of China's investments went into the manufacturing sector in SSA. Further quantitative analysis of the determinants of FDI flows in ten[7] selected countries in SSA by Jaiblai and Shenai (2019) provided interesting perspectives on key determinants of FDI in SSA. According to them, FDI flows (though their findings are inconclusive due to data limitations) generally appear to have been attracted to countries with better quality infrastructure, smaller markets, lower income levels, and with higher openness as well as of significant depreciation in exchange rates (Jaiblai and Shenai: 2019). Conventional understanding and empirical evidence, on the other hand, suggest that market size, cost of factors of production (such as labour and land), taxation policies, effectiveness of rule of law and political risk, abundance of natural resources, income levels, etc. are key determinants of FDI flows.

Available data on SSA's FDI stock shows that the EU27 + United Kingdom remains, by far, the largest contributor to the region with an average FDI stock of USD 160 billion in 2015, although this has gone down to USD 120 billion in subsequent years (Figure 5.7). Until 2014, the USA followed the EU as the second source of FDI stock in SSA, with about USD 29 billion in that year. However, the USA has ceded its second place to China since 2015 onwards. In 2016–2018, the average Chinese FDI stock in SSA was about USD 38.7 billion. However, the distinction between Chinese development finance and FDI flows

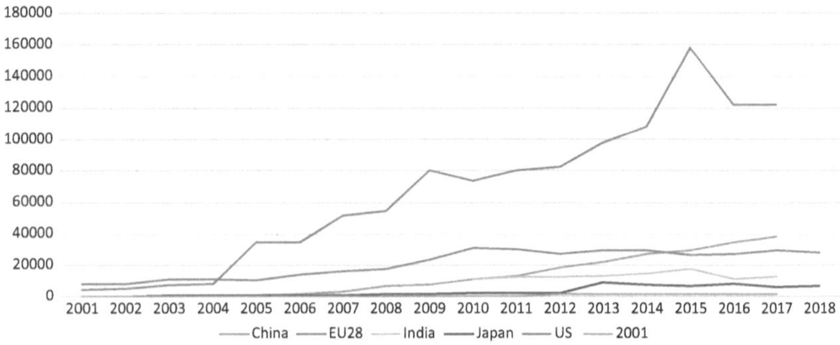

Figure 5.7 FDI stock of SSA by traditional and non-traditional partners in USD millions (2001–2018).

Source: UNCTADstat (2019).

is blurred as China provides blended finance to developing countries including SSA. This includes supporting Chinese State-Owned Enterprises (SOEs) as part of the development grants, concessional loans, and credits to finance SSA's needs, particularly in physical infrastructure such as the transport and power sectors. As from 2006 onwards, India followed in the footsteps of China, surpassing Japan, to become the fourth most important contributor of FDI stock in SSA. In 2017–2018, India's FDI stock in SSA reached about USD 13 billion. Japanese FDI stock has nevertheless improved between 2012 and 2018, growing from USD 2.4 billion to USD 6.9 billion, which is nearly half of the FDI stock of India in 2018. The increase in the Japanese share in recent years is partly due to an increasing sectoral focus of its FDI (to agriculture and regional infrastructure) and partly due to a joint India-Japan partnership for Asia-Africa Growth Corridors, which was discussed earlier in this chapter.

Besides FDI stocks, closer examination of annual FDI inflows to SSA provides interesting insights. Although, the EU27 (+UK) remains the largest investor in SSA during 2001–2018, China has emerged as the top investor in SSA, particularly between 2016 and 2018 (Figure 5.8). Annual inflows to SSA from Japan and the USA have also continued to decline, though moderately (when compared with the fall in flows from the EU) between 2012 and 2018, making India the second largest contributor of FDI flows to SSA. The decline in EU's FDI flows is consistent with a general disengagement in direct investment capital circulating between the EU and the rest of the world (Eurostat: 2019). A recent World Bank policy research paper also reported that the EU's capital flows to SSA suffered a steep decline due to its member states' sovereign debt crises of 2011–2013 and the 2014 plunge in international oil prices (Calderon et al.: 2019). Subdued commodity prices can also be regarded as further reasons for the steep decline in EU and US FDI inflows to SSA. Moreover, the FDI flows from the USA to SSA are also heavily concentrated only in three countries: Mauritius, Nigeria, and South Africa.

Despite the global slowdown in FDI flows (UNCTAD: 2018), FDI to SSA has continued to increase, with China and India becoming the largest contributors.

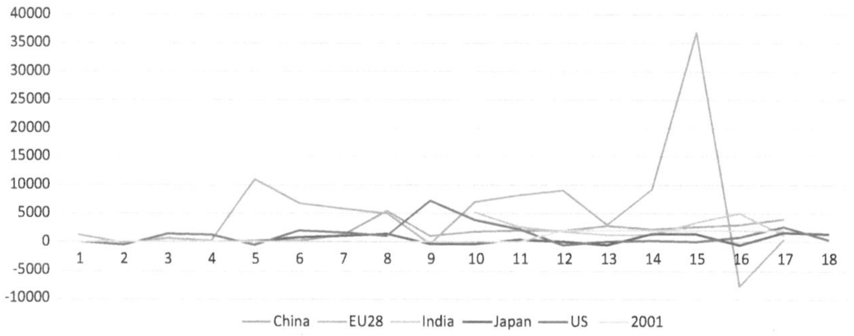

Figure 5.8 FDI inflows to SSA by traditional and non-traditional partners in USD millions (2001–2018).

Source: UNCTADstat (author's calculation).

In 2017, Chinese FDI flows to SSA reached USD 4 billion. Interestingly, flows from India surpassed those of China in 2016 when it slightly exceeded USD 5 billion, before declining to USD 2.6 billion in 2017. India increased its engagements with countries in SSA by establishing ICT centres, technology centres, a centre for geoinformatics applications for rural development, entrepreneurship centres, and vocational training centres, etc. However, China remains the top FDI home country for SSA in annual flows. Chinese investments (SOEs and private firms) in SSA have come in various forms, sizes, and industries, including infrastructure development, establishing and managing Special Economic Zones[8] (SEZs) and/or Industrial Parks. Moreover, although only very few countries in SSA are to benefit directly from the Chinese Belt and Road Initiative[9] (BRI), China is poised to allocate USD 1 trillion to build transport and trade logistics installations such as ports, highways, and railways, connecting regions across the world (Yueh: 2019). China also supports Chinese companies' cooperation and engagement with the African side, including SOEs. China particularly encourages its financial institutions such as Exim Bank and the China Development Bank (CDB) to provide export credit and export credit insurance for key projects in SSA such as railways, telecommunications, and power projects undertaken by Chinese companies, with the premise that risks are under control. This is expected to continue in the years ahead. The Beijing Action Plan (2019–2021) adopted by the summit of the Forum on China-Africa Cooperation (FOCAC) in 2018 indicates that China will encourage Chinese (private sector) companies to invest at least USD 10 billion in Africa in the next three years. The government of China supports Chinese companies to forge alliances of corporate social responsibilities and Africa's efforts to harmonize policies, laws, and regulations pertaining to private sector investment in national and regional projects. During the summit, Chinese President Xi Jinping declared that China would allocate further funding (to the tune of USD 60 billion) to African countries for various investment and development activities as part of its development finance efforts (consisting of grants, concessional loans, and credits).

Early 2000s, Chinese development finance and (public and private) investments were in resource-rich countries of SSA and heavily concentrated in the extractive sectors. Chinese development finance (including grants and loans) to Nigeria doubled from USD 3 billion in 2003 to USD 6 billion in 2005 with gas and oil accounting for 75 percent (Oyeranti et al.: 2010). However, this has changed since 2006 as China financed infrastructure and power development in Nigeria heavily, with USD 5 billion in that year – accounting for almost 70 percent of China's total public and private investment in SSA (Oyeranti et al.: 2010). In Ethiopia and Kenya, China finances infrastructure development mainly in roads and railways as well as in the manufacturing sector (see Chapter 6). In Uganda, China finances (grants, loans, and FDI) the development of the power (electricity sector), road (expressway), agriculture, and forestry sectors (Golub et al.: 2011). In Mauritius, in recent years, China has been funding the expansion of the airport terminal at the Mauritius International Airport and the development of a "Smart-City" (SEZ) project (Xinhua: 2018). In Zambia, although Chinese investments are primarily resource-seeking, there has been an increase in Chinese involvement in road and railway construction and other projects such as the construction of the national Malaria Control Centre and the Central Statistical Office. In fact, Zambia-China trade, investment, and economic relationships mirror the dominant global engagement of China (*Zambia Daily Mail*, 7 January 2019).

As shown in Figure 5.9, Chinese FDI inflows and development finance to SSA have been evenly distributed between the countries of SSA that have natural resource wealth and "others". Chinese investments have substantially increased in infrastructure development, manufacturing, and services. This includes countries that are known to be non-oil or non-mineral producers and exporters, such as Ethiopia.

There has been a substantial increase both in FDI stocks, flows as well as development finance (loans, grants, and credits) to SSA, and the various sectors,

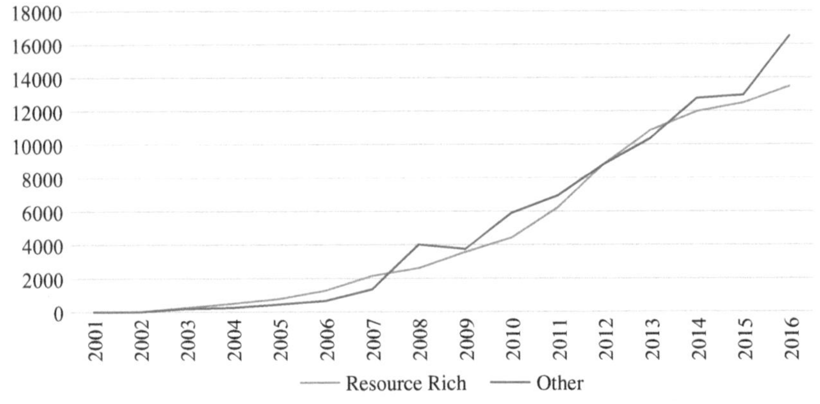

Figure 5.9 Chinese FDI stock and development finance in natural resource-rich and other countries of SSA in USD millions (2001–2018).

Source: UNCTAD FDI Statistics (2019).

including manufacturing, infrastructure, and energy (power) sector, albeit to various degrees. However, despite increased Chinese financial flows to SSA, the productive capacities of the region remain the lowest or weakest among the developing regions. The low level of productive capacities (see Chapter 3) is the main cause and consequence for the absence of structural economic transformation in SSA, lack of inclusive growth, poor job creation, and overall underdevelopment. The reasons for such a vicious circle include (but are not limited to): (i) a huge investment gap in infrastructure financing and resources needed to foster productive capacities and structural economic transformation. Even with an unprecedented increase of the Chinese outward investment and finance flows to SSA, when compared to other developing regions, the share of SSA in global flows is miniscule. This is consistent with the findings and conclusions of Wolf and Cheng (2018) who argued that the vast majority of Chinese outward FDI flows go to Asian countries, fast-growing markets in Europe and South America. (ii) There are very limited institutional and human resource capacities in Africa to direct FDI flows to productive sectors outside of the extractive sectors, improve the quality and enhance the impact of FDI as well as monitor effective execution of projects. For instance, although there is growing Chinese engagement in Nigeria's infrastructure and manufacturing sector, the economy of Nigeria is still dominated by exports of oil and gas, indicating little or no impact from increased Chinese investment on the country's export diversification. There is continued and problematic dependence of Nigeria on the export of fuel, where fuel exports accounted for more than 90 percent of the country's exports between 1995 and 2017 (Adunbi and Stein: 2019). (iii) There is a mismatch between policy ambitions and commitments to transform the economies, as well as huge gaps between policy formulation and implementation (or outcome); (iv) weak ownership capacities of countries of SSA in project formulation (design), implementation and follow-up as well as lack of clearly defined strategy to engage with China so as to effectively benefit from Chinese investment; and (v) focus on short-term apparent satisfaction or complacency by countries of SSA with Chinese investment in helping to manage poverty by creating employment opportunities for unskilled labour and low-value-added exports rather than transforming economies through skill formation, enhancing production linkages, and fostering technological capabilities. While managing poverty is not bad in itself in the short run, overemphasis on poverty reduction has the tendency to lock countries in a suboptimal economic status quo rather than transforming their economies for sustained and inclusive growth and development. Therefore, the countries of SSA should focus more on long-term economy-wide gains than short-term benefits in attracting and targeting FDI, including from China.

5.3 SSA's Partnerships and Development Finance Flows

There are stark conceptual and political variations between the Chinese ODA flows to SSA and those from developed countries (member countries of the Organisation for Economic Cooperation and Development's (OECD's) Development Assistance Committee – DAC). Conceptually, China still considers itself a developing country and thus its financial assistance to developing countries including SSA is enshrined in principles guiding "South-South Cooperation", centred on "strategic partnerships". Politically, China adopted eight principles,[10] governing the provision of its development assistance to developing countries, including SSA (Chin and Frolic: 2007). This variation in approaches and definitions of development assistance led to political controversies between DAC members and non-DAC members (consisting of China, Brazil, India, Russia, and South Africa) during global discussions related to principles governing development finance. This includes the application of principles of aid-effectiveness and transparency in development aid[11] aimed at improving the quality, effectiveness, transparency, and impact of development aid. There has been a series of discussions on the need for a coordinated exchange of statistical information and data on development aid, assessments of its impacts and outcomes, and building effective states in beneficiary countries.

However, non-DAC members (often led by China) have maintained that their development finance is qualitatively different from Western development aid and should not be governed by traditional aid principles (Fuchs, Strange, et al.: 2017). Instead, non-traditional donors, including China, opted for voluntary standards, which allow non-DAC members to voluntarily report on their aid allocations or disbursements, including to the OECD Credit Reporting System. There is also a concern regarding Chinese loans to SSA, which generally bear higher interest rates and have shorter repayment schedules than concessional loans from developed countries. In recent years, despite several initiatives by bilateral and multilateral creditors to ease the external indebtedness of heavily indebted poor countries (HIPCs, predominantly in SSA), several countries of the region have relapsed into the vicious circle of poverty, underdevelopment, and external debt distress. Zambia has become the "first African country to default on its debts since the COVID-19 pandemic, leading to fears that a debt tsunami could engulf the continent's most heavily indebted nations as the financial impact of coronavirus hits" (*The Guardian*, 25 November 2020). However, Zambia will not be the last as several countries in SSA are grappling to contain the spread and contagion of COVID-19 amidst mounting external indebtedness, including from borrowing from China and the private sector.

Another important distinction between Chinese and OECD-DAC development finance is the composition and definition of what is termed "development aid". Although China applies some of the OECD principles in the allocation of its development finance or loans to SSA (see Chapter 4), there are clear distinctions as to the composition of development finance allocations. As argued by several authors including (Brautigam: 2010, 2011, Grimm et al.: 2011), the Chinese development finance package includes a blend of investment and aid (concessional and non-concessional financing) including other flows such as preferential export buyer's credit, natural resource-backed loans, and lines of credit. However, China excludes financial aid related to the military and scholarships – both of which belong to the category of Other Official Flows (OOFs). In some cases, part of Chinese allocations is considered as "Vague Official Finance" (VOF). This category of flows captures officially financed projects where there was not enough information about the project's terms and conditions of finance or intent, which is difficult to categorize as ODA or OOF.

From the perspective of development aid, Chinese development finance flows (as with flows from the OECD-DAC countries) focus on "development projects and/or programmes". With both China and OECD-DAC, funding for such projects or programmes is channelled from government institutions to government institutions in recipient countries. One stark similarity between Chinese development finance and ODA from DAC countries is that, in both cases, there are complex institutional arrangements[12] to plan, manage, coordinate, and monitor flows of development finance to developing countries, including SSA.

Variations in approaches, concepts, definitions, and politics as well as composition and guiding principles in ODA between the OECD and China may be justifiable. This is particularly due to variations in the motivation, rationale, and historical relations between donors and recipient countries as well as temporal differences between China's rise as a global economic powerhouse and traditional donors. However, a more challenging aspect of Chinese development finance is the absence of consistent and internationally comparable data and statistical information on the scale, country focus, and sectoral distribution. This glaring lacuna in data and statistical information forced analysts and researchers to heavily rely on media-driven databases (Fuchs, Strange et al.: 2017) and project-based statistical information (Guillon and Mathonnat: 2018).[13] This gap has not only made international comparison of Chinese development finance arduous, but it has also undermined the quality and reliability of policy research and analytical work. This, in turn contributed to poor capacities in the formulation and implementation of evidence-based policies in recipient countries, making it difficult to precisely map effective and mutually beneficial (future) relationships between recipient countries and the People's Republic of China. Moreover, the lack of official and internationally comparable data and statistics on Chinese development finance drew suspicions, misconceptions, and misinterpretations, particularly in Western countries and mainstream media, regarding the motivation or reasons behind the ever-expanding Chinese engagement in Africa. Despite these limitations, the pledges of Chinese aid to Africa have increased more than 12-fold between 2006 and 2018 – from USD 5 billion in 2006 to USD 60 billion in 2018.[14] Consequently, the combined Chinese development finance flows (including credits and loans) to SSA have substantially increased over the years, reaching more than USD 135 billion in 2017 (see Chapter 4, Table 4.2). This amount is consistent or comparable with the amount of Chinese development finance reported in "Aiddata's Media-Based Data Collection on Chinese Official Finance" as discussed by Fuchs, Strange et al. (2017), and Guillon and Mathonnat (2018).

However, there are significant variations in the terms of data between various sources with respect to the magnitude and country focus of Chinese development finance (export credit, natural resources backed or commercial, and concessional loans). Some sources indicate that between 2000 and 2015, the top SSA recipients of Chinese development finance were Côte d'Ivoire (with USD 4 billion), Ethiopia (USD 3.7 billion), Zimbabwe (USD 3.6 billion), Cameroon (USD 3.4 billion), Nigeria (USD 3.1 billion), Tanzania (USD 3.0 billion), and Ghana (USD 2.5 billion). There are variations in the amount of annual country-specific distribution of Chinese development finance in SSA. For instance, as discussed in Chapter 4 (Table 4.2), in 2006, the total Chinese financial disbursement to SSA was about USD 6 billion. While Chinese development finance to SSA continues to rise, ODA flows from key development partners (EU, USA, and Japan) have tended to decline or remain stagnant in recent years. The flows from the EU28 (27 plus U.K.) have substantially declined from a peak of USD 18 billion in 2009 to USD 13.3 billion in 2017. The commitments from the USA have shown a modest increase from USD 9.3 billion to USD 11.6 billion during the same period, although actual disbursements are lower than the pledges.

Likewise, Japan's commitments have slightly improved from USD 1.6 billion to USD 1.8 billion during the same period (Figure 5.9). Irrespective of definitional, conceptual, and composition differences or variations in development resources configuration, none of the developed countries (individually) were able to match development finance flows from China during the period under consideration. In fact, aid commitments from DAC countries in 2017 (in 2016 constant prices) stood at about 0.31 percent of their combined Gross National Income (GNI), which is lower by far than the internationally agreed aid target of 0.7 percent (OECD-DAC Statistics: 2018). The top nine recipients in SSA of ODA from DAC countries (Ethiopia, Nigeria, Tanzania, Kenya, DRC, South Sudan, Uganda, Mozambique, and Somalia) accounted for about 51 percent of ODA flows to the region in 2017.

Most of the countries that have been top recipients of the Chinese development finance are also those in the list of countries attracting the highest DAC ODA flows. However, closer examination of sectoral aid distribution (allocation) shows a big gap between the Chinese (Chapter 4, Figure 4.6) flows and those from the DAC members, notably the EU, USA, and Japan, as shown in Figure 5.10. The sectoral distribution of Chinese development finance (in all its forms) concentrates in economic sectors such as transport, power (energy), and mining which receive, respectively 30.6 percent, 24.1 percent, and 15.4 percent. The communications and other sectors each receive, respectively 6 percent and 23.9 percent of total flows (Figure 4.6). However, closer examination of ODA flows from the EU, USA, and Japan to SSA shows that the share of the economic sectors in beneficiary countries in their combined aid allocations remain lower than that of the social sectors during 2008–2017 (Figure 5.11). That is, more aid from DAC members targets social sectors (education, health, and public services) whereas flows from China focus on economic sectors.

An increasing share of ODA allocation to the social sectors by traditional donors of SSA only shows the increasing needs of the sectors. It is also an indication of the continued dependence of the countries of SSA on external resources

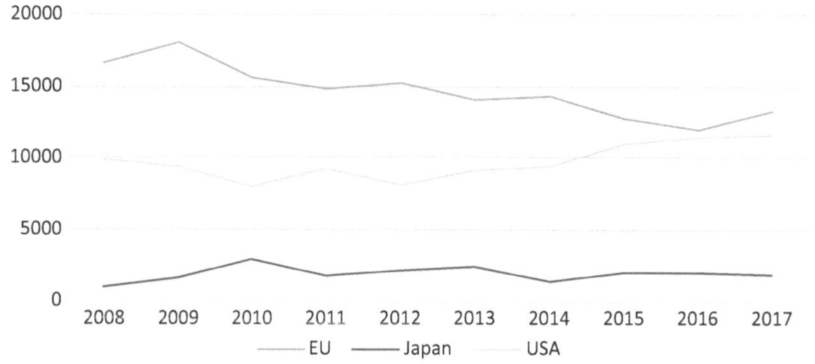

Figure 5.10 Bilateral ODA commitments of EU, Japan, and USA to SSA in USD millions (2000–2017).

Source: OECD-DAC Statistics (2018) (author's computation).

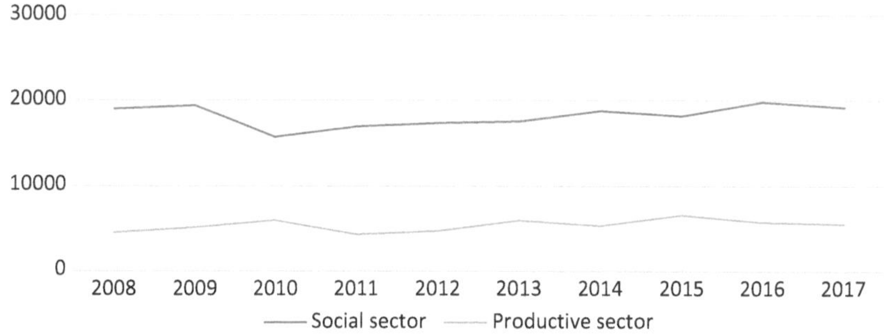

Figure 5.11 Distribution of ODA between social and economic sectors in USD millions (2008–2017).

Source: OECD-DAC Statistics (2018) (author's computation).

flows even to finance the provision of basic social services to their citizens. The current COVID-19 pandemic may accentuate the imbalance in the allocation of development resources between the social and economic sectors. However, such an increasing focus on the social sectors (if it occurs) at the expense of economic sectors will have a detrimental impact on fostering productive capacities and structural economic transformation in SSA. The increased share of ODA allocations to the social sectors (principally education and health) is not bad because such supports are critically important in building human capital component of the productive capacities. The problem is when such an allocation is made at the expense of core productive sectors and when the productive sectors fail to generate inclusive growth, employment and sustainable development. Weak or unbalanced allocation of development aid penalizes growth sustainability and undermines employment creation, capital accumulation, and the overall improvement of the wellbeing of the population – which will have important adverse repercussions on sustainability of growth and development.

Closer examination of the US and EU ODA flows and sectoral[15] allocations show the pattern of overall DAC ODA flows to, and sectoral distribution in, SSA. While social sectors consistently receive a higher share than the production sectors,[16] in the case of the USA, the share of the social sector indicates consistent expansion, while that of the production sector has been on a persistent decline throughout the period reviewed (Figure 5.12(a)).

As with the share of productive sectors, the share of US ODA for transport and communications infrastructure (Figure 5.13(a)) as well as to industry and mining (Figure 5.13(b)) has been consistently declining, whereas the contribution of Japan to both areas has improved during the 2008–2019 period. The EU's share, though volatile, remains higher than the allocations of the USA and Japan to both sectors. The declining share of allocations of the USA to transport and communications infrastructure is dramatic and alarmingly substantial (from nearly USD 800 million in 2008 to about USD 55 million in 2017). Coincidentally, the fall in the USA's allocation to the transport and communications sector has been

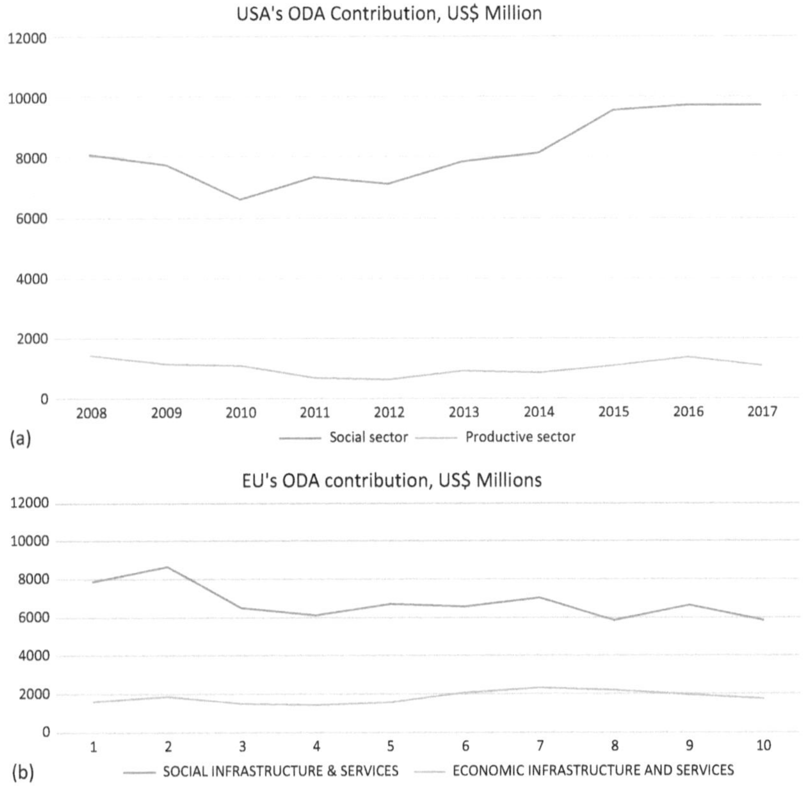

Figure 5.12 Distribution of ODA between social and productive sectors of SSA in USD millions (2008–2017): EU and USA.

Source: OECD-DAC Statistics (2018) (author's computation).

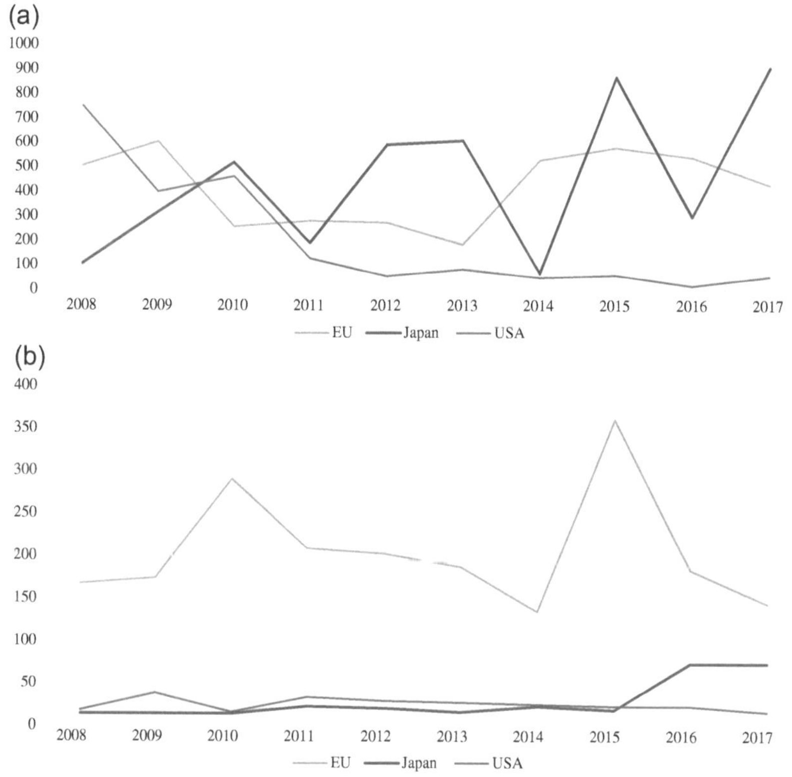

Figure 5.13 ODA to transport and communications. industry, mining and construction (2008–2017): EU, Japan, and USA.

Source: OECD-DAC Statistics (2018) (author's computation).

compensated by the huge push from the Japanese allocations to the sector, which skyrocketed from USD 105 million in 2008 to USD 905 million in 2017 (Figure 5.13(a)). These sectors or areas of aid allocation are key to the process of fostering productive capacities and structural economic transformation in SSA, and more encouragingly, these are the sectors where substantial development finance from China has been destined or concentrated (Chapter 4, Figure 4.6).

5.4 Conclusion and Lessons

The key lessons from Chapter 5 are that (i) the increased trade of SSA with traditional partners and China has exacerbated persistent deficits in SSA trade balances, and weak trade integration into domestic development policies. Instead of helping the countries to diversify their exports (including value addition) or transform economies, the relations have indeed entrenched SSA's commodity dependence; (ii) despite favourable market access granted by developed countries, market entry remains the most costly and pervasive demand-side constraint to exports of SSA; (iii) the primary commodity-driven "growth model" pursed by SSA has failed to improve the socioeconomic landscape of the countries and undermined the capacity of trade to foster productive capacities and structural economic transformation; (iv) as with international trade, flows of FDI from traditional partners, China and India have little or no impact on the gross fixed capital formation of SSA and the building of productive capacities to promote structural economic transformation; (v) ODA flows from the OECD-DAC favour social sectors over the productive sectors despite the fact that the latter is key to the inclusivity and sustainability of economic growth, with multiplier effects on the social sectors particularly in the long run. Increased ODA flows and sectoral allocation, especially from the traditional donors, show the heavy dependence of countries of SSA on ODA to deliver basic social services to their citizens. Such a trend perpetuates more dependence on external assistance, especially when the increased allocations to the social sectors penalize the productive sectors which are fundamental in enhancing productive capacities and structural transformation in SSA, and finally (vi) China's development finance, more than traditional ODA allocations, went to transport infrastructure, communications, and energy (power). However, this has not significantly improved transport and energy components of the productive capacities index of SSA as a group or as individual countries (see Chapter 3, Figures 3.5 and 3.6 on the transport and energy components, respectively).

The sum of Chinese investment or development finance alone cannot bridge the huge gap in infrastructure financing in SSA. This also shows that the benefits from increased investment in physical infrastructure alone could be short-lived. This is particularly the case if equal attention is not paid to the production sectors of the economy (notably industrial or manufacturing and agriculture) as well as export diversification in the allocation of public investment. In fact, allocation of external finance to the production sectors of SSA, including industry and agriculture, from all the sources was not significant during the years closely examined. This is particularly due to the policies pursued by many countries in SSA, including through Structural Adjustment Programmes (SAPs) and Poverty Reduction Strategy Papers (PRSPs). These externally imposed policies have significantly diminished the role of the state in industrial development (Stiglitz: 2001, Brautigam: 2019). Consequently, the diminishing role of public investment in the industrial or manufacturing sectors has also led to premature deindustrialization in SSA, as reflected by the lack of improvement in the manufacturing value-added (MVA), structural change component of the productive capacities index as shown in Chapter 3 (Figure 3.7) and Chapter 4.

The challenges discussed or limitations analyzed in the contexts of SSA's trade, investment, and ODA flows are diverse and complex. However, there is an interesting and even encouraging trend that seems to have been emerging in the region's trade and economic ties with China and the triad of traditional donors (EU, USA, and Japan). That is, increasing relations between SSA and China is a blessing for SSA as combined OECD ODA flows have tended to decline in recent years. Moreover, the analysis reveals an emerging trend of "specialization" in the delivery of development finance to SSA. That is, China and India need to continue to focus on economic sectors (notably manufacturing, energy or power, and transport infrastructure); Japan on agriculture and communications technologies (see Figure 5.12(a)); the EU and USA on social sectors. This trend of specialization is beneficial to SSA and the development partners alike in sharpening the areas of focus within their respective political or conceptual development narratives and relations with beneficiary countries. This also shows complementarity (not competition), particularly between China and the larger traditional development community in support of countries of SSA. While China and other non-DAC countries continue in improving their allocation to the economic sectors, the EU and USA focus on social sectors.

Both non-DAC and DAC countries should view their respective roles as complementary – as opposed to the current widespread view of competing agencies for strategic, economic, and political dominance in SSA. However, the overall development orientation of the countries of SSA should be the gradual and strategic withdrawal from the current heavy dependence on external sources of development finance. An increasing dependence of SSA on external finance for development will continue to undermine the predictability and sustainability of policy interventions making socioeconomic progress unstable and vulnerable to various negative shocks. In sum, the economies of SSA should focus their efforts in fostering productive capacities and structural economic transformation, with a view to generating and sustaining inclusive growth and production transformation as well as breaking away from aid dependency. As shown in Chapter 1 (Figure 1.1), the most aid-dependent countries of SSA are the least performers in terms of economic growth. Likewise, the development experiences of East Asia and Vietnam discussed in Chapters 7 and 8 clearly indicate that sustainable growth is driven by endogenous growth factors, although favourable exogenous factors can play a complementary role in facilitating economic growth and production transformation. This means that the countries of SSA should implement home-grown (indigenous) policies that seek country-specific solutions to the development challenges facing each of the countries of the region, including by tapping into global trade and investment opportunities.

Notes

1 The ACP-EU partnership agreements were negotiated every five years, leading to four Lomé Conventions (Lomé I–Lomé VI), covering the period 1975–2000 and almost all the countries of SSA, Caribbean, and Pacific states, most of which have colonial ties with Europe. The Lomé convention was replaced by the Cotonou Agreement in 2000, which itself paved the way for the ongoing negotiations on the Economic Partnership Agreement (EPA).

2 Countries that are not eligible for AGOA benefits are: Central African Republic, DRC, Equatorial Guinea, Eritrea, Eswatini, The Gambia, Somalia, South Sudan, Sudan, and Zimbabwe.

3 For an increasingly important share in SSA's imports and exports in recent years, India, which is not part of the research question, is included in the comparison of trade flows and directions. The inclusion of India is only for the purpose of compar-

ing trade flows and direction as well as examining the evolving dynamic economic relations between SSA and the two major economic powerhouses of the developing region.

4 As argued by Rodrik: 2016, "pre-mature deindustrialization", which has become the characteristic feature of low-income countries, refers to a phenomenon whereby developing countries run out of opportunities for industrialization sooner and at much lower level of income compared to the early industrializers.

5 Notable market access initiatives include the EU's Everything But Arms (EBA) initiative for the least developed countries (33 of the current 46 are in Africa); the Africa Growth and Opportunity Act (AGOA) of the USA (benefiting 39 of the 48 countries of SSA); and several bilateral market access offers.

6 In international trade, the current account is part of the balance of payments that records a given countries or territory's transactions with the rest of the world, specifically its net trade in goods and services, its net earnings on cross-border investments, and its net transfer payments over a defined period, usually a year.

7 Countries covered by the study are Cameroon, Côte d'Ivoire, Liberia, Mali, Mauritania, Niger, Nigeria, Sierra Leone, and Senegal.

8 Starting from 2007 several countries in SSA (Ethiopia, Mauritius, Namibia, Nigeria, and Zambia) have successfully established special economic zones and/or industrial parks, although the SEZ in Namibia was abandoned in 2015.

9 The Road and Belt Initiative (RBI) or One Belt, One Road (OBOR) is the initiative of the Government of China to build infrastructure, encompassing 65 countries from Southeast Asia to Central Asia to Africa. From Africa, 40 out of the 54 countries have signed to RBI with operationalization already begun in Djibouti, Ethiopia, and Kenya.

10 These include: (i) ensuring quality and mutual benefits, (ii) respecting sovereignty with no aid conditionality, (iii) providing interest-free loans or low interest loans, (iv) helping recipients to become independent, (v) building projects that require little investment and time to execute, (vi) providing quality equipment and materials at market prices, (vii) ensuring effective technical assistance, and (viii) paying Chinese experts according to local standards in beneficiary countries (for more details on the principles, see Chin and Frolic: 2007).

11 These are contained in the Paris Declaration (2005), Accra Agenda for Action (2008), and the outcome document of High-Level Forums on aid effectiveness held in Busan (2011) and Nairobi (2016).

12 In the case of China, the Premier provides overall political or strategic guidance on aid priorities. The Ministry of Commerce (MOFCOM), through its Department of Foreign Aid (DFA), oversees grants and interest-free loans. The Chinese Exim Bank and the China Development Bank deal with concessional and non-concessional loan as well as export credits. The Ministry of Finance is responsible for debt relief and contributions to multilateral institutions. The Ministry of Foreign Affairs (MOFA) reviews project proposals coordinates with MOFCOM and organizes the FOCAC summit.

13 AidData's Media-Based Data Collection (MBDC) is a research lab, Global Research Institute, based at the College of William and Mary, in Williamsburg, Virginia. It consists of Chinese Official Finance to Africa and information on thousands of Chinese-financed projects in 50 African countries (available at https://www.aiddata.org/publications/aiddatas-media-based-data-collection-methodology, http://china.aiddata.org, and http://china.aiddata.org/datasets/1.0).

14 The pledges were made at various FOCAC summits and conferences, which have been held since 2006 as: USD 5 billion in 2006, USD 10 billion in 2009, USD 20 billion in 2012, and USD 60 billion at the 2018 FOCAC Summit.

15 The main headings of the OECD's DAC ODA distribution by sector consists of aggregates of individual projects by sector in eight broad sections: social infrastructure, economic infrastructure, production sectors, multisector, programme assistance,

humanitarian aid, and unspecified. However, it does not refer to the types of goods or services provided. DAC classifies emergency and disaster relief in cash or in kind, including emergency response, relief food aid, short-term reconstruction relief and rehabilitation, disaster prevention and preparedness as humanitarian aid. This category excludes aid to refugees in donor countries. Direct food aid for countries that have persistent food insecurity falls under programme assistance and not in the category of humanitarian aid.

16 Production sectors in the DAC aid allocation includes vast economic sectors such as agriculture, fishing and forestry, crop and livestock development; provision of production requisites such as farm machinery and fertilizer, irrigation, pest control, veterinary services; services to the agricultural sector, fishing and forestry (including tree crops); conservation and extension, land reclamation; land and soil surveys, land and water use; agricultural construction; storage and transport facilities. Allocations to agricultural development banks are also included under this heading together with industry, mining and construction, trade and tourism including export promotion, trade, commerce, and distribution; banking (including industrial development banks); and hotel and other tourist facilities.

Biographical references

ADB. (2017). *Country Operations Business Plan: Vietnam 2018–2020*. Internal Document, Asia Development Bank. Available at: https://www.adb.org/sites/default/files/institutional-document/379881/cobp-vie-2018-2020.pdf.

Adunbi, O., and Stein, H. (2019). The Political Economy of Chinese Investment in Nigeria: Prometheus or Leviathan? In *China-Africa and an Economic Transformation*. Edited by A. Oqubay, and J. Y. Lin. Chapter 10. Oxford University Press, Oxford, 192–215.

Alam, M. B., and Gupta, A. K. (2011). Destination Africa: China, India, and Japan. *Indian Foreign Affairs Journal*, 6(2), 187–200.

Brautigam, D. (2010). China, Africa, and the International Aid Architecture. Africa Development Bank Group. Working Paper No. 107, April 2010.

Brautigam, D. (2011). Aid with Chinese Characteristics: Chinese Aid and Development Finance Meet the OECD-DAC Regime. *Journal of International Development*, 23(5), 752–764.

Brautigam, D. (2019). Chinese Loans and African Structural Transformation. In *China-Africa and an Economic Transformation*. Edited by A. Oqubay, and J. Y. Lin. Chapter 13. Oxford University Press, Oxford, U.K., 265–281.

Calderon, C., Chuan-Pole, P., and Kubota, M. (2019). Drivers of Gross Capital Inflows: Which Factors Are more Important for Sub Saharan Africa? Policy Research Working Paper 8777. World Bank Group, African Region, Office of the Chief Economist.

Chen, G., Geiger, M., and Fu, M. (2015). *Manufacturing FDI in Sub Saharan Africa: Trends, Determinants, and Impact*. World Bank, Washington, DC.

Chin, T. G., and Frolic, B. M. (2007). *Emerging Donors in International Development Assistance. Partnership & Business Development Division (PBDD)*. International Development Research Center (IDRC), Ottawa.

Chow, C. K. D., Sheldon, I., and McGuire, W. (2018). How the United States Withdrawal from the Trans-Pacific Partnership (TPP) Benefits China. Public Law and Legal Theory Working Paper Series No. 451, The Ohio State University. August 7, 2018.

Cornelissen, S. (2012). Japan's Role in Africa: Principles, Pragmatism and Partnership. *African-East Asian Affairs*, 70, 4–12

Eurostat. (2019). European Union Statistics. Available at: https://ec.europa.eu/eurostat/371.

Fuchs, A., Strange, A. M. *et al.* (2017). Chinas' Development Finance to Africa: A Media-Based Approach to Data Collection. Available at: https://www.researchgate.net/publication/2560616663.

Garcia-Santana, M., Pijoan-Mas, J., and Villacorta, L. (2016). Investment Demand and Structural Change. CEPR Discussion Paper No. DP11636, November 2016. Available at: https//ssrn.com.

Golub, S., Bernhardt, A., and Liu, M. (2011). Development and Trade Strategies for LDCs 2001–2010 and Looking Ahead. Unpublished background paper for UNCTAD in the run up to the Forth United Nations Conference on LDCs.

Gould, D. M., Ruffin, R. J., and Anderson, M. D. (1996). Trade Deficits: Causes and Consequences. Federal Reserve Bank of Dallas. *Journal of Economic Review*, Fourth Quarter.

Grimm, S., Rank, R., Schickerling, E., and McDonald, M. (2011). *Transparency of Chinese Aid: An analysis of the Published Information on Chinese External Financial Flows*. Center for Chinese Studies, Stellenbosch University, London. Available at: http://www.ccs.org.za/wp-content/uploads/2011/09/Transparency-of-Chinese-Aidfinal-for-print.pdf. Accessed on 2 February 2020.

Guillon, M., and Mathonnat, J. (2018). What Can We Learn from Chinese aid Allocation Motivations from New Available Data? A Sectoral Analysis of Chinese Aid to African Countries. HAL Open Access Archive. Available at: https://hal.archives-ouvertes.fr/hal-01777484.

Hamoni, S. (2008). Trade Balance and the Terms of Trade in G-7 countries: Panel Cointegration Approach. *Journal of Applied Econometrics and International Development*, 8–2, 13–22.

International Monetary Fund, the World Bank, and the World Trade Organization. (2010). Making Trade an Engine of Growth for All: The Case for Trade and for Policies to Facilitate Adjustment. Available at: https://www.wto.org/english/news_e/news17_e/wto_imf_report_07042017.pdf.

Jaiblai, P., and Shenai, V. (2019). The Determinants of FDI in Sub Saharan Africa: A Study of Data from 1990–2017. *International Journal of Financial Studies*, 7(43), 1–31.

Kassim, L. (2016). The Revenue Implications of Trade Liberalization in Sub Saharan Africa: Some New Evidence. School of Economics, University of Kent Discussion Papers, KDPE1605.

Kharoubi, E. (2011). The Trade Balance and Real Exchange Rates. Bank of International Settlement (BIS). *BIS Quarterly Review*, 33–42.

Lawrence, Z. R. (2018). *Why the Focus on Trade Deficit is Misleading: Policy Brief*. Peterson Institute for Economics, Washington, DC.

Michalowski, T. (2012). Foreign Direct Investment in Sub Saharan Africa and its Effects on Economic Growth of the Region: Challenges of the Global Economy. Working Papers. Institute of International Business, University of Gdansk, 2012, No. 31.

Nordic Africa Institute-NAI. (2018). Africa's Mineral Economies: Breaking their Dependence on Mining. Policy Note No. 6, Nordic Africa Institute (NAI), October 2018.

Obi, C. (2019). The Changing Dynamics of Chinese Oil and Gas Engagements in Africa. In *China-Africa and An Economic Transformation*. Edited by A. Oqubay and J. Yifu Lin, Chapter 9. Oxford University Press, Oxford, 173–191.

Okoro, A. S. (2013). Deficit Financing in Nigeria. *International Journal of Accounting Research*, 1(2), 49–54.

Organization for Economic Co-operation and Development Assistance Committee (DAC) Statistics. (2018). Available at: https://www.oecd.org/dac/financing-sustainable-development/development-finance-standards/official-development-assistance.htm#:~:text=ODA%20data%20and%20trends%202021&text=ODA%20provided%20by%20members%20of,in%20real%20terms%20from%202020.

Oskawe, P., and Verick, S. (2007). Current Account Deficits in Sub Saharan Africa: Do they Matter? Proceedings of the African Economic Conference, 2007.

Owusu, Y. F. (2007). Post-9/11 U.S. Foreign Aid, the Millennium Challenge Account, and Africa: How Many Birds Can One Stone Kill? *Africa Today*, 54(1 Fall), 3–26. https://www.jstor.org/stable/27666872.

Oyeranti, A. O., Babatunde, M. A., Ogunkola, E. O., and Bankole, S. A. (2010). *The Impact of China-Africa Investment Relations: A Case Study of Nigeria*. The African Economic Research Consortium (AERC), Nairobi, Kenya, 28 February 2010. AERC Collaborative Research on China-Africa.

Panda, J. (2017). The Asia-Africa Growth Corridor: An India-Japan Arch in the Making? *Focus Asia Perspective & Analysis*, No. 21, August 2017.

Schmieg, E. (2019). EU and Africa: Investment, Trade, Development: What a Post-Cotonou Agreement with the ACP States Can Achieve, a commentary, German Institute for International and Security Affairs, No.1, January 2019.

Shafaeddin, S. M. (2005). Trade Liberalization and Economic Reform in Developing Countries: Structural Change or De-industrialization? Discussion Paper No. 179, UNCTAD.

Stiglitz, J. (2001). *Globalization and its Discontent*. Penguin Books, London.

The Guardian. (2020). Zambia's Default Fuels Fears of African 'Debt Tsunami' as Covid19 Impact Bites, 25 November 2020. https://www.theguardian.com/global-development/2020/nov/25/zambias-default-fuels-fears-of-african-debt-tsunami-as-covid-impact-bites.

UNCTAD. (1996). *Trade and Development Report*. United Nations Publication, New York and Geneva.

UNCTAD. (2016a). *Trade and Development Report*. United Nations Publication, New York and Geneva.

UNCTAD. (2017c). *Key Statistics in International Trade, United Nations Conference on Trade and Development (UNCTAD)*.United Nations, Geneva.

UNCTAD. (2018). *World Investment Report: New Industrial Policies*. United Nations Publication, New York and Geneva.

UNCTADStat. (2019). Available at: https://unctadstat.unctad.org/EN/.

UNECA. (2011a). Minerals and Africa's Development: The International Study Group Report on Africa's Mineral Regimes, November 2011.

USIT. (2018). U.S. Trade and Investment Relations with Sub Saharan Africa: Recent Developments. United States International Trade Commission April 2018.

UNCTAD. (2019b). *Economic Development in Africa 2019 Report: Made in Africa-Rules of Origin for Enhanced Intra-African Trade*. United Nations, New York and Geneva.

Wolf, C., and Cheng, S.-K. (2018). Chinese FDI in Angola and Ethiopia: Between Flying Geese and Resource Colonialism. Industrial Development, Construction and Employment in Africa (IDCEA) Working Paper 02, SOAS, University of London.

World Bank. (1993). *The East Asian Miracle: Economic Growth and Public Policy*. Oxford University Press., New York.

WTO. (2018). *World Trade Statistical Review 2018*. World Trade Organization, Geneva, Switzerland.

Xinhua News Agency. (2018). New Smart City Offers Glimpse into Booming Mauritius-China Cooperation, 28 July 2018.

Yueh, L. (2019). China's Economic Emergence and the Implications for Africa. In *China-Africa and an Economic Transformation*. Edited by A. Oqubay, and J. Y. Lin. Chapter 2. Oxford University Press, Oxford, 19–34.

Zambia Daily Mail. (2019). Chinese Investment Helps Improve Zambia, 17 January 2019.

6 China in Angola and Ethiopia

The case studies discussed in this chapter allow comparative analysis of the challenges facing Angola and Ethiopia in developing their productive capacities, despite their increased ties with China and against their own comparative advantages. The two countries are chosen because of their historical and socioeconomic similarities and differences. Their similarities lie in earlier domestic political governance and ideological relationships with the "Eastern Bloc", including China, and a history of protracted (ideological) armed conflicts,[1] with devastating socioeconomic outcomes. Over the last 20 years, both countries have also shown, with varying degrees, changes in the relative sectoral composition of their respective GDP figures. These changes, as discussed in later sections of this chapter, show the "wrong type" of structural transformation, which is not associated with industrialization, manufacturing, export diversification, creation of decent jobs, and building technological capabilities.

Angola and Ethiopia also possess their own specific or unique geopolitical, historical,[2] socioeconomic, and demographic characteristics. Today, Angola is an oil-exporting economy whereas Ethiopia is emerging as a service-driven economy, with agriculture still playing an important role as a source of Gross Domestic Product (GDP), employment, and trade. Moreover, the central government's dependence on external resource flows is much lower in Angola compared to that of Ethiopia (Figure 6.4). Another area of difference between the two countries is in population dynamics and urbanization. The percentage of rural population of Angola is estimated at about 34 percent, with agriculture employing 49 percent of the country's total active population in 2018. In Ethiopia, the rate of urbanization is slower and still more than 80 percent of the country's population resides in rural areas, with agriculture contributing more than 40 percent to GDP in 2010, and more than 80 percent of exports. Recent estimates show that the share of agriculture in the GDP of Ethiopia has gone down to 31.2 percent in 2018, while the respective shares of industry and services grew to 27.3 and 36.5 percent during the same year (www.statista.com). In Angola, despite agriculture employing nearly half of the labour force, its share in GDP is only about 10 percent in 2017 (www.gfmag.com). The industrial and services sectors contributed, respectively, 42.2 and 46.8 percent in the same year. Over the last couple of decades, the share of the traditional sector (agriculture) in GDP and employment of Angola

DOI: 10.4324/9781003295334-6

has declined, driven by the discovery of oil and other extractive resources. This signals a shift from low-skill and labour-intensive agricultural activities to the capital-intensive mining sector (with low employment, value addition, and economic diversification). In the two countries, despite variations in sectors, there is an emerging trend of the wrong type of transformation. This is demonstrated by their low Productive Capacities Index (PCI) scores (including category-specific scores), high export commodity and market concentration, and low and declining Manufacturing Value-Added (MVA) share in GDP, rigidities inherent in the mining and agriculture sectors in terms of export diversification and employment.

6.1 Angola's Current Socioeconomic Conditions

Today, Angola is the second largest producer and exporter of oil (and natural gas) in SSA and the largest exporter of these products to China from the region. In 2019, oil accounted for 50 percent of its GDP,[3] 75 percent of government revenue,[4] and 93 percent of its merchandise exports.[5] Although Angola has transitioned from an agriculture-based to extractive resources-driven economy, the overall economic management and post-war governance[6] of the country manifest typical characteristics of a "paradox economy". This kind of economy mirrors the abundance of natural resources alongside generalized poverty, substantial cronyism, corruption, nepotism, and mismanagement (plundering) of public resources.[7]

Angola's political governance has long been characterized by dictatorship or authoritarian rule with anaemic corruption. This is typical of what some economists describe as "resource curse". Consequently, despite massive inflows of Foreign Direct Investment (FDI), increased development finance including from China and large export revenues, Angola's economy failed to foster productive capacities and structural economic transformation. The economy remains one of the most dependent on the export of primary commodities in SSA and, hence, persistently vulnerable to negative external shocks. This situation is expected to further worsen with the COVID-19 pandemic. Weak productive capacities are causes and consequences of socioeconomic vulnerability which in turn locks large chunk of the population in multidimensional poverty.

Closer examination of the Angola case reveals other internal challenges facing the country. These include systemic weakness in policy formulation implementation and coordination capacities. Angola also suffers from weak performance of the domestic private sector and a lack of linkages between domestic and foreign firms and between small and large firms. Angola's economy is one of the most fragmented with few or no forward and backward linkages between the key sectors (agriculture, mining, manufacturing, and services). Moreover, Angola is one of the most expensive countries in the developing world; a large percentage of consumer goods (including food) are imported.[8]

6.2 Ethiopia's Current Socioeconomic Conditions

Ethiopia is the second most populous country in Africa, after Nigeria, and it is one of the 33 least developed countries in the region. The country has been registering fast economic growth in the last couple of decades and is described as one of the fastest growing economies in the developing world in recent years. However, the impact of such an accelerated economic growth on job creation and poverty reduction has been negligible and the country's productive capacities and structural transformation remain one of the weakest in SSA. The lack of productive employment in the country, declining agricultural productivity, and MVA as well as the "servicification" of the economy, can stall efforts to foster productive capacities and structural economic transformation in the country. Over the years, in a typical Developmental State model under a regime of "Revolutionary Democracy",[9] and with a view to reversing the country's wrong type of structural economic transformation, Ethiopia has scaled up investment (Ali: 2019) in transport infrastructure, urban housing, and power or electricity generation. The large proportion of resources invested in transport infrastructure (particularly road and rail) comes from the government's own capital expenditure and external loans from China, the World Bank, and development partners. Despite the increased investment in road transport infrastructure, on all indicators, used to assess the transport component, Ethiopia's performance is not different from the average of SSA and lower by far than that of other developing countries. The Grand Ethiopia Renaissance Dam (GERD) which is being built on the Blue Nile through domestic resource mobilization and remittances, when completed, is expected to radically alter electricity generation capacity and consumption in the country.

6.3 Comparative Economic Growth of Angola and Ethiopia

Angola's growth performance after the transition to peace in 2002 had been consistently positive and much better than the pre-2002 period. However, during the 2008–2009 global financial and economic crises, economic growth collapsed as the country's economy contracted by more than 10 percent (Figure 6.1). Such a vulnerability to external economic shocks is the consequence of Angola's excessive dependence on the export of primary commodities (largely oil) whose

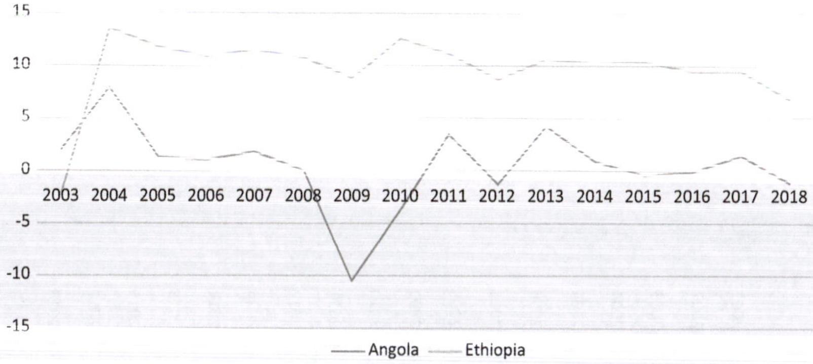

Figure 6.1 GDP growth rates of Angola and Ethiopia (2003–2018).

Source: World Bank Data (2020).

international prices are spectacularly volatile. Consequently, its average economic growth between 2002 and 2018 was 0.4 percent, which is almost identical to its pre-war growth performance. In contrast to that of Angola, the economic growth of Ethiopia in the post-1991 period has remained spectacular with an average annual growth rate of 8.9 percent between 2002 and 2018 (Figure 6.1). However, Ethiopia remains one of the poorest countries in SSA in terms of Gross National Income (GNI) per capita, which is about USD 600 in 2015 (Figure 6.2(a)). Despite much slower growth rates in SSA, Angola has managed to become a middle-income country with a GNI per capita of USD 4,520 in 2015 (latest available data).

Both Angola and Ethiopia will continue facing daunting challenges in building their respective productive capacities to transform their economies. Despite Ethiopia's higher economic growth, the country has much less potential than Angola to become an upper-middle-income country sooner. Angola can also build its productive capacities and transform its economy quicker than Ethiopia, provided that the country funnels its commodities rent to transformational development.

Between 2000 and 2012, the net Official Development Assistance (ODA) received as a percentage of the total expenditure of the Government of Ethiopia

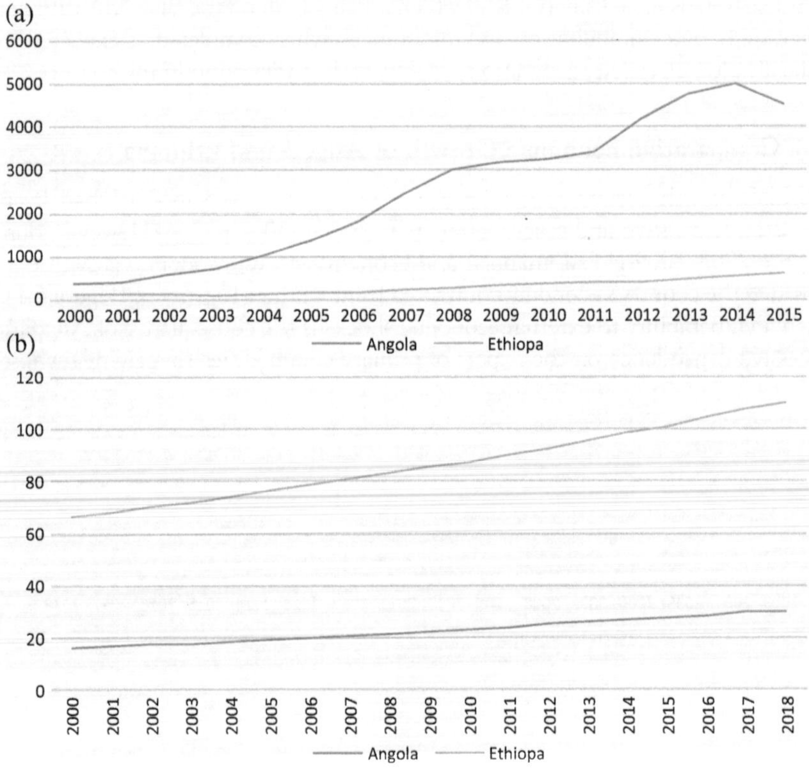

Figure 6.2 Angola and Ethiopia: (a) GNI per capita, Atlas method, and (b) population (millions).

Source: World Bank Development Indicators (2020).

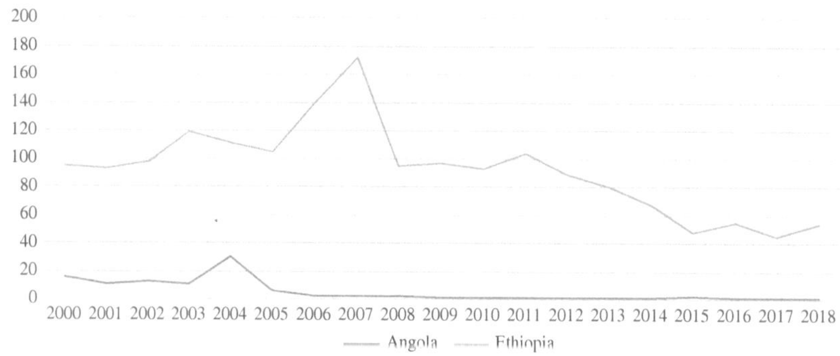

Figure 6.3 Angola and Ethiopia: net ODA[10] Received as percent of central government expenditures (2000–2018).

Source: World Development Bank Data (2019).

was substantial, reaching as high as 170 percent in 2007. This share has gone down significantly in subsequent years and the trend is consistent with an overall trend observed in many countries in SSA, such as Ghana and Mozambique (Castel-Branco: 2008). However, nearly 60 percent of the public expenditure of Ethiopia is still dependent on ODA flows (Figure 6.3). Such a high level of dependence on external sources of finance makes policy formulation and implementation greatly influenced by the predictability and sustainability of external financial resources. Such a problem undermines capacities to exercise ownership of development policies and to enhance aid effectiveness in addressing development challenges facing recipient countries.

Angola's dependence on external aid has been substantially reduced and is consistently lower than that of Ethiopia and most countries in SSA (Figure 6.3). This is precisely because post-war Angola emerged as an oil exporter and mining sector-led economy, which not only reduced its dependency on external finance but has also helped Angola to invest in Sovereign Wealth Funds,[11] particularly during extractive commodity super cycles or boom periods. The Angola Sovereign Wealth Fund, which boasted an amount of USD 5 billion in 2016, has the objective of addressing socioeconomic gaps and vulnerabilities of the poorest sections of the society (Chen: 2019).

6.4 Angola-China Partnership: What Impact?

Most African countries view China as a strategic partner in their development efforts, mainly due to their growing dissatisfaction and frustration with "patronizing attitudes" of traditional developed-country partners and their institutions (Oqubay and Lin: 2019). Western development partners push for good governance and respect for human rights in SSA as defined by their value systems. From the perspectives of African political elites, the Chinese stance of non-interference in the domestic affairs of African countries seems to have been among the key reasons driving Africa-China economic relations. This includes Chinese engagement with countries often characterized by the West as "rogue states" such as Libya, Sudan, and Zimbabwe.

China's direct engagement in Angola officially began in 1983 when China opened diplomatic ties with the country. This led to increased defence cooperation between the two in the 1990s. The end of the civil war in Angola in 2002 heralded a shift in China-Angola relations from an exclusive focus on defence or military cooperation in the 1990s to expanded trade, development finance, and investment relations with a particular focus on post-war reconstruction and development programmes. The current China-Angola partnership is influenced by natural resources and cheap labour (human resources), China's continued demand for raw materials to finance its rapid transformation, a search for markets, and particularly for its labour-intensive manufactures and low-tech firms. SSA, including Angola, has become home or a location for some of China's labour-intensive industries (Lin and Xu: 2019) and as a growing market for its low-skill, labour-intensive manufactures. Another factor driving Africa-China relations, including with Angola and Ethiopia, is China's interest to advance its foreign policy objectives, including winning the support of Africans for its "One China Policy".[12] A further reason is the West's reluctance to change its long-standing narrative about Africa's governance, human rights, and political enterprise. Consequently, in a relatively short period, China has emerged as the largest destination for Angola's exports of crude oil, absorbing nearly 50 percent of the country's total petroleum exports in 2016, which accounted for 12 percent of Chinese total imports of oil in that year (Begu, Vasilescu et al.: 2018). Angola has become the second largest supplier of oil to China after Saudi Arabia and the top exporter to China in SSA.

Regarding Chinese development finance[13] (Angola became the top recipient between 2002 and 2018, with a combined amount of USD 43 billion against USD 143 billion to SSA during the same period (see Chapter 4, Table 4.1). On FDI, China has also emerged as a top investor in Africa in a country-by-country comparison and the second largest investor after the EU28 (EU27 plus U.K.), surpassing traditional development partners such as the USA and Japan (see Chapter 5, Figure 5.7). Chinese total investment (stock) in SSA reached USD 38.7 billion in 2017 accounting for nearly 90 percent of total Chinese FDI stock in Africa (Table 6.1). The Chinese FDI stock in Angola has grown from about zero in 2003 to USD 2.3 billion in 2017, bringing total Chinese external financial flows (FDI plus loans) to the country to more than USD45 billion.

Chinese FDI flows and stocks are destined for countries with natural resources-driven and non-extractive resources-based economies alike (see also Chapter 5, Figure 5.8). However, in the case of Angola, the preponderant share of Chinese finance is concentrated in the extractive sectors and infrastructure, supporting the sectors. Such a concentration is not unique to Chinese investment stocks or flows as investments from traditional development partners of Angola (such as Portugal) are dominant in the extractive sectors (Wolf and Cheng: 2018). There is a lack of accurate and internationally comparable data and statistics on spill-over effects of Chinese FDI in Angola particularly in technology transfers,

Table 6.1 Chinese FDI Stock in SSA by Destination (USD Millions)

Region/Economy	*2003*	*2005*	*2010*	*2011*	*2012*	*2013*	*2014*	*2015*	*2016*	*2017*
Africa	491	1,595	13,042	16,244	21,730	26,186	32,350	34,694	39,877	43,296
North Africa	27	618	1,978	3,152	3,178	3,767	5,113	5,323	4,973	4,618
Algeria	6	171	937	1,059	1,305	1,497	2,452	2,532	2,552	1,834
Egypt	14	40	337	403	459	511	657	663	889	835
Libya	1	33	32	68	65	109	109	106	211	367
Morocco	4	21	56	89	95	103	114	156	163	318
Sudan	1	352	613	1,526	1,237	1,507	1,747	1,809	1,104	1,202
Tunisia	2	2	3	6	6	14	15	21	16	15
Other Africa	464	977	11,064	13,092	18,552	22,418	27,237	29,371	34,905	38,679
Angola	0	9	352	401	1,245	1,535	1,214	1,268	1,633	2,260
Benin	8	19	39	40	48	50	69	87	103	104
Botswana	2	18	179	200	220	231	262	321	438	297
Burkina Faso	–	–	–	–	–	4	9	–	0	0
Burundi	–	–	7	7	9	10	13	12	12	10
Cameroon	6	8	60	62	80	148	178	207	367	424
Cape Verde	–	1	5	5	12	15	15	15	15	15
Central African Rep.	–	2	47	51	51	60	57	46	36	16
Chad	–	3	80	108	194	321	405	423	397	412
Comoros	–	–	4	4	5	5	5	5	5	5
Congo	–	13	136	142	505	695	989	1,089	783	1,126
DRC	0	25	631	709	970	1,092	2,169	3,239	3,515	3,884
Côte d'Ivoire	8	29	33	35	40	35	64	127	180	304
Djibouti	–	0	12	18	18	31	40	60	125	233
Equatorial Guinea	9	17	86	99	405	261	208	232	237	396
Eritrea	2	0	13	14	104	105	107	119	378	217
Ethiopia	5	30	368	427	607	772	915	1,130	2,001	1,976
Gabon	24	35	125	127	128	168	180	244	257	385
Gambia	–	1	1	1	1	1	1	1	4	5

(*Continued*)

Table 6.1 Continued

Region/Economy	*2003*	*2005*	*2010*	*2011*	*2012*	*2013*	*2014*	*2015*	*2016*	*2017*
Ghana	7	7	202	270	505	835	1,057	1,274	1,958	1,575
Guinea	14	44	136	168	235	339	419	383	418	76
Guinea-Bissau	–	–	27	27	27	27	67	69	70	675
Kenya	26	58	222	309	403	636	854	1,099	1,103	1,543
Lesotho	0	1	9	9	9	9	11	11	7	7
Liberia	6	16	82	115	154	196	230	289	297	320
Madagascar	28	50	230	254	275	286	353	348	298	766
Malawi	1	1	32	30	49	254	258	258	259	291
Mali	12	13	48	160	211	317	343	307	320	395
Mauritania	2	2	46	75	106	108	101	106	193	236
Mauritius	13	27	283	606	701	850	580	1,097	1,176	961
Mozambique	2	15	75	98	337	508	654	725	782	873
Namibia	1	2	47	60	95	349	982	380	454	480
Niger	13	20	379	430	125	242	198	565	525	666
Nigeria	32	94	1,211	1,416	1,950	2,146	2,323	2,377	2,542	2,862
Rwanda	3	5	42	59	64	73	111	124	89	99
STP	–	–	0	0	0	0	0	0	0	0
Senegal	3	2	45	45	102	83	130	126	150	214
Seychelles	0	4	19	24	77	103	114	160	247	231
Sierra Leone	–	18	41	52	58	108	148	196	189	184
South Africa	45	112	4,153	4,060	4,775	4,400	5,954	4,723	6,501	7,473
South Sudan	–	–	–	0	11	26	19	36	37	48
Togo	5	5	58	67	98	123	136	129	119	113
Uganda	1	5	114	126	141	384	464	722	1,006	576
Tanzania	7	62	308	407	541	716	885	1,139	1,192	1,280
Zambia	144	160	944	1,200	1,998	2,164	2,272	2,338	2,687	2,963
Zimbabwe	37	42	135	576	875	1,521	1,696	1,799	1,839	1,748

Source: UNCTAD/MNE Database.

innovation, export diversification, and in fostering productive capacities and structural economic transformation. This could be due to four key factors: first, the low level of initial conditions in the country given the ravaging impacts of civil wars on infrastructure, institutions, and the overall economy, which undermine the impact of Chinese investment on Angola's economy. Second, the technology mismatch and language barriers as well as a low level of domestic capacity to absorb new technologies, which in turn undermines the formation of economy-wide linkages (Tang and Pigato: 2015).

Third, wrong domestic priorities and defective incentive structures of host governments that target large multinational firms at the expense of domestic Small and Medium-sized Enterprises (SMEs). And (fourth), a weak capacity to negotiate and enforce terms and conditions that facilitate transfers of technology from Chinese FDI firms and enterprises and foster business linkages between these and domestic enterprises. As with the rest of SSA, large multinational companies and firms are more favoured in Angola than domestic SMEs, as open investment regimes grant lucrative incentives and unfettered access to bigger firms which dominate production networks and value chains. This limits opportunities for fostering linkages between larger foreign and smaller domestic firms as well as the capacities of domestic firms to become internationally competitive and technologically innovative. Without vibrant and dynamic domestic firms, the capacity of Angola to build productive capacities and kick-start structural economic transformation will continue to be serious challenges.

More puzzling and at times problematic China-Angola relations relate to international trade between the two. Angola's total merchandise exports have soared (in value) from less than USD 10 billion in 2000 to USD 70 billion in 2012 before deteriorating to USD 27.7 billion in 2016 – the lowest level in recent decades (Figure 6.4(a)). In 2018, the value of total merchandise exports of Angola bounced back to about USD 40 billion. The percentage share of China in Angola's total exports has leaped nearly four-fold in the last two decades (Figure 6.4(b)) – from less than 11 percent in 2001 to nearly 46 percent in 2018. In value terms, this increase in the share of China has shown an impressive magnitude – from USD 4 billion in 2000 to USD 34 billion in 2012 before it reached the lowest level (USD 12 billion) in 2016. As with the total merchandise exports of the country, its imports from China have shown modest increase to about USD 18 billion in 2018 (Figure 6.5(a)).

Such a significant share of Angola's exports to China will have three important implications: first, as discussed in Chapter 5, Angola's increasing exports to China are the result of a change in the direction of its trade from traditional partners to China rather than creating new trade flows. Second, in the absence of export diversification, increasing the trade of Angola with China and other traditional partners can limit the country's scope to take advantage of intra-African trade (UNCTAD: 2013) as Angola trades more with China than Africa. Third, it leads to heavy market concentration with an increased risk of the continued vulnerability of Angola, emanating from its overdependence on a single market and single commodities for such a dominant share of its exports. This means that any external or internal

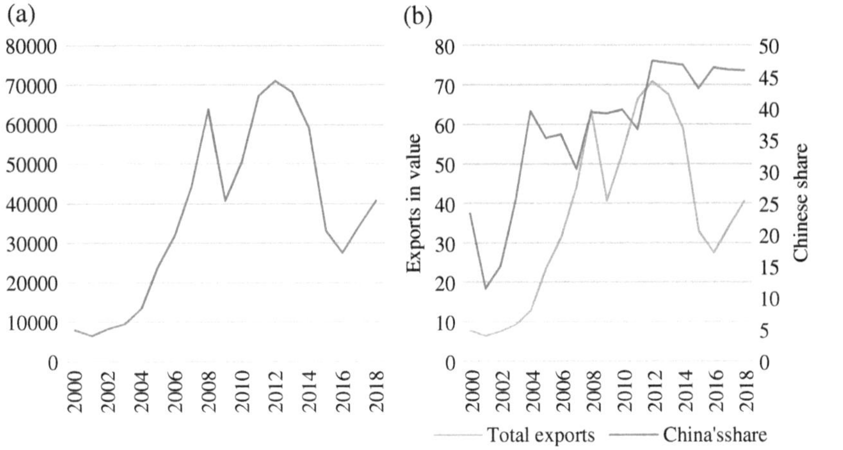

Figure 6.4 Angola's merchandise exports to the world and China's share (percent), 2000–2018.

Source: UNCTADstat (2019).

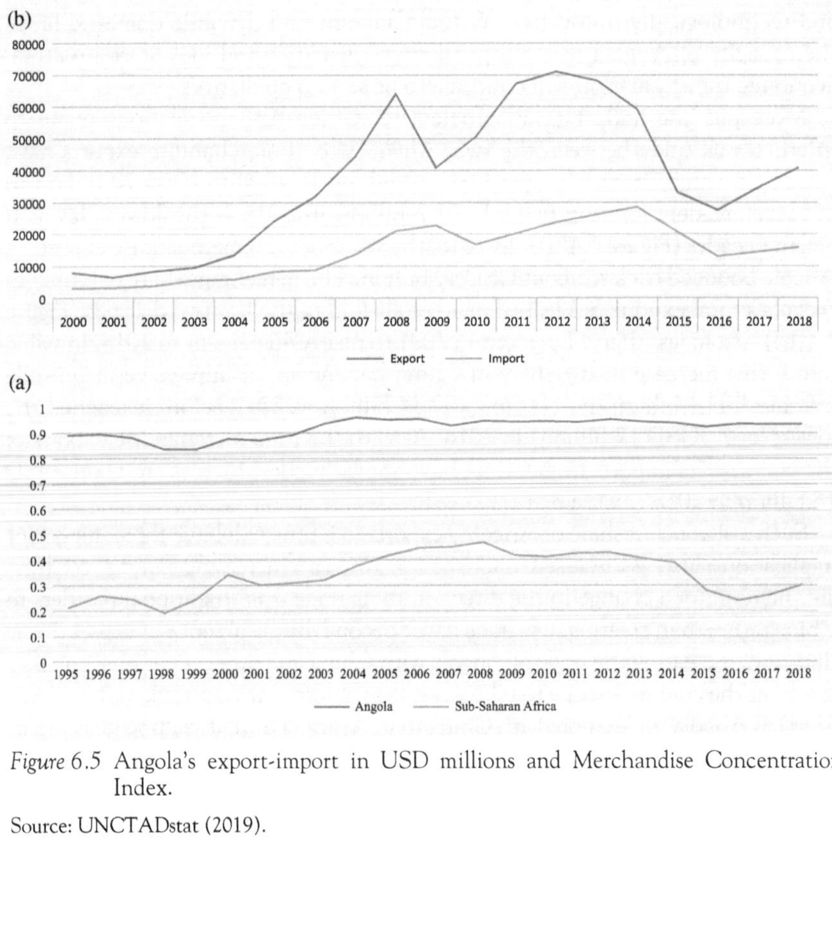

Figure 6.5 Angola's export-import in USD millions and Merchandise Concentration Index.

Source: UNCTADstat (2019).

negative shock – economic, political, or otherwise – that exposes China (such as the current COVID-19 pandemic) will have direct consequences on Angola's trade and development prospects, further amplifying the country's vulnerability to external shocks. Already, Chinese exports and imports have sharply contracted, global export- and import-oriented firms as well as travel and tourism are suffering from the destabilizing effects of COVID-19. COVID-19 has already made international oil prices plummet (see Chapter 1), with disastrous consequences for Angola's oil exports, which account for more than 90 percent of the country's export earnings. China-Angola trade relations are against the widely held view and empirical evidence regarding of the role of international trade in accelerating poverty reduction and development of nations.

In successful developing countries, deliberate strategies to enhance international trade (particularly exports) played a critical role in long-term growth (Dollar: 1992). Outward-oriented trade and investment policies played an important role in facilitating a virtuous circle of investment, innovation, and poverty reduction and maximizing dynamic gains – all of which are key in fostering export competitiveness (UNCTAD: 2008a). However, maximizing benefits from international trade requires carefully formulated and effectively implemented trade policies, and vibrant institutions capable of taking advantage of global trade and investment opportunities. Sound policies and vibrant institutions are instrumental in fostering productive capacities to relieve binding constraints to trade, and realigning interventions and incentive structures to the comparative advantages of Angola and SSA as a region.

Angola's increasing exports in value made the country one of the few in SSA with a positive trade balance. Thanks to its oil exports, Angola managed to sustain positive trade balance throughout the last two decades (Figure 6.5(a)). However, the country's dependence on a single market (China) (Figure 6.5(b)) and a single commodity (oil) has increased over the years instead of decreasing even in comparison with the average level of SSA as shown in product (export) concentration (Figure 6.5(b)). In contrast, SSA's export concentration index[14] has remained below 0.5, whereas that of Angola has increased from 0.84 in 1991 to 0.93 in 2018.

An important lesson from the above diagnostics is that the form of Angola's integration into the global economy and its trade pattern with China is typical of that of SSA – driven by high natural resources or the natural capital component of the productive capacities (Chapter 3). This phenomenon shows the potential that Angola and SSA as a region hold for fostering productive capacities and structural transformation, if properly harnessed. However, during the years under study, Angola's productive capacities are lower than SSA's average PCI (Figure 6.6.), which itself is lower by far than the rest of the developing regions (Chapter 3).

The evolution of Angola's productive capacities and economic transformation is identical to the trends observed in SSA. Angola's preponderant dependence on the extractive sectors for exports, investments, or government revenues makes the country more vulnerable to external economic shocks and related

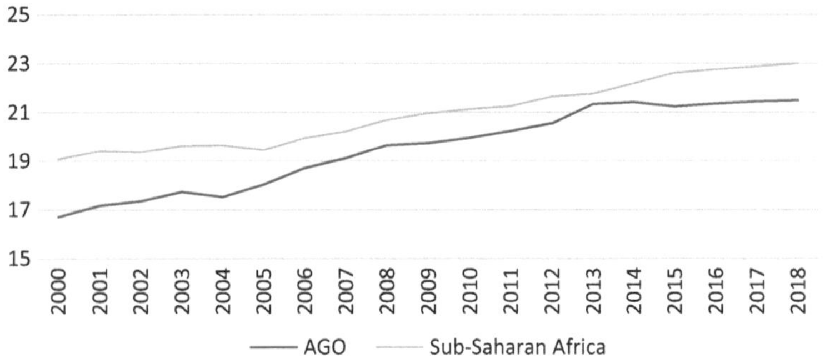

Figure 6.6 Productive capacities in Angola and SSA (2000–2018).

Source: UNCTAD Global Productive Capacities Index (PCI).

crises. Despite modest progress in fostering productive capacities in Angola and SSA during the last nearly two decades (Figure 6.6), the levels are still far below those of the developing regions (Chapter 3 Figure 3.11). In Angola, the country's natural endowments and increased GDP per capita combined with substantial FDI inflows, development finance, and expanding trade with China, have not led to significant improvements in the overall productive capacities of the country. Consequently, the country's overall productive capacities remain low. This does not mean that there has not been any progress in the country since the end of the war in 2002. Angola has reduced its dependence on external finance or development aid (Figure 6.3) and achieves higher GNI per capita, which increased from less than USD 1,000 in 2000s to nearly USD 5,000 in 2014–2015 (Figure 6.2(a)).

However, such improvements in the GNI per capita have not impacted the income poverty level in Angola. Instead, Angola has seen an increase in extreme (monetary or income) poverty from 44.5 percent in 1995 to 47 percent in 2018, although there is significant variation between various data sources. The World Bank data[15] (www.worldbank.org) show that extreme poverty (poverty head count ratio at USD 1.90 a day) in Angola has increased from 32.3 percent in 2000 to 47 percent. Moreover, the UNDP (2019) estimates that 36 percent of Angolans still live below the internationally defined poverty line. The Human Development Index (HDI)[16] value of the country stood at 0.574 in 2019 and it ranked 149th out of 189 countries. Similarly, on the measure of Multidimensional Poverty Index (MPI),[17] Angola is one of the countries in SSA with the highest proportion of people in multidimensional deprivation. Not only is Angola unable to reduce the proportion of people in extreme (income or monetary) poverty, but the MPI for the country also stood at about 58.5 percent in 2016 where the intensity of poverty (the average deprivation experienced by poor people) was 55.2 percent during the same year. The gap between natural capital and economic wellbeing in Angola is the result of its low productive capacities even when compared with the average for SSA. Angola's performance on PCI is weaker in all components measured, except natural capital component (Figure 6.14), which reflects the country's dominant extractive sector.

Several policy lessons can be drawn from the high level of intensity and generalized poverty observed in Angola. First, the high economic growth achieved by Angola during the commodities boom (2002–2006) has not translated into poverty reduction. Although high economic growth is critically important for poverty reduction, it is not a necessary and sufficient condition by itself. Adequate emphasis should be placed on the quality, form, sources, and durability of growth rather than the quantity of growth only. That is, for growth to have a robust impact on poverty, it must create quality employment opportunities with improved income levels, and it should be inclusive and sustainable. Second, Angola will continue to face complex development challenges if it continues its heavy reliance on the extractive sectors for its development indefinitely. This is because extractive sectors are capital-intensive by their nature and are not the best way to generate jobs and redistribute income. Third, extractive sector-driven growth may further entrench commodity dependence (Figure 6.6) and accentuate systemic vulnerabilities and rent-seeking behaviours in the country. Fourth, there is an overall lack of economy-wide improvement in Angola in terms of productivity, value-added by domestic producers (export diversification), and long-term structural transformation. However, there is no doubt that Angola is in a fortunate position to build its productive capacities and accelerate the process of structural transformation, provided that the country channels its natural resource wealth into productive transformation. Lastly (fifth), further problems, often observed in countries with natural resource wealth such as Angola, reside in the appreciation of the domestic currency in relation to foreign currencies with negative consequences, particularly on the manufacturing sector. Angola's manufacturing sector has been historically weak even in comparison with SSA (Figure 6.7) during 2000–2018.

The implication of the weak manufacturing sector is that the sectoral shift in the GDP composition discussed earlier masks systemic problems facing Angola. When combined with high commodity dependence, it signals the wrong type of transformation – a change from low-skill, low-productivity traditional agriculture to low-skill and low-productivity service sectors or to inefficient or uncompetitive industrial sectors as well as capital intensive mining sector. Although industrialization is not the only avenue for poverty reduction or employment and income generation, empirical and historical evidence suggests that without industrialization and a vibrant manufacturing sector Angola and other countries of SSA may not be able to address their persistent development challenges and a continued lag in productive capacities and structural economic transformation. In this context, the country has not fully reaped significant benefits from its partnership with China. Increased China-Angola trade, economic, and investments relations have further heightened the country's dependence on the export of primary commodities and market concentration, with China serving as the single most important buyer for Angola's natural resource-based exports.

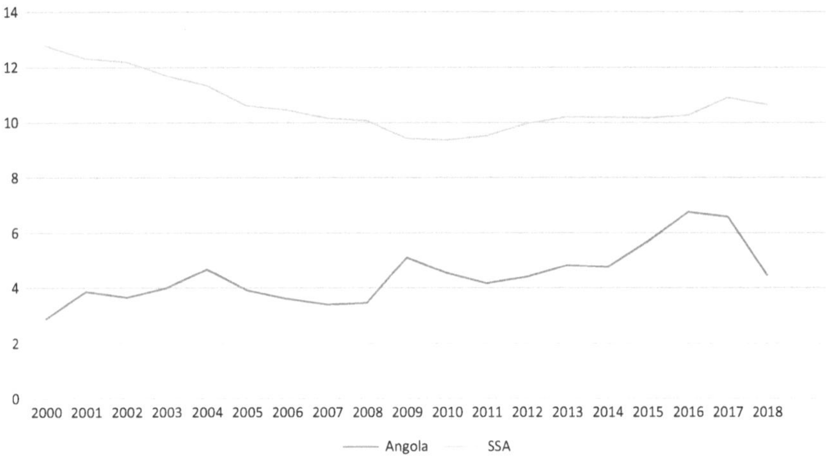

Figure 6.7 Manufacturing value-added as percentage of GDP: Angola and SSA (2000–2018).

Source: World Bank Data (2019).

Nevertheless, there is considerable room for Angola to take advantage of an increased partnership with China, including by formulating and implementing comprehensive, multisectoral, and coherent policies and strategies centred on strong institutional coordination, and fostering productive capacities. This calls for a shift away from the current fragmented or disjointed project-based interventions. The key for Angola is to invest rents from its natural resource wealth in removing structural constraints, improving human capital resources, building infrastructure, and rehabilitating its agriculture and manufacturing sectors. Angola can also learn from the successful experience of Vietnam in unlocking binding constraints on its economic development, facilitating the attainment of quality growth and harnessing its comparative advantages for fostering productive capacities and structural transformation. Gradualism, persistence, experimentalism, pragmatism, and state-driven policy formulation, sequencing and implementation are key characteristics of Vietnam's transformational development. Diversifying the sources of growth in parallel with catalyzing engines and drivers of growth played an important role in propelling Vietnam as one of the most vibrant and dynamic economies in the developing world in a short period of time (Chapters 7 and 8). Angola can also learn from the experience of China itself – the country that has successfully transformed its economy to become the world's second largest in about four decades of successful growth and transformation (Yueh: 2019). Vietnam's experience in harnessing natural resources such as oil, coal, and zinc for socioeconomic transformation (Chapter 7) and Chinese experience in building industries that are consistent with the country's comparative advantages (Monga: 2019) can provide useful lessons to the countries of SSA such as Angola.

6.5 China-Ethiopia Partnership: What Impact?

From a historical perspective, China-Ethiopia relations[18] are recent when compared with Ethiopia's relations, particularly with Western countries and Japan. China opened its embassy in Addis Ababa only in 1970, a few years before the overthrow of Emperor Haile Selassie's government by the Dergue[19] in 1974. The end of the Ethiopian political instabilities of the 1980s and 1990s, and the overthrow of the military regime in 1991, offered the Ethiopian economy yet another opportunity and hope to undergo multiple transitions[20] at the same time (Chole: 1992), and enhanced its relations with the West and China.

China-Ethiopia relations have gained a momentum over the last couple of decades and turned around the tides of negative characterization of China's role in Africa by the West. Against pessimistic views widespread in the West, the robust Chinese engagement in Ethiopia gave new perspectives and hopes. This was because Ethiopia does not have known or commercially viable natural (extractive) resources such as oil: it has a predominantly agrarian and backward economy. These facts partly nullify claims that China's engagement in Africa was primarily extractive (mineral) resource-driven and that Chinese interest in Africa is in search of markets for its labour-intensive manufactures. China-Ethiopia relations are indeed described as a "classic win-win situation" (Chakrabarty: 2016). Moreover, from the Ethiopian and Chinese political elites, China and Ethiopia have fostered "genuine partnerships based on mutual respect and non-interference in the domestic affairs of Ethiopia".

Chinese official finance has increasingly been directed towards building transport infrastructure, telecommunications, energy (electricity), and low-cost urban housing in Ethiopia. Moreover, Chinese FDI flows went to the manufacturing sector of Ethiopia. Ethiopia has also been benefiting from Chinese market access grants aimed at facilitating or boosting exports. Cheru and Oqubay (2019, pp. 285–286) went far in arguing that "Ethiopia is one of the few African countries that had taken a more strategic approach to engage China, while maintaining strong ties with its traditional partners". While their arguments sound plausible, they have not provided substantial comparative evidence as to how the Ethiopian approach towards China is qualitatively different from the rest of SSA. Nor have they provided statistically or empirically supported justifications as to whether China's expanded engagements in Ethiopia had brought about any substantive or qualitative changes in the productive capacities and structural economic transformation of Ethiopia.

On a case-by-case examination, during the last two decades or so, Angola is by far the largest recipient of Chinese finance in SSA (USD 43 billion), followed by Ethiopia (USD 13.8 billion). The share of the top ten recipients of Chinese finance including Angola and Ethiopia during 2000–2017 was over USD 100 billion (nearly 70 percent of the total). While most of the top recipients are mineral or fossil-fuel producing and exporting countries, Ethiopia is largely a producer and exporter of agricultural commodities, with a fledgling manufacturing sector. Ethiopia's share is channelled largely through Exim Bank of China (58.5 percent) and credit via suppliers or export credit (30.3 percent), which brings the share of interest-bearing loans to 88 percent of the total disbursements. Consequently, Ethiopia is among the countries of SSA that have seen growing external indebtedness to China over the years (see Chapter 4, Figure 4.7).

Chinese FDI stock (both by State-Owned Enterprises (SOEs) and private) in Ethiopia has continuously increased from about USD 5 million in 2003 to USD 363 million in 2010, which increased to a further USD 915 million in 2014 (Table 6.1). The largest Chinese FDI stock in Ethiopia was registered in 2016 when it reached USD 2.2 billion. It is important to indicate that data and statistics on Chinese FDI in Ethiopia is inconsistent,[21] often with larger variations between various sources (see also Wolf and Cheng: 2018). Despite variations in FDI statistics, China remains the leading investor in Ethiopia based on the number of projects recorded in the country, with the largest contribution to employment. Cheru and Oqubay (2019) reported that during 2000 – 2017, the total number of Chinese manufacturing enterprises that were operational in Ethiopia were 407 with many more in the initiation phase, followed by India (123) and EU (60). The total FDI stock recorded by the Ethiopian National Bank and the Ethiopian Investment Commission during 2000–2017 is in the magnitude of USD 5.65 billion, of which China accounts for USD 1.976 billion (about 35 percent).

At the domestic level, with the support of donors and international financial institutions, Ethiopia has been undertaking wide-ranging policy and institutional reforms since 1992[22] with the aim to maximize the positive impact of trade and investment on development by removing distortions and biases. The principal objectives of these policy measures were also intended to gradually reduce the role of the state in the economy, remove economy-wide distortions, reduce inefficiencies, and build export competitiveness as a prelude to a free-market economic system (Manyazewal and Shiferaw: 2019). However, these trade policy objectives of Ethiopia have not been met. The volume and value of the country's exports have remained negligible (USD 2.8 billion in 2018), even by the standards of SSA.

At sectoral level, policies, institutional arrangements, and incentive structures (such as access to export credit and exemptions from export taxes) aimed at boosting coffee exports – the country's historically dominant export item – have fallen short of the intended objectives. Although Ethiopia established the Ethiopian Commodities Exchange (ECX)[23] and provided incentives for coffee producers and exporters, these measures failed to enhance the country's coffee exports. Cramer and Sender (2019) argue that Ethiopia's coffee exports in 2014/15 were only 30 percent of what had been targeted for that year under the first cycle of the country's Growth and Transformation Plan (GTP-1), and the trends, thus far, are far short of the targets contained in GTP-2. This is because, in some cases, the reform programmes focused exclusively on the demand side of the equation with little or no attention given to supply side challenges. In some other cases, while the quality of policies has improved over the years, institutional, human, and financial capacities to implement them remain woefully inadequate, leading to disappointing outcomes.

Table 6.2 Chinese Development Finance (Loans, Grants, Credits) to African Governments 2000–2017, by Lender Institutions (USD Millions, Unadjusted)

Country	*Exim Bank*	*CDB*	*Supplier's Credits*	*Other*	*Total*	*SSA*
Algeria	0	0	0	9	9	N
Angola	8,272	26,589	22	8,262	43,145	Y
Benin	1,686	0	0	223	1,909	Y
Botswana	90	0	0	841	931	Y
Burkina Faso	0	0	0	0	0	Y
Burundi	36	0	0	50	86	Y
Cameroon	5,034	2	2	523	5,561	Y
Cape Verde	43	0	0	6	49	Y
Central African Rep.	0	0	60	43	103	Y
Chad	586	0	0	4	590	Y
Comoros	39	0	0	0	39	Y
Congo	4,812	0	238	20	5,070	Y
Côte d'Ivoire	2,710	0	0	73	2,783	Y
Djibouti	1,261	0	150	56	1,467	Y
DRC	3,325	0	0	20	3,345	Y
Egypt	767	2,600	0	54	3,421	N
Equat'l Guinea	1,198	0	478	23	1,699	Y
Eritrea	589	0	0	16	605	Y
Ethiopia	8,069	655	4,165	907	13,796	Y
Gabon	450	0	0	285	735	Y
The Gambia	0	0	0	0	0	Y
Ghana	1,585	1,000	599	315	3,499	Y
Guinea	273	0	335	38	646	Y
Guinea-Bissau	0	0	0	0	0	Y
Kenya	7,878	867	0	155	8,900	Y
Lesotho	27	2	0	8	37	Y
Liberia	50	0	0	0	50	Y
Libya	0	0	0	0	0	N
Madagascar	435	0	0	0	435	Y
Malawi	262	0	0	0	262	Y
Mali	909	0	0	80	989	Y
Mauritius	414	0	0	78	492	Y
Mauritania	381	0	0	50	431	Y
Morocco	1,022	0	0	8	1,030	N
Mozambique	2,018	179	0	93	2,290	Y
Namibia	270	0	223	45	538	Y
Niger	332	0	352	19	703	Y
Nigeria	4,903	0	390	0	5,293	Y
Rwanda	222	0	0	68	290	Y
S. Tome & Principe	0	0	0	0	0	Y
Senegal	1,998	0	0	21	2,019	Y
Seychelles	34	0	0	0	34	Y
Sierra Leone	48	0	176	0	224	Y
Somalia	0	0	0	0	0	Y
South Africa	0	3,131	0	688	3,819	Y
Sudan	5,027	0	598	870	6,495	Y

(*Continued*)

Table 6.2 Continued

Country	*Exim Bank*	*CDB*	*Supplier's Credits*	*Other*	*Total*	*SSA*
South Sudan	158	0	0	0	158	Y
Swaziland	0	0	0	0	0	Y
Tanzania	2,378	200	0	62	2,640	Y
Togo	773	0	0	80	853	Y
Tunisia	143	0	0	3	146	N
Uganda	3,110	0	0	71	3,181	Y
Zambia	3,760	1,002	673	3,199	8,634	Y
Zimbabwe	2,692	40	290	266	3,288	Y
TOTAL	**80,561**	**36,772**	**8,751**	**19,645**	**145,729**	

Source: Johns Hopkins SAIS China Africa Research Initiative (by Lucas Atkins, Deborah Brautigam, Yunnan Chen, and Jyhjong Hwang 2017, "Africa-China").

Overall, the performance of the trade sector of Ethiopia is disappointingly poor. Consequently, the contribution of trade to foster productive capacities and structural economic transformation remains weak. The total merchandise trade of Ethiopia (exports and imports) was about USD 18.3 billion in 2018 – about 22 percent of GDP, which is estimated by the World Bank at about USD 80.2 billion during the same year. While the country's share of trade in GDP is consistent with the average level for developing countries including SSA, what is worrying (more in the case of Ethiopia) is the preponderance of imports (in value terms). Imports have continued to outstrip the country's exports between 2000 and 2018, reaching USD 15.5 billion in 2018 against exports of USD 2.8 billion in the same year. Consequently, Ethiopia's trade deficit has continued to deepen, reaching USD 12.6 billion in 2018, which is about 15.7 percent of GDP, 81 percent total trade, and 450 percent of the country's exports. An increasing share of imports in the country's trade can be justifiable, given the development (investment) needs of the country such as imports of intermediate goods, machinery, and components.

However, the stagnant export sector and the continuously bulging gap between imports and exports is particularly troubling. Such a huge gap between imports and exports shows several challenges facing Ethiopia. First, earnings from the export of primary commodities are unable to pay for the country's imports of manufactured goods. Second, the deficit in trade balance has been financed through FDI, loans, drawing from international reserves, or ODA often at the expense of financing the country's productive capacities and structural transformation. Lastly, not only has the performance of Ethiopia's external sector remained poor, but it can also be the source of increased external indebtedness, deteriorating terms of trade, increasing capital flight, job losses, and persistent external economic shocks as well as vulnerabilities of the country's economy in the years ahead.

During the period under investigation (2000–2018), Ethiopia's trade with China (Figure 6.9(a)) has skyrocketed, reaching about USD 754.6 million (USD 302.2 million exports and USD 493.5 million imports) in 2018.The combined trade with China in 2000 was less than USD 350 million. However, as with the country's total trade, Ethiopia has continued to incur persistent and growing trade deficits with China, with imports from outstripping its exports to China. Therefore, while China offered an alternative export market and expanded opportunities as a source of imports, this has not substantially increased Ethiopia's exports when compared to its imports from China. Ethiopia's increasing trade with China has not contributed to diversifying its exports – vertically or horizontally (Figure 6.9(b)).

In fact, Ethiopia's overall trade with the world and its direction (Figure 6.8(a)) mimics the country's trade flows with China (Figure 6.8(b)), clearly showing the dominant weight of China in the country's imports and exports flows or direction. The Chinese share in Ethiopia's total trade (in value) has increased from about 4 percent in 2000 to 28 percent in 2018 (Figure 6.8(b)). Imports to Ethiopia from China has leaped from about USD 77 million in 2000 to a little above USD 5.6 billion in 2015 (the highest in a decade) representing a 77-fold increase. This has modestly decelerated to USD 4.9 billion in 2018. When compared with the early 2000s, the increase in imports in recent years has been substantial, especially when compared to stagnant exports of the country to China (Figure 6.8(a)).

During the same period, Ethiopia's exports to China have also increased significantly from the lowest level of USD 2 million in the early 2000s to about USD 302.1 million in 2018. Ethiopia has always maintained a negative trade balance with China, which increased from about USD 78 million in 2000 to a whopping USD 5.33 billion in 2015 – an increase of about 640 percent before modestly improving in 2018 (with a deficit of USD 4.6 billion). It appears to be the case that decades of trade liberalization policies and related reform programmes undertaken by Ethiopia have led to a substantial increase in imports over exports, leading to persistent and bulging trade deficits. This also means that countries such as Ethiopia cannot take advantage of preferential market access granted to them by their trading partners such as China unless they effectively unlock binding constraints on their productivity and overall supply side challenges facing their trade sector and their economies.

The poor outcome of reforms and adjustment programmes result from the lack of indigenous capabilities, low level of intergenerational capital accumulation,

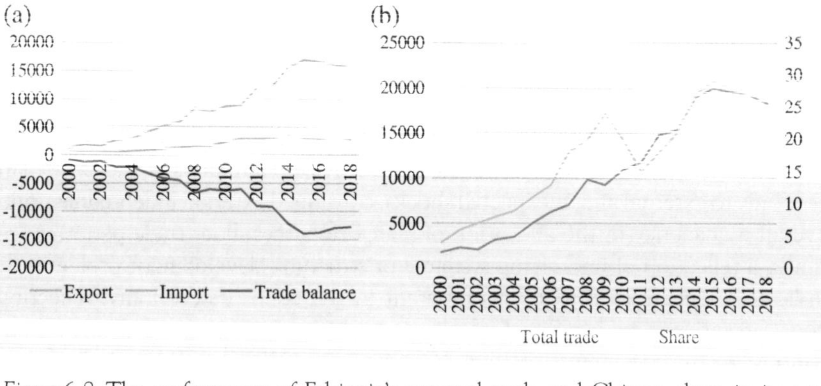

Figure 6.8 The performance of Ethiopia's external trade and Chinese share in its total trade (2000–2018).

Source: UNCTADstat (2020).

technological learning, and innovation or productive capacities. Externally prescribed policies place more emphasis on policy formulation and articulation than implementation. That is, they seek to perfect articulation although the key problems lie in implementation. This situation is further compounded by inadequate and unsustainable financing of the reform programmes given the increased dependence of Ethiopia and SSA as a whole on external finance and limited scope for domestic resource mobilization.

When the trade deficit is persistent, systemic, and expanding over time, it can pose a daunting challenge for developing countries such as Ethiopia, contributing to the balance of payments crisis. The bulging trade deficit of Ethiopia can increase the external indebtedness of the country, significant job losses, and entail a shift in the allocation of development resources away from productive sectors to permanently financing the trade deficit. The lagging export sector and expanding trade deficit is only half the problems facing Ethiopia's external sector performance. Equally troubling is the country's export basket, which is increasingly dominated by primary agricultural commodities, accounting for nearly 80 percent of total exports (Gebrehiwot: 2019). International prices for primary agricultural commodities are spectacularly low, volatile, and susceptible to shocks in global demand and/or supply. Ethiopia's exports to China are predominantly unprocessed agricultural produce, consisting of sesame seeds, oilseeds, leather, and spices (Cheru and Oqubay: 2019).

Ethiopia's merchandise export concentration coefficient has also increased over the years when compared to that of SSA (Figure 6.9(b)), indicating lack of structural change – diversification or transformation in the country's trade sector. Tesfachew (2019) argues that while Ethiopia's modern (sophisticated) exports have increased from zero percent in 2005 to 1 percent in 2015, its primary agricultural exports have fallen only marginally, from 90 percent in 2005 to 85 percent in 2015. Nevertheless, Ethiopia's trade integration pattern with China is not unique but it is identical to countries of SSA such as Angola and Nigeria – the two largest oil exporting economies in SSA. For instance, Adunbi and Stein (2019) argue that the trade relations between Nigeria and China remain problematic as Nigeria's trade deficit has continued to expand due to its export of primary products and imports of manufactured goods from China. Their arguments are like those advanced earlier and specifically blamed Chinese textile exports as the main causes of destroying the vibrant textile sector of Nigeria (Muhammed et al.: 2017).

Although Ethiopia's export concentration coefficient is lower than Angola's, it has also increased when compared with SSA's average score during the same period. These problems are behind the persistent vulnerabilities of the Ethiopian economy to external and unexpected shocks, continued external indebtedness, and overall inefficiency in the allocation of scarce resources. Poor trade performance is also a reflection of underlying systemic or structural development problems. It indicates a deep-rooted weakness inherent in the country's economy, reflecting poor capacities in trade policy formulation and implementation. This is in sharp contrast to the argument of Cheru and Oqubay (2019) that Ethiopia "exhibits a high-degree of political ownership and reasonably well-developed institutional capacity for implementation of policies and strategies" (p. 285). The evidence

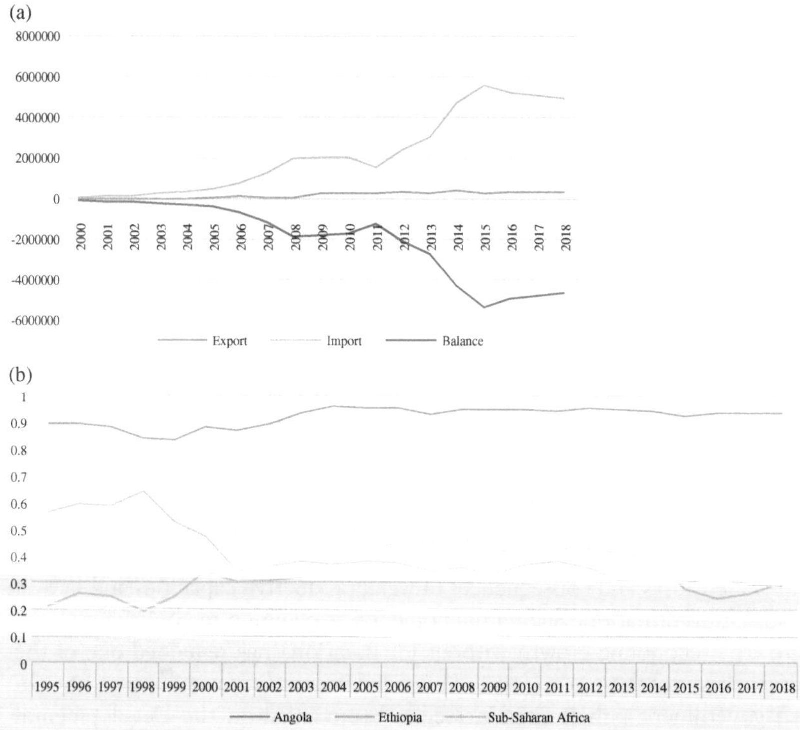

Figure 6.9 Ethiopia's trade with China in USD thousands, and its Merchandise Export Concentration Coefficient.

Source: UNCTADstat (2020).

presented in this book shows that the increasing share of China in the country's trade may further entrench commoditization and market concentration problems that are the characteristic features of the economies of SSA. However, problematic trade performance can also provide opportunities for Ethiopia to formulate and implement targeted and country-specific strategies to improve its trading position (Cheru and Oqubay: 2019, pp. 288–289). This calls for concerted efforts to design, sequence and implement integrated, coherent, and holistic development policies and strategies centred on fostering economy-wide productive capacities, export diversification (value addition), and structural economic transformation.

6.5.1 *Ethiopia's Economic Growth and Productive Capacities*

Despite successive modernization and industrialization endeavours since the early 19th century (Bekele: 2019), Ethiopia's economy continues to be traditional. The country's economy continues to be dominated by primitive agriculture and farming methods: informal, micro, and small enterprises with persistently declining MVA (indicative of premature deindustrialization). Ethiopia's economy also faces the challenges of bulging trade deficits, rising unemployment, weak productive capacities, and absence of structural economic transformation. Successive internal and inter-ethnic conflicts as well as wars with neighbouring countries have further compounded the challenges of achieving transformational growth, centred on fostering productive capacities and structural economic transformation. Consequently, Ethiopia remains one of the poorest countries in the world with a GNI per capita of USD 600 in 2015 (Figure 6.2).

The World Bank data shows that Ethiopia has managed to significantly reduce the proportion of its people living in extreme poverty (on less than USD 1.90 per day) from 71 percent in 1991 to 32 percent in 2015 and to 30.8 percent in 2018. However, the country's MPI shows that 83 percent of the Ethiopian population was in multidimensional poverty in 2016. The intensity of poverty (the average deprivation experienced by poor people) stood at 58.54 percent during the same year. Such a dismal performance in reducing multidimensional deprivation in Ethiopia is observed against the backdrop of high economic growth of the post-1991 economy (Figure 6.1), which is considered one of the fastest in the developing world in recent years. The widening gap between high economic growth performance and meagre social outcomes (with massive multidimensional deprivation) are causes and consequences of weak productive capacities and lack of economic transformation. Such a phenomenon is common in SSA where "jobless growth" (economic growth without job creation) has remained one of the defining features of these economies. This trend goes against a wide range of well-crafted government policies and strategies[24] (modelled on the Developmental States of East Asia). Consequently, as with Angola, the productive capacities of Ethiopia remained lower even by comparison with the average level for SSA, although it has shown improvement in recent years (Figure 6.10).

Raising the productivity of the sector through targeted investment is critically important. However, the modernization of Ethiopia's rainfed agriculture dominated by the fragmented and rudimentary farming methods of small households can pose daunting challenges to raise the productivity of the sector and to kick-start the process of structural transformation. This is in line with the arguments of the most recent study undertaken by the staff of the World Bank (Fuglie et al.:

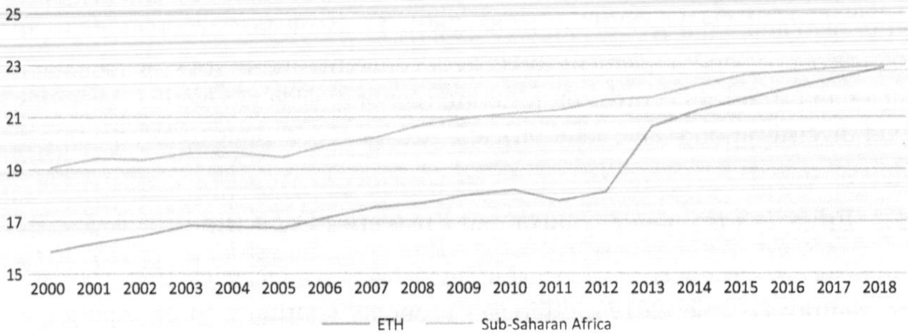

Figure 6.10 Productive capacities of Ethiopia and SSA (2000–2018).

Source: UNCTAD's Global Productive Capacities Index (PCI).

2020), which confirms that the lag in agricultural productivity in poor countries has seriously undermined their efforts to converge with advanced developing and developed economies. Within the agriculture sector, Ethiopia has shown an example of within-sector transformation, though minimal. In a short period, the country has become the second largest exporter of flowers in SSA after Kenya. In 2018, Ethiopia earned USD 230 million from exports of flowers (www.floradaily.com). This represents a more than 56 percent increase over the level for 2008, which was about USD 130 million. This is more remarkable as Ethiopia is a newcomer to the flower industry (which started only in the 2000s). The success of Ethiopia's flower industry is due to the combination of several factors: strong desire and commitment of the government to develop the sector, provision of targeted incentives, effective collaboration with the private sector, supportive donor governments (facilitating investments and granting market access), and air connectivity between Ethiopia and major flower destinations in Europe (Gebreeyesus and Iizuka: 2010).

The sector has been dominated by foreign firms, benefiting from the government's incentives such as the provision of land, tax holidays, and import duty exemptions. The government also created a semi-autonomous agency to provide dedicated services to horticulture exporters and insulate the industry from the normal bureaucracy (Golub et al.: 2011). The flower industry is capital-intensive and may show the signs of transformation within the agriculture sector if progress is sustained even after the gradual withdrawal of state-donor support to floriculture. However, so long as this positive change or trend has not been accompanied by growth and modernization across the agriculture sector (such as the production and export of food and cash crops), the scope and extent of transformation will be very limited. Moreover, although the improved performance of the flower industry and the agricultural sector of Ethiopia was driven by the Ethiopian government's strong policy commitment, still high transport costs reduce the use of modern agricultural inputs (Fuglie et al.: 2020) to further improve productivity growth in agriculture and enhance the role of the sector in output and employment.

Due to weak transformation (value addition) of other export items and poor sectoral linkages (between the agriculture and industry), Ethiopia's exports to China continue to be dominated by primary agricultural produce, whereas the country's imports from China consist of finished manufactured goods, machinery, iron and steel, construction materials, power generation, transmission equipment, and industrial spare parts (Cheru and Oqubay: 2019). The dependence of Ethiopia's exports on primary agricultural produce is in contrast to the view that Chinese investments in the country are productive which are spread across a wide range of manufacturing projects. Against these claims, what is observed is that the MVA of Ethiopia as a percentage of GDP is far below the average of SSA for 2000–2018 (Figure 6.11).

Ethiopia's declining trend in the MVA is accompanied by the dominance of very small, informal and a consistently small number of large enterprises (Shiferaw and Soderbom: 2019). This reflects not only premature deindustrialization, but it is also a sign of weak productive capacities, poor linkages between FDI to firms

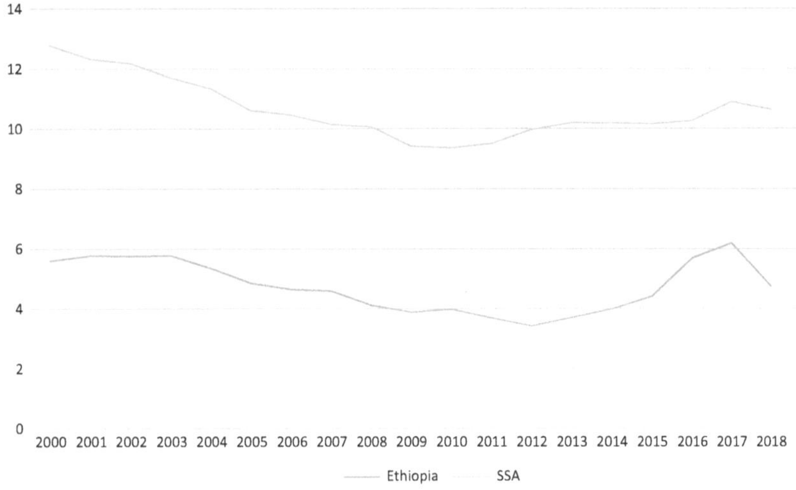

Figure 6.11 Manufacturing value-added as percentage of GDP: Ethiopia and SSA (2000–2018).

Source: World Bank Data (2019).

and domestic enterprises, and sheer lack of structural economic transformation in the country. The persistently falling share of MVA in the GDP of Ethiopia is consistent with the overall trend documented in Africa. Lin and Xu (2019) provided statistical and empirical evidence that the shares of manufacturing in output and employment in Africa today are smaller than they were in the 1980s. The authors argue that in 2017, SSA's average share of MVA was only 10 percent, down from 20 percent in the 1980s. Ethiopia's MVA has continued to decline despite the increasing share in GDP of industry and the services sectors.

In sum, underdeveloped agriculture whose productivity is stagnant or declining, a precipitous decline in MVA, and persistently bulging trade deficits severely constrain or hinder the process of fostering productive capacities and structural transformation in Ethiopia and Angola. In fact, for countries such as Ethiopia, the key to kick-starting the process of structural transformation is to enhance agricultural productivity and by shifting the sector from resource (land and labour) – driven to productivity growth – led by increasing Total Factor Productivity (TFT) in the sector (Fuglie et al.: 2020).

6.6 Comparative Productive Capacities in Angola, Ethiopia, and SSA

The overall trends in fostering the productive capacities and structural economic transformation of Angola and Ethiopia represent SSA (Figure 6.12). The level of overall productive capacities (in Angola, Ethiopia, and SSA as a whole) has slightly improved over the years, although the changes are too little to transform respective economies, and to bring them to the level of other developing

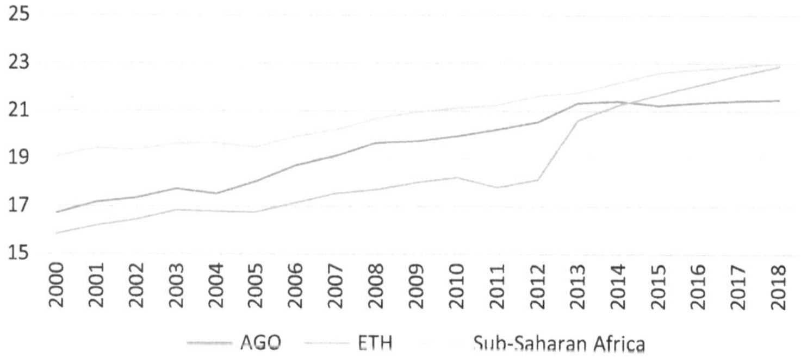

Figure 6.12 Productive capacities of Angola, Ethiopia, and SSA (2000–2018).
Source: UNCTAD's Global Productive Capacities Index (PCI).

regions. To maximize the partnership with China, the countries of SSA must be in the "driving seat" to chart the course of their development paths. They need to develop ownership of their development polices and strategies. They should also develop home-grown, clear, coherent, and comprehensive policies and strategies to target Chinese FDI and development finance to sectors where they have comparative advantages.

SSA's huge natural capital potential (Chapter 3), if fully harnessed and the rents are captured in fostering productive capacities and structural transformation, the region can achieve sustained, inclusive, and transformational development. The starting point for SSA should be in clearly understanding key binding constraints on development and designing policy interventions consistent with each country's comparative advantages or resource endowments. Although transformation can start within a given sector, the shift in policies and resources from traditional to modern sectors and from traditional to modern (technology-intensive) activities is key to fostering sustainable productive capacities and structural economic transformation. Such shifts are crucial for sustaining growth, improving wellbeing, and protecting the environment. The reality of SSA is that modern sectors, notably the manufacturing sector that helped China and other economies in East Asia to technologically leapfrog and gradually converge in income with developed economies, have been caught in a downward spiral since the 1980s (see Figure 6.13).

The poor performance of the manufacturing sector in Angola and Ethiopia, as well as SSA as a region, reflects their overall weakness along the eight components of productive capacities. The lag in the energy (electricity) component of productive capacities of SSA undoubtedly negatively affects the performance of the manufacturing sector. Likewise, the poor performance of SSA (including Angola and Ethiopia) in the transport, structural change, and ICT components (Figure 6.14) reflects the problems facing the manufacturing sector in embracing modern, vibrant, and competitive firms as well as technologically sophisticated production systems discussed later in this chapter. In essence, the poor

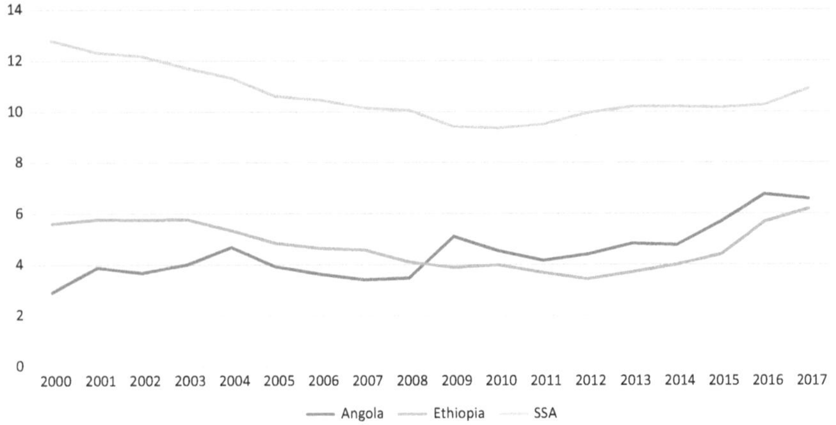

Figure 6.13 Manufacturing value-added as percentage of GDP: Angola, Ethiopia, and SSA (2000–2018).

Source: World Bank Data (2019).

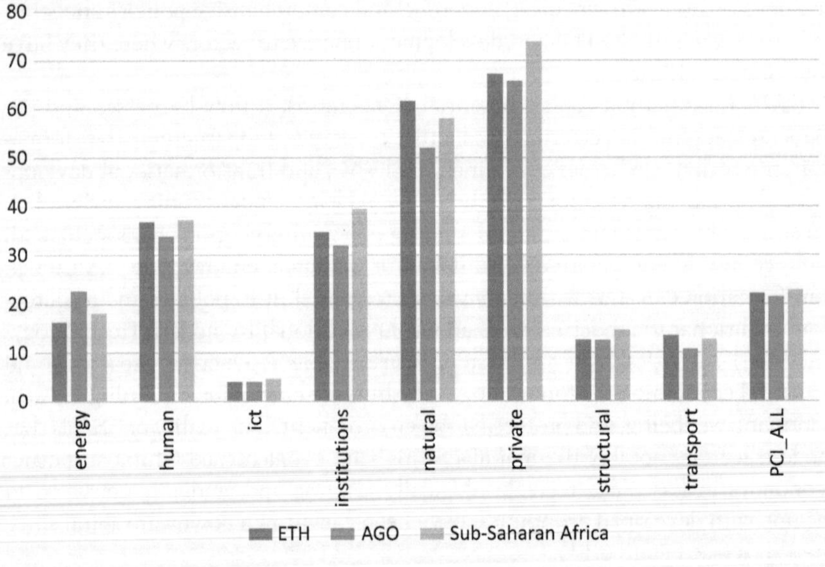

Figure 6.14 Angola, Ethiopia, and SSA: performance along the eight components of productive capacities (2018).

Source: Computed from UNCTAD's Productive Capacities Index (forthcoming).

performance in the transport and energy components of the productive capacities is in sharp contrast to an increasing amount of investment (including from China) that went into transport infrastructure and the power sector in countries such as Angola, Ethiopia, Kenya, Nigeria, and several other countries of SSA. As discussed in the preceding chapters, transport, and power (electricity generation) are two areas enjoying a large proportion of Chinese development finance, including investment from Chinese SOEs. Alongside the promotion of outward foreign investment by Chinese firms, China also pledges to undertake massive investments in large international transport infrastructure (Huang: 2016). This is principally through the Belt and Road Initiative (BRI) particularly in Ethiopia, Angola, Kenya, and Nigeria. SSA (including Angola and Ethiopia) also performed poorly on human capital component, especially. This is despite the fact that, for several decades, a sizeable proportion of public finance, including from external sources, have gone to the social sector with a focus on education and health.

Overall, the productive capacities of Angola and Ethiopia, as in the rest of SSA, are far too low and weak to dent their complex development challenges. In the case of Ethiopia, there is sectoral variation of the extent of China's engagement or partnership. While Ethiopia's exports to China are largely dependent on raw agricultural commodities, Chinese FDI including from SOEs goes to the manufacturing sector (Cheru and Oqubay: 2019) and the loans are largely financing physical infrastructure such as transport, communications, and low-cost urban housing. In the case of Angola and several other countries in SSA, extractive resources have been key to attracting growing interest on the part of development partners, including China. These resources are also the main factors behind intensified competition or rivalry between major global players poised to gain political and economic influence on the African continent. This notwithstanding, if natural capital is fully harnessed and resource rents are adequately geared towards socioeconomic transformation, SSA holds significant potential for transformational development. What is needed now is to put in place the right mix of comprehensive, consistent, and coherent economic policies centred on fostering productive capacities and structural transformation. Improvements in the regulatory and governance environment and the overall institutional framework for effectively harnessing the potential in natural resources can play complementary and facilitative roles in kick-starting inclusive and sustained economic growth that could substantially improve the socioeconomic performance of the countries concerned. In the early phases of Vietnam's reforms, the foundation for its transformation was the agriculture sector. Policies and strategies based on targeted state subsidies to agriculture with a focus on the production of food (rice, cassava, coffee, sugar) and fishery sectors were central in improving the socioeconomic landscape of Vietnam, including the standards of living of the rural population.

6.7 Evidence from Enterprise Survey Data

Globally, firms and enterprises play a critical role in employment creation, technological acquisition, adoption, innovation, and learning – processes which are vital for the fostering of productive capacities and structural economic transformation (Lee et al.: 2011). For instance, following in the footsteps of Japan and later South Korea and China, Vietnam has successfully managed to move up the value chain. As in China, Vietnam has developed vibrant, competitive, innovative, and technologically advanced domestic firms (Chapters 7 and 8). Moreover, Chinese firms have also become multinational, significantly investing at home and abroad (Yueh: 2019). Yueh also emphasized that dynamic and innovative firms have altered the Chinese economy from cheap, low-skill manufacturing hubs to an economy with technologically sophisticated firms and production structures with a growing outward orientation. This means that, for SSA, improving the overall business environment and the provision of targeted incentives to fledgling SMEs is an urgent matter if the declining role of the manufacturing sector both in output and employment is to be reversed.

A major part of firms in developed and developing countries belong to the category of SMEs, which represents 90 percent of all firms and 70 percent of employment (ITC: 2017). In SSA, SMEs account for 90 percent of businesses and 60 percent of employment (ITC: 2018), although the majority among them – more than 98 percent – are informal, micro, or small, with medium-sized enterprises accounting for only 1.5 percent, and large firms representing 0.5 percent (Fjose et al.: 2010, Salifu: 2020).

Despite their critical socioeconomic contributions, SMEs in SSA face a series of obstacles, which collectively undermine their potential and limit competitiveness. They suffer from the consequences of economy-wide weaknesses in productive capacities and structural transformation. These include lack of access to dependable (predictable) and affordable supply of energy (electricity), poor ICT and transport connectivity, weak financial and banking sectors as well as regulatory inefficiencies and institutional hurdles. Relaxing these constraints is key to realizing the full potential of the SMEs sector in SSA by enhancing productivity or capacity utilization (see below), business and export competitiveness, as well as catch-up in ICT and the digital economy.

Technological leapfrogging and ICT connectivity constitute the most pervasive challenge and barrier to SME competitiveness in SSA (ITC: 2015, 2018). Moreover, the evidence gathered through the World Bank's Enterprise Survey[25] confirms the low-level performance of firms in Angola, Ethiopia, and SSA in terms of capacity utilization,[26] employment creation, investments in fixed assets, technology, and innovation as well as infrastructure, among other things. Average capacity utilization is an important indicator of the performance of firms in contributing to production transformation at industry level. According to the Enterprise Survey's latest (2018) edition, although there are variations across countries, firms in developed countries have an average capacity utilization of about 85 percent. In advanced developing countries, firms' capacity utilization rates are converging with that of the developed countries. In 2018, Brazil had 81.4 percent, East Asia 78 percent (on average), South Africa 79.6 percent. The performance of firms in China is higher than the average for developed countries, with 87 percent in the same year.

The performance of firms on capacity utilization rates in SSA is the lowest of all countries covered by the survey in 2018, with an average value of about 70 percent (Figure 6.15). In other words, that capacity underutilization rate in SSA was 30 percent during the same year. The overall capacity utilization rates for Angolan and Ethiopian firms were the lowest even when compared to the

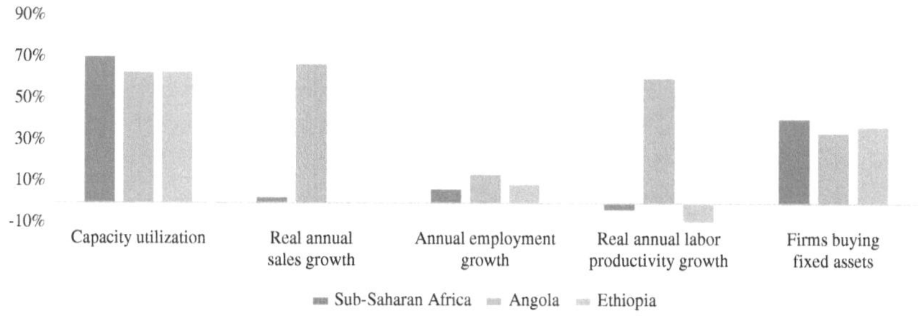

Figure 6.15 Firm-level evidence on capacity utilization and overall performance[27]: Angola, Ethiopia, and SSA.

Source: World Bank Enterprise Survey (2018).

average for SSA (62.5 percent for Angolan firms, 63.3 percent those of Ethiopia and 70 percent for SSA as a region). From the policy perspective, this means that, while building new productive capacities is crucially important, the countries of SSA should simultaneously endeavour to enhance the utilization rates of the existing capacities of their firms and enterprises.

During the same year, the real annual labour productivity in Ethiopia and SSA (average) were in negative territory, whereas their respective real growth rates in annual sales were not even reported in the survey year. On the other hand, Angolan firms show much higher level of real growth in sales (66.9 percent). The labour productivity rate for Angolan firms was at 60.3 percent in 2018, which is much higher than the average for SSA (−3 percent) and that of Ethiopia (−8.7 percent), despite their respective investments in fixed assets being almost comparable. The high productivity of labour in Angola may be induced by the capital intensity of the oil economy, which is a characteristic feature of investments (capital and technology) in extractive sectors, which tend to enhance the productivity of labour.

The overall poor performance of firms in Ethiopia is despite improved market access conditions in major trading partners of the country (USA,[28] EU, China, and other bilateral preferential market access offers), the relatively cheap cost of labour, proactive government policies, and incentives in supporting the private sector, and a relatively growing middle-class and large domestic market. This means that a long-standing mantra of mainstream economic orthodoxy and neo-liberals that "getting policies right" and "one-size-fits-all" approach to overcome complex challenges of development is overly simplistic, misguided, and plagued by systemic fallacies.

Sound policies, if not backed by vibrant and dynamic institutions and adequate human, financial, and technical resources for their implementation, could not resolve binding constraints on development. While it is too early to assess the impact of the recent developments in Ethiopia in building large industrial parks and export processing zones, there is growing optimism, at least at the political or policy level, as to whether it is possible to make Ethiopia SSA's manufacturing hub.

In the case of Angola, although real labour productivity seems higher, key problems facing Angolan firms are diverse. These include the high cost of intermediate goods, a low-skill labour force, poor linkages between foreign and local firms, and the dominance of large foreign companies especially in the mineral and oil sectors, with little or no positive impact on manufacturing firms. The oil-driven economy of Angola has the tendency to penalize firms in the manufacturing and agricultural sectors through the appreciation of the local currency, pushing up the cost of production and making exports excessively expensive, thereby rendering them unproductive and internationally uncompetitive.

Other important firm-level evidence that is directly relevant for productive capacities or structural transformation narratives, relates to the innovation and technology problems of firms in Angola, Ethiopia, and SSA as a region. For countries of SSA such as Angola and Ethiopia, the full realization of their development objectives requires them to go beyond their current low-skill, low-technology production, and exports. They should embrace technology, innovation, technological knowhow, and learning (Tesfachew: 2019). Based on selected indicators of competitiveness and level of technological development, Tesfachew argues that Ethiopia lags behind comparable countries (Bangladesh and Kenya) and countries with which it intends to gradually converge (South Korea and Vietnam) in technology and innovation. This argument is consistent with the data presented in the World Bank Enterprise Survey on key indicators of technology and innovation, which are believed to help countries of SSA in technological leapfrogging and catch-up.

Whereas 34 percent of firms in Angola were using technology licensed from foreign companies, which is by far higher than the global average of 23.6 percent, only 7 percent of firms in Ethiopia reported using such technologies, which is 50 percent less than the average for SSA (15.4 percent). However, despite the high proportion of firms using foreign technologies in Angola, there were no firms in the country that have reported the introduction of either new products and/or services, or process innovation in the year of survey. For comparison, in China 43.6 percent of firms introduced new products and/or services, whereas 58 percent reported process innovation during same period. The average proportions for all countries covered in the survey were 28.6 percent and 37.2 percent, respectively, for introducing new products/services, and process innovation. Interestingly, in the case of SSA, the average percentage of firms introducing new products and/or services was 43.2 percent, which is by far higher than the global average and equivalent to the performance of Chinese firms. As regards process innovation, the proportion was 38.4 percent in SSA against 37.2 percent global average, and 58 percent Chinese firms (Figure 6.16). This shows that firms in SSA are ready and capable to introduce new products and services as well as new processes, provided they have access to technology. The performance of firms in Ethiopia on the same indicators was 25.6 percent and 32.6 percent, respectively. A more serious concern regarding firms in SSA and their persistent lag behind the rest of the developing regions is in the area of Research and Development (R&D) expenditures. The percentage of firms that spent on R&D in SSA (on average) in

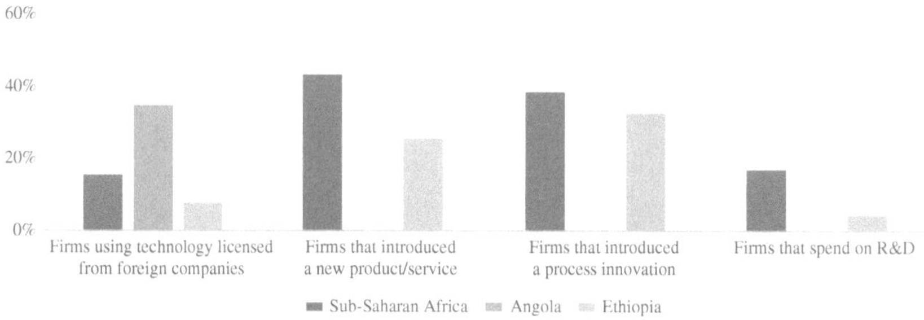

Figure 6.16 Innovation- and technology-related performances.

Source: World Bank Enterprise Survey (2018).

2018 was 16.9 percent, and for Ethiopia the percentage was a meagre 4.4 percent, against 38.7 percent for China and 23.6 percent for all countries covered in the 2018 survey database.

A further critically important area, which is undermining the performance of firms in SSA, is electricity infrastructure, more than transport or water supply. This is a direct reflection of the overall poor performance of SSA in energy component of productive capacities discussed in the preceding sections and chapters. Various studies have identified the challenge of providing reliable and affordable electricity, the high cost of infrastructure and related services as the most important impediments to productivity, competitiveness, and growth of the manufacturing firms in Africa in general and SSA in particular (Mbeakeani: 2007, Eifert et al.: 2008). UNCTAD (2008b, 2015) also documented that the quality of infrastructure, particularly electricity infrastructure, is one of the pervasive challenges in SSA, undermining industrialization, export diversification, and value addition in the commodities sectors where SSA has comparative advantages. While power outages in developed countries are minimal and are at acceptable levels in advanced developing countries, firms that experience repeated and long power outages in Angola were 87.7 percent, in Ethiopia 80 percent, and 76.2 percent in SSA as a whole in 2018 (Figure 6.17). In SSA (on average) 41.2 percent, in Angola 35.7 percent, and in Ethiopia 33.3 percent of firms identified electricity as a major constraint during the same year. Globally, among the countries surveyed 58.1 percent experienced power outages of short duration, against 37 percent in China in 2018. The percentage of firms that identified electricity as a major constraint for all countries in the survey was 33.3 percent and only 1.8 percent in China in the same year.

6.8 Policy Implications for Transformation

Several lessons can be drawn from the case studies of Angola and Ethiopia discussed in this chapter. First, the two countries exhibit the characteristic feature of SSA's weak productive capacities and lack of structural economic

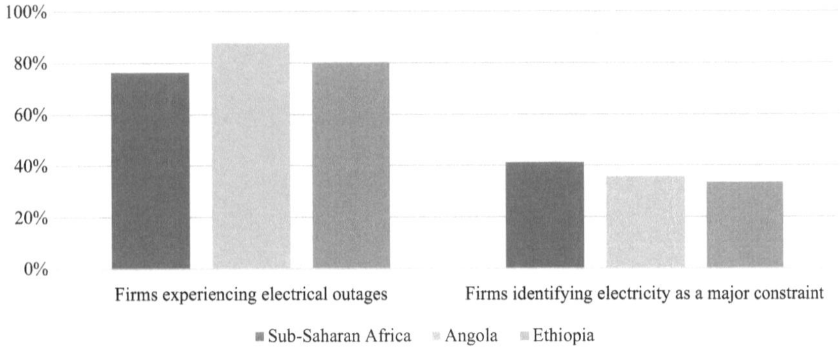

Figure 6.17 Electricity as key infrastructure undermining firm-level performance in Angola, Ethiopia, and SSA.

Source: World Bank Enterprise Survey (2018).

transformation, which lead to persistent socioeconomic vulnerabilities. Second, the complex and persistent challenges facing them are despite increasing trade, investment, and financial relations with China and traditional development partners. Although trade, finance, and FDI are key drivers of productive capacities development, their respective contributions are not automatic. Governments or policymakers need to have a strategic approach to trade, FDI, and development finance (they need to focus more on long-term gains than short-term benefits). Third, the quality of policies and institutions matter in catalyzing and calibrating the role of trade, investment, the private sector, and development finance. This is a fundamental prerequisite to enable countries to alleviate the effects of binding constraints and exploit comparative advantages to accelerate the fostering of productive capacities and structural transformation for socioeconomic development. Policies and strategies that support the growth and expansion of vibrant, dynamic, and competitive enterprises and firms, which can absorb technologies, innovate, learn and upgrade production and productivity are key to accelerating the process of transformational development. This calls for rebalancing incentives which are skewed to attract FDI at the expense of domestic investment and local firms.

Fourth, the role of Developmental States that tapped into the potential of open trade and investment regimes was important in transforming the economies in East Asia and Vietnam. However, in the context of SSA, open trade and investment policies have miserably failed in helping these countries to grow and catch up with the rest of the developing regions. Home-grown policies and strategies that are flexible and consistent with the initial conditions, institutional capabilities, and offer opportunities to experiment and implement as well as learn from others are critically important. Finally, the rise of China and its robust engagement in SSA offers ample opportunities for SSA economies such as Angola and Ethiopia. Fully exploiting these opportunities lies in the hands of the African countries themselves. They need to address the infrastructure gap and other limitations in their domestic policies, regulatory, and institutional environments. These include effectively tackling corruption and mismanagement of natural resource rents (particularly in extractive sector-driven economies) as well as rationalizing their incentive structures for firms and enterprises. The countries of SSA should formulate and implement indigenous policies that broaden the sources of economic growth and mobilize drivers and engines of such growth as Vietnam has successfully accomplished.

There is also recognition that governments alone cannot address the lag of SSA in building productive capacities and fostering structural economic transformation. Governments are responsible for formulating policies and strategies aimed at enhancing industrialization, facilitating the transfer of capital, technology, and know-how. However, the private sector is central in introducing innovation, enhancing learning, improving production processes as well as technology diffusion, which are necessary conditions to foster productive capacities and structural economic transformation. Several countries in SSA have established special economic zones, export processing zones, and/or industrial parks to enhance the role of the private sector by reducing transaction costs and removing entry barriers, facilitating skills formation, technology, and knowledge transfers. However, the objectives of governments in providing incentives have largely focused on fighting extreme poverty, generating foreign currency and promoting low-skill manufacturing and service sectors. While these objectives are important and necessary, they have the tendency to limit the scope for fostering productive capacities and economic transformations. For instance, governmental incentives in SSA countries tend to focus more on poverty-reducing firms and enterprises as opposed to firms that innovate, export, and compete internationally. Incentives and sectoral policies (such as agriculture, industry, and trade) should focus on increasing the technological content of production and exports to tap existing comparative advantages or rediscover latent comparative advantages. The countries of SSA should also focus on facilitating and enhancing linkages between domestic and foreign firms, across economic sectors and among small and large firms.

Notes

1 Angola's armed conflict between pro-Marxist People's Movement for the Liberation of Angola (MPLA) and Total Independence of Angola (UNITA) began immediately after the independence of the country in 1975 and ended in 2002. As with Angola, Ethiopia's internal wars which started with the Ethiopian Socialist Revolution in 1974 ended in 1991 with the independence of Eritrea and making Ethiopia landlocked. However, after a brief period of relative peace, the Ethiopian-Eritrean war (1998–2000) reignited. Angola's (1975–2002) and Ethiopia's civil wars (1974–2000) are considered proxy wars between the Eastern or Communist bloc and the Western or Capitalist bloc.

2 Angola gained its independence from Colonial Portugal in 1975, while Ethiopia remains a symbol of independence and anticolonial struggle in SSA save for the five years occupation by Fascist Italy (1936–1941). Also, Ethiopia is less prosperous than Angola in terms of Gross National Income per capita (Figure 6.2(a)) with a much

higher population (about 110 million) against 30 million inhabitants of Angola (Figure 6.2(b)).

3 CIA World Factbook: Angola Economy 2020. https://theodora.com/wfbcurrent/angola/angola_economy.html
4 Ibid.
5 World Trade Organization: Breakdown in Angola Export Data (2019). Available at: https://www.wto.org/english/res_e/statis_e/daily_update_e/trade_profiles/AO_e.pdf.
6 Angola held the latest national election in 2017, which led to a change in the political leadership of the country for the first time in 38 years. Although the ruling party (Movement for the Liberation of Angola – MPLA) which has led the country since independence in 1975 is still in power, one of the continent's long-serving leaders was replaced following the national election.
7 The ex-president's daughter, the richest woman in Africa, is facing serious charges for using family ties to enrich herself by plundering public resources including from the state oil company Sonangol. She was designated by her father as the CEO but later removed from that responsibility by the current president. She is also accused of involvement in shoddy business including money laundering. Likewise, the son of the ex-president was the first to stand trial following the 2017 election for stealing millions of dollars from the Angolan Sovereign Wealth Fund, which he oversaw from 2013 to 2018.
8 According to various statistics (FAO, UNCTAD, and the World Bank), Angola spends on average USD5–6 billion a year on food imports and daily consumables, although there are ongoing efforts to reduce dependence on imported food. According to the most recent data of the World Bank Development Indicators, the country's food imports in total merchandise imports was reported at 19.83 percent in 2018 (https://data.worldbank.org/).
9 Between 1991 and 2018, Ethiopia was ruled by the Ethiopian Revolutionary Democratic Front, a coalition of ethnically federated parties, which came to power after the end of 17 years of rebellion and protracted armed conflict against the military regime that had ruled the country from 1974 to 1991.
10 The World Bank's definition of net official development assistance (ODA) refers to disbursements of loans made on concessional terms (net of repayments of principal) and grants by official agencies of the members of the Development Assistance Committee (DAC), by multilateral institutions, and by non-DAC countries. It includes loans with a grant element of at least 25 percent (calculated at a rate of discount of 10 percent).
11 These are funds which are often set up with capital from fiscal surpluses, balance of payments surpluses, foreign currency operations, or commodity exports, and usually they are invested in foreign financial assets for macroeconomic purposes.
12 The "One China Policy" is a long-standing policy of the People's Republic of China that firmly stands on principles that "there is only one China in the world, and Taiwan is part of China".
13 Including credit, natural resources-backed loans, concessional loans, grants, and credits.
14 The values are from UNCTAD's export or product concentration index. The index measures the degree to which exports of a given economy or of groups of economies are concentrated on a few products, rather than being distributed in a more homogeneous manner among several products. The concentration index is computed by Herfindahl-Hirschmann (HH) concentration coefficient. The values range from 0 to 1 where "0" means perfectly (infinitely) diversified exports and 1 means a unitary (single product) export (for details and computation formula, see UNCTADstat at www.unctad.org).
15 The World Bank's poverty data for Angola can also be found at: http: //povertydata.worldbank.org/poverty/country/AGO.

16 The Human Development Index (HDI) is a statistical tool developed by the United Nations Development Programme (UNDP). It is a composite index of life expectancy, education, and per capita income indicators, which are used to rank countries on yearly basis.
17 The Multidimensional Poverty Index (MPI) is jointly developed by the United Nations Development Programme (UNDP) and the Oxford Poverty and Human Development Initiative (OPHI) of the University of Oxford. MPI measures multiple deprivations of household and individual level in education, health, and standards of leaving. The MPI is different from the World Bank's poverty measures as it consists of multiple deprivations beyond income. The index measures the incidence of multi-dimensional deprivation a headcount of those in MPI and its intensity (the average deprivation score experienced by poor people) along the key indicators of health, education, and standards of living.
18 See Geda and Degefe: 2005, Geda and Meskel: 2010, Adem: 2012, Shinn 2014, Brautigam: 2019, Cheru and Oqubay: 2019). They discussed China-Ethiopia relations in varying degrees of details and perspectives.
19 The group of soldiers that overthrew the reign of Emperor Haile Selassie (the last monarchy of Ethiopia) in 1974, and ruled Ethiopia until 1991.
20 The economy transitioned, on the one hand, from centralized (socialist) economic system to a "Developmental State" -led mixed economic system, and on the other hand, from a "war economy", to peace, stability, and economic revival with some level of uncertainty due to the cessation of Eritrea in 1991.
21 For instance, according to the Ethiopian Investment Commission, the value of Chinese FDI stock in Ethiopia was USD851 million (Cheru and Oqubay: 2019) which is in a stark contrast with the UNCTAD data shown in Table 6.1. Such a variation in data and FDI statistics could possibly be the result of several problems such as accounting errors, double counting, reporting pledges (not actual flows) in the records, combining loans from China with FDI, or combining stocks and annual flows at a particular time or period.
22 The reforms include, among other things, enacting laws for open investment regimes; privatizing State-Owned Enterprises (SOEs); liberalizing imports through rationalization of duties and tariffs; simplifying licencing procedures on trade and investment; removing taxes on exports; providing incentives for export-oriented firms; devaluing the national currency (the Birr); introducing managed or controlled floating (or fixed-floating) exchange rate on foreign currency; liberalizing foreign currency-denominated bank accounts for savings, and prioritizing transport infrastructure in public investment.
23 The Ethiopian Commodity Exchange (ECX) was established in 2000 by the Government with a view to modernizing the commodity trade of the country, enhancing market transparency and efficiency by introducing real-time price information, and serving as a marketplace for buyers and sellers with standardized contracts to ensure quality and deliver at remunerative prices. ECX is also designed to facilitate the integration of producers of agricultural commodities to the regional and global trading system by cutting out the middlemen.
24 These include the country's Agriculture Development-Led Industrialization (ADLI) which tacitly favours domestic investment against foreign investors (World Bank: 2009).
25 The World Bank's enterprise surveys are available at (https://www.enterprisesurveys.org/. The 2018 enterprise survey of the Bank covered 158,000 firms from 144 countries in manufacturing, construction, retail, and other services. The Bank's survey assesses the overall environment facing firms by using about 100 indicators.
26 In the survey capacity utilization is defined as the percentage of resources (labour and capital) used in the production of finished goods to meet demand. In normal times, the ideal capacity utilization of 80 percent for productive resources for firms is sought.

27 The 2018 *World Bank Enterprise Survey* includes country-specific surveys for Angola and Ethiopia which were undertaken, respectively, in 2010 and 2015.

28 The USA has decided to remove Ethiopia from the list of countries in SSA benefiting from AGOA starting from 1 January 2022, due to recent increasingly tense diplomatic relations between the two, and accusations of the Government of Ethiopia on reported "gross human rights violations" in the northern part of the country as the result of the ongoing internal inter-ethnic wars.

Bibliographical references

Adem, S. (2012). China in Ethiopia: Diplomacy and Economics of Sino-Optimism. *African Studies Review*, 55(1), 143–160. Available at: www.jstor.org/stable/41804135. (Accessed on 13 March 2020).

Adunbi, O., and Stein, H. (2019). The Political Economy of Chinese Investment in Nigeria: Prometheus or Leviathan? In *China-Africa and an Economic Transformation*. Edited by A. Oqubay, and J. Y. Lin. Chapter 10. Oxford University Press, Oxford, 192–215.

Ali, N. S. (2019). Infrastructure and Economic Transformation in Ethiopia. In *The Oxford Handbook of the Ethiopian Economy*. Edited by F. Cheru, C. Cramer, and A. Oqubay. Oxford University Press, Oxford, 191–212.

Begu, L. S., Vasilescu, M. D. et al. (2018). China-Angola Investment Model Sustainability. 12th International Conference on Business Excellence, 22–23 March 2018, Bucharest, Romania.

Bekele, S. (2019). Ethiopia's Transition from a Traditional to a Developing Economy: 1809–1960s. In *The Oxford Handbook of the Ethiopian Economy*. Edited by F. Cheru, C. Cramer, and A. Oqubay. Oxford University Press, Oxford, 17–31.

Brautigam, D. (2019). Chinese Loans and African Structural Transformation. In *China-Africa and an Economic Transformation*, Edited by A. Oqubay, and J. Y. Lin. Chapter 13. Oxford University Press, Oxford, U.K., 265–281.

Castel-Branco, C. N. (2008). Aid Dependency and Development: A Question of Ownership? A Critical View. Working Papers' Collection of the Institute of Social and Economic Studies (IESE), Mozambique.

Chakrabarty, M. (2016). Ethiopia-China Relations: A classical Win-win Situation. World Review of Political Economy. *Journal of the World Association for Political Economy*, 7(2) Summer 2016., 226–248.

Chen, J. (2019). Financing the Sustainable Development Goals: The Role of African Sovereign Wealth Fund. *International Law and Politics*, 51, 1259.

Cheru, F., and Oqubay, A. (2019). Catalysing China-Africa Ties for Africa's Structural Transformation: Lessons from Ethiopia. In *China-Africa and an Economic Transformation*. Edited by A. Oqubay, and J. Y. Lin. Oxford University Press, Oxford, 282–309.

Chole, E. (1992). Ethiopia at the Crossroads: Reflection on the Economics of the Transition Period. Dialogue, *Journal of Addis Ababa University Teachers Association*, 3rd Series, Vol. 1, 1 March 1992, Addis Ababa.

Cramer, C., and Sender, J. (2019). Policy, Political Economy, and Performance in Ethiopia. In *The Oxford Handbook of the Ethiopian Economy*. Edited by F. Cheru, C. Cramer, and A. Oqubay. Oxford University Press, Oxford, 249–268.

Dollar, D. (1992). Outward-Oriented Developing Economies Really Do Grow More Rapidly: Evidence from 95 Countries, 1976–1985. *Economic Development and Cultural Change*, 40(3), 523–544.

Eifert, B., Gelb, A., and Ramachandran, V. (2008). The Cost of Doing Business in Africa: Evidence form Enterprise Survey Data. *World Development*, 36(9), 1531–1546.

Fjose, S., Grunfled, L. A., and Green, C. (2010). SMEs and Growth in Sub-Saharan Africa: Identifying SME Roles and Obstacles to Growth, MENON-publication no. 14/2010. June 2010.

Fuglie, K., Madhur, G., Aprajita, G., and William, F. M. (2020). *Harvesting Prosperity: Technology and Productivity Growth in Agriculture*. The World Bank, Washington, DC. https://doi.org/10.1596/978-1-4648-1393-1.

Gebrehiwot, B. A. (2019). Trade Policy in Ethiopia 1991–2016. In *The Oxford Handbook of the Ethiopian Economy*. Edited by F. Cheru, C. Cramer, and A. Oqubay. Oxford University Press, Oxford, 230–248.

Gebreeyesus, M., and Iizuka, M. (2010). Discovery of Flower Industry in Ethiopia: Experimentation and Coordination. *Journal of Globalization and Development*, 2. https://doi.org/10.1515/1948-1837.1103. Available at: https://www.researchgate.net/publication/227378568_Discovery_of_Flower_Industry_in_Ethiopia_Experimentation_and_Coordination/citation/download.

Geda, A., and Degefe, B. (2005). *Conflict, Post-Conflict and Economic Performance in Ethiopia*. Palgrave Macmillan, London.

Geda, A., and Meskel, A. G. (2010). *Impact of China–Africa Investment Relations: Case Study of Ethiopia*. African Economic Research Consortium Collaborative Research on the Impact of Chain on Africa, African Economic Research Consortium (AERC), Mombasa, Kenya. http://dspace.africaportal.org/jspui/bitstream/123456789/32411/1/Ethiopia--China_Eth_Invest_Fina.pdf?1.

Golub, S., Bernhardt, A., and Liu, M. (2011). Development and Trade Strategies for LDCs 2001–2010 and Looking Ahead. Unpublished background paper for UNCTAD in the run up to the Forth United Nations Conference on LDCs, 2011.

Huang, Y. (2016). Understanding China's Road and Belt Initiative: Motivation, Framework and Assessment. *China Economic Review*, 40(C), 314–321.

International Trade Centre. (2015). *SME Competitiveness Outlook 2015: Connect, Compete and Change for Inclusive Growth*. ITC, Geneva. Available at: https://www.intracen.org/SMEOutlook/.

International Trade Centre. (2017). *SME Competitiveness Outlook 2017. The Region: A Door to Global Trade*. ITC, Geneva. Available at: https://www.intracen.org/SMEOutlook/.

International Trade Centre. (2018). *Promoting SME Competitiveness in Africa: Data for De-Risking Investment*. ITC, Geneva. Available at: https://www.intracen.org/SMEOutlook/.

Lee, K., Jee, M., and Eun, J.-H. (2011). Assessing China's Economic Catch-Up at the Firm Level and Beyond: Washington Consensus, East Asian Consensus, and the Beijing Model. *Industry & Innovation*, 18, 487–507. https://doi.org/10.1080/13662716.2011.583463.

Lin, J. Y., and Xu, J. (2019). China's Light Manufacturing and Africa's Industrialization. In *China-Africa and an Economic Transformation*. Edited by A. Oqubay, and J. Y. Lin. Chapter 13. Oxford University Press, Oxford, 265–281.

Manyazewal, M., and Shiferaw, A. (2019). Economic Policy and Structural Transformation in Ethiopia. In *The Oxford Handbook of the Ethiopian Economy*. Edited by F. Cheru, C. Cramer, and A. Oqubay. Oxford University Press, Oxford, 137–158.

Mbekeani, K. (2007). The Role of Infrastructure in Determining Export Competitiveness. Framework Paper. Available at: https://pdfs.semanticscholar.org/18c3/941e006fc1f3f60

dce786854837bd99fc435.pdf?_ga=2.5002291.1652695529.1585833181-894806755.1563973926.

Monga, C. (2019). The Meanings and Global Externalities of China's Economic Emergence. In *China-Africa and an Economic Transformation*. Edited by A. Oqubay, and J. Y. Lin. Oxford University Press, Oxford, 35–57.

Muhammed, M., Mukhtar, M., and Lola, G. (2017). The Impact of Chinese Textile Imperialism on Nigeria's Textile Industry and Trade, 1960–2015. *Review of African Political Economy*, 44(154), 673–682.

Oqubay, A., and Lin, J. Y. (2019). Introduction to China-Africa and Economic Transformation. In *China-Africa and Economic Transformation*. Edited by A. Oqubay, and K. Ohno, Oxford University Press, Oxford, 1–18.

Salifu, K. (2020). Contributions of Small & Medium Enterprises to Economic Development in Sub Saharan Africa. *International Journal of Academic Accounting, Finance & Management Research (IJAAFMR)*, 4(3), 63–78.

Shiferaw, A., and Soderbom, M. (2019). The Ethiopian Manufacturing Sector: Productivity, Export, and Competitiveness. In *The Oxford Handbook of the Ethiopian Economy*. Edited by F. Cheru, C. Cramer, and A. Oqubay. Oxford University Press, Oxford, 651–668.

Shinn, D. (2014). Ethiopia and China: Two Former Empires Connect in the 20th Century, 13th International Conference of Africanists, 27–30 May 2014. Institute for African Studies. Russian Academy of Sciences, Moscow, Russia.

Tang, W., and Pigato, M. A. (2015). China and Africa: Expending economic ties in an evolving global context, No. 95161, pp. 1–40. Investing in Africa Forum. The World Bank.

Tesfachew, T. (2019). Technological Learning and Industrialization in Ethiopia. In *The Oxford Handbook of the Ethiopian Economy*. Edited by F. Cheru, C. Cramer, and A. Oqubay. Oxford University Press, Oxford, 721–741.

UNCTAD. (2008a). *The Least Developed Countries 2008 Report: Growth, Poverty and Terms of Development Partnership*. United Nations Publication, New York and Geneva.

UNCTAD. (2008b). *Economic Development in Africa 2008 Report. Export Performance Following Trade Liberalization: Some Patterns and Policy Perspectives*. United Nations, New York and Geneva.

UNCTAD. (2013). *World Investment Report*. United Nations, New York and Geneva.

UNCTAD. (2015). *Facilitating the Participation of Landlocked Developing Countries in Regional and Global Commodity Value Chains*. United Nations, New York and Geneva.

UNCTADstat. (2019, 2020). Available at: https://unctadstat.unctad.org/EN/Index.html.

Wolf, C., and Cheng, S.-K. (2018). Chinese FDI in Angola and Ethiopia: Between Flying Geese and Resource Colonialism. Industrial Development, Construction and Employment in Africa (IDCEA) Working Paper 02, SOAS, University of London.

World Bank. (2009). Towards the Competitive Frontier: Strategies for Improving Ethiopia's Investment Climate. The World Bank Report No. 48472-ET, June 2009. Document of the World Bank.

World Bank Data. (2019). World Bank Open Data. Available at: https://data.worldbank.org/.

Yueh, L. (2019). China's Economic Emergence and the Implications for Africa. In *China-Africa and an Economic Transformation*. Edited by A. Oqubay, and J. Y. Lin. Chapter 2. Oxford University Press, Oxford, 19–34.

7 Vietnam's Experience in Fostering Productive Capacities and Structural Transformation

Vietnam's experience reveals how policies and strategies identify sectors of comparative advantages and how these are effectively harnessed as key drivers and enablers of transformation. It also demonstrates how government interventions, finance and institutions are aligned to unlock binding constraints to economic growth. Unlike the countries of SSA, Vietnam followed carefully selected and sequenced policies and strategies. As discussed in this and Chapters 8 the country has tacitly rejected laissez-faire policy prescriptions from outside, corrected market distortions, and espoused Developmental State principles. These have been complemented by entrepreneurial state functions and accelerated capital accumulation by rediscovering its comparative advantages, primarily in the agriculture sector. Indeed, in less than three decades, Vietnam has become one of the few star performers in the developing world in economic growth and poverty reduction with the right type of transformation. It has successfully shifted away from a traditional agriculture-led economy to a manufacturing- and services-driven economy. The chapter argues that while SSA exclusively depends on exports of primary commodities and a limited number of export markets such as China, Vietnam has reduced its dependence on natural resources and strategically maximized global trade and investment opportunities by penetrating a wide range of markets and economies across the world.

7.1 Economic Growth and Development: Luck, Miracle, or Hard Work?

Compared with many developing countries, Vietnam has excelled SSA in almost all measures, benchmarks, and development indicators of productive capacities. Why has Vietnam succeeded in fostering productive capacities and structural economic transformation, while others, particularly in SSA, have failed? What are the main sources and drivers of learning (both technological and policy) and catch-up in countries such as Vietnam? Why do some countries quickly catch up, while others lag and remain locked in low productivity and low-value production and poverty traps?

Vietnam's performance on UNCTAD's global Productive Capacities Index (PCI) (www.pci.unctad.org) is impressive, following in the footsteps of East Asian economies. On the PCI, East Asian economies, which serve as an

DOI: 10.4324/9781003295334-7

inspiration and role model for Vietnam, converge with developed economies in all the eight categories of the index, while SSA continues lagging behind other developing regions. East Asia's outstanding performance is an indication of the right type of fast and deep transformation in their respective economies. They have not only substantially reduced the proportion of their population living in extreme poverty, but also quickly become either upper-middle income or high income countries and significantly improved the living standards of their citizens in a relatively short period. The overall socioeconomic progress seen in these economies is nothing short of a "miracle", as described by the World Bank (Deyo: 1987, World Bank: 1993). Most of these countries were in the same or similar socioeconomic conditions as countries of SSA in the 1960s and 1970s. Their convergence and catch-up with industrialized economies provide indisputable evidence that development is neither inevitable nor impossible. The question is: why is it that Asian "latecomers" such as Vietnam were able to learn from the dynamic economies of the Asian region and register noticeable progress, while other latecomers in Africa are having difficulties despite their increasing trade, development finance and investment ties with China? What can SSA learn from the experiences of successful economies such as Vietnam, keeping in mind that the learning curve, as discussed in subsequent sections, is not flat?

The focus on Vietnam's experience is for five crucially important reasons. First, Vietnam's development experience is relatively new or fresh and it is still in the making, with lots of hope but also with some risks, pitfalls, and uncertainties. Thus, current, and future Vietnamese policies and strategies which aim to sustain and further deepen progress can provide useful lessons for the countries of SSA. Second, the level of economic development and the prevalence of poverty in Vietnam only a few decades ago was almost identical to those in SSA today. Third, as with most countries in SSA, the economy of post-1986 Vietnam was predominantly agrarian. It has gradually embraced extractive resources such as oil, coal, and zinc in the early phases of the reform processes. Fourth, Vietnam has quickly reduced its dependence on extractive resources by diversifying exports into manufactured and technologically sophisticated industrial products and services as well as harnessing the potential in agriculture, all of which can offer fresh lessons to several resource-dependent countries of SSA. Finally, Vietnam's path to growth and development as well as political and institutional landscapes have been influenced by its experience with colonialism, armed conflicts, a command economy (centralized economic policymaking), and, more recently, by its transition to a market economy, often with prescriptions from international financial institutions (IFIs). All of these are identical to the experiences and development paths of many countries in SSA, including Ethiopia and Angola, discussed in Chapter 6. Moreover, the "China factor" has been less relevant in Vietnam's growth and transformation processes than endogenous or domestic factors of growth. Unlike SSA countries, Vietnam does not depend on China alone for its trade, investment, and technology acquisition. Instead, it pursued diversified sources of growth alongside expanded partnerships with several countries, although it shares borders and development experience with the world's (unarguably) second largest economy – China.

Although there were stark similarities in initial socioeconomic conditions between Vietnam and today's poorly performing economies of SSA, the learning curve is not flat. Rather, it is steep and complex due to several underlying differences in initial fundamentals: geography (location within a dynamic region), binding constraints on development, institutions, culture and mindset, climate, and environmental conditions. These differences dictate the choice of growth paths and influence priority-setting processes, sequencing interventions, and the types and qualities of institutional and human resource capabilities. The way priorities are set, policy interventions are sequenced and coordinated, and how governments lead investments in infrastructure and other capabilities (e.g., R&D) in the implementation of development policies are key factors that distinguish SSA from the Asian economies, including Vietnam.

There are also significant variations not only between Vietnam and SSA countries, but also among the countries of SSA. However, as argued earlier, heterogeneity or variation both between and within countries offer ample opportunities for policy "possibilism" (Cramer et al.: 2020). Irrespective of heterogeneity, there are important lessons to be drawn. These include understanding how binding constraints are identified, comparative advantages defined or articulated, priorities set, interventions sequenced, and financial and human resources realigned with policy priorities. A lot can also be inferred from how market and government institutions guide transformational policy interventions or how incentive structures are provided and targeted to sectors of comparative advantages. Therefore, heterogeneity does not brush aside the importance of learning from the experiences of various countries and regions. Instead, understanding heterogeneity is key to learning what works best, what does not and why.

Experience shows that while learning from advanced developing countries, latecomers need to focus more on long-term development objectives than short-term policy gains (Oqubay and Tesfachew: 2019a, 2019b). In this regard, latecomers need to realign their operational strategies and interventions as well as incentive structures with their long-term development visions – with a focus on the fostering of productive capacities and structural economic transformation. Emphasis should particularly be placed on "self-discovery" – such as knowing comparative advantages (latent or revealed), understanding key binding constraints to growth and development, realigning policy interventions to address constraints, and more importantly, learning from successes and failures of one's own policies and strategies. This should include how to enhance backward and forward linkages within economic sectors, and between firms (large and small, foreign and domestic). This also requires strategically and systematically hooking into the global production and supply networks, maximizing spill-over effects, and technological learning (Alcorta and Tesfachew: 2020). Moreover, while successful development experiences can provide a useful starting point for latecomers, it is equally important to understand that not all successes come without experimentation, failures, and necessary corrective measures. In addition to drawing lessons from successful experiences, it is equally important to discern lessons from failures of policies or strategies as well as corrective measures undertaken.

The discussions in the preceding chapters demonstrate SSA's challenges in making policies work for growth and poverty reduction. The wide-ranging policies and strategies implemented in SSA have not led to achieving the objectives of sustained growth, employment, and poverty reduction (Stiglitz: 2001, Easterly: 2002, Nayyar, 2006). Poor policy outcomes are also due to weak domestic institutions, misalignment of development aid, and misguided market access opportunities from traditional and emerging development partners (Chapters 3, 4, and 5). The combination of internal and external less propitious policy and economic conditions have accentuated the socioeconomic vulnerability of SSA and the region's persistent lag behind the rest of the developing regions in fostering productive capacities and structural transformation.

Figure 7.1 compares productive capacities between SSA, the developing economies of Asia, and China. It clearly shows the widening gap in productive capacities between SSA and developing Asia. The linearly increasing trend in the overall productive capacities of SSA is the result of a relatively higher or dominant role of the natural capital component (as discussed in Chapters 3 and 4). The dominance of natural capital can indicate the potential that SSA holds for future development (if carefully harnessed). Without the right policies and institutions, it can also intensify cronyism and corruption as well as entrench increased dependence on commodities rather than facilitate economic diversification or structural transformation (UNCTAD: 2020a). If the natural capital component is omitted from the comparison, the level of SSA's productive capacities could have been far lower than that of the Asian economies. Comparison of economies on the PCI helps to broadly understand the evolution of economy-wide productive capacities and the degree of transformation taking place, if any. However, it does not provide clues or evidence about specific productive capacities-centred development policies and strategies and how these have been implemented in a country over the period examined. These are discussed in detail in later sections of this chapter as well as in chapter 8.

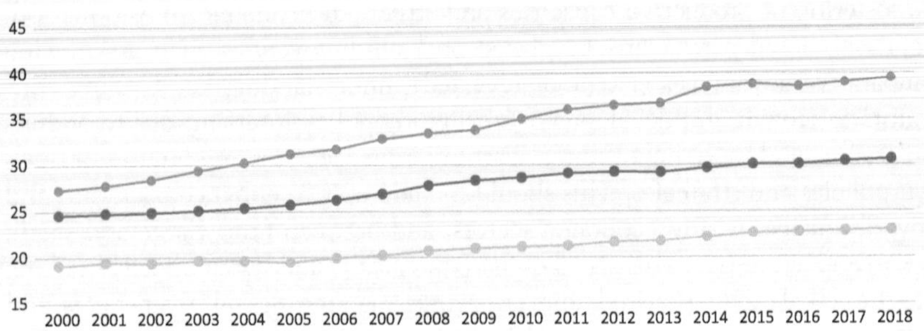

Figure 7.1 Productive Capacities Index in SSA, Asia, and China (2000–2018).

Source: Computed from UNCTAD's Global PCI.

While the rest of Asia has maintained a steady increase, China's performance on productive capacities is exceptional. SSA's performance, which has started from a lower position in the 2000s, remains as such throughout the period investigated. The low level of PCI in SSA is disappointing not only in comparison with other regions but also vis-à-vis the needs of the region to generate and sustain economic growth. Unfortunately, increasing Africa-China trade, finance, and investment structures as well as those with Western partners discussed earlier have not been predisposed to facilitate the fostering of productive capacities in SSA. This has increased the region's socioeconomic vulnerability and its continued dependence on external aid and economic conditions. Weak productive capacities made economic growth and exports more vulnerable to adverse external shocks when compared with Asia, Latin America or China (Figures 1.2 and 1.3. in Chapter 1). The dip in the average GDP growth rates in 2008–2009 reflects the impact of the global financial and economic crises which reveal weak productive capacities and the systemic and structural vulnerability in economies of SSA. The shock is more pronounced in the case of SSA than Asia, Latin America or China.

It is evident that the remarkable performance of the developing economies of Asia in the PCI is due to such top-performing East Asian economies as Hong Kong, Malaysia, Singapore, South Korea, Taiwan, Thailand, and recently Vietnam. China's exceptional performance in the index (Figure 7.1) also reflects the country's phenomenal production transformation which it achieved in less than three decades. In fact, Asia's overall index scores could have been by far higher than SSA and increasingly converge with that of China had it not been for the relatively lower values of countries such as Afghanistan, Bangladesh, Cambodia, Lao PDR, Myanmar, Nepal – all of which belong to the United Nations category of LDCs, which also includes 33 countries in SSA.

In terms of historical economic indicators, in 1970 Namibia had a GDP per capita of USD 3,035 (at 2015 constant prices). This was 47 percent higher than

Table 7.1 Selected East Asian and Sub-Saharan African Countries: GDP Per Capita in USD at Constant Prices (2015)

Economies	*1970*	*1980*	*1990*	*1995*	*2000*	*2010*	*2018*
Botswana	606	1,689	3,690	4,042	4,654	5,747	7,173
Hong Kong	6,977	13,054	21,270	2,593	27,173	38,406	45,870
Taiwan	1,810	4,076	7,839	10,790	13,967	19,975	24,431
Congo	1,437	1,813	2,237	1,991	1,942	2,521	2,012
Dem. Rep. of Congo	1,291	1,022	850	485	351	404	507
Côte d'Ivoire	1,787	1,812	1,422	1,293	1,322	1,182	1,650
Ghana	1,142	962	891	953	1,044	1,411	1,964
South Korea	2,045	4,171	9,512	13,502	16,859	25,455	31,231
Malaysia	1,579	3,055	4,139	5,727	6,393	8,248	11,057
Namibia	3,035	3,313	2,752	2,921	3,149	4,179	4,767
Nigeria	1,555	1,924	1,614	1,437	1,474	2,442	2,553
Singapore	6,783	13,871	23,356	30,193	34,760	47,977	58,692

Source: UNCTADstat (2020).

Malaysia's, 40 percent higher than that of Taiwan, and 32 percent higher than South Korea's in that year (Table 7.1). Likewise, Congo, Zaire (now Democratic Republic of Congo – DRC), Côte d'Ivoire, Ghana, and Nigeria had GDP per capita comparable to that of Taiwan and Malaysia in 1970 and slightly lower than that of South Korea. A decade earlier (in the 1960s), South Korea was one of the world's poorest countries with per capita GDP of USD 79 (Kicox: 2012). In the 1970s, the only East Asian economies that had higher GDP per capita than the then star performers of SSA were Hong Kong and Singapore. Half a century ago, the newly independent economies of SSA (Namibia was a colony then) were in a better position to invest in education, health, technology, infrastructure, and overall productive capacities than most Asian economies. However, in 2018 (48 years later), the GDP per capita of Taiwan was USD 24,431 whereas that of Namibia stood at USD 4,767. Within SSA, Namibia's performance can still be considered as outstanding. When compared with East Asian economies (which it outstripped in the 1970s), Namibia's performance today is starkly inferior. Hong Kong had a GDP per capita five times higher than that of Namibia in 2018, South Korea six times, and Malaysia nearly three times higher. In the same year, the DRC saw its GDP per capita plummet by more than 50 percent and Côte d'Ivoire by almost 7 percent, while the increase in Ghana and Nigeria was too small to bring about any meaningful change in their socioeconomic conditions when compared with their performance in the 1970s (Table 7.1).

The outstanding socioeconomic transformation of Asian economies has raised pertinent questions. How have they been able to transform their socioeconomic conditions in a relatively short period, while other developing countries, particularly in Africa, could not substantially raise their per capita income, reduce poverty, and generate decent jobs for their citizens? What can regions and countries lagging behind learn from the successful development experiences of East Asian countries? The answers to such questions vary significantly, and still today there has not been agreement or consensus on key sources and drivers of growth and development in East Asia. In some cases, the debates range along the schools of thought. For instance, mainstream economic traditions (neoclassical) and their heirs or custodians (including the World Bank and the International Monetary Fund) have credited the post-war economic growth and development to market fundamentals and institutions that allow such fundamentals to function. The Bank's frequent reports and policy research papers (World Bank: 1991) argue that, over the previous 40 years, market fundamentals had worked well, in sync with public policy. Accordingly, selective public policies, which allow markets to function without hindrance (with governments intervening only in areas where markets are inadequate) have been the main drivers of growth and development. The 1993 policy research (report) of the Bank, whose arguments were in perfect consonance with its previous reports, builds its analysis on the successful experience of Japan and other East Asian economies. The Bank's reports arrived at two important conclusions, which have had significant ramifications for the ensuing conceptualization of development theories (narratives) and understanding of national experiences. First, more open economies accompanied by free competition, increased investment in human capital (education and health), and total factor productivity have been key drivers of the accelerated socioeconomic transformation in East Asia. Second, sound domestic micro- and macroeconomic policies and capable institutions that function in sync with market forces matter for raising per capita incomes in the region and the "East Asian Miracles" (World Bank: 1993).

As with the World Bank, the International Monetary Fund's 1994 World Economic Outlook was entitled "The East Asian Miracles: Building a Basis for Growth" (IMF: 1994). Not only the title, but also the findings and conclusions of the IMF were akin to those covered in the preceding two (1991 and 1993) reports of the World Bank. In continuing with the Bank's earlier assertions, the IMF argues that the East Asian economies continued and sustained growth and transformation, were driven by a combination of physical and human capital accumulation, allocation of these resources to highly productive investments, market-oriented economic policies, and tailored government interventions (IMF: 1994). The Bank, the IMF, and mainstream (orthodox) traditions argue that getting the market fundamentals right and fostering institutions that allow the market to function freely are key to enhancing allocative efficiency, maximizing returns on investment, augmenting total factor productivity, and boosting economic growth and development. Accordingly, the interplay of market forces, with little or no government intervention but combined with human and physical capital accumulation, is a key ingredient for transformational growth and development in East Asian economies. The World Bank and the IMF were particularly apprehensive of State-Led Industrialization (SLI) and a strategy of Import Substitution (IS) vigorously pursued by East Asian economies, which they argue lead to unfettered government intervention in market through tariffs, State-Owned Enterprises (SOEs), exchange controls, or direct or indirect subsidies. These conclusions intensified subsequent discourse and protracted debates on the respective roles of the market and state institutions (public policy) in the process of development.

Contrary to the World Bank's and IMF's assertions on the central role of free market and selective state interventions in East Asian economies, Ajit Singh and several other notable economists provided empirical evidence and substantial arguments on the critical role of governments. Singh argued that governments in Japan and South Kora "were not reluctant bystanders" or mere facilitators of the functioning of market forces; nor were they operated in perfect harmony with market forces as claimed by the World Bank, the IMF, and other mainstream (orthodox) traditionalists (Singh: 1994). Instead, the governments of Japan, South Korea, and many other countries in East Asia, have intervened heavily through various market corrective (as it happens, highly protectionist) measures. These include (but are not limited to): effective import controls which were instituted to protect domestic firms and industries, rationalization of foreign currency allocations, subsidized credits to domestic firms and industries, highly aggressive state-led interventions in technology policies, restrictions in foreign investment and company ownerships, state-led investments in R&D and related capabilities, and building a vibrant and competitive domestic enterprises sector.

Obviously, these measures stifle the role of the market, fetter free competition, and strengthen the role of the state in fostering institutional and human resource capacities for public policy formulation and implementation. This means that as with Vietnam currently, governments in Japan and other East Asian economies were at the centre of building domestic productive capacities and enhancing structural economic transformation.

Institutionally, a more robust analysis of the East Asian development experience emerged from UNCTAD and its research staff. UNCTAD (1994) placed emphasis on the critical importance of protective fiscal and monetary policies that encouraged corporate profits of domestic firms over household savings and public investments as drivers of transformational development in the East Asian countries. It argues that high corporate profits in Japan, South Korea, and elsewhere in East Asia, led to increased domestic corporate savings and investments as opposed to raising dividends, profit sharing, or capital pay-outs in the form of financial returns or disbursements. Akyuz and Gore (1996) further argue that a rapid pace of capital accumulation, creation of a conducive environment for modern and dynamic private business, which is consistent with the national development priorities as well as capable institutions that maximized the nexus between investment and profit, have played a critical role in enhancing productivity growth in the East Asian economies.

Kim and Lau (1994), in their analysis of the experiences of Hong Kong, Singapore, South Korea, and Taiwan, emphasized the crucial role of economy-wide capital accumulation in the countries' accelerated socioeconomic transformation, growth, and development. In a further study on this group of countries, Young (1994, 1995) argued that, by far the most important source of the extraordinary post-war growth and development of the four economies lies in augmented total factor productivity and accumulation, particularly in the non-agricultural economy and manufacturing, and gains from total factor accumulation and sectoral allocation of resources.

By slightly diverting from the above-discussed arguments on sources and drivers of growth and transformation in East Asian economies, Rodrik (1994) provided analytical insights on the importance of "initial conditions" that helped to kick-start the process of accelerated growth and unprecedented post-war economic development in East Asia. His substantive arguments which were also corroborated by sound data, emphasized that the "1960s initial conditions of the East Asian economies explain a large fraction of their growth performance". This argument has greatly influenced subsequent analysis of the development experiences of nations, shifting the focus away from a simplified quantitative model-based analysis to a more realistic and evidence-based empirical analysis of the role of initial conditions in economic development.

Notwithstanding the above-mentioned differences, an important conclusion that emerges from the close examination of the East Asian success stories (including Vietnam's) is that there is no one (single) or uniform path to economic growth and transformation even within countries of the same region. In some of these countries, capital accumulation and an increase in employment (labour participation) have played a critical role in building economy-wide productive capacities and kick-starting the process of structural economic transformation. In others, outward-oriented investment and export strategies have played a pivotal role in transformational and sustained economic growth and development. Moreover, in many of these countries, productivity growth of all factors of production is responsible for their exceptional socioeconomic performance. In all successful cases, the role of the state in directing and sequencing priorities as well as calibrating interventions and incentive structures combined with the initial conditions in each of the countries examined, played decisive or determining role in productive transformation. It is safe to conclude that the combination of managed openness and the Developmental State interventions with entrepreneurial acumen have contributed to outstanding economic growth and fostering productive capacities with profound structural economic transformation in successful economies of Asia. These policy conclusions will have implications in the conceptualization of new productive capacities-centred policies and strategies for accelerating transformational growth and development in SSA.

From the above-mentioned discussions, we can learn that development is a complex process which requires continued experimentation, self-discovery, emulation, and application of difficult or competing policy options. The question is how did – Vietnam – learn from the East Asian experience? How did it manage to register growth and transformation with substantial increases in income and reduction in poverty? How do the development paths followed by Vietnam differ from those pursued by the countries of SSA, despite similar historical and socioeconomic background? As with the East Asian experience, there is no consensus on the reasons behind Vietnam's successful transformation. Some arguments focus on the form of economic governance and the role of the state. Others place emphasis on outward-oriented export and investment-led strategies. The focus of export and investment-led strategies on labour-intensive manufacturing sectors has also been at the centre of the discourses on Vietnam's development experience. Some other analyses place emphasis on the combination of the Developmental State and market-oriented reforms as central to successful productive capacities-led transformation of the country. As argued throughout this book, the underlying differences in economic development between and within nations are explained by differences in their ability to foster productive capacities and the type of structural transformation. More importantly, Vietnam's pragmatic, forward-looking and home-grown policies and strategies, as well as institutional capabilities to effectively implement them, are key lessons that the countries of SSA should draw as key for their own development processes. This is analyzed further in the following sections of the chapter.

7.2 The Impact of Economic Growth on Poverty Reduction in Vietnam: Any Lessons?

The World Bank's open data (https://data.worldbank.org/) shows that in 1990, the average GDP per capita for low-income countries of SSA was USD 663 (at current USD) whereas that of Vietnam was USD 95. In the 1990s, the ratio of people living with less than USD 1.90 a day[1] was 54.9 percent and 52.9 percent, respectively, in SSA (average) and Vietnam. The socioeconomic conditions in Vietnam were almost similar or identical to most countries of SSA, except that the average GDP per capita of SSA was almost seven times higher than that of Vietnam. A relatively higher GDP per capita means that SSA had better capacities for saving and investment than Vietnam. Moreover, as with the countries of SSA, 80 percent of the national income of Vietnam originated from the agriculture sector in the 1980s (Nguyen Thi et al.: 2016, Tarp: 2017). Likewise, Vietnam's economy was dominated or characterized by small-scale production (subsistence and traditional agriculture) in the 1980s and 1990s. Vietnam was also characterized by a large informal sector, high unemployment rates, material and technological scarcity, as well as insufficient food and consumer items. These characteristic features have been familiar descriptions or manifestations of SSA for several decades in the past and to date.

SSA and Vietnam also share geopolitical historical similarities. Like SSA, Vietnam had also suffered the consequences of colonialism[2] and destructive wars of independence).[3] At independence, the country was one of the poorest in the region, characterized by a high illiteracy rate, poor standards of living, underdeveloped infrastructure, a backward economy, and rudimentary farming methods. With such a very weak and excessively vulnerable economic structure, the country entered a resistance war against the USA in 1955, which is also known as the "Second Indochina War" (Schlight: 1986). The external occupation of Vietnam also ignited internal wars in the country – between the North (supported by USSR and China) and the South (supported by the USA and its regional anti-communist allies such as Australia, South Korea, Thailand, and the Philippines) – for almost 20 years (1955–1975). These wars have further destroyed the socioeconomic fabric of Vietnam and pushed the nation into continued economic deterioration, with rampant destitution and grim prospects for its economic revival. The proxy wars of the Cold War era were not actually "cold" for several countries of SSA such as Ethiopia and Angola (see Chapter 6) and Vietnam. Therefore, the 1970s, 1980s, and 1990s development challenges of Vietnam were almost identical to those of several economies of SSA. These encompass the rehabilitation and reconstruction of the economy, rebuilding socioeconomic institutions and infrastructure, and the provision of basic needs (food, medicine, potable water, schools, health facilities, etc.) to the population.

However, between the mid-1980s and early 2000s, Vietnam repaired its dilapidated economic infrastructure, reversed the decline in socioeconomic conditions, and subsequently, laid the foundation for sustained transformation. The country managed to achieve high economic growth (7.5 percent on average) with substantial poverty reduction and job creation. Consequently, the GDP per capita has jumped from USD 95 in 1990 to USD 390 in 2000 while the proportion of its population living in extreme poverty declined from 54.9 percent to about 30 percent during the same decade.

Since the end of the Second Indochina War in 1975, Vietnam followed a centralized or socialist economic system. A mixed economic management was gradually introduced by the mid-1980s. The state played a critical role not only in the management of the economy but also in guiding economic policy interventions and enhancing public ownership of the means (or instruments) of production, including land and large SOEs. Consequently, Vietnam's economy has become relatively more diversified (at least horizontally), combining the agriculture and extractive industries (with the discovery of oil, coal, and zinc). Between the 1980s and 1990s, the annual production of steel, cement, electricity, and zinc grew by between 8 and 12 percent. Also, in a very short period, Vietnam emerged as a regional rice producer and exporter – a major change for an economy dominated and driven by subsistence agriculture, and for a country that was food-insecure a decade earlier (Nguyen Thi et al.: 2016). With the combination of increased agricultural produce, booming extractive sectors, and state-led intervention in the economy, the overall socioeconomic performance of Vietnam continued to improve with unprecedented speed in poverty reduction (Figure 7.2). The country maintained consistent annual GDP growth of above 6.5 percent during nearly the last 20 years. Consequently, between 2000 and 2018, GDP per capita has jumped six-fold, from USD 390 in 2000 to nearly USD 2,500 in 2018, and the percentage of population living in extreme poverty went down from 30 percent in 2000 to a mere 1.9 percent in 2018 (Figure 7.2).

The question is what did Vietnam do that most developing countries, particularly those in SSA, have not been able to do? To answer this question, it is important to examine three interrelated fundamental issues in Vietnam's experience: (a) policy formulation, implementation, and coordination and the role of the state in these; (b) global influences and regional dynamism; and (c) how the country fostered productive capacities and structural economic transformation.

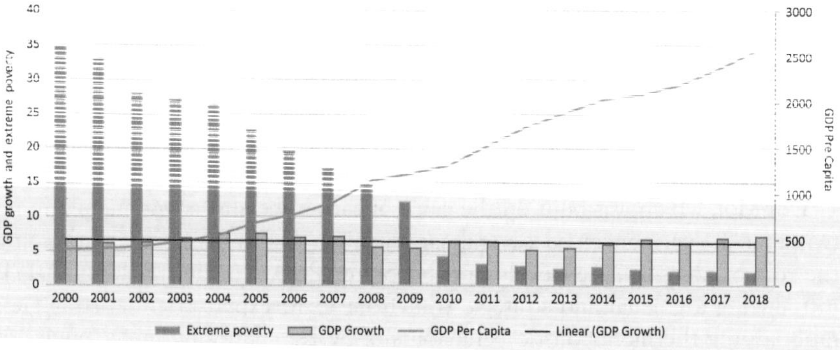

Figure 7.2 Vietnam: annual GDP growth, GDP per capita at current USD, and extreme poverty[4] trends (2000–2018).

Source: World Bank open data source (https://data.worldbank.org/).

7.2.1 Policy Formulation, Implementation, and Coordination in Vietnam

Following the end of colonization and the subsequent wars, Vietnam pursued command or centralized economic planning until the mid-1980s, with a focus on a regional dualistic approach: socialist industrialization in the north and agriculture-led development in the southern part of the country. The priority for the then socialist government was the rehabilitation and reconstruction of the war-ravaged economy, while consolidating central planning and the role of the state in it (Masina: 2006). Consequently, SOEs dominated the early phases of industrialization of Vietnam particularly in the north and in some urban growth poles such as Ho Chi Minh City and Hanoi (Nguyen Thi et al.: 2016). At the same time, socialist agriculture (through cooperatives and collectivization programmes and distribution of land) clearly defined the socialist (public) ownership in the sector, particularly in the southern regions. The dual sector policy approach was based on careful examination and understanding of regional comparative advantages of the country. The socialist system was not successful in modernizing the economy by fostering a competitive and productive industrial sector (Nguyen et al.: 2016). However, it laid the foundation for improved and accelerated social outcomes by ensuring an equal distribution of land, investing in modern infrastructure, and promoting universal access to education and healthcare both in urban and rural areas, although minorities in remote mountainous areas remain isolated or are further marginalized (Masina: 2006). In SSA, during the same period, agriculture was ignored as most economies of the region became extractive sector-driven, conflicts and policy prescription weakened state institutions, and economies continue to be vulnerable to external shocks, notably, the 1970s oil price and the 1980s external debt crises.

"Perestroika" in the USSR and the winds of inevitable change in several former socialist bloc countries, made changes in policy direction inevitable in Vietnam. In 1986, Vietnam's political leadership made two quick and bold decisions, which reshaped the country's subsequent policymaking processes: a transition from a centrally planned (socialist) economic system to gradual and carefully sequenced "socialist-oriented free-market system"; and insertion into the regional economic arrangements (Nguyen Thi et al.: 2016). In December 1986, Vietnam officially launched the country's major economic renewal and renovation programme called "Doi-Moi"[5] – meaning "Renovation" (Malesky et al.: 2011, Nguyen Thi et al.: 2016).

Doi-Moi, which was built on the gains of earlier socialist economic planning (Masina: 2006), conceived several far-reaching sets of measures: reinforcing the role of post-socialist Developmental State (PSDS) model (Bolesta: 2017); introducing a gradual and strategic shift from IS to export-oriented strategies; rationalizing the monopolistic behaviours of SOEs; addressing inefficiencies of the command economy; encouraging the participation of domestic and foreign private sector in the economy and boosting public investments (Nguyen Thi et al.: 2016). These have led to a gradual dismantling of features of the command economy such as price controls, foreign currency rationing, and agricultural cooperatives.

The reform process also included a strong political commitment to address inequality via income redistribution policies and balanced regional growth through state interventions. Further areas of focus of Doi-Moi were on deeper trade liberalization and integration into the global economy. This included membership to the World Trade Organization (WTO) in 2007, regional economic grouping and negotiating bilateral trade arrangements with key export markets. Doi-Moi and the accompanying strategies have been successfully implemented. The successes were the results of better policy formulation and implementation capacities centred on effective institutional coordination. These were further facilitated by timely information flows between institutions – top-down, bottom-up, horizontally, vertically, and diagonally (Nguyen Thi et al.: 2016). Vietnam has also built key semi-state agencies, such as chambers of commerce and industry, business associations, and private sector federations. These were key to coordinating business entities and facilitating state-business relations between SOEs and the emerging private sector. Meanwhile, politically continuing with the socialist tradition, Vietnam maintained a broader coalition and public participation in economic policy formulation and decision-making.

In Vietnam, Doi-Moi has proved successful, with the state and market forces functioning in tandem. Trade liberalization and integration processes have been carefully sequenced and managed. Economic growth has been robust at 6.6 percent even during the Asian financial crisis of 1997–1998, which had a relatively minimal impact on Vietnam (Kokko: 1998). This led to a diminishing of extreme poverty levels over the years with more distributional gains, by virtue of which Vietnam became "less unequal" by developing world standards (Malesky et al.: 2011). Contrary to the case of Vietnam, SSA's liberalization policies failed dismally and the dependence of the region on external aid has increased (Chapter 1), integration into the global economy through market access (preferential trade) and investment facilitation could not improve the share of Africa in global trade (Chapter 5) and SSA's marginalization in global production and trade continued unabated.

In Vietnam, since the launch of Doi-Moi, industrial output has grown by an annual average of 15.2 percent, contributing to 34 percent of the GDP. Manufacturing accounted for 87 percent of the total industrial output in 2016. Likewise, total exports have been increasing by an average of 18.1 percent since the reform (Nguyen Thi et al.: 2016). The bulk of imports into Vietnam consist of capital and intermediate goods such as fuel, steel, and fertilizers as well as semi-finished electronic components. These were deliberately selected, enjoying import-tariff reduction and removal of quotas whereas higher import tariffs and stringent licence requirements were imposed on consumer goods (Kokko: 1998). The World Bank noted that exports in labour-intensive manufacturing, particularly garments, footwear, leather, and leather products played a critical role in enhancing the country's export competitiveness. They grew from about 13 percent in 1992 to 37 percent in 1997 (World Bank: 1999). The Bank also described the performance of Doi-Moi as remarkable, noting a "significant rise in rice export in which Vietnam has transitioned, in a few years, from being a net rice-importer into the world's second largest exporter in 1998 after China". Currently, Vietnam holds fifth and fourth positions in global rice production and exports, respectively. What we have seen in SSA on the other hand, is decreasing agricultural production and productivity, increasing commoditization of trade (Chapters 1 and 4) and declining manufacturing value-added in GDP, high export and market concentration, and servicification of the economy (Chapter 4) all of which are vivid signs of premature deindustrialization (Chapter 4).

Despite the starkly positive performance of Vietnam, there has been (there still is) consistent pressure on the country to embrace orthodoxy. Mainstream traditionalists have been calling on the government to limit the role of the state in economic decision-making. The calls were to embrace the Structural Adjustment Programmes (SAPs) of the 1980s and Poverty Reduction Strategy Papers (PRSPs) of the 1990s – all of which have failed in SSA. There was consensus between Vietnam's policymakers and development partners on poverty reduction being a binding theme and key component of the growth and transformation objectives of the country. However, there was no agreement as to how to view poverty reduction (i.e., as a goal by itself or the source of economic growth). Vietnam's policymakers did not view poverty reduction as an outcome of economic policies. Rather they view it as a "resource" for further growth and development. This was a widely-shared view, particularly in East Asia, that if poverty was reduced, it was not for its own sake but rather to expand domestic demand and market opportunities, which can further generate incentives for the domestic production of goods and services. The creation of a domestic market through poverty-reducing incentives and interventions for local produce was seen as a necessary condition for escaping dependency and succeeding in economic development (Myrdal in Lundberg: 1974, Masina: 2006).

The Government of Vietnam has successfully and radically changed, the socioeconomic conditions of the country for the better. However, advocates of neoliberalism caution that the success achieved by Vietnam through Doi-Moi cannot be sustained without further and deeper reforms. The prevailing orthodoxy, mainly imposed by the IFIs called for sustained structural reforms despite their recognition of the "remarkable achievements" of Doi-Moi. The prescribed reforms are in line with the established mainstream neoliberal tradition.[6]

The failure of the SAPs and PRSPs of the 1980s and 1990s in most of SSA and other developing regions raised questions about the relevance of these programmes. These concerns coupled with the Asian financial crisis of 1996–1997 and the 2008–2009 global financial and economic crisis prompted the search for a new, viable, and sustainable model of economic governance and policymaking. Consequently, the so-called Washington Consensus has come under heavy scrutiny, which further intensified the call for post-Washington Consensus in development discourse (Lin: 2015). These developments may have helped Vietnam to tacitly, and technically, reject the orthodox policy prescriptions. The country persisted with its strategic planning model while gradually embracing "socialist free-market" approaches. This phenomenon, though theoretically sounding contradictory, describes a system where governments and markets complement each other. In refashioning economic policymaking along the state-market divide, Vietnam has created a dichotomy of the state functions. This delineated, however vaguely, the respective roles of the bureaucracy and the political leadership with strong linkages between the two and by building capable institutions. Functionally, the bureaucracy focuses on designing and implementing economic policies with little or no apparent political interference. The political leadership, on the other hand, focuses on building national and political consensus, mediating real or perceived tensions or conflicts, balancing regional distribution (allocation of productive resources), and ensuring effective governance at all levels (Malesky et al.: 2011, Nguyen Thi et al.: 2016). These were lessons drawn from the experiences of "East Asian Miracle" economies. In effect, Vietnam tacitly rejected externally imposed economic policy prescriptions and expanded its "policy space"[7] in formulating and implementing home-grown policies. This was done on the strength of Vietnam-specific circumstances, while at the same time, learning from the successful experiences of other East Asian economies in recalibrating the "post-socialist Developmental State model" (Bolesta: 2015, 2017).

Since the launch of Doi-Moi in 1986, Vietnam has implemented seven five-year plans.[8] Each of these had a set of measurable goals, targets, and objectives. The plans tackled a series of development challenges, achieved sustained economic growth, and created jobs and incomes with substantial transformation in the country's economy. Earlier strategic plans – those implemented during 1985–1990 and 1990–1995 – had several goals and targets. These included ensuring gradual and smooth transition from a fully centralized economic system to a mixed economic system (*socialist free market*), fostering institutional and human resource capacities for policymaking and implementation, ensuring income distribution and balanced regional development, kick-starting industrialization with a focus on agri-processing and labour-intensive manufacturing, effectively harnessing natural resources for socioeconomic development, diversifying the economy, and gradually reducing the dependence on subsistence agriculture. In all these, the state assumed a central role. In the implementation of the plans, efforts have also been made to generate and meet domestic demand for local produce, and enhance the contribution of the service sector in socioeconomic development of the country (Nguyen Thi et al.: 2016). The service sectors which were given particular emphasis were construction services (buildings and transport infrastructure), telecommunications, tourism, consultancy services, banking and finance, audit, and insurance services.

Immediately after the launch of Doi-Moi, the Government of Vietnam introduced successive deliberate policies to further promote agricultural production and agri-processing. These include (see Chapter 8) increased sugarcane plantations for sugar production, enhancing the production of coffee, rice, forestry, livestock, and fishery, etc., which have greatly contributed to the growth and expansion of the rural economy of Vietnam. The second wave of five-year strategic plans covering (1995–2000, 2000–2005, 2005–2010, and 2010–2015), consolidated the gains of the previous decade in parallel with mobilizing private investment, facilitating Foreign Direct Investment (FDI) flows into the manufacturing sector and knowledge-intensive services (Nguyen Thi et al.: 2016). This phase of the planning also saw the establishment of Export Processing Zones (EPZs), Industrial Zones (IZs), and Industrial Parks (IPs), which laid the foundation for Vietnam's industrialization and structural economic transformation. These also marked a significant change in policy approaches in Vietnam with an expanded role for SME-focused private sector. The 2015–2020 strategic plan focuses on further deepening of structural transformation drive of the government with a focus on carefully selected industries where Vietnam has comparative and competitive advantages (such as agri-processing, paper, textiles, leather and footwear, electronics, chemicals, mechanical engineering, ICT, steel, gasoline as well as careful and sustainable exploitation of natural resources (Ministry of Planning and Investment, 27 December 2018). Concrete outcomes of the various planning phases and their contributions to foster productive capacities and structural transformation are discussed in more detail in Section 7.3 of this chapter.

7.2.2 Harnessing Global and Regional Dynamism: Impact on Domestic Policymaking of Vietnam

Despite contentious debates about the pros and cons of the globalization process, there is substantial evidence that the process has created opportunities for many, but risks and pitfalls for many others. The globalization process (largely driven by the advances in ICT, and open trade and investment boundaries) has created unprecedented wealth and prosperity for many nations and peoples. However, it has also accentuated marginalization, exclusion, and economic deprivation for many others (Nayyar: 2006). This is the case in weaker, vulnerable economies, isolated and remote regions, rural communities, and disadvantaged urban centres. This calls for the continued efforts of policymakers and stakeholders to put in place the right mix of policies and strategies aimed at maximizing the opportunities of globalization while minimizing its adverse consequences.

In Vietnam, prior to Doi-Moi, the country's political relations had been limited mostly to the socialist bloc. The pre-1986 economic policymaking of the country was also within the socialist model and guiding principles characterized by public ownership of the means of production. The actors and stakeholders in the domestic economic policymaking processes of Vietnam expanded immediately after Doi-Moi. The influence of Washington-based institutions, donors, civil society actors, and regional economic groupings have increasingly become important in the country's policymaking processes. The mechanisms or means of exerting external influence on the domestic policymaking were diverse. In most cases, these have been through an expanded role of international agencies in domestic policymaking, policy prescription, conditional funding (financial support), and through direct influence on priority-setting processes. With the opening-up of the political and policymaking space, "internationalization" of domestic policymaking has become inevitable. However, this has led to tensions and controversies within Vietnam itself and with its pro-free market development partners and ideologues. Within Vietnam, the immediate and unavoidable tension was between the vanguard of an earlier (old) socialist system (including its institutions and mindset) on the one hand, and the fear of the new (unknown) capitalist-oriented market principles on the other hand (Masina: 2006). For instance, the political leadership wanted to balance the speed and depth of the reform (Doi-Moi) without compromising national sovereignty and independent policymaking. Dismantling State Owned Enterprises (SOEs) and enhancing the role of the private sector in the economy have been pushed by the ardent advocates of free competition but this was viewed as politically costly by the Government of Vietnam (Nguyen Thi et al.: 2016). The 2003 joint report of the World Bank and the International Finance Corporation (IFC), recognized the progress made in Vietnam in "levelling the playing field". However, it has warned that there are still systemic biases in the business environment against the private sector. The report also argued that these can be eliminated only through deeper reform of the state sector and by improved access to capital and land for the private firms (World Bank and IFC: 2003). The report further argued that the reform "should include measures to corporatize SOEs, diversify ownership (including domestic and foreign private sectors) and manage State assets efficiently" (World Bank and IFC: 2003).

There have also been growing tensions between the reformers and the socialist establishment concerning potential reform-induced inequalities, particularly between the urban and rural areas. This included the fear that the reform might lead to a further marginalization of citizens in remote and inaccessible areas, although Vietnam has been successful in reducing social inequality quicker than many developing countries (Malesky et al.: 2011). Further tensions in policy and economic decision-making in Vietnam were also observed between the growing influence of international consultancy (largely from the IFIs who view themselves as modernizers), and Vietnam's scholars and think tanks who saw themselves as custodians of the local knowledge, culture, and mindset which play a key role in influencing policymaking processes. While the former group dominated the policymaking environment by advocating faster, deeper, and extensive reforms, the latter groups (though positively impressed by the results of the reform process) were uncertain about the sustainability of achievements and implications of the reform for social wellbeing (Malesky et al.: 2011). The top political leadership of Vietnam and the policymaking environment were trapped in between the neoliberal orthodoxy and the gradual post-socialist Developmental State vision (Bolesta: 2017).

However, the Government of Vietnam tacitly and carefully navigated the tides. It systematically resisted the imposition of the neoliberal doctrine on domestic policymaking during the actual negotiations, though this was not evident in open policy declarations. Judging from the slow pace and persistence in policy reforms pursued by the government, with the state playing a central role, Vietnamese decision-makers stood firm against policy prescription from outside. The role of the state in Vietnam was not limited to guiding policy interventions, but it included measures, such as controlling the country's financial institutions, mobilizing savings, directing subsidies and credits to economic activities that would accelerate economic growth and transformation, gradually privatizing SOEs, and selectively liberalizing international trade, etc. (Masina: 2006). These measures and gradual approaches to market-based reforms were in stark contrast to the pervasive discourse established by mainstream (neoliberal) traditions, IFIs, and their advocates. In SSA, as discussed earlier, policy prescription from outside has effectively replaced the role of national governments and the internationalization of SSA's policymaking environment has become evident with the World Bank and the IMF becoming de facto ministries of finance in Africa.

Interestingly, by rejecting the orthodox dogma and learning from the experiences of other East Asian economies, Vietnam has established national development banks and capital markets to trade bonds and equities. The government's credit allocation has been behind "the extraordinary industrial development of Vietnam rather than commercial lending or external borrowing" (Nguyen Thi et al.: 2016). Moreover, the country's sustained and robust economic growth discussed earlier, has led to an increase in aggregate savings, household (disposable) income and significant poverty reduction, improved living conditions as well as other extraordinary social outcomes notably in health and education.

Another fascinating aspect of Vietnam's policymaking process was the conscious selectivity of global policies and institutions and adapting them to local needs and conditions as appropriate for the country's transformational growth. For example, while the government had technically and tacitly rejected the free market mantra pushed by the Washington Consensus, the country went through cumbersome accession negotiations to join the WTO in 2007, joining the multilateral trade body six years after China's membership.

At one level, this is remarkable for a country that follows a dirigiste Developmental State model to have joined the WTO – the organization that drives the global free-trade agenda. At another level, it shows that the political decision-making process of Vietnam has been pragmatic and selective in strategically and gradually integrating the country into the global economy and multilateral trading system. Multilateral trade rules governed by the WTO are complex, in terms of content, sectoral coverage, policy implications and decision-making processes within the organization itself (Hoekman and Kostecki: 1995). The rule and key decision-making processes in WTO are driven by major economic and trading powers, which sometimes impose the rules on others but ignore them when it suits them. As Nayyar (2006) argues, "major trading countries resort to unilateral exercise of power, ignoring the rules because small countries do not have the economic strength even if they have the legal right to retaliate". Vietnam joined the WTO fully cognizant of the limitations to policy space that full membership in WTO implies. WTO membership involves commitments and obligations to fully liberalize trade, reduce all sorts of protections, remove inefficiencies and distortions in international trade as well as accept national treatment clauses.[9] All these commitments and tough conditions which Vietnam agreed to as a full member of WTO were thought to have wider implications and detrimental impacts on Vietnam's transformational growth.

In parallel with joining the WTO, Vietnam had also negotiated and consolidated bilateral trade relations and agreements with key players such as the USA, concluded in 2000, and Japan, in 2008. The most significant one of these was the US-Vietnam Trade Agreement (US Chamber of Commerce: 2019), which was seen as the basis for the normalization of economic and diplomatic relations between the two nations.

The signing of the US-Vietnam agreement has eased the challenges Vietnam would have faced in negotiating the terms and conditions in its accession to WTO. This is because Vietnam in its agreement with the USA had introduced trade policies that are compatible or consistent with WTO rules and regulations. The USA would facilitate (at least, not hinder) Vietnam's entry into the WTO as it had already signed bilateral trade deals with Vietnam before its accession to the WTO in 2007. After more than two decades, the results of the bilateral agreement with the USA have been remarkable with trade in goods between the two countries reaching USD 59 billion in 2018 from just USD 1.5 billion in 2000. In effect, the USA has become the third largest trading partner of Vietnam (in value), and the first export destination (US Chamber of Commerce: 2019). According to UNCTAD's statistics, while the USA accounts for 19.9 percent of Vietnam's exports, Vietnam's imports from the USA were only 4.4 percent in 2018. As Vietnam runs a trade surplus with the USA in the range of USD 36–40 billion, there was growing concern that President Trump's "Make America Great Again" slogan may stall the negotiations foreseen for 2018–2019. However, this was tacitly pushed forward, and it is expected to be concluded by President Biden's administration. Overall, Vietnam's achievements are in sharp contrast to the fears and concerns prevalent prior to the signing of the agreement in 2000 that it may not have sufficient "policy space" to manoeuvre, given the imbalance in economic and negotiating powers between the two countries.

Vietnam has also strategically tapped into trade and business opportunities with Japan, thanks to the bilateral trade agreement signed in 2008, immediately after the country's accession to the WTO. Japan remains the largest source of Official Development Assistance (ODA) flows to Vietnam with a cumulative amount of USD 56 billion over the last 20 years, accounting for 80 percent of ODA flows to Vietnam. In subsequent years, Japanese average annual ODA flows to Vietnam (largely in the form of loans) amounted to USD 1.5 billion, largely devoted to the infrastructure sector and technical assistance. Japan is also the second largest foreign investor and the fourth largest trading partner of Vietnam (Dezan Shira & Associates: 2020). Data from World Integrated Trade Solutions (WITS) shows that bilateral trade between the two countries doubled between 2008 and 2017, reaching USD 33.5 billion in 2017 from about USD 17 billion in 2008, with Vietnam registering a trade surplus of about USD 250 million in 2017.

The renovation launched in 1986 (Doi-Moi) has also greatly contributed to opening up and consolidating Vietnam's relations with the Association of Southeast Asian Nations (ASEAN). This was a major policy shift in Vietnam's political leadership as Vietnam had consistently criticized ASEAN, historically viewing it as anti-Vietnam and pro-USA (Amer: 2015). The earlier mutual mistrust and tensions between the vibrant economic bloc (ASEAN) and Vietnam was further intensified during the country's military conflict with Cambodia in 1978. The bloc strongly opposed the presence of Vietnam in one of its member countries, Cambodia (Masina: 2006). However, Vietnam quickly realized the importance of regional political and diplomatic support it desperately needed against Cambodia. In essence, the conflict with Cambodia had the opposite effect and strengthened or reinforced Vietnam's interest in engaging more with ASEAN (Amer: 2015).

Gradually, with the deepening of the domestic reform processes, and after the formal settlement of the Cambodian war in 1991, Vietnam formally normalized its relations with ASEAN and joined the bloc in 1995 (Amer: 2015). Vietnam has expanded its trade and productive integration with ASEAN. The trade of Vietnam with the bloc grew from less than USD 2 billion in 1995 to USD 19 billion in 2014 (Thanh: 2017). The strategic move and integration of Vietnam into the global economy by negotiating bilateral, regional, and multilateral trade agreements was forward-looking. Vietnam has strategically and selectively integrated itself into the global trading system (WTO) which expanded its trade and economic ties with key global players (not only with the USA and Japan but also with the EU, South Korea, Taiwan, and Singapore as well as ASEAN). In all its engagements, Vietnam has maintained its policy space and pursued gradual and sequenced market-based policy and institutional reforms. Furthermore, the political leadership of Vietnam technically and tacitly resisted (or minimized) the influence and domination of its policymaking processes by the Washington-based institutions including IFIs. Such a strategic and "smart" move was the result of the conviction, pragmatism, and determination of its policymakers to use trade as an engine of growth and development, while maintaining or safeguarding its policy space.

There was another area of contention or controversy between the advocates of the Washington Consensus and Vietnam's leadership during the early phases of the reform process. This relates to the opening-up of political and economic space to international and national civil society and Non-Governmental Organizations (NGOs). Once again, pragmatism prevailed in Vietnam's decision whether to allow international and national civil society and NGOs to operate in the country. Indeed, Vietnam opened and expanded a space for such entities. Consequently, the number of international and domestic NGOs grew from 114 in 1991 to 500 in 2010 (Tran: 2018). By 2018, Vietnam had links and relationships with over 1,200 international NGOs, 500 of which had operations on the ground with a total budget of USD 1.47 billion for the 2014–2018 period (Vietnam Times: 2019).

International, or foreign NGOs are confined to activities that focus on the delivery of technical or specialized services, particularly in humanitarian or disaster-related emergencies. Key areas defined for the engagement of civil society entities and NGOs are limited to poverty reduction, humanitarian relief, and professional development (CIVICUS et al.: 2006). This carefully and deliberately established that division of labour is in sync with the government's longstanding view that NGOs and civil society entities should focus on "social rights" as opposed to "human rights", with a focus on grassroots, communities, and disadvantaged groups. This has effectively banned the involvement of non-state actors in advocacy for political rights, press freedoms, rule of law, and the fight against corruption (CIVICUS: 2006, Tran: 2018). International NGOs are also obliged by law to forge strong ties and networks with local NGOs and Civil Society Organizations (CSOs), particularly Vietnam's Mass Organizations of the socialist era, which have more influence on national policies than other types of CSOs (CIVICUS et al.: 2006, Tran: 2018). Foreign and local NGOs are also tamed to build collaborative, non-adversarial, or non-critical relationships with government and public institutions (Tran: 2018). In fact, "international NGOs are not entirely autonomous from State machinery but rather they are intertwined, with foreign NGOs having been run by (100 percent) Vietnam's staff" (Tran: 2018).

Unlike conflictual relationships in SSA (see Chapter 9), the relationship between the Government of Vietnam and NGOs provides a unique insight and perspective as to how to best balance political space and economic decision-making, without upsetting mutual interests and collaborative relationships. Although there is no critical evaluation of the role of the local and foreign NGOs in Vietnam's economic growth and development, there is an overall positive assessment that they have been important in providing critical services and conveying the needs and priorities of the local population to the government, particularly in rural and in accessible areas. A clear demarcation or division of tasks and roles between the government, NGOs, and CSOs (particularly Mass Organizations) has played an important role. It enhanced the participation and membership of citizens in non-state actors in socioeconomic development, notably at community or local levels. Popular participation in national and international NGOs and CSOs is substantial – nearly 75 percent of the adult population belongs to at least one entity (predominantly Mass Organizations), and more than 60 percent participates in more than one entity (Taylor et al.: 2012). Why do such partnerships lead to astounding success in Vietnam while SSA's historical and contemporary ties with traditional donors and China have miserably failed? The answer to this and related questions lies in the synergetic outcome of policymaking, sequencing priorities, realigning interventions, and diversifying and recalibrating domestic growth sources.

7.2.3 *Policymaking in Vietnam: Implications for Productive Transformation*

Unlike the countries of SSA, Vietnam has fully tapped bilateral, regional, and global opportunities through selective and cautious integration, while maintaining its domestic policy space. The country has carefully balanced its post-socialist Developmental State vision with that of the neoliberal tradition, rejecting, when necessary, the imposition of policy prescriptions from outside. Vietnam's political leaders have also unlocked some of the binding constraints to the country's development. They carefully managed the transition from a socialist economy to a mixed economic system based on strategic planning, without upsetting the social, cultural, and institutional balance. Vietnam has continued with its pro-poor and egalitarian social policies inherited from the socialist system (Molesky et al.: 2011). It achieved universal education and expanded access to basic health services for citizens in the early phases of the reform. It facilitated access to productive assets such as land and capital to the poor – a measure which forms the foundation for building productive assets of the population. Above all, pragmatic and forward-looking policies helped Vietnam to succeed in transformational development. Such policies also facilitated the country's beneficial integration into the regional economic and political blocs, forge comprehensive bilateral trade agreements and join the multilateral trading system (WTO).

Successive strategic plans have effectively replaced socialist planning. These strategic plans were conceived as part of the overall vision of renovation (Doi-Moi) and have substantially altered the socioeconomic landscape of Vietnam. The country achieved accelerated, sustained, and inclusive economic growth together with continued industrialization and export diversification. By 2010, when the sixth five-year strategic plan was completed, the share of agriculture in the economy of the country has gone down to 15 percent from about 80 percent in the pre-reform period, while industry and services accounted for 44 percent and 41 percent, respectively (Nguyen Thi et al.: 2016). Currently, agriculture contributes only 14 percent to the GDP and 37 percent to employment. The annual average growth of the industrial output and total exports remained robust at 15.2 percent and 18.1 percent, respectively, during the post-1986 period. Within industry, the manufacturing sector accounted for a whopping 87 percent of total industrial output in 2018, a huge leap when compared to less than 20 percent early in the reform process. This shows fundamental and long-term, or the right type of structural transformation as opposed to SSA's wrong type of transformation (see Chapter 8).

Similarly, the relative share of the state in Vietnam's aggregate investment and GDP, went down to 42 percent in 1995 while that of non-state domestic actors and FDI firms has continued to rise. This was against total public ownership prior to the 1986 reform (Trinh et al.: 2019). This share further shrunk to 33 percent in 2018, while the combined share of the domestic non-state actors[10] and FDI firms progressively increased to nearly 67 percent in 2018. Of the 67 percent, the share of non-state actors was 42.3 percent, whereas that of FDI firms was 23.4 percent in the same year (Trinh et al.: 2019). In terms of GDP contribution, the state sector accounted for only 28.63 percent in 2017, while the non-state sector contributed 41.7 percent and that of the FDI firms 19.63 percent in 2017 (Trinh et al.: 2019). In absolute values, in 2019, the FDI stock (in about 31 mega-projects) reached the total registered capital of USD 363 billion – accumulated realized capital being estimated at about USD 212 billion – accounting for 58.4 percent of total registered capital (Ministry of Planning and Investment, 15 August 2020). The savings to GDP ratio had jumped from less than 10 percent in the 1980s to less than 15 percent in 1990 and to 36 percent in 2004 (Nguyen Thi et al.: 2016), before declining to 26 percent in 2018. The recent declining proportion was due to a more proportionate (faster) increase in GDP than to declining savings levels. In terms of employment, the share of agriculture declined from 73 percent in 1980 to about 46 percent in 2010 (Nguyen Thi et al.: 2016). According to the latest ILO-modelled data available on the World Bank Development Indicators Database and Trading Economics, the employment share of agriculture further declined to 37 percent in 2019 (WBDI: 2020b; TradingEconomics: 2020). These are clear signs of the solid productive capacities and profound (right type) structural economic transformation of Vietnam discussed in detail in Chapter 8.

In sum, the outcomes of policies and strategies pursued by Vietnam over the last 35 years are simply remarkable and unprecedented in the recent history of economic development. Most of the policies and measures which the country has been undertaking are similar or identical to those pursued by many developing countries, including SSA. What distinguishes Vietnam particularly from countries of SSA, is its pragmatism, determination in implementing policies, and farsightedness in sequencing priorities, identifying binding constraints, and realigning interventions and incentive structures, as well as the coordinated implementation of its strategic plans. While the content and articulation of policies are rather similar across the developing world (nearly all of which embraced the Washington Consensus), Vietnam can offer unique insights into policy implementation and coordination. As can be seen from Figure 7.3, the poverty-reducing impact of economic growth in Vietnam has been robust, faster, deeper, and sustained.

The GDP per capita of Vietnam was lower than the average for SSA in 2000 (Figure 7.3(a)) and, by far, lower than that of Angola and Nigeria. During the same year, the percentage of population living on less than USD 1.90 a day was higher than in Angola and slightly lower than in Ethiopia (Figure 7.3(b)). Throughout the 2000–2018 period, Angola maintained a much higher GDP per capita than Vietnam. Nigeria did the same until 2016 and likewise the average for SSA until 2013. Only Burkina Faso, Ethiopia, and Rwanda had GDP per capita levels lower than that of Vietnam during the same period. Except for Angola, most countries of SSA have managed to reduce the percentage of their population living in extreme poverty, albeit in varying degrees. Angola's case shows the mismatch between growth rates in GDP per capita and the poverty reduction. The World Bank, which has been crediting the precipitously declining rate of extreme poverty in SSA for its decades of policy prescriptions, has recently acknowledged that the absolute number of poor people in the region has rather been constantly rising (World Bank: 2016a). The World Bank's newly issued report entitled *Poverty in a Rising Africa* described the phenomenon of continuously increasing number of people in extreme poverty in SSA as "sobering".

The gap in GDP per capita growth between selected countries of SSA and Vietnam on the one hand and the variation in poverty impact of growth on the other is startling. In the case of Vietnam there is robust poverty-reducing impact of growth. Such a phenomenon is in sharp contrast with the paradoxical

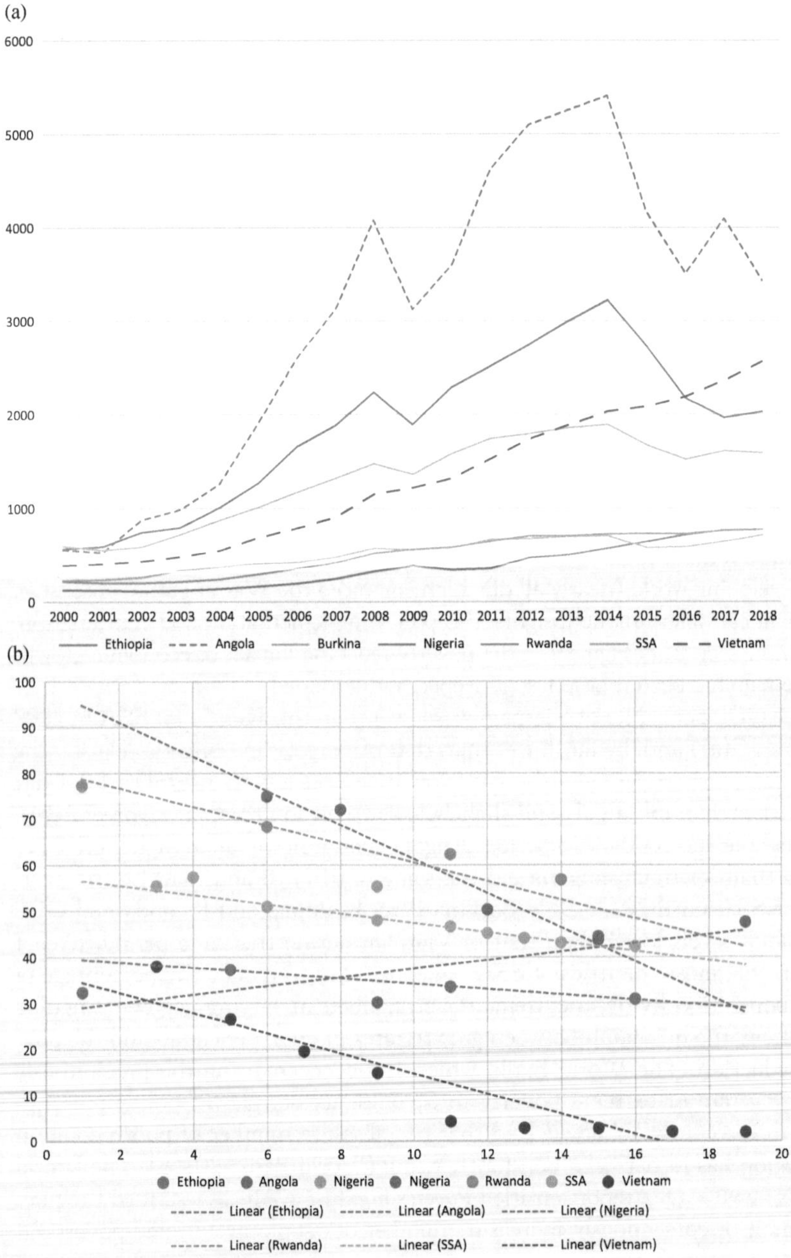

Figure 7.3 Economic growth and poverty reduction in Vietnam and selected countries of SSA. (a) GDP per capita at current USD (2000–2018); (b) percentage of population living on less than USD1.90/day (2000–2020).

Source: World Bank (2020).

relationships between growth and poverty reduction seen in SSA. A more worrying trend is the inverse relationship between the high growth of per capita income and poverty reduction in Angola and many other extractive resource-driven economies of SSA. Such a relationship casts a shadow on the importance of high (quantity) economic growth in poverty reduction and emphasises the need to pay due attention to the form and sources of quality growth. The extractive sector-driven growth model, which is the main feature of SSA's growth story, is capital-intensive and has little or no impact on job creation, income distribution, and poverty reduction. Such a phenomenon particularly indicates missed opportunities to capture natural resource wealth (natural capital) in fostering productive capacities and structural economic transformation for sustained and inclusive growth and sustainable development in SSA.

It also shows a wastage and misuse of rents from natural resources, which undermines state-building and capital accumulation, fuels corruption, cronyism and kleptocracy, and leads to violent conflicts and political instability – which, combined, can lead to a "natural resource trap" (Collier: 2007). Angola has registered impressive GDP per capita growth since 2000, from about less than USD 800 to USD 5,400 in 2014 (the highest in recent years) before it declined to less than USD 3,800 in 2018, which is still higher than the level in Vietnam (Figure 7.3(a)). However, during the same period not only was the absolute number of poor people been on the rise in Angola, but also was the share of people living in extreme poverty. The percentage of population in extreme poverty in Angola consistently increased from about 30 percent in 2000s to 47.6 percent in 2018, whereas that of Vietnam dramatically declined from about 30 percent in 2000 to a mere 1.9 percent in 2018, despite a relatively lower growth in GDP per capita in the latter (Figure 7.3(b))

The key factor which delineates socioeconomic transformation in Vietnam and SSA is the variation in overall productive capacities which expanded the sources and the quality of economic growth in Vietnam. In the early 2000s, the gap between Vietnam and the countries of SSA in productive capacities was not significant. However, afterwards Vietnam distanced itself significantly in fostering economy-wide productive capacities (Figure 7.4). The key policy implication of this is that higher economic growth alone, though necessary, is not in itself a sufficient condition for sustained and substantial poverty reduction. Achieving higher economic growth should be viewed neither as an exclusive target of policies nor as an end. Instead, policies and strategies should focus on diversifying sources of growth, maximizing drivers of growth and meticulously addressing the distributional aspects of growth. As discussed in Chapter 8, Vietnam's success lies in broadening the sources of economic growth, identifying sectors of comparative and competitive advantages (with multiplier effects), and harnessing natural capital and rents from extractive resources to accelerate capital accumulation. Vietnam also used such rents to provide targeted incentives (including state subsidies) to mobilize the domestic and foreign investments that are crucial in fostering productive capacities and kick-starting the process of structural economic transformation.

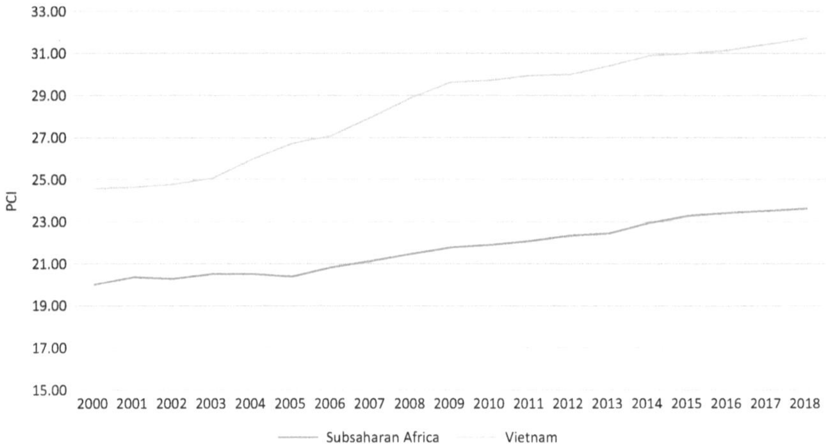

Figure 7.4 Evolution of productive capacities in Vietnam and SSA (average) (2000–2018).
Sources: UNCTAD Global Productive Capacities Index (PCI).

Why is high economic growth having little or no impact on poverty reduction in SSA whereas the reverse is the case in Asian countries such as Vietnam? There are four main plausible reasons to reckon with. First of all, distributive policies matter. Vietnam's elite political institutions such as the Central Committee (CCOM) of the Communist Party of Vietnam (CPV), Council of Ministers and State Council, and the bureaucracy were empowered with wider room for economic decision-making and distributive policies (Molesky et al.: 2011). There has been a strong commitment of the political leadership to income distribution policies by rationalizing government expenditures on public goods such as infrastructure, education, and health as well as to deliberate state intervention in reducing development gaps between regions and communities (Masina: 2006). Growth-friendly decision-making such as the allocation of increased budgets for poor communities and rural areas, targeting private investments in such jurisdictions, and directly financing large-scale projects in marginalized areas (with multiplier effects on jobs and incomes) have played key roles in maximizing the impacts of Vietnam's economic growth on poverty reduction. Growth-facilitating policies of the government also include a strong commitment to reduce inequality and create opportunity through tax or fund transfer equalization, which also have played an important role in making growth inclusive, poverty-reducing, and development-facilitating. In all these processes, economic growth played a paramount role in financing welfare and the country's capital formation needs, particularly by funnelling rents from natural resources to infrastructural, institutional, and socioeconomic development. The reform process in Vietnam (Doi-Moi) was built on the socialist model of the 1960s, 1970s, and 1980s. It is deliberately designed to ensure universal access to education, health, and productive assets (such as land tenure in the rural areas). Consequently, the reform has contributed to a sustained and robust economic growth with significant poverty reduction in the country (Molesky et al.: 2011).

Second, the sources of growth matter more than the quantity of growth. Whereas growth in SSA has been largely driven by a few single sectors (such as extractive sectors), the sources of growth in Vietnam are widespread with consistently improving capital accumulation, economy-wide productive capacities, and transformation within and across sectors of growth. Forward and backward linkages between the agricultural, industrial, and services sectors, expanding knowledge-intensive services (such as ICT, banking, and financial services) and supportive export diversification strategies have played a pivotal role in transforming Vietnam. The country has quickly changed from one of the poorest countries in the developing world to one of the few vibrant economies in a relatively short period. For instance, the 1991–1995 strategic planning successfully fostered agri-processing industries (such as the sugar industry), side by side with transformation-supporting agriculture (commercial and food), forestry and fishery (see Chapter 8). These were carefully identified and targeted sectors that accelerated growth and transformation, particularly in rural areas of Vietnam (Nguyen Thi et al.: 2016).

Third, the quality of growth also matters. The commodity or extractive sector-driven economy in SSA has commonly resulted in "jobless growth" or "enclave-based" growth – a phenomenon characterized by high economic growth in one sector and weak job creation, which can partly be explained by structural factors (Martus: 2016). Extractive-driven or enclave-based growth also causes authoritarianism and corruption, and, in some cases, fuels protracted civil wars (see Chapter 6). It entails the wrong and misleading type of transformation. Contrary to SSA, in Vietnam the production of steel, coal, zinc, and oil has complemented or boosted industrialization (heavy and light industries). The discovery and exploitation of natural resources in the early phase of the reform has improved aggregate income and enhanced local demand. The increase in aggregate demand, in turn, accelerated the development of agriculture, forestry, and fishery as well as agri-processing. Resource rents also facilitated the continued growth and expansion of the infrastructure and service sectors such as education and health, including in rural areas (Nguyen Thi et al.: 2016). Consequently, over time, the employment share of agriculture has continued to decline from 73 percent in 1980 to less than 37 percent in 2018. The respective employment shares of the industrial (manufacturing) and service sectors were 20 percent and 43 percent, respectively (Statista: 2019). As discussed earlier, four out of five jobs created in rural areas were off-farm jobs. The contribution of agriculture to the national output has also gone down from 80 percent in the 1980s to less than 14 percent currently.

Finally, coherent, and consistent trade, industrial, and other sectoral policies played a critically important role in ensuring the sustainability of growth through transformational development. The industrial, infrastructural, investment, and other micro- and macroeconomic policies have boosted production and productivity, especially in manufactured goods. Likewise, the country's trade policies have been "international market-seeking" for exports. Vietnam has pursued such export-led strategies in parallel with a carefully targeted and managed IS strategy. The country's open trade policies combined with investment-friendly strategies made Vietnam attractive for FDI. These policies have been free from external influences and prescriptions, which would have otherwise limited the space for governments and domestic stakeholders to formulate and implement nationally owned and home-grown strategies. Through the post-socialist Developmental State model pursued by Vietnam, the country has made consistent efforts to expand its policy independence. The lower the dependency on foreign policy prescriptions (which was the case with Vietnam), the more the economic resilience or the weaker the transformational shocks (Masina: 2006, Bolesta: 2017).

7.3 Economic Growth, Productive Capacities, and Structural Transformation in Vietnam

Whereas growth in SSA remains enclave-based, Vietnam's growth has been economy-wide (driven by diverse sectors and different growth poles). This has led to accelerated and complex transitions through the right type of transformation in less than four decades (since 1986). The transformation observed in Vietnam has included multiple transitions in policymaking and socioeconomic perspectives: (i) from a centrally planned (command) and state-led economy to an export- and private capital (investment)-led economy; (ii) from an impoverished rural, subsistence agriculture-led economy to a vibrant urban growth pole-driven economy; (iii) from a net rice-importing and food-insecure economy to currently being the fifth largest producer and the fourth exporter of rice in the world; (iv) from an extractive sector (agriculture and mining)-driven economy to one driven by manufacturing and service sectors; and (v) from a primitive industrial base to the foundations that will enable the country to embrace the Fourth Industrial Revolution (Industry 4.0). These transitions and transformation occurred in Vietnam's economy in parallel with one another, vertically, horizontally, simultaneously, or in some cases sequentially. Vietnam's multiple transitions from a centrally planned to a hybrid economic system have led to consistent economic growth. These successes are due to a combination of several factors: determined efforts to strategically harness the country's comparative advantages, ability to identify key binding constraints on development, and realigning interventions in a development-driven post-socialist state model. The post-socialist Developmental State of Vietnam can be described as pragmatic and forward-looking. It has clearly demonstrated its ability to generate and sustain economic growth, build key institutions and vital infrastructure and sequence reforms and interventions through strategic planning that has favoured industrialization and transformation. These include the provision of transport infrastructure, ICT connectivity, and building overall institutional capabilities as key enablers of fostering productive capacities and structural economic transformation.

In short, not only has Vietnam successfully transitioned from a centralized economic system to a mixed economic policy model, but it has also altered the economy's ownership structure. The share of non-state and FDI in Vietnam's aggregate investment ownership increased from nil (or negative) in the 1970s and early 1980s to 65.7 percent in 2017 (see above), whereas the share of the state sector dropped from 100 to 34 percent during the same period. In international trade, the share of FDI-generated exports increased from 27 percent in 1995 to 47.02 percent in 2000 and reached a whopping 72.5 percent in 2017 (Trinh et al.: 2019). According to data from the country's Foreign Investment Agency of the Ministry of Planning and Investment (MPI), Vietnam continues to be an important destination for FDI in the region with annual FDI flows reaching USD 38.2 billion (about 14 percent of GDP) in 2019 – a 7.2 percent increase over 2018 levels. The agency also reported that in 2018, Japan was Vietnam's top FDI source (USD 8.5 billion), followed by South Korea (USD 7.9 billion), and Hong Kong (USD 7.8 billion). However, in terms of FDI stock, South Korea is the leading investor with a total FDI value of USD 62.5 billion, followed by Japan (USD 57 billion) (MPI: 2018, Dezan Shira & Associates: 2019). At the sectoral level, manufacturing and processing continue to lead investment, accounting for a total of 65 percent of registered investment capital (MPI: 2018). What is more interesting is the increasing role of Vietnam's domestic firms, which invested USD 183 million in 69 projects in 2018 alone (MPI: 2018). The average combined overall output from non-state actors (households, foreign, and domestic firms) reached 61 percent in 2017 (Trinh et al.: 2019), with large state ownership being confined to mining, electricity, gas, steam, and air-conditioning distribution (Nguyen Thi et al.: 2016). In 2019, FDI was the source of 70 percent of the country's export revenue, with manufacturing (and processing) sectors accounting for more than 85 percent of the total industrial output, 40 percent of the country's GDP and 40 percent of the labour force in 2018 (World Bank: 2018b).

Vietnam's abundant, well-trained, and relatively cheap labour, smooth transportation services, proximity to larger regional markets and FDI-friendly policies made the country mainly attract efficiency-seeking or export-oriented FDI. Key factors that made Vietnam an important destination for FDI include a continued improvement in the overall investment environment such as political stability, favourable taxation terms, and Free Trade Areas (Busch: 2017). A rapidly growing middle class, urbanization and expanding markets, trained labour force, and cost competitiveness have also played vital role. The cost of labour in Vietnam is estimated to be 46 percent of that in China and 57 percent of that in Thailand (Dezan Shira & Associates: 2019). Deep structural economic transformation in Vietnam is also associated with the country's continued and expanded urbanization trends. As discussed in the report of the World Economic Forum (2015), the urban population of Vietnam grew from 13 million in 1986 to 23 million in 2005, and 36 million in 2019 (Statista: 2019). Cities have become strong growth poles, with urban areas growing twice as fast as the national average economic growth, "through positive agglomeration effects such as larger and efficient labour markets, lower transaction costs, easier and faster knowledge spill-over effects and effective markets and distribution services" (World Economic Forum: 2015). The shift from a rural or agriculture-driven economy to dynamic urban centre-driven economic growth has greatly assisted Vietnam in consolidating its manufacturing and processing sector-driven economy. Urbanization has also led to an increased domestic demand not only for agricultural produce but also manufactured goods and a variety of services. As Vietnam grows wealthier and income per capita increases, the "consumer class", which spends USD 5.50 or more per person per day, is rapidly expanding from about 49 percent in 2010 to over 70 percent in 2016 (World Bank: 2019). "Approximately 89 percent of urban dwellers belong to the consumer class, compared to around 66 percent of the rural population" (World Bank: 2019d). As has been the case in several East Asian economies, the growth in domestic demand has been critically important in sustaining growth and transformation in Vietnam as the country strategically moves to integrate itself into the regional and global economy as well as the global production networks and supply chains.

Unlike countries of SSA, post-1986 Vietnam has successfully fostered productive capacities by harnessing the productive resources, entrepreneurial capabilities, and production linkages (forward and backward sectoral linkages, business linkages between foreign and domestic firms, and among conglomerates and SMEs). These can be seen from the country's policy efforts and results in recalibrating the role of natural and human capital formation, harnessing the role of ICT, using electricity to enhance production and productivity. ICT and energy have also been key in kick-starting and deepening structural changes in exports, expanding growth-facilitating infrastructure (soft and hard), fostering institutional capacities, and promoting the growth and development of the private sector. Each of these categories – in isolation or in combination – provides a "productive capacity-facilitating framework". The next chapter provides further insights into how Vietnam fostered economy-wide productive capacities and fostered the right type of structural economic transformation by harnessing the potential in the agriculture sector in the early phase of the reform process. The key policy lesson for SSA is that without fostering requisite productive capacities no nation ever grew and developed, and hence the countries of SSA should prioritize capital accumulation and the fostering of economy-wide productive capacities as a foundation for structural transformation, inclusive growth, and sustainable development.

Notes

1 Poverty data is not available for all countries and regions for all the years. Moreover, because of revisions in PPP exchange rates, poverty rates for individual countries cannot be compared with poverty rates reported in earlier editions. Nevertheless, the World Bank open data provides discrete (country-specific) time series data on poverty headcount ratio at USD 1.90 a day which is the percentage of the population living on less than USD 1.90 a day at 2011 international prices.

2 Vietnam had been colonized by France for six decades, beginning from the late 1880s to 1940 as part of the "French Indochina" (consisting of Cambodia, Lao PDR, and Vietnam). It was briefly occupied by Japan during the Second World War and until

1945, although Japan left the administration to French officials and troops, which it evicted in 1945 (Starr: 1991).

3 The end of the First Indochina War (1945–1954) heralded the independence of Vietnam in 1954 (Starr: 1991.

4 The World Bank estimates extreme poverty based on a poverty headcount ratio at USD 1.90 a day (2011 Purchasing Power Parity) (percent of population) from primary household survey data obtained from government statistical agencies and World Bank country departments poverty headcount ratio at USD 1.90 a day is the percentage of the population living on less than USD 1.90 a day at 2011 international prices.

5 The Doi-Moi strategy had four broad goals: transitioning from a centrally planned economy to a market economy, shifting from agrarian production to a manufacturing and services-driven economy, fostering migration from rural to urban areas, and changing Vietnam from a closed to an open export-driven and globally integrated economy.

6 These include (but are not limited to) reducing the role of the state in economic decision-making; rationalizing state budget and social expenditures; privatizing parastatals or SOEs; deepening trade liberalization; undertaking financial reforms including privatization of the banking and insurance sectors, devaluing, or realigning the currency; revamping investment laws and removing remaining market distortions and inefficiencies in resources allocation (World Bank: 1999, 2002; Masina:2006).

7 There is no universally agreed or accepted definition of what is meant by "national policy space" but generally it refers to a space for national development policy formulation and implementation which has increasingly been crowded out by international agreements, aid conditionality, market forces, and "internationalization" of domestic policy environment.

8 These were implemented during 1986–1990, 1991–1995, 1996–2000, 2001–2005, 2006–2010, 2011–-2016, and 2016–2020.

9 WTO national treatment clauses are the foundations or cornerstones of multilateral trade agreements that prohibit discrimination between imported and domestic products in taxation or between domestic and foreign firms in the provision of tax exemptions and incentives.

10 Non-state sectors include domestic private sector, collective ownership, and households.

Bibliographical references

Akyuz, Y., and Gore, C. (1996). The Investment-Profit Nexus in East Asian Industrialization. *World Development*, 24(3), 461–470.

Alcorta, L., and Tesfachew, T. (2020). Special Economic Zones and Export-Led Growth: An Industrial Policy Imperative. In *The Oxford Handbook of Industrial Hubs and Economic Development*. Edited by A. Oqubay, and J. Y. Lin. Chapter 18 pp (323–344). Oxford University Press, Oxford.

Amer, R. (2015). Vietnam-ASEAN Relations: Retrospective, Asia Dialogue, 14 April 2015. Available at: https://theasiadialogue.com/2015/04/14/vietnam-asean-relations-a-retrospective/#:~: text=Vietnam%20acceded%20to%20the%20Treaty,first%20official%20meeting%20in%201994.&text=This%20displayed%20a%20remarkable%20shift,a%20period%20of%2020%20years.

Bolesta, A. (2015). *China and Post-Socialist Development*. Published by Policy Press, University of Bristol, Bristol.

Bolesta, A. (2017). The Post-Socialist Developmental State in Asia. In *Post-Communist Development: Europe's Experiences, Asia's Challenges*. Edited by A. Bolesta. Collegium Civitas, Warsaw, 71–98. ISBN: 978-83-61067-59-7.

Busch, M. (2017). The Missing Middle: A Political Economy of Economic Restructuring in Vietnam. Lowy Institute. Available at: https://www.jstor.org/stable/pdf/resrep17556.pdf?refreqid=excelsior%3Aa569af65baf57f9ee6fa3eff68c48f11.

CIVICUS, VIDS, SNV, UNDP. (2006). The Emerging Civil Society: An Initial Assessment of Civil Society in Vietnam, Hanoi, March 2006.

Collier, P. (2007). *The Bottom Billion: Why the Poorest Countries are Falling Behind and What Can Be done About It*. Oxford University Press, New York.

Cramer, C., Oqubay, A., and Sender, J. (2020). *African Economic Development: Evidence, Theory and Policy*. Oxford University Press, Oxford.

Dezan Shira & Associates. (2019). Asia Briefing: An Introduction to Doing Business in Vietnam 2018–19. Available at: https://www.asiabriefing.com/store/book/an-introduction-to-doing-business-in-vietnam-2018-7633.html.

Dezan Shira & Associates. (2020). Vietnam Briefing: Growing Economic Cooperation between Japan and Vietnam. https://www.vietnam-briefing.com/news/growing-economic-cooperation-japan-vietnam.html/, accessed on 25 June 2020.

Deyo, F. C. (1987). *The Political Economy of the New Asian Industrialization*. Cornel University Press, Ithaca, NY.

Easterly, W. (2002). *The Elusive Quest for Growth: Economist's Adventures and Misadventures in the Tropics*, First MIT Paperback Edition, Massachusetts Institute of Technology.

Hoekman, B. M., and Kostecki, M. M. (1995). *The Political Economy of the World Trading System: From GATT to WTO*. Oxford University Press.

International Monetary Fund. (1994). The East Asian Miracles: Building a basis for growth, Finance and Development. Staff Studies for the World Economic Outlook. *Quarterly Publication of the International Monetary Fund and the World Bank*, 31(1), 1–4.

KICOX. (2012). Industrial Park Development Strategy and Management Practices of South Korea. Korea Industrial Complex Corporation (KICOX) and Ministry of Knowledge Economy (MKE), Knowledge Sharing Programme.

Kim, J., and Lau, L. J. (1994). The Sources of Economic Growth of the East Asian Newly Industrialized Countries. *Journal of the Japanese and International Economies*, 8(3), 235–271.

Kokko, A. (1998). Vietnam: Ready for Doi Moi II? *ASEAN Economic Bulletin*, 15(3), 319–327. In Southeast Asia's Economic Crisis: Origins, Lessons, and the Way Forward. December 1999. Published by ISEAS- Yusof Ishak Institute. Stable URL: http://www.jstor.com/stable/25773546.

Lin, J. Y. (2015). The Washington Consensus Revisited: A New Structural Economics Perspective. *Journal of Economic Policy Forum*, 18(2), 96–113.

Lundberg, E. (1974). Gunnar Myrdal's Contribution to Economic Theory. *The Swedish Journal of Economics*, 76(4), 472–478. Published by Wiley on behalf of The Scandinavian Journal of Economics. http://www.jstor.com/stable/3439253.

Malesky, E., Abrami, R., and Zheng, Y. (2011). Institutions and Inequality in Single-Party Regimes: A Comparative Analysis of Vietnam and China. *Comparative Politics*, 43(4), 401–419.

Martus, B. (2016). Jobless Growth: The Impact of Structural Change. *Public Finance Quarterly*, 2016(2), 244–264.

Masina, P. (2006). *Vietnamese Development Strategies*. Routledge Taylor and Francis Group, London.

Ministry of Planning and Investment, Foreign Investment Agency (FIA). (2018). Vietnam Lures USD 34.46 billion FDI in 2018. *Vietnam Investment Review*, 27 December 2018.

Available at: https://www.vir.com.vn/vietnam-lures-3546-billion-usd-fdi-in-2018-64870.html.

Ministry of Planning and Investment (Vietnam). (2020). Brief on the 2019 Foreign Direct Investment, 15 August 2020. Available at: http://www.mpi.gov.vn/en/Pages/tinbai.aspx?idTin=45020&idcm=122.

Nayyar, D. (2006). Development through Globalization. UNU-WIDER Research Paper No. 2006/29, March 2006. United Nations University.

Nguyen, T. A., Luu, M. D., and Trinh, D. C. (2016). The Evolution of Vietnamese Industrialization. In *Manufacturing Transformation: Comparative Studies of Industrial Development in Africa and Emerging Asia*. Edited by C. Newman, J. Page, J. Rand, A. Shimelis, M. Soderbom, and F. Tarp. Chapter 12. UNU-WIDER Studies in Development Economics. Oxford University Press, Oxford, U.K. 236–276, 235–256.

Oqubay, A., and Tesfachew, T. (2019a). Technological Learning in Africa: Catch-Up in the Aviation Industry. In *How Nations Learn: Technological Learning, Industrial Policy and Catch-Up*. Edited by A. Oqubay, and K. Ohno. Chapter 11 pp (235–260). Oxford University Press, Oxford.

Oqubay, A., and Tesfachew, T. (2019b). Learning to Catch-Up in Africa in the Cement Industry. In *How Nations Learn: Technological Learning, Industrial Policy and Catch-up*. Edited by A. Oqubay, and K. Ohno. Chapter 13 pp (285–308). Oxford University Press, Oxford.

Rodrik, D. (1994). King Kong Meets Godzilla: The World Bank and The East Asian Miracle, CEPR Press Discussion Paper No. 944. https://cepr.org/publications/dp944.

Singh, A. (1994). How did East Asia Grow So Fast? Slow Progress Towards an Analytical Consensus. University of Cambridge. MPRA Paper No. 53435. Available at: https://mpra.ub.uni-muenchen.de/53435/1/, accessed on 15 June 2020.

Schlight, J. (1986). The Second Indochina War. Proceedings of a Symposium, 7–9 November 1984. Airlie, Virginia. Center of Military History. United States Army, Washington, DC..

Starr, J. M. (1991). *The Lessons of the Vietnam War*. Center for Social Studies Education, Pittsburgh, PA.

Statista. (2019). Online Database: Vietnam Urban Population. Available at: https://www.statista.com/statistics/603397/vietnam-urban-population/#:~: text=The%20major%20urban%20cities%20are,Da%20Nang%20and%20Bien%20Hoa.&text=Vietnam's%20urbanization%20rate%20was%20at%2035.92%20percent.

Stiglitz, J. (2001). *Globalization and its Discontent*. Penguin Books, London.

Tarp, F. (Ed.). (2017). Growth, Structural Transformation, and Rural Change in Viet Nam: A Rising Dragon on the Move. UNU-WIDER Studies in Development Economics, ISBN 978-0-19-879696-1. Oxford University Press, Oxford. Available at: http://doi.org/10.1093/acprof:oso/9780198796961.001.0001.

Taylor, W., Nguyễn, T. H., Phạm, Q. T., and Huỳnh, T. N. T. (2012). A Comparative Study of Civil Society Organizations in Hanoi and Ho Chi Minh City. HANOI, October 2012.

Thanh, V. T. (2017). ASEAN and Member States: Transformation and Integration. Vietnam Country Report. ASEAN@50, Vol. 3, 2017.

Tran, Q. (2018). Analyzing the Partnership between International Non-Governmental Organizations and the Vietnamese Government in the Post-Reform Period. School of Public Policy. Central European University.

TrendEconomy. (2020). Vietnam Imports and Exports: Dairy produce (birds, eggs, natural honey edible products of animal origin), 2008–2019. Annual International Trade

Statistics by Country, 10 February 2020. Available at: https://trendeconomy.com/data/h2/Vietnam/04.

Trinh, B., Thai, N., and Anh, B. (2019). Foreign Direct Investment (FDI) in Vietnam's Economy. *Theoretical Economics Letters*, 9. http://doi.org/10.4236/tel.2019.94064.

UNCTAD. (1994). *Trade and Development Report*. United Nations Publication, New York and Geneva.

UNCTAD. (2020a). *Productive Capacities Index: Focus on Landlocked Developing Countries*. United Nations Publication Issued by the United Nations, Geneva.

UNCTADStat. (2020). https://unctadstat.unctad.org/EN/.

U.S. Chamber of Commerce. (2019). *The Next Stage of US-Vietnam Relations: A Blueprint to Deepen Trade and Investment Ties, 10 May 2019*. Available at: https://www.uschamber.com/sites/default/files/vietnam_white_paper_final_website.pdf, accessed on 30 June 2020.

Vietnam Times. (2019). More than 500 Foreign NGOs Operate Regularly in Vietnam, 10 December 2019. Available at: https://vietnamtimes.org.vn/more-than-500-foreign-ngos-operate-regularly-in-vietnam-17237.html.

World Bank. (1991). *World Development Report: The Challenge of Development*. Oxford University Press, World Bank, New York. Available at: https://openknowledge.worldbank.org/handle/10986/5974.

World Bank. (1993). *The East Asian Miracle: Economic Growth and Public Policy*. Oxford University Press.

World Bank. (1999). Vietnam: Export Performance in 1999 and Beyond. An Informal Economic Report of the World Bank Vietnam Consultative Group Informal Mid-Year Review. World Bank Country Office.

World Bank. (2002). *Vietnam: Country Procurement Assessment Report: Transforming Public Procurement*. World Bank Country Office 2002, Vietnam.

World Bank. (2016a). *Transforming Vietnamese Agriculture: Growing More from Less*. The World Bank, Washington, DC.

World Bank. (2018b). *Taking Stock: An update on Vietnam's Recent Economic Developments*. The World Bank. Available at: http://documents1.worldbank.org/curated/en/536421528929689515/pdf/127168-WP-TakingStockENG-PUBLIC.pdf.

World Bank. (2019). Connecting Vietnam for Growth and Shared Prosperity. Vietnam Development Report, Hanoi, Hong Duc Publishing. World Bank Group, December 2019.

World Bank. (2020b). World Bank Development Indicators (WBDI) Database: Vietnam. Available at: https://data.worldbank.org/indicator/SL.AGR.EMPL.ZS?locations=VN.

World Bank and International Finance Corporation. (2003). *Informality and the Playing Field in Vietnam's Business Sector*. World Bank and International Finance Corporation (IFC), Washington, DC.

World Economic Forum. (2015). Why Efficient Cities are Crucial to Vietnam's Transformation. Available at: https://www.weforum.org/agenda/2015/11/why-efficient-cities-are-crucial-to-vietnams-transformation/.

Young, A. (1994). Lessons from East Asia: A Contrarian View. *European Economic Review*, 38(3–4), 964–973.

Young, A. (1995). The Tyranny of Numbers: Confronting the Statistical Realities of the East Asian Growth Experience. *The Quarterly Journal of Economics*, 110(3), 641–680.

8 Vietnam's "Right" Type of Transformation

8.1 Transformation in and from Agriculture

Unlike the wrong types of sectoral shifts in the GDP of SSA, what has been observed in Vietnam is deep, qualitative, and the right type of structural transformation. Since the 1986 Doi-Moi, Vietnam's economy has undergone fundamental changes. The agriculture sector, which itself has undergone transformational changes, served as a springboard to the economy of Vietnam (FAO: 2005, JICA: 2013). Key processes in agricultural transformation include modernizing production techniques, enhancing productivity, and removing supply- and demand-side constraints to the sector. The transformation observed in agriculture is largely due to the sector's augmented total factor productivity (JICA: 2013), distributive policies (land use rights), and the incentives provided by the government in ensuring access to agricultural inputs such as fertilizers. Revenues from extractive resources (oil, coal and zinc) as well as power generation (electricity) are also behind the state's capacity to finance infrastructure, farm subsidies, and expanding the social sector (education and health) including in rural areas. Land use rights further assisted in improving access to productive assets and the entitlements of poor households. The growing rate of urbanization, improvements in household incomes, and enlarging the middle class have generated high aggregate domestic demand for agricultural produce, which in turn, has contributed to an improved income for the rural population. Moreover, regional trade agreements, improved methods of farming and the growth of Total Factor Productivity (TFP) have played an important role in the transformation of Vietnam's agriculture sector (World Bank: 2016b). Such an improvement was not limited to the production of staple food (such as rice). Rather it includes the production of diverse food and industrial crops such as coffee, sugarcane, livestock, cassava, rubber, and fisheries (JICA: 2013). Consequently, Vietnam has emerged from a net food-importer and food-insecure nation status in the 1980s to the fifth largest producer and the fourth largest exporter of rice in the world, after India, Thailand, and the USA in 2019 (www.worldstopexports.com/rice-exports-country). The country is now known as the "Rice Bowl of the World". Vietnam's agricultural average GDP growth rate has been 3.6 percent for the last couple of decades, exceeded only by China among leading agricultural producers

DOI: 10.4324/9781003295334-8

in the world, with significant impact on poverty reduction, particularly in the rural areas (JICA: 2013).

The sustained changes seen in Vietnam's agricultural sector demonstrate that structural transformation can occur not only across sectors but also within sectors. This has been supported by increased rural investment by the state (including in infrastructure such as rural electrification), often through rents from extractive (mineral) resources and integrated rural development strategies. Along with increased production, agri-processing and agri-business played an important role in generating high yield, value addition, and lifting the living standards of the rural population. To illustrate this, the role of four key subsectors (sugarcane, coffee, livestock, and fishery) is closely examined hereunder. These sectors played vital roles in accelerating structural transformation in rural areas, while forging linkages with the rest of the economy. The development of regional and global value chains (including handling, transportation, processing, conversion, distribution, and marketing) has further accelerated the transformation of Vietnam's agriculture sector (World Bank: 2016b). Vietnam has carefully chosen subsectors and products that foster linkages, increase exports, and improve employment, and accordingly it sequenced policies and incentives to unlock binding constraints to the chosen sectors and products.

8.1.1 *Commercial Crops: Sugarcane Production*

Vietnam's sugarcane plantation started in the 1960s and grew at an average rate of 7.25 percent between 1969 and 2018, reaching 17.9 million tonnes[1] in 2018 from just 886,000 tonnes in 1969 (https://knoema.com/atlas/Viet-Nam). Exports of sugar and sugar confectionary reached about USD 210 million in 2013 and to USD 264 million in 2019 (Trend Economy, 10 February 2020). This was against sugar imports worth of USD 340 million and USD 378 million, respectively, in 2013 and 2019. The selection of the production of sugar came as part of the country's Import Substitution (IS) strategy. Notwithstanding its moderate trade imbalance on sugar, the huge jump in Vietnam's production of sugarcane has been accompanied by an expansion of sugar processing mills, predominantly in the northern part of the country. The northern region was chosen to take advantage of an extra supply of electricity generated from sugarcane by-products or bagasse (GIZ: 2017), contributing to the electrification of local rural areas. Thus, in 2017, 10 of 41 sugar processing firms were producing electricity from sugar by-products, with a total generation capacity of over 186 million kWh (GIZ: 2017). This was important in meeting the energy demand for Vietnam's integrated rural development strategy, expansion of non-farm jobs, rapid structural economic transformation, and reducing carbon emissions (GGGI: 2018). Forward and backward linkages between agriculture (sugarcane plantations) and industry (sugar processing mills) as well as energy services have played a vital role in expanding job opportunities (on- and off-farm), improving the quality and efficiency of social sectors such as health and education in rural areas.

8.1.2 The Coffee Subsector

The pre-reform coffee export destinations were confined to former socialist countries, principally the USSR and China (World Bank: 2004). Yet, in less than three decades, Vietnam has become the world's second largest producer and exporter of coffee after Brazil (ICO: 2019). In the last 30 years, Vietnam's coffee production has skyrocketed 100-fold (from 18,400 tonnes in 1986 – the beginning of Doi-Moi – to a whopping 1.8 million tonnes in 2018 (ICO: 2019), with coffee now accounting for 10 percent of the country's total agricultural exports and nearly 30 percent of the GDP in central highland regions where it predominantly grows. Ninety percent of the (mostly Robusta) coffee produced is exported, with an average annual turnover of USD 3.5 billion in 2018, up from about USD 210 million in 1995 (Business Wire, May 2017). The growth of Vietnam's coffee sector was designed to meet a rising trend in global coffee consumption and lags in production in SSA.

The commercial coffee sector also provides jobs and income for more than 500,000 farmers (ICO: 2019), with about 1 million additional smallholder farmers growing coffee as part of their overall agriculture (JICA: 2013). Not only has Vietnam's coffee sector seen production transformation in the last three decades, but it has also undergone several changes: first, with the launch of Doi-Moi (Renovation), the role of the state in coffee production has continuously decreased, which currently accounts only for about 5 percent of the total production. Private farms generate 95 percent of the production and exports. Second, an increased intensity of processing and value addition. Currently, there are more than 100 coffee processing mills all over Vietnam, with an average processing capacity of 1.5 million tonnes a year (ICO: 2019, Ministry of Agriculture and Rural Development of Vietnam: 2020). More than 176 facilities roast and grind coffee, 8 factories produce instant (soluble) coffee, while another 11 are devoted to mixed instant coffee processing. Despite all the efforts, nearly 83 percent of total coffee exports of Vietnam are still in raw beans (USDA: 2019). Value addition in the coffee sector requires addressing current limitations[2] identified by various studies (World Bank: 2013, JICA: 2013 and USDA: 2019). Due to such systemic challenges, in 2018,[3] only about 10 percent of the coffee exported was in deep processing (soluble or instant), which the government aims to increase to at least 25 percent by 2020–2022 (*Vietnam Plus*, 8 July 2020). Although the overall domestic value addition in the coffee sector is currently low, there is significant potential for increasing the share in parallel with improving packaging, branding, transportation, marketing, and other related services.

Third is the diversification of export destinations. Exported exclusively to socialist economies only prior to the 1986 reform, Vietnam's coffee production has since penetrated major global markets and exported to over 70 countries (World Bank: 2013), with the EU being its largest importer followed by the USA. Fourth, Vietnam has heavily invested in improving the quality and safety[4] of its coffee by meeting international public and private standards[5] (ICO: 2019). This is done through increased allocation of financial resources for the education and training of coffee farmers, processors, traders, and associations. Vietnam has also established quality assurance and control centres, compliance certification programmes, standards bodies, and mechanisms for information sharing regarding the benefits of meeting quality and safety standards for building export competitiveness.

Finally (fifth), Vietnam's coffee production has shifted from traditional farming (plantations) methods to technology-intensive and R&D-driven farming methods. Coffee farmers began increasingly applying advanced agricultural production technologies with the support of the government and the private sector. For instance, there have been consistent efforts to expand the production and export of better-quality Arabica varieties by "hybridizing and grafting the variety suitable for the local soil and climatic conditions with increased resistance to pests and diseases as well as have high productivity" (ICO: 2019). The role of the Government of Vietnam in making the coffee sector a vibrant rural industry (World Bank: 2004) remains central. This includes reforming and liberalizing the coffee subsector, facilitating individual land-use rights for farmers (FAO: 2005), and enhancing public investment in the sector. Further measures include the provision of interest-free loans or credits at preferential rates to private smallholder farmers, encouraging individual farmers to engage in coffee cultivation and production, providing better coffee seeds and high-yield varieties, and deregulation of key farm inputs such as chemical fertilizers at cheap or subsidized prices.

8.1.3 The Livestock Subsector and Its Linkages

The demand for dairy products has continued to increase in Vietnam particularly from the 2000s onwards, driven by demographic pressure, improved household incomes, and overall standards of living of the population (FAO: 2005, JICA: 2013). Consequently, the livestock subsector has undergone a major transformation, gradually shifting from subsistence to commercial production (Hostiou et al.: 2016). Doi-Moi, which galvanized the socioeconomic transformation of Vietnam, has played a vital role in making the sector vibrant and dynamic. The livestock sector has shifted from communal (collectivized) and traditional breeding and rearing to a commercial (private) or market-oriented production system. The expansion of commercial livestock rearing has resulted in increasing the country's import bills both from the supply and demand sides. On the demand side, the slower pace of supply response to the reform processes (than the rise in domestic demand) increased the country's imports of dairy products from USD 307 million in 2000 to USD 715 million in 2005 (JICA: 2013). On the supply side, the deepening of the reform and the shift in ownership and production systems in livestock boosted the need for animal feed and veterinary medicine to control animal diseases, which increased the import bill from USD 600 million in 2005 to USD 2.2 billion in 2010 (JICA: 2013). However, Vietnam has successfully modernized the livestock sub-sector and has become self-sufficient in poultry meat, egg production, other meat, and dairy supplies to its growing population (estimated at about 97.3 million in 2020). Improvements in the subsector include domestic production of animal feed, which has increased from less than 20 percent in early 2000s to 66 percent in 2015 (Hostiou et al.: 2016). Vietnam has also introduced modern and scientific breeding and production systems, including crossbreeding of high-yield species. The country has equally improved the quality of animal feed and established institutions and regulations to enhance food safety and quality standards for its expanding domestic and international markets.

Further efforts in developing the livestock subsector focused on the reorganization of animal husbandry and the introduction of large-scale farms, which helped some dairy producing companies to build their own large-scale farms and dairy supply chains (Hostiou et al.: 2016). In 2018, the total import value of dairy products including birds, eggs, and natural honey was estimated at about USD 170 million, which decreased to USD 153 million in 2019. In 2018 and 2019, the export of this commodity group was, respectively, USD 243 million, and USD 264 million (*TrendEconomy*, 10 February 2020).

The livestock subsector has served as a springboard for the diversification of exports into labour-intensive manufacturing (leather and leather products and footwear) as well as associated economic activities with substantial job creation, improved incomes, and sustained poverty reduction, particularly in rural areas. The livestock subsector is a classic case of "within and across sectoral" structural transformation, providing incontrovertible evidence for a visible shift (transformation) from low and subsistence productivity activity to higher productivity activity. And, subsequently, from low to higher value added, and from low technological content to the embodiment of higher technological sophistication of outputs and production processes.

The livestock sector has also been key in generating employment due to its labour-intensive characteristics while giving rise to export-oriented industrialization with an increased participation of domestic and Foreign Direct Investment (FDI) firms. In 2017, there were a total of 1,711 enterprises (Leather, Footwear, and Handbag Association (LFASO): 2017) in the leather and leather products sector, representing a 55 percent increase when compared to the number in 2010 (1,104). The number of enterprises in footwear grew by 55.5 percent (from 645 in 2010 to 950 in 2017), whereas those in handbag production grew from 411 to 710, representing a whopping 72 percent increase during the same period. Accordingly, in 2017, roughly 30 percent of the enterprises were foreign or FDI-based but had a nearly 70 percent share in exports. The remaining 70 percent were domestic enterprises with an average share of 29.7 percent in exports. The share of State-Owned Enterprises (SOEs) was less than 1 percent in the same year. Vietnam emerged third in the top ten exporters of leather footwear in the world after China and Italy (Hoang and Pham: 2016). The total global market share of the country in 2017 was 10.9 percent in value or USD 5.6 billion and 11.6 percent in the quantity produced (supply) or 232 million pairs the same year. The total footwear and handbag exports of Vietnam grew from USD 10.4 billion in 2013 to USD 18.1 billion in 2017, accounting for 10 percent of the country's total exports in value. The dominant destinations for Vietnam's exports of footwear and handbags (in 2017) were the USA (35.9 percent), EU (30.6 percent), China (6.4 percent), Japan (6.3 percent), South Korea (2.8 percent), and others (18 percent) (LEFASO: 2017).

In terms of employment, between 2006 and 2016 manufacturing employment increased twofold from 2.3 million to 6.7 million (UNIDO: 2019). Forty-three percent of the total manufacturing jobs were in the textile, apparel, leather, and footwear subsector. Employment in the leather and footwear sector alone increased from 800,000 workers in 2011 to 1.2 million in 2016 (UNIDO: 2019, p. 20), with women accounting for 70–80 percent of the labour force. During the same period, the share of agriculture in GDP and employment substantially declined from 80 percent and 76 percent, respectively, in 1986 to less than 14 percent and 37 percent in 2020. In 2019, the employment shares of the manufacturing and services sectors were 19 percent and 44 percent, respectively, each accounting for 44 and 43 percent of the GDP in that year (Statista: 2020). Such an unprecedented structural shift – the right type of transformation towards service – and manufacturing sector-driven output and employment have led to a continued growth in job creation, income generation, and substantial poverty reduction in Vietnam (World Bank: 2018c).

The success in Vietnam's labour-intensive manufacturing (leather footwear, leather apparel, and leather handbags) is the result of carefully sequenced steps towards industrialization. This involves identifying sectors of spill-over effects, exploiting actual and latent comparative advantages, and simultaneously addressing key binding constraints. Before building a complete value or supply chain in the leather and leather products sector, Vietnam prioritized the development and optimization of upstream parts (or the lowest or initial phases in the value chains). Early in the reform process, Vietnam realized that its leather and footwear industry had no comparative advantage in downstream[6] phases of the value chain (such as design, branding, marketing, and sales). The only obvious comparative advantage it had in the leather and footwear industry was cheap labour (Masina and Cerimele: 2018). However, this has gradually changed with an increasing participation of FDI enterprises, which brought capabilities in R&D, technology, design, branding, packaging, distribution services, among others. The participation of FDI firms has greatly contributed to the gradual transformation of the sector, with a dominant share in exporters of leather and leather products as well as footwear to the international markets. These enterprises are also the largest source of formal or regular employment in Vietnam, although they represent only about 30 percent of the total number of enterprises in the leather and leather products supply chain.

The focus of Vietnam on the lowest echelon of the value chain (upstream) has helped the country to understand the structure of export markets and their requirements before starting to manufacture for exports. It has prioritized understanding market requirements and networking with key industry actors and players prior to engaging in processing and value-adding. This has helped Vietnam to gain knowledge about the overall governance structure of globally dispersed production and supply networks of leather and leather products including footwear.

These strategies were key to Vietnam's effective and beneficial integration into regional and global value chains in leather and leather production or supply. Improvements in the upstream phase of the supply chain have helped Vietnam in gradually building its leather and footwear industry, with further growth and expansion of the subsector. The country began reaping the advantages of regional and global trading opportunities in labour-intensive manufacturing products. This has further boosted Vietnam's potential to enhance production and productivity and become the manufacturing hub in a region, with enhanced competitiveness and deepened structural transformation.

8.1.4 *Fishery Sector and Aquaculture*

In 2018, the total global production of fish was 178.8 million tonnes – natural capture (90 million tonnes) and aquaculture (87.8 million tonnes) – and had an estimated export value of USD 166 billion the same year (FAO: 2019). While captured fish has stabilized at around 90 million tonnes per year for the last two decades, the production of cultured fish grew from 32 million tonnes in 2000 to 87 million tonnes in 2018 (up 172 percent). The rapid growth in the aquaculture subsector has been central in sustaining the constantly increasing global demand for fish (FAO: 2018). Prior to the 1986 reform, Vietnam's fishery sector and aquaculture subsector[7] were under the socialist (centralized) economic system. The total exports (in value) of the captured fish and aquaculture sector was USD 11.2 million in 1980 (Leh: 2017), predominantly traditional and artisanal, with little or no value addition or industrial-scale production. However, with its abundant water resources (freshwater, brackish, and marine), Vietnam has quickly realized the potential the fishery sector holds for its structural economic transformation. The sector has gradually emerged as a vital economic activity in contributing to sustained and inclusive economic growth, export diversification, and poverty reduction in post-reform Vietnam, the sector being identified as key to experimenting its gradual but well sequenced transition from a command (socialist) economy to a mixed economic model (Kim A.T.N: 2017). Indeed, the sector has become an entry point for the participation of the private sector (domestic and foreign) with strong support from the government through well-targeted incentives, institutional and policy supports (Kim A.T.N: 2017).

Thirty-one years after the launch of Doi-Moi, in 2017, Vietnam emerged as the fifth largest producer of fish and the fourth largest producer of aquaculture[8] in the world (FAO: 2017, UNCTAD: 2017d), with the total fishery production of 6.7 million tonnes of which 3.64 million tonnes (54.3 percent) were from aquaculture (FAO: 2017). Vietnam's total export value of fish hit USD 8.6 billion the same year, which grew to USD 10 billion in 2018, up 20.2 percent (European Parliament: 2018). This represents a six-fold increase over the level in 1990, which, on average, was about USD 1.5 billion back then. In 2018, the country was also the third largest exporter of shrimp in the world (second in Asia after India but ahead of the region's leading producers (China, Indonesia, and Thailand). Vietnam has also emerged as the third largest importer of shrimp in the world (after the USA and EU) during the same year, for reprocessing and reexport (FAO: 2019). Intensive and extensive shrimp farming[9] accounted for 55 percent of the total fishery production and 70 percent fishery exports in 2018 (Kim A.T.N: 2017). The fishery sector remains an important driver of socioeconomic transformation in Vietnam, contributing 4–5 percent to the GDP, 4–5 percent of the workforce (employment), 30 percent of animal protein intake, and 40 percent of total food production in Vietnam in 2018 (Kim A.T.N: 2017).

The biggest success for Vietnam's fishery came from aquaculture, which accounts for 55 percent of the total fishery production of the country, generating close to 80 percent of fishery export revenue in 2018. Also, the fishery sector (aquaculture, capture, processing, and distribution) all along its value chain employs as many as 10 million people (5 percent of the current labour force). Nearly 80–90 percent of the employees are women, and close to 80 percent of the employment is in the aquaculture subsector. While many developing countries, especially in SSA, failed to develop their aquaculture subsector, Vietnam has become the second largest producer and exporter of cultured fish in Asia – the region that boasts perfecting the science and the industry of aquaculture.

There are several factors that have led Vietnam's aquaculture subsector to become an "industry" in its own right. These include: (i) effective and modern governance and management frameworks for aquaculture development; (ii) availability of high-quality seed (fingerlings) and fish feed; (iii) facilitated access to finance, land, and water resources particularly for small producers and rural households; (iv) advances in technology and innovation; and (v) integrated environment management, marketing, and export penetration. Further factors that are behind the expansion and development of the aquaculture subsector include Research and Development (R&D); effective linkages between R&D facilities and the aquaculture farms and the industry; increased participation of the private sector, including in supporting R&D institutions as well as teaching and technical training centres; high level of Public-Private Partnerships (PPPs) in aquaculture development and effective risk mitigation systems through subsidized insurance schemes to fish farmers, lower premiums for farms as well as targeted government subsidies or incentives[10] to mobilize the country's private sector as well as the participation of foreign enterprises in the production and export of fisheries (UNCTAD: 2020b).

Fishery growth and expansion, as well as the sector's contribution to export diversification and transformation in Vietnam, has been boosted through the growth and expansion of the fisheries and seafood processing industry. "There were about 570 industrial plants and manually operated entities, producing fishery products with a combined value of USD 6 billion in 2011" (JICA: 2013). This includes significant value addition along the key value chains such as fishing, aquaculture, production, processing, transport, and retail marketing, consisting of primary and secondary activities (Kim and Jolly: 2018). Value addition or industrial-scale seafood processing has also generated auxiliary services such as water and electricity provision, management services including facilitating the choice of technology, procurement, transport, and other related infrastructure such as cold storage (Kim and Jolly: 2018).

The key factors for the successful transformation or value addition in the fishery sector include (but are not limited to) integrated and coherent fishery, agriculture, industrial, and trade policies; large-scale production and sustainable supply of fish; clear identification of sources of competitiveness (cost advantage, product and services differentiation and picking value-creating activities); investing in modern technology, marine fishing boats,[11] quality assurances, and certification; and ability to penetrate global fisheries and seafood markets (Kim and Jolly: 2018). Overall, success for Vietnam from aquaculture and the captured fish has led the country to transform the sector into one of the vibrant manufacturing hubs in terms of seafood processing (such as processed food, frozen fish, frozen premium shrimp, fish paste, fish feed, etc.). One important factor, which distinguishes Vietnam from other developing countries, is the degree to which it has managed to penetrate external markets. Today, the country exports fish and seafood to 161 countries (Leh: 2017), largely to Australia, ASEAN, China, EU, Hong Kong, Japan, Russia, South Korea, Singapore, Taiwan, and the USA. In terms of the broad strategy, the country followed an export-led investment strategy in the fishery sector (as in many other sectors), targeting primarily fisheries with high-value, high-return, and high global demand such as big shrimp (prawns), pangasius, tuna, mollusc, crabs, and others. Vietnam has also deliberately expanded the production and export of these species, which not only attracts private capital and technology but also brings high value and high return on investment (Leh: 2017).

Vietnam has harnessed its comparative advantages in key productive sectors (including agriculture) and became one of the fastest growing economies in the world. In less than four decades, it emerged as one of the few star performers in the developing world, lifting millions out of poverty. It can serve as a model for developing countries such as those in SSA. Vietnam's experience in tapping domestic comparative advantages and global opportunities, enhancing investments in institutions and infrastructure, fostering private sector development, and attracting and targeting FDI. Such economy-wide and profound transformation can provide useful practical lessons to the economies of SSA. Over the last three decades Vietnam's economy has transformed from traditional agriculture-driven to a manufacturing and services-driven economy. The GDP of the country has grown from USD 14 billion in 1980 to USD 260 billion in 2019 – almost 19-fold. Consequently, the poverty level has gone down from about 35 percent in 2000 to 1.9 percent in 2020 (see Figure 7.3). Although the relative share of agriculture in GDP and employment has significantly diminished over the last three decades (as the share of the other sectors become dominant), the role of agriculture in the socioeconomic transformation of Vietnam is still significant. This is particularly important given that 63 percent of the total population still resides in rural areas in 2019, although this is much lower than the 81 percent in 1980 (World Bank Blog: 9 September 2019). In examining Vietnam's transformational growth, it is vital to closely examine how the country has used key enablers and accelerators of productive capacities and structural economic transformation.

8.2 Key Enablers and Accelerators of Vietnam's Transformation

Vietnam has developed capabilities in various areas with a focus on key enablers and accelerators of transformational growth. The country's development policies were centred on building key "enablers" that the country needs to develop productive capacities and transform its economy. These include: (i) enhancing the energy (electricity) supply, (ii) building human resources (human capital), (iii) enhancing transport infrastructure; (iv) harnessing the potential of ICT for economic growth, (v) altering export structures through diversification and value addition, and (v) building institutional capabilities as a foundation for industrialization, transformation, and export competitiveness. How Vietnam has harnessed and used each of these enablers and accelerators, and how it realigned policy interventions and incentives, consistent with productive capacities narratives, is discussed below.

8.2.1 *The Power (Electricity) Sector in Post-reform Vietnam*

The power sector of Vietnam was underdeveloped before the launch of Doi-Moi. The country had one of the poorest energy infrastructures in Asian continent and the developing world with the sector severely hampered by successive external, regional, and internal wars as well as the US embargo (World Bank: 2020b). In 1985 – one year prior to the launch of Doi-Moi – only "9 percent of all households with an average power consumption of 65 kWh/year (which is equivalent to domestic lighting) had electricity in the country" (World Bank: 2020c). However, in less than 25 years (i.e., by 2011), 99.5 percent of communes and 95.5 percent of villages across Vietnam had electricity (JICA: 2013), and by 2018, 100 percent of communes and 99 percent of rural households had electricity. An average per capita consumption hit 2,100 kilowatt hours (kWh) the same year (World Bank: 2020c), with Vietnam emerging 23rd in the world and 2nd in ASEAN bloc in total energy production[12] and supply (Energy Vietnam – EVN: 2018).

This progress has been achieved under Electricity Vietnam (EVN), which was established in 1994 as a SOE (EVN: 2018). The trend has continued to increase by 10 percent a year (World Bank: 2020c, EVN: 2018), and the installed capacity reached 220,000 megawatts (MW) or 220 billion kW in 2018. The total energy supply reached about 251,000 MW in 2019 and projected to increase by a factor of 2.4 in the next five years (EVN: 2020). SOEs still dominate the production and supply of electricity where the share of EVN was 60 percent and other SOEs 13 percent in 2018. However, the role of private investments (domestic and foreign) has increased over time and reached 27 percent in 2018 (EVN: 2018). The availability of reliable electricity at affordable cost[13] is behind the fostering of industrialization, export diversification, and agricultural transformation. It also drives the complete electrification of households (including in rural areas) and improvements in the efficiency of the social sector such as education, technical and vocational training, health, and the services sector such as commerce, banking and finance, construction, ICT, etc. The energy sector has also had multiplier effects in expanding jobs and creating employment opportunities particularly in rural areas (World Bank: 2018c).

Building on the 2004 Electricity Law and learning by doing, the Government of Vietnam is determined to continue to further modernize the energy sector in the years ahead. This includes establishing a regulatory authority (Energy Regulatory Authority of Vietnam – ERAV) and the Electricity Power Trading Company (EPTC), enhancing operational and financial efficiency, ensuring balanced asset (capital-liability) ratio through business plans, and transitioning to clean or renewable energy sources. Policy directions of the government also aim at issuing new laws and formulating and implementing key energy policies with a focus on introducing corporate governance and administration for the sector. Vietnam has also seen a gradual shift in the country's energy mix – from excessive dependence on coal and natural gas towards renewable energy sources, albeit at slow speed. According to Vietnam Energy Profile,[14] in 2020, the share of coal and gas in the total energy mix of the country was 49 percent (down from nearly 75 percent in the 1980s). during the same year, the share of hydroelectricity was 30 percent and solar 24 percent, up respectively from less than 10 percent and 1 percent in the 1980s. Further efforts include a commitment to improve the quality of human resources, labour productivity, and introduce mechanisms for cost savings, while enhancing power production and business efficiencies of the electricity sector (World Bank: 2020c). With the aim of sustaining the availability of reliable and affordable electricity in the years ahead, Vietnam is also preparing to introduce further reforms in a number of critically important areas (EVN: 2018): (i) substantially increasing (public and private) investment in energy infrastructure and expansion of sources of power generation in the national grid projects, (ii) expediting investment in power grid development to absorb renewable energy sources such as solar energy, and (iii) applying technological advances and efficiencies of the fourth industrial revolution for applications in power production and business activities.

8.2.2 *Building Human Capital*

The post-colonial Government of Vietnam prioritized human development-centred tasks along with ensuring the sovereignty and independence of the country. Its immediate objectives were then guided by a motto: "fight against hunger, fight against illiteracy and fight against enemy invasions" (Ministry of Education and Training of Vietnam: 2015). Vietnam was then characterized by poverty, high illiteracy rates, and poor healthcare systems in the Asian continent. However, after the end of the Second Indochina War, the socialist government laid the foundation for promoting the universal access of citizens to education and health in urban and rural areas, although there was unequal opportunity for minorities in remote mountainous areas. Building on the gains from the socialist system on education and health outcomes, Doi-Moi further revolutionized the country's education and health sectors by enhancing public investment, introducing administrative governance and reforms as well as by providing free universal education and healthcare services particularly to urban poor and rural communities.

In 2018, Vietnam boasts more than 15 million students[15] (46 percent girls) in primary and secondary schools, 1.7 million university students, and 87,000 students in vocational and technical schools across the country (General Statistics Office of Vietnam: 2020). The country has also invested in building schools, reaching (on average) 28,000 schools[16] between 2014 and 2018, 235 universities in 2018 (Statista: 2020), and more than 1,000 technical and vocational schools (Tvet Vietnam: 2019). Moreover, in 2018, 100 percent of Vietnam's 11,000 communes had kindergarten, primary, and lower secondary schools, while nearly 15 percent had secondary schools (General Statistics Office of Vietnam: 2020). The primary gross enrolment ratio reached 111 percent in 2018, with girls slightly ahead of boys with 111.85 percent and 109.46 percent, respectively (WENR: 2017, UNESCO: 2020). Whereas the proportion of boys is higher than that of girls in secondary school, female participation in tertiary schools leads that of the boys by 31.72 percent against 25.53 percent in 2018 (UNESCO: 2020). Along with this impressive performance, the country has also made remarkable progress in improving the quality of education and its participation in international educational services. As noted by the World Bank (2017a), Vietnam's students performed much higher than those of developing countries and were at par with those from developed countries in the 2015 PISA.[17]

Another critical area for human capital formation in Vietnam is improvements in health and healthcare services. Despite its relatively lower per capita income, Vietnam's health and healthcare services continued to perform on a par with Thailand's and Indonesia's, and far better than several developing countries with a higher per capita income (including many in SSA). According to General Statistics Office (GSO) of Vietnam, in 2018, there were 1,420 hospitals (1,189 public and 231 private); 303,515 hospital beds and 400,000 health workers of which 80 percent were doctors, assistants to doctors, nurses, and medical technicians (GSO: 2019). Fully 100 percent of the 11,000 communes across the country's 60 provinces had clinics with 7.6 doctors per 100,000 population during the same year (PricewaterhouseCoopers: 2014). Similarly, Vietnam's health expenditure continues to increase, reaching USD 12 billion in 2013 or 6.5 percent of the GDP, with a per capita expenditure of USD 130 (twice the level in 2007).

Recent reports and statistics (Statista: 2020) indicate that in 2019, the health expenditure of the country reached USD 17 billion or 6.6 percent of the GDP, which brings per capita expenditure to USD 170 the same year. Moreover, as of 31 October 2018, 82.33 million Vietnamese (87.62 percent) were covered by healthcare insurance (Vietnam Plus: 2018) with a plan to reach 95 percent coverage by 2020–2021. With these investments and expansion of health and healthcare services, Vietnam has recently managed to significantly reduce child mortality rates. Nearly, 97 percent of children received immunization in 2019.

This is a higher level than the rate in some developed countries (WHO and UNICEF: 2019). The maternal mortality rate has also declined by almost 75 percent since the 1990s while average life expectancy increased to 75.3 years in 2019, up from 69 years in 1986 (UNDESA: 2019).

The progress in education and health boosted the World Bank's Human Capital Index[18] of Vietnam to 0.67 in 2018. This was much higher than the average for developing countries and greater than the level in countries in the upper middle-income category (World Bank Blogs, 9 September 2019). As far as the Human Development Index (HDI) of the United Nations Development Programme (UNDP) is concerned, Vietnam's value consistently improved from 0.475 in 1990 to 0.693 in 2018, positioning Vietnam 118th out of 189 countries (UNDP: 2019b). These improvements in the human development and human capital indices are consistent with the performance of Vietnam in the 2019 Productive Capacities Index of UNCTAD (2020b), both in aggregate values and across the values of the categories. Such an impressive performance is an indication of the rapid and deep transformation observed in Vietnam over the last 30 years. Paradoxically, the countries of SSA have increased their expenditures on their education and health sectors, including through the allocation of Official Development Assistance (ODA) (Chapter 5), although the results thus far have been disappointing. The question is what has Vietnam done that those countries of SSA have failed to do to foster their human resources capital? The difference lies both in the quantity and quality of investments made as well as policy reforms Vietnam has been undertaking to realign the social sectors with its development priorities or objectives. Not only has Vietnam substantially increased investment in education and health, but it has also revamped and reformed these sectors as part of its overall reforms (renovation) processes

Learning from best performing countries in the region such as Singapore and South Korea, Vietnam devoted substantial financial resources to education and made significant interventions at the policy, operational, and institutional levels. From a policy perspective, Vietnam's education system was centralized in terms of management and strategic planning, resource allocation, and harmonized teaching across the country. However, the schools were given autonomy in developing curricula and setting competitive testing standards. According to OECD (2014) and UNESCO (2015), Vietnam has also taken key operational steps, emphasizing several areas of strategic significance to the education sector. Some of these steps included: designing "smart curricula" that facilitate pupils' deep learning of core concepts and mastery of skills as well as practical application (with a focus on mathematics, sciences, and humanities); enhancing critical thinking, creativity, and problem-solving techniques; valorizing and professionalizing the teaching profession; enhancing pedagogical contents of the teaching staff and incentivizing continuous upgrading of their knowledge and technical skills; and instituting continuous testing of students. Further actions which Vietnam has undertaken on education relate to building institutional frameworks, such as new accreditation and quality assurance mechanisms, establishing national qualification frameworks consistent or in line with the ASEAN Qualification Reference Framework

(AQRF), internationalizing the Vietnamese education system through outbound education and making education transnational, and increasing the role of the private sector in the delivery of education services (OECD: 2014, UNESCO: 2015).

Vietnam's policymakers and political leadership also view the delivery of quality health as key to foster social and political cohesion as well as for sustained economic growth and development. Specific actions include developing advanced and inclusive family planning and elaborate national healthcare systems with clear targets and strategies, providing universal health insurance coverage, and establishing special healthcare funds. Further actions relate to availing voluntary and subsidized health insurance for the rural population; educating the youth to raise awareness about healthcare and reproductive health; expanding the numbers of village health workers and health centres; building hospitals, ensuring antenatal consultations, and expanding skilled birth attendants; improving nutrition, access to food, basic hygiene and reducing malnutrition; as well as increasing the doctor-patient ratio (WHO: 2014).

8.2.3 *Transport Infrastructure and Connectivity*

The role of the Government of Vietnam has been central in the industrialization and transformation process of the country. This includes the provision of a state-of-the-art transport infrastructure, ICT connectivity, and building overall institutional capabilities as key enablers of productive capacities and structural economic transformation. Regarding transport infrastructure, Vietnam has developed diverse modes of transport and networks to serve as a gateway to the world and to connect its urban and rural sectors. These include road[19] and air[20] transport, inland waterways,[21] maritime transport,[22] and railways.[23] The last several decades have seen rapid changes in the magnitude and extent of transportation services, expansion of infrastructure, and a substantial increase in public investment. In implementing the country's Transport Infrastructure Plans (Transport Master Plans) and sectoral strategies, Vietnam has been investing, on average, 5.9 percent of GDP in infrastructure. This shows an increase of 11.1 percent – which ranks Vietnam in the second place in the region behind the Philippines' 12.6 percent (6.6 percent of GDP). The country has been ahead of most of its other neighbours such as Malaysia, Singapore, and Thailand, each spending 5.1 percent, 3.3 percent, and 3.4 percent of their respective GDP on physical infrastructure (*The ASEAN Post*, 28 September 2018). In absolute values the annual investment of Vietnam in infrastructure was USD 11 billion in 2011 but this level has quickly increased over the last few years to an average amount of USD 15 billion in 2017–2019 (Global Infrastructure Outlook: 2020). This is projected to further increase to an average of USD 22 billion a year during 2020–2030 period and to a further USD 25 billion a year until 2040.

However, such an impressive growth in infrastructure investment in Vietnam covers only 83 percent of the projected investment needs of the country in the sector. The projected cumulative amount of infrastructure investment need is expected to reach USD 605 billion by 2040, while the projected actual investment hovers around USD 503 billion (or 83 percent) by then. There will be an estimated financing gap of USD 102 billion in 2040, of which the gap in the road sector alone is expected to reach USD 55 billion followed by water-based transport infrastructure of USD 23 billion of the total investment gap (Dezan Shira & Associates, *Vietnam Briefing*, 21 August 2020). The Asian Development Bank (ADB: 2017) and the World Bank (2019) also projected that Vietnam's need for infrastructure investment will be USD 25 billion per year of which nearly 65 percent will come from the national government budget while the remaining 35 percent is expected from ODA, borrowing, FDI, and the domestic private sector. In 2015, of the total investment of USD 15.5 billion in infrastructure, USD 10 billion (64.5 percent) was from government coffers whereas USD 5.5 billion (35.5 percent) was from other sources (World Bank Blog, 21 February 2019). The boost in investment in transport infrastructure is driven by economic growth and an enlarging middle class; continuously expanding urban centres and increasing population; an unprecedented expansion in exports including manufacturing and services sectors; growing participation in regional and global production networks and value chains and increased imports. An increase in investment in infrastructure has in turn been a key factor in boosting economic growth, employment, and poverty reduction.

Transport infrastructure has multiple functions beyond transporting goods and passengers and enhancing export competitiveness. The sector has multiplier effects in developing, modernizing, and transforming other sectors such as agriculture, industry (manufacturing), services, and public utilities (Vietnam National Transport Strategy: 2020). Therefore, the increasing investment trends in the sector are the results of several push and pull factors in the country's efforts to modernize and expand transport infrastructure and logistics in all its forms. These include (but are not limited to) the building of new expressways, highways, exchange centres, transport-transit systems, airports, railways, waterways, and maritime ports as well as improving the governance of the transport sector. Availability of quality and efficient transport and logistics are also key to facilitating the engagement of the private sector both as user and provider of logistics, which is critically important for enhancing the participation of Vietnam in regional and global production and supply networks. For instance, as of March 2018, Vietnam had about "296,469 enterprises registered for business in logistics-related fields, focusing mainly on dynamic regions which have convenient ports and road systems" (Hoai: 2018 in Pham Linh and Nguyen Huong: 2020).

The efforts and achievements of Vietnam in building transport infrastructure are consistent with and supportive of the country's economic transformation from subsistence agriculture-led (traditional) economy to modern and dynamic manufacturing and service sector-driven economy in Southeast Asia, and from one of the poorest nations to one of the few vibrant economies in the world. According to several studies (JICA: 2013, Hoai: 2018 in Pham Linh and Nguyen Huong: 2020, General Statistics Office: 2020), the transport sector is the "lifeblood" of Vietnam's dynamic growth and transformation. Between 2015 and 2018, the total volume of goods transported by road accounted for an average of 24.2 percent, maritime (sea) transport 55.4 percent, inland waterways 18.6 percent, rail 1.5 percent, and air 0.3 percent. The average growth rate for goods transported by road was 110 percent, against 103 percent for maritime traffic, 106 percent for inland waters or rivers, 99.3 percent for railways, and 119 percent for airfreight during the same period (Hoai: 2018 in Nguyen Linh and Nguyen Huong: 2020). In 2019, while maritime transport accounted for 80 percent of imports and exports, its share in domestic cargo service was only 4.7 percent with no share in domestic passengers (Ministry of Transport of Vietnam: 2019). On the other hand, the share of road transport was 77 percent for domestic cargo and 94.5 percent of domestic passengers. During the same year, the share of waterways in domestic freight and passengers was 17.6 percent and 4.2 percent, respectively, whereas that of railways was 0.35 percent (cargo) and 0.19 percent (passengers).

The transport sector of Vietnam is expected to continue to attract investment, and by 2020 the road sector was projected to account for 56 percent of the total investments in the infrastructure sector, followed by railways (22 percent), public transport (15 percent), aviation (5 percent), and sea and waterways (2 percent) (Urban Development Management Center: 2016). The higher shares of road transport and railways indicate the enlarging demand for such infrastructure in urban areas due to the fast rate of urbanization, increasing demographic trends, improved household incomes, and the growing manufacturing sector that requires expanded infrastructure and logistics. For instance, private vehicles and motorcycles account for 80–90 percent of total vehicles in the country (Urban Development Management Center: 2016). Road transport also accounts for the lion's share of domestic passenger traffic and cargo transport. The allocation of high investment to road transport is consistent with the country's long-term objectives and strategies. The aim is to enhance road connectivity of regional, interprovincial, urban, and rural centres and create a competitive environment for the participation of the private sector. The strategies also aim to improve road safety and environmental standards by periodic assessment of the impact of roads on the natural environment and the population at large (Ministry of Transport, 2020). The focus on road transport and connectivity shows the drive of the Government of Vietnam to build export competitiveness and further enhance its participation in value chains. Currently, the participation in value chains accounts for nearly 70 percent of the country's exports and geographically covers the largest economic corridors[24] and growth poles (World Bank: 2019).

These efforts led Vietnam to consistently improve its global competitiveness and participation in regional and global trade. Consequently, in 2019, Vietnam ranked 67th out of 141 countries compared (improving a whopping ten points over the previous year) in the overall Global Competitiveness Index, ahead of some of the BRICS[25] (except China, Russia, and South Africa) and several other relatively more advanced developing countries, such as Argentina (World Economic Forum: 2019). The country has also performed better than it did in previous years in infrastructure (77th out of 141 countries compared) and it outperformed most of its peers in air connectivity (ranking 22nd) and road density (58th), transport infrastructure (66th). Areas where Vietnam has been lagging behind comparable countries on the index include road connectivity (104th), air transport efficiency (104th) and the quality of transport infrastructure (103rd). Despite these impressive records, Vietnam still faces several challenges in infrastructure. These include improving quality standards of the transport infrastructure, reducing the negative impact of the sector on the environment, making it more climate-resilient, attracting the private sector through PPPs, and meeting international safety standards. These call for consistent and continued efforts of the government in developing transformation-centred and value chain-oriented support infrastructure (World Bank: 2019). Otherwise, the progress seen in Vietnam in infrastructural development over the last three decades has been simply outstanding or exceptional.

8.2.4 *Information and Communications Technology (ICT)*

Vietnam's ICT sector is where one observes deeper and accelerated revolution and evolution. ICT has emerged as a sector and acts as a key enabler of transformation in other sectors (Kaila: 2017). As enabler, the ICT sector contributes to improving the sharing of market information, enhancing the efficiency of business transactions, and the delivery of other key social sectors such as education and health, and services sectors such as tourism and travel, energy, commerce, banking, and financial services. As a sector (including telecommunications) the annual GDP contribution (in value) reached USD 6.2 billion in 2018, with ICT expenditure (investment) consistently growing from USD 5.5 billion in 2015 to USD 65 billion in 2018. Out of this increase in expenditure, investment in hardware accounted for 89 percent, software 4 percent, and services 7 percent (Spire: 2019). The ICT sector in Vietnam has indeed become a source of economic growth, export diversification, and investment (including FDI), while employing a nearly 800,000-strong labour force in 2018 (MIC: 2019, Spire: 2019).

A more striking ICT revolution in Vietnam is seen as enabler of other sectors such as e-commerce, travel, hotels, transportation, and more importantly the manufacturing sector as well as the expansion of the digital economy. The digital economy accounted for nearly 4 percent of the GDP in 2018, the highest in Southeast Asia (*Vietnam Investment Review*, 16 February 2019). The same year, manufacturing was the driver of FDI inflows to Vietnam, where the production of telephone components, textiles, and electronics have accounted for USD 43 billion, USD 25 billion, and USD 23 billion, respectively, making Vietnam a hub for manufacturing and export of ICT-related goods in Southeast Asia (MIC: 2019, Spire: 2019; TMA Solutions: 2019). The combined FDI investment share of telephone components, electronics, including computer parts was USD 66 billion in 2018. Vietnam has also become a magnet for leading technology firms (particularly Samsung, LG Electronics, Nokia, and Intel) not only as a location to build manufacturing facilities for hardware, but also as an emerging hub to develop software and application-based services. These were accompanied by transfers of technology, knowhow, and best practices which are key for further transformation in the ICT sector (*Vietnam Investment Review*, 16 February 2019).

According to the Ministry of Information and Communication (MIC), the ICT sector in Vietnam is preparing for further and deeper transformation of the country's economy by embracing digital economy – Fourth Industrial Revolution (Industry 4.0). This transformation of the sector is expected to entail further shifts from telecommunication services and infrastructure to the digital ICT sector. Such a shift is centred on or driven by building new skills and jobs, facilitating R&D services, fostering new ICT-savvy societies, all of which are necessary to lay the foundation for the new industrial revolution.

Vietnam's readiness for Industry 4.0, both as producer and consumer of ICT-related products and services, can be seen from the unprecedented growth and expansion in ICT users and internet-based economy. The mobile phone penetration rate reached 139 percent, with a total of 143.3 million subscriptions – 152 per 100 people in 2019. The same year, the internet-based economy grew at about 40 percent a year – the fourth fastest growth rate in ASEAN and 70th in the world (TMA Solutions: 2019). Regarding the internet, 50 percent (nearly 48 million) of the total population were using internet in 2018 (TMA Solutions: 2019), up from only 16.1 percent in 2006 and 28.4 percent in 2014 (Keila: 2017). In 2017, Vietnam ranked 21st out of 193 countries in broadband internet subscription numbers (ITU: 2017), although it ranked 108th globally and 17th regionally in the overall ICT Development Index in the same year (ITU: 2017). In terms of access, broadband internet users in Vietnam reached about 13 million in 2018 against fewer than 10,000 in 2003 (ITU Data: 2020), while the country boasted 49 million 3G subscribers in 2017. There are some variations in data on internet access. Whereas most national and regional sources put the proportion of people with internet access at 50 percent, the latest analysis by the World Bank argues that "82 percent of the population in Vietnam has access to mobile broadband internet, while only 12 percent have access to fixed broadband" (World Bank: 2019). Notwithstanding this, there were about 29 million mobile social media accounts and 62 million social media users in Vietnam in 2018 (TMA Solutions: 2019). Out of the total 48 million who have access to the internet, in 2018, 97 percent were mobile phone users, 72 percent smartphone, 43 percent laptop (or desktop), and 13 percent tablet users in 2018.

The revolution and evolution of the ICT sector has facilitated and enabled the country's overall economic growth and transformation. The rapid expansion of the ICT sector has become vital for the country's efforts to further expand growth sources, deepen structural transformation and usher in Industry 4.0. For Industry 4.0 to happen, Vietnam has been undertaking further giant initiatives which include: (i) establishing smart cities,[26] expanding start-ups and mobilizing investments; (ii) putting in place a National Innovation Programme;[27] (iii) rolling out state-of-the-art 4G and next generation or 5G services;[28] (iv) IT-based skills formation[29] and developing e-governance;[30] and (v) enhancing transformation in the industrial (manufacturing), agriculture, and services sectors in preparation for Industry 4.0 (MIC: 2019, Spire: 2019, TMA Solutions: 2019, *Vietnam Investment Review*, 16 February 2019). To fully implement this ambitious transformation agenda, Vietnam has already boosted investment in the ICT sector. It has been laying infrastructural, institutional, and regulatory foundations for the sector to continue to thrive in the coming decade and to usher in Industry 4.0.

The government has already embarked on a major task to develop a national strategy for Industry 4.0, under the responsibility of the Ministry of Planning and Investment (MPI) with specific, time-bound targets (Spire: 2019, MIC: 2019). For instance, by 2025 all administrative agencies would provide level-4 online public services via technology-2025; 100 percent online payments for public services would be realized; fibre optic and mobile broadband internet (4G and 5G) would cover all communes; 100 percent internet penetration would be achieved, and by 2030, the ICT sector would add between USD 28 billion and USD 62.1 billion to the GDP, which is equivalent to an increase of 7–16 percent (Spire: 2019).

The ICT sector has been driving and deepening Vietnam's structural economic transformation in recent years. It has also been acting as enabler of transformation in other sectors such as industry and the services sectors and facilitator of domestic, regional, and global integration of Vietnam's economy. The sector has particularly contributed to efficiency in the delivery of services, including public administration in urban and rural areas. It has greatly improved the efficiency of business, transport, information, and communication as well as education and health services. Overall, the digital economy of the country has been thriving, growing at 40 percent a year, with e-commerce alone registering 13.8 percent annual growth (World Bank: 2019). Between 2020 and 2025, e-commerce is forecast to grow by 35 percent a year and cloud computing by 65 percent, deepening further the role of ICT in socioeconomic transformation in Vietnam. In 2018, almost 40 percent of Vietnam's participants in e-commerce were SMEs, with investment in existing e-commerce and e-commerce-related SMEs almost trebled from USD 291 million in 2017 to USD 889 million in 2018 (World Bank: 2019).

However, there are remaining challenges that must be effectively resolved to accelerate further growth and improvements in the sector. The bottlenecks include the need to continuously upgrade the technical skills and capacities of ICT professionals, revamp supplier development initiatives, and enhance an entrepreneurial ecosystem with managerial knowhow and ease of bureaucracy (Sturgeon and Zylberberg: 2017). Despite these gaps and limitations, the ICT sector has shown an outstanding performance and achievements in deepening Vietnam's structural transformation. The key success factors that have propelled the ICT sector to such a high level are those that have assisted Vietnam in fostering its economy-wide productive capacities and structural transformation. These include sustained and continued economic growth that helped to increase aggregate income, investment, and capital accumulation; growing middle class and expanding urbanization; the country's continued and expanded participation in regional and global production networks and value chains; building human capital and creating a technology-savvy population (both as consumers and producers of ICT products and services); increasing targeted investment by the government and the private sector; attracting FDI and leading firms to the ICT sector and continuously growing consumption of ICT for information and communication.

8.2.5 Banking and Financial Services

Vietnam's fast economic growth and transformation has been supported by a dynamic and flexible banking and financial services sector. The sector has been further facilitated and accelerated by increased FDI flows, remittances, the advent of e-commerce, ICT, dynamic entrepreneurship, expanded imports and exports of the country. Without reforming the sector, a centrally planned and state-controlled "mono-banking sector" of Vietnam could not have effectively responded to the nation's expanded needs. In this context, Vietnam's policymakers have intensified the reform of the sector as an integral part of and consistent with the socialist market-oriented economic renovation (Doi-Moi) – i.e., gradual, and carefully sequenced. The initial wave of reforms focused on changing the management systems within the State-Owned Banking and Financial Sector. This was done by separating the legislative, political, and operational roles, duties, and functions of the sector. Consequently, the reforms led to the separation of the large State-Owned Commercial Banks (SOCBs) from the State Bank of Vietnam (SBV)[31] and revamping the Joint Stock Banks (JSBs), each with distinct roles or functions in the economy (Kovsted et al.: 2003).

The SBV is the country's central bank. It is responsible for trading in treasury bills, overseeing inter-bank transactions in domestic currency, and managing the domestic market for foreign currency exchanges. Moreover, the SBV monitors and supervises all credit institutions and banks in Vietnam to ensure that they comply with domestic laws and policies. The SOCBs, on the other hand, carry out standard banking operations[32] (both primary and secondary operations) in accordance with the country's financial laws and regulations. As with the SBV and SOCBs, the Vietnam JSBs are state-owned financial institutions and their key roles and functions are to support sectors such as trade or industry.[33] These early phase reforms have transformed the sector from an exclusive and tightly controlled, state-owned into a semi-autonomous and flexible banking and financial sector, with the state still playing dominant (direct and indirect)[34] functions, ownership, and management roles. The state maintained its central role despite international pressures to transform the banking and financial sector from exclusively government-owned to private sector-led independent banking and financial sector, guided by market forces and free competition (Kovsted et al.: 2003).

The sustained economic growth and transformation of Vietnam necessitated a further deepening of the reform of the banking and financial sector of the country. Growth with transformation requires world-class banking and financial institutions that are capable of creating macroeconomic stability, sustaining economic growth, and further deepening structural transformation (Leung: 2009). The banking and financial sector is vital in guiding and allocating funds or investments into productive sectors and high-growth economic activities (King and Levine: 1993). The Government of Vietnam has, therefore, initiated a second wave of reforms[35] of the sector (Leung: 2009). This phase has led to gradually abolishing credit cooperative systems (Kovsted et al.: 2003). Consequently, the role of foreign bank operations increased, with permission to take national currency (Dong) deposits, and gradually increasing their market shares (Leung: 2009). However, the control and administration of exchange rates remain with the state banks. Moreover, "although the Vietnamese government has stopped using the financial sector as a direct instrument for the implementation of productive sector policies, considerable indirect government control of financial sector activities persists" (Kovsted et al.: 2003).

The overall outcomes of the reforms of the banking and financial sector of Vietnam are remarkable and surpassed all expectations. Banking services have shown exponential growth from barely 200,000 private bank accounts in 2001 to 86 million ATM/Debit and credit cards by 2018, 3005 points of sale (PoS), 18500 ATM, 72.7 million private bank accounts, with 43.2 million people having bank accounts, representing 60 percent of the country's population 15 years old and above [in 2018] (World Bank Project, 25 June 2019).

With the outstanding expansion of users of banking services, the share of SOCBs in the country's banking system has diminished steadily from nearly 100 percent of loans and deposits in the economy in the pre-reform period to 50 percent in 2018, with astronomical growth in securities market[36] (World Bank Project, 25 June 2019). Today, the banking sector of Vietnam is regarded as sound, fast expanding, and the largest segment of the country's financial system when measured by deposits or credits (Vuong: 2019). The reform has also altered institutional aspects both within and outside of the sector. The role of Foreign-Owned Banks (FOBs) and (domestic) Privately-Owned Banks has significantly increased, while other development-facilitating banks such as the Bank of Investment and Development (BID), Technology and Commercial Joint Stock Bank (TCJSB), Social Policy Banks (SPBs), etc. have been established to respond to the changing socioeconomic and technological landscapes of the country. These specialized banks have been operating side by side large State-Owned Banks such as SOCBs, JSCBs, with the SBV playing the role of the central bank. The reforms have further facilitated the growth and expansion of non-bank financial institutions and services. These include insurance and securities companies, financial leasing companies, investment funds, and development funds – all of which have collectively propelled the banking and financial sector of Vietnam to a different level (Vuong: 2019). The gradual and strategically sequenced reforms in the banking and financial sector have played critically important roles in modernizing the sector, creating a stable microeconomic and macroeconomic environment, and sound monetary and fiscal policies.

8.2.6 *Institutions*

Institutions play a part in guiding policy formulation, implementation, and setting the rules of engagement as well as driving socioeconomic transformation. They are equally important in determining the incentive structure in transformational growth. Educational and health institutions, R&D, innovation, and technology centres, etc. are all agents of change and transformation. There is increasing consensus on the need for and important role of institutions in economic development from both historical and contemporary perspectives. Yet, there have also been serious contentions and disagreements on several institutional aspects.[37] Vietnam's institutions have continued to be centralized in terms of governance, structure, and management for more than six decades. This, with gradual gravitation towards mixed economy-based decision-making, seems to have functioned well for the country. Pragmatism, learning from others, adaptation to changing circumstances, and being forward-looking have characterized decision-making processes in Vietnam since 1986. Its institutions have become predictable within a centralized authority and have clearly defined rules, regulations, and responsibilities with a division between political leadership and bureaucracies. The country's success in fostering productive capacities and structural transformation is the result of solid institutions, which are capable of formulating and implementing growth-friendly, home-grown, and transformational development policies.

The World Bank acknowledged remarkable economic growth and poverty reduction as tangible gains for the people of Vietnam in terms of welfare and improvements in accessing quality services (World Bank: 2017b) and attributed these to the country's policymaking and the capacity of the state in "delivering education, health, power (electricity), rural roads, rural electrification, water supply and sanitation services" (World Bank: 2016c). Likewise, the IMF credited the socioeconomic success of Vietnam to macroeconomic stability, stepped-up economic reforms, and inflows of FDI which are enabling structural transformation with a potential for further growth (IMF: 2018a). Despite such a public recognition, the two institutions persisted in calling for a further deepening of market-based reforms with the focus on privatizing the SOEs and strengthening the domestic private sector, with a presumed objective of boosting labour productivity. The prescribed institutional reforms are also claimed to enhance the efficiency of infrastructure in parallel with ensuring increased government effectiveness, developing market institutions, and improving transparency and accountability in banking and monetary policies (World Bank: 2016c, 2017b, IMF: 2018b).

There is no divergence of views or opinions on the need for continued institutional reforms. However, there is no empirical or historical evidence to substantiate the claims that institutional reforms should necessarily be market-based or driven by market fundamentals. Institutions require cognitive, normative, and regulative elements for their effective functioning (Scott: 1995, cited in Nguen and Trinh: 2018). They must consider specific local circumstances – political, cultural, governance, and overall business environment (North: 1991). Therefore, the motivation for institutional reform should go well beyond market signals and be accompanied by incentive structures and realigning these with the overall policy objectives of the government. It should play a vital role in creating conducive conditions for R&D, facilitating technology transfers, and accelerating innovation. Institutional reforms also need in-built flexibility to respond or adapt to new challenges and external shocks, including environmental or climate change-induced vulnerability (Nguen and Trinh: 2018). Vibrant institutions require growth-friendly and development-oriented government policies and strategies, stable legal and political frameworks, and the allocation of adequate human and financial resources to enable them to formulate and implement policies (Chand et al.: 2001). All these cannot be addressed by market forces (demand and supply) alone. For instance, in the absence of adequate financial, technical, and human resources, it will be difficult or impossible for governments to effectively address key constraints to their countries' development (Chand et al.: 2001).

Within its centralized institutional arrangement and mixed economy-based policymaking, Vietnam has developed vibrant institutions. As discussed earlier, its institutional framework distinguishes, however vaguely, between bureaucracy and political decision-making processes. This tacit but conscious distinction seems to have been functioning well and has gradually led Vietnam's transitions with deepened structural transformation. Vietnam's transformation has been in production and productivity as well as changes in the sectoral share of employment and GDP contributions. Fostering human capital, ICT, energy, and infrastructure-building have played central role in socioeconomic changes. Undoubtedly, institutions, policymaking capabilities, and governance capacities (Phung, Visseren-Hamakers, and Arts: 2015) have equally played an important role in Vietnam's growth and transformation. The distinction between politics and bureaucracy particularly, makes political interference in economic decision-making less frequent, disruptive, or obvious (Masina: 2006). The country also developed organizational structures with a clear delineation of duties and responsibilities between the various agencies. But it has deliberately made such a distinction less clear (vague), which often makes dialogue with donors challenging. This notwithstanding, there are important political, hierarchical, and institutional setups – formal and informal – with implications for policy formulation, implementation, coordination, and oversight (Datta and Mendizabal: 2018). These involve the state, the Communist Party of Vietnam (CPV), the Fatherland Front[38] and the military. The role of the state is generally defined in party and government guidelines. Accordingly, the National Assembly sets long-term vision and medium-term strategic plans,[39] while the state manages and provides public services, overseeing and assuring the provision of quality services (World Bank: 2016c, SRV Resolution No. 142/2016/QH13 dated 12 April 2016, FAO: 2017).

In parallel with building state (public) institutions, Vietnam has gradually opened up space for the private sector and civil society and enhanced public-private dialogue through enacting new laws and codes. It has instituted regular consultations among the newly established Vietnam Chambers of Commerce and Industry (VCCI),[40] the Private Sector Associations, and Private Sector Forum. Vietnam's private sector generated "40 percent of the GDP, employed more than 80 percent of the labour force, and had a total investment of USD 27.1 billion in 2018 – the highest investment level compared to the SOEs" (ASEM Connect, 21 December 2019, 4 June 2020). However, the formal (officially registered and licensed) private sector contributes only about 10 percent to the GDP, which is significantly lower than that of the SOEs and the informal sector (private households). Despite the dominant informality of the domestic private sector, Vietnam's performance in the World Bank's Doing Business[41] has continued to improve, increasing from 62.6 in 2016 to 69.8 (out of 100) in 2020, with Vietnam ranking 70th out of 190 economies compared (World Bank Doing Business: 2020).

Vietnam has also been credited for its efforts to continuously improve corporate governance, which is critically important for the continued growth and expansion of the private sector and its role in the country's economy. Although a lot remains to be done, ongoing efforts include beefing up the functioning and oversight role of the State Securities Commission and moving towards international best practices. Improved corporate governance is also viewed as equally important for enhancing the performance and management of public companies (SSC and IFC: 2019). With a view to further enhancing the role of the private sector, the government needs to take further steps in several areas of interest to the sector. These include easing registration and bankruptcy declaration for SMEs, facilitating access to credit on preferential terms and creating formal structures for continuous public-private sector dialogue. Dialogue between SOEs, large and small firms as well as between foreign and domestic firms is vital for the country's efforts to enhance the role of the private sector in development. Fostering beneficial and productive linkages between SMEs and large firms along the supply chains and facilitating the sharing of industry and market information between and among firms or enterprises are also critically important in enhancing the role of the private sector (World Bank: 2018a).

Institutions have played an important role in facilitating the strategic and beneficial integration of Vietnam into the global economy. This includes identifying priority sectors with comparative advantages and those with multiplier effects, articulating binding constraints to development and realigning incentives to unlock bottlenecks. They were particularly important in mapping intervention areas and sequentially implementing policies and strategies for maximizing impact and efficiency gains. For instance, carefully negotiated bilateral, regional, and multilateral trade and economic relations, discussed in Chapter 7, have greatly assisted Vietnam in taking advantage of regional and global trade, investment, and economic opportunities. Moreover, Vietnam's institutions have facilitated and enabled the country to draw practical lessons from other successful economies in East Asia, which helped it perfect its own policies and strategies. Although the country's institutions recognize the importance of learning from other successful and less successful experiences, they have equally realized that learning cannot be effective without local and technical knowledge. Hence, priority was given to understand country-specific challenges and seek home-grown solutions by fostering knowledge and technical skills as well as enhancing policy coordination. Vietnam's political leadership and policymakers have rightly placed emphasis on fostering human capital, enhancing technical and operational skills as well institutional capabilities for effective and successful learning, experimentation, and emulation of policymaking. As with several newly industrializing East Asian economies such as South Korea, Taiwan, and Hong Kong, Vietnam's institutions quietly or tacitly followed export- and investment-led economic diversification strategy in parallel with IS strategies. These have been pursued not as conflicting but mutually supportive and complementary strategies. For example, the country pursued aggressive export diversification strategies in sectors where it has comparative advantages[42] in parallel with carefully identified goods for IS with a focus on consumer items for which there is high domestic demand and which it had been massively importing despite comparative advantages, such as rice, sugar, and dairy products. The priority attention given to these items made Vietnam self-sufficient and one of the largest producers and exporters in the world in less than three decades.

In pursuing its development policies and strategies and in the context of its institutions, Vietnam has also gradually built national consensus on the reform processes. It has effectively mobilized all stakeholders (including the private sector and civil society actors) in the country's development. For instance, there was full understanding and awareness within the CPV and policy governance structures that economic growth, job creation and poverty reduction are essential for the political survival and continuity of centralized but gradually market-oriented system (Masina: 2006). Public (mass) mobilization[43] for action against poverty and development has been central to the state machineries and the governing party's (CPV) vision. However, there have been concerns that participation does not necessarily entail empowerment in key decision-making processes (Kwak: 2019). There also appears to have been a distinction between popular participation and that of members of the CPV, as the latter enjoy greater access to decision-making processes with better income and other privileges (Markussen and Quang-Thanh: 2018). Notwithstanding this, the CPV governs through a combination of legitimacy, consensus, and tacit coercion, and by clearly articulating organic linkages between the party and the people when it comes to political governance. Accordingly, "all State power belongs to the people of Vietnam and is based on an alliance between the working class, the peasantry, and the intelligentsia" (SRV National Assembly: 2013–3). Governance based on popular legitimacy, solidarity, and consensus is not unique to Vietnam but have been viewed as compatible with the political culture and core principles of ASEAN and its member states over the last 50 years (CustomsNews, 9 August 2017). In all these processes, Vietnam's institutions (political leadership and bureaucracy alike) have played paramount roles. In the context of a declaration that "state power belongs to the people of Vietnam", sustained and inclusive economic growth (which maximized societal welfare) has assisted in fostering the legitimacy of the state machinery in decision-making and solidarity between the state and the people of Vietnam as well as enhancing "governance by consensus".

The overall socioeconomic transformation in Vietnam has been accelerated by fostering capital accumulation (including human capital formation), industrialization, investments, and export diversification. Building infrastructure such as energy (power), transport, and other utilities, harnessing the potential of ICT, and transforming the rural (agriculture) economy, etc. have played critical roles in the country's structural economic transformation. The banking and financial sector has also played a key role in catalyzing and facilitating the fostering of productive capacities and structural economic transformation. The combination of these engines and enablers of growth and fostering vibrant institutions have laid solid foundations for Vietnam's sustained and deeper transformation.

Unlike in SSA, Vietnam's growth and transformation processes as well as key enablers and drivers of the process have been endogenous to the economy. External factors such as ODA, external borrowing, FDI, and imports of capital goods have not been decisive. They have only played complementary or facilitating roles. The country has also emerged as an important manufacturing hub in Southeast Asia and an important trading nation. In 2020, despite the disruptive impact of COVID-19, Vietnam was among the few countries that posted positive economic growth (3 percent) during the COVID-19 pandemic, although this was far lower than the forecast of 6.7 percent (Spire: 2019). The contribution of agriculture to the growth rate has significantly diminished over the years and was expected to remain at a mere 3.7 percent in 2020, whereas manufacturing, construction, and services were projected to contribute 12.6 percent, 9.1 percent, and 6.9 percent of the growth, respectively. Manufacturing not only has been the largest source of economic growth in Vietnam, but it has been also the destination for the largest share of FDI (28 percent) and the driver of exports of the country. The structural change of Vietnam's exports (discussed in the following section) is an indication of the country's profound transformation and the fostering of productive capacities. In all these processes Vietnam's institutions have played vital roles in balancing the pressure of neoliberalism with the development priorities (visions and ambitions) of the country.

8.2.7 *Trade "Openness"*

With the world merchandise trade having bounced back from its fall in 2016 (WTO: 2019), Vietnam continued to register outstanding performance in its exports, with a 13.2 percent increase in 2018 when compared to the level in 2015 (UNCTADstat: 2020). As discussed above, the GDP of Vietnam skyrocketed from USD 14 billion in 1980 to USD 244.5 billion in 2018 (UNCTADStat: 2020, World Bank Data: 2019) and to a whopping USD 260 billion in 2019. During the same year, the total trade (exports and imports of goods plus services) reached USD 615 billion, bringing the country's trade growth to GDP ratio to 236 percent and its exports to GDP ratio to 108 percent (UNCTADstat: 2020). Although Vietnam and China started with the same level of trade to GDP ratio of less than 20 percent in 1980 (Tarp: 2017), in 2019, the share of Vietnam's trade in GDP was nearly seven times higher than that of China (35.68 percent the same year: World Bank Data: 2019). This makes Vietnam one of the most open economies in the world, against the widely held views that centralized, or "socialist free-market economies" are tightly closed economies. Notwithstanding its high degree of trade openness, Vietnam's ranking in the global Trade Enabling Index (TEI) lags behind several countries on the Asian continent (World Economic Forum and Global Alliance for Trade Facilitation: 2016). In 2016, Vietnam ranked 73rd out of 136 economies compared, whereas Singapore topped the list, while Hong Kong was 3rd, South Korea 27th, Taiwan 35th, Malaysia 37th, China 61st, Thailand 63rd, and Indonesia 70th (WEF and GATF: 2016).

Its increased openness to international trade would have exposed Vietnam to external economic shocks – financial, economic, or health-related such as the COVID-19 pandemic. However, thus far, Vietnam has been carefully navigating through the tides of negative external shocks. The country managed to successfully contain the impact of the 1997–1998 Asian financial crisis (Kokko: 1998) and global financial and economic crisis of 2008 2009 (Nguyen et al.: 2016). With the forecast of economic growth for 2020 of 6.7 percent, Vietnam is also expected to contain negative socioeconomic impacts of COVID-19, although the full impact of the pandemic on the global economy is still looming large. The credit in averting the impact of negative external shocks on Vietnam goes to carefully managed and sequenced beneficial integration into the global economy. An increasing middle class, enlarged domestic demand, and policies centred on the fostering of productive capacities are among factors that help Vietnam to avert or contain the impact of external shocks on the country's economy. Vietnam's beneficial integration into the global economy has also been facilitated by its selective bilateral, regional, and multilateral trade and economic relations with key countries both within and outside of the continental Asia. Its major trading partners are in East Asia, North America, and Europe and mostly reached by sea and air, through two airports, five seaports and five border crossings. With all its major trading partners (except China), Vietnam has maintained surpluses in its trade balance thanks to capacities to export to all parts of the globe. This is an outcome of determined efforts of the Government of Vietnam to achieve geographic (export market) diversification along with product diversification, penetrating global markets and seizing opportunities. The largest individual trading partners (in alphabetical order) are China, Japan, Hong Kong, South Korea, and the USA (Figure 8.1).

As for imports, all the major suppliers are from the Asian continent with China accounting for 27.5 percent of total imports of the country, followed by South Korea (22 percent), Japan (7.9 percent), Thailand (5 percent), the USA (4 percent), and others (33.2 percent) in 2018 (UNCTADstat: 2019). Vietnam's trade surplus with the USA is estimated between USD 36 and 40 billion a year, followed by its surplus with Japan (USD 40 million). The only major trading partner with which Vietnam runs a trade deficit is China with a

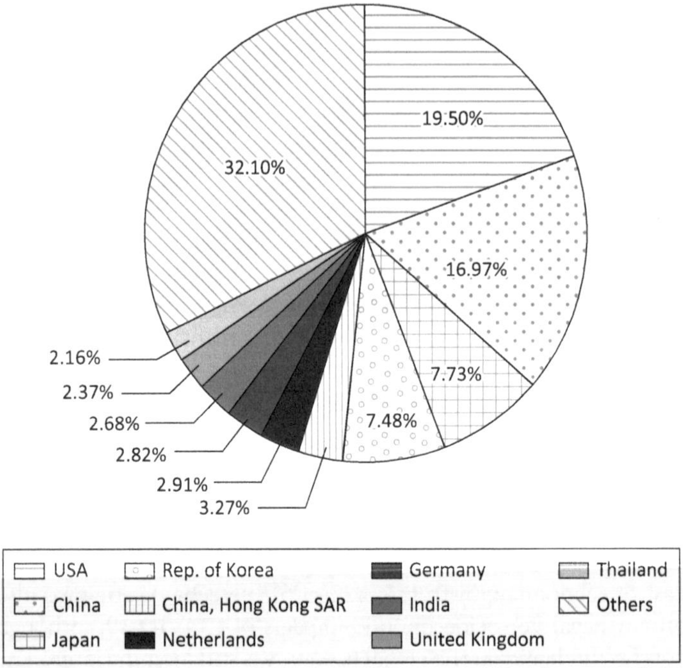

Figure 8.1 Trade partners of Vietnam (2018): exports.
Source: UNCTADstat (2020).

magnitude of USD 20 billion in 2018 which further increased to about USD 29 billion in 2019 (*Hanoi Times*, 21 November 2019). According to UNCTADstat, Vietnam's total merchandise trade was USD 580.1 billion in 2019 – USD 264.2 billion exports and USD 253.9 billion imports. The trade surplus in goods was USD 10.3 billion – a substantial increase from USD 6.8 billion in 2018. The latest data obtained from the Observatory of Economic Complexity (OEC) shows that the service trade of the country for the same year was USD 34.9 billion (of which USD 16.6 billion service exports and USD 18.3 billion imports: OEC: 2020).

In parallel with intensifying bilateral, regional, and multilateral trade and economic agreements, Vietnam has also diversified its exports both in number, volume, and structure. The number of products exported by Vietnam increased by about 126 percent between 1995 and 2018 – from 199 products to 250 (UNCTADstat: 2020). During the same period, the number of products imported from all nations, notably from Asian developing economies (see Figure 7.5) remains at about 260. Vietnam has quickly and substantially increased the number of products it exports to the average level of the world and that of the developing economies, which shows supply capacities and the extent of export diversification in the country over the last 23 years examined. As discussed above, Vietnam's exports of goods and services have also spiked over the last two decades from USD 36 billion in 2005 to USD 280.8 billion in 2019 (UNCTADstat: 2020).

A more profound transformation observed in Vietnam's international trade is a change in the structure, technological sophistication, and composition of its exports, with the manufacturing sector playing an important role in the growth of exports and GDP. While exports of primary agricultural commodities (such as coffee and rice) and extractive products (such as petroleum and related products) have significantly diminished over the years (Figure 8.2), the role of value-added and technologically sophisticated industrial and manufactured products (such as broadcasting equipment and accessories, telephones, computer parts, automatic data processing equipment and components, integrated circuits, cathode valves and tubes, textiles and footwear, leather and leather products) have taken a central place as top export earners (Figure 8.3).

The manufacturing sector has also become a key driver of growth in FDI and the overall economy. Vietnam's export basket has become ever larger and diversified as the country's industrial base expands and its economy-wide productive capacities increase. The share of petroleum and petroleum products which accounted for nearly 25 percent of the country's total exports (in value) in 2000 went down to less than 3 percent in 2018. Likewise, the share of rice and coffee also diminished from about 15 percent in early 2000s to less than 3 percent in 2018. The decline in relative shares of agricultural and extractive resources has been compensated, particularly by an impressive increase in the share of telecommunications equipment, electronics, and parts in the country's total exports.

8.3 Conclusions

The evidence presented in Chapters 7 and 8 clearly indicates that economic growth and development are outcomes of carefully selected, sequenced, and effectively implemented policies and strategies. Vietnam's sustained and inclusive economic growth, export diversification, and technological sophistication as well as investments (including FDI) are behind increasing aggregate income, capital accumulation, and fostering productive capacities and structural transformation. Building human and technical capabilities, fostering a dynamic ICT sector, supply of predictable and productivity-enhancing energy (electricity), and scaling-up investment in transport infrastructure are key success factors in Vietnam's continued growth and transformation centred on manufacturing in Asia. Kick-starting transformation in the agriculture sector with a focus on cash and food crops, fisheries, and livestock is a further source of growth and transformation of Vietnam. These success factors have been further facilitated by dynamic, predictable, and flexible institutions and continuously growing banking and financial sectors. These have guided and facilitated the country's continued and accelerated socioeconomic transformation through endogenous enablers and drivers. External factors such as ODA, borrowing, FDI, and imports of capital goods have played complementary or facilitating – not determining or decisive – roles.

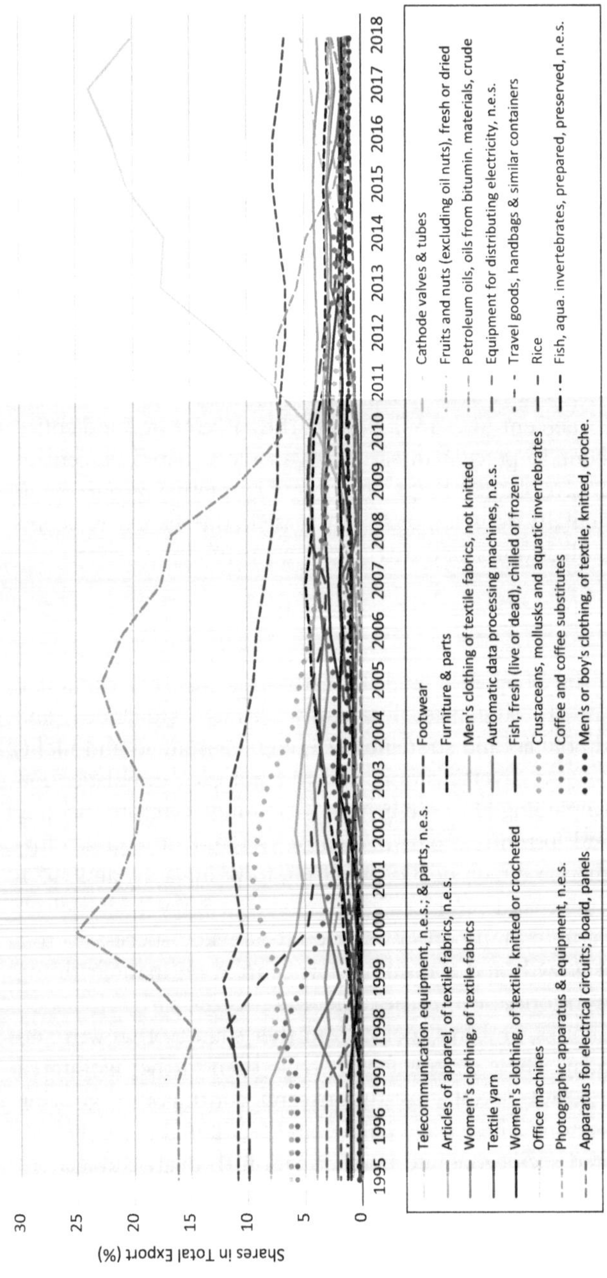

Figure 8.2 Change in the structure of Vietnam's exports and share (1995–2018).

Source: UNCTADstat: 2020.

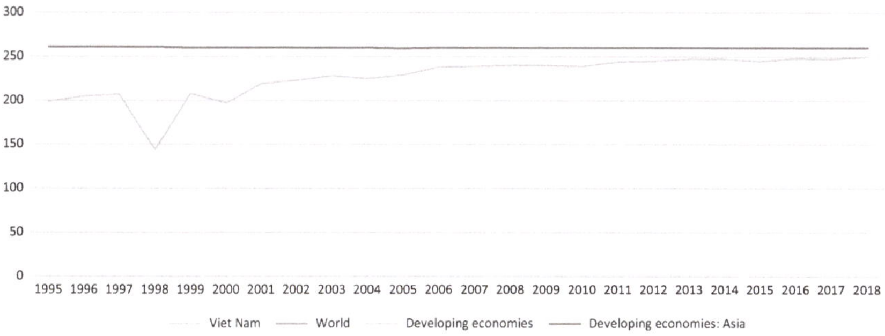

Figure 8.3 Number of products exported: Vietnam, developing economies, and world (1995–2018).

Source: UNCTADstat (2020).

What are the policy lessons from Vietnam's experience with implications for SSA, given the region's growing partnership with China? What worked in the case of Vietnam and why? The next chapter (Chapter 9) seeks to provide a response to and justifications for these and related questions.

Notes

1 A tonne, which is commonly referred to as metric ton (USA), is used in the chapter as a metric unit of mass equal to 1,000 kilograms.

2 The key limitations in the sector include (but are not limited to) the fragmentation in the production and supply of coffee cherries, lack of contractual obligations to ensure regular supplies by farmers, disconnect between firms and processing mills, shortage of investment (capital) to modernize coffee processing mills and upgrading their capacities, limited opportunities for training and capacity-building as well as information sharing among coffee farmers.

3 In 2018 Nestlé inaugurated a new Nescafé Dolce Gusto Capsule (90 percent of which is for export). Bien Hoa Vinacafé Joint Stock, Len's Coffee LLC, Starbucks, Phuc Long Trading, and Anni Coffee all are well-established coffee processing and exporting enterprises in Vietnam.

4 By the end of 2017, more than 300,000 ha, accounting for more than 50 percent of the total coffee growing area of Vietnam (600,000 ha), were certified by initiatives including Common Code for Coffee Community (4C), VietGAP, and/or RFA (ICO: 2019, USDA: 2019).

5 Norms were established by such programmes as the Common Code for Coffee Community (4C), Vietnam's Good Agricultural Practice (VietGAP), and followed the EU's Good Agricultural Practice (GAP), Rainforest Alliance, etc. (ICO: 2019).

6 The upstream part of the value chain refers to activities that are close to the exploitation of natural resources (without adding value), whereas downstream parts relate to value adding or transforming natural resources into manufacturing the final product.

7 The fisheries sector in Vietnam is vast, covering marine fisheries, inland fisheries, and aquaculture.

8 There are three sources of cultured fish in Vietnam: freshwater, which accounts for 82 percent of production; brackish water aquaculture (15 percent of production), and marine aquaculture (3 percent of production).

9 The Mekong River Delta provides 70 percent of cultured fish production, 80 percent of cultured shrimp, and nearly 90 percent of Vietnam's export rice (Leh: 2017).

10 Government subsidies include the provision of high-quality seeds (fingerlings), credits to fish farmers at preferential rates and insurance against risks and disasters as well as extension services such as training and advisory services to the fishing communities and associations in rural areas.

11 The number of marine fishing (registered) vessels has increased from 44,000 in 1991 to 95,000 in 2006 and to 110,000 in 2016 (Kim A.T.N: 2017).

12 The sources of power in Vietnam are hydro (40 percent), coal (39.5 percent), and natural gas (18.88 percent), with the remaining balance (1.67 percent) percentage being imported from China and Lao PDR.

13 Between 2009 and 2018, electricity power has increased nine times but remains below full cost recovery (World Bank: 2020c).

14 For details, see https://www.trade.gov/country-commercial-guides/vietnam-power-generation-transmission-and-distribution and https://ourworldindata.org/energy/country/vietnam

15 Of these, 7.8 million students were in elementary school, 5.14 million in lower secondary schools, and 2.4 million in upper secondary schools in 2018.

16 The number includes, 15,000 primary schools, 10,321 lower secondary and 2,399 upper secondary schools during the same period.

17 PISA is the OECD's Programme for International Students Assessment of 15-year-old students in reading, mathematics, and science skills.

18 The Human Capital Index of the World Bank measures the level of human capital that a child born today can expect to attain by age 18. The index is designed to show how improvements in the current health and education outcomes shape the productivity of the next generation of workers. (For more details, see https://www.worldbank.org/en/publication/human-capital.)

19 According to the General Statistics Office and the World Bank (2019b), as of 2016, the total length of the road network, excluding village roads, reached over 300,000 km, including about 1,000 km of expressways – a fully access-controlled toll road system.

20 In total, Vietnam has 23 airports, most of which are undergoing major upgrading in the context of the 2015–2020 Master Plan, which also includes the construction of new airports with a total investment of USD 13.4 billion. Of these the most important project that attracts increasing attention is Long Thanh International Airport with a total investment outlay of USD 6.7 billion for phase 1 (BBGV: 2018).

21 Vietnam boats an extensive network of natural waterways, including nearly 16,000 km of managed navigable routes carrying significant traffic around the Red River Delta and Mekong Delta areas.

22 Vietnam has a total of 3,200 km of coastline, with 224 river ports, 8,000 landing stages, 45 seaports, and 200 terminals (World Bank: 2019b).

23 Vietnam's railway is relatively underdeveloped by regional standards and has a network of 3,200 km with a limited capacity in terms of passenger (5 percent) and goods (2 percent) transportation. The Master Plan on railway transport development for 2010–2030 is expected to increase the rail network capacity and encourage local manufacture of new wagons and locomotives (World Bank: 2019).

24 The key corridors include Hanoi–Ho Chi Minh City, Hanoi–northern Chinese borders, North–South coastline and between the central highlands and the south and connecting major export processing zones, industrial parks, seaports, and airports (World Bank: 2019, Hoai, A (2018) in Pham Linh and Nguyen Huong: 2020).

25 "BRICS" stands for the association of five major emerging economies: Brazil, Russia, China, India, and South Africa.

26 Currently there are four new Smart Cities, which are being developed in the north, centre, and south of the country: The Hanoi Smart City, Da Nang Smart City, the Dong Nai province Smart City, and The Binh Duong Smart City. The overall objec-

tive of the Smart Cities project is to experiment e-government and modernize urban services by introducing "*smart* traffic systems, smart power grids, smart water management systems, smart environment and smart manage waste" (Spire: 2019).

27 The programme is designed to build an innovation ecosystem through further funding of scientific and research infrastructure of the national innovation centre to be established in Hanoi, which is expected to host 40 large technology companies, 150 start-ups, and 15 venture investment funds.

28 This is intended to further develop the ICT infrastructure including by issuing more licenses for 3G, 4G, and 5G networks across all the provinces and focusing on wireless rather than fixed line connectivity as key for Industry 4.0.

29 The aim is to strengthen technological skills amongst all levels of the country and to provide digital skills training for 500,000 employees of small and medium-sized enterprises (SMEs).

30 E-Government is needed to deepen regulatory reforms with the aim to ease digitization in the government, remove hurdles and encourage local business to adopt technology and facilitate technology transfer.

31 The State Bank of Vietnam (SBV) acts as the central bank of the country with authority to supervise, facilitate and organize the banking sector. It regulates the issuance of banknotes, maintaining currency reserves, securing monetary stability, managing the currency and credit systems, formulating, implementing, and monitoring monetary policy, managing the circulation of banknotes and coins, managing foreign exchanges and acting as the banker's bank (see Corporate Finance Institute at: https://corporatefinanceinstitute.com/resources/careers/companies/top-banks-in-vietnam/.

32 The primary functions of the SCOBs include maintaining deposits, facilitating withdrawals, providing loans for investment, and collecting interests on loans. Their secondary functions, on the other hand, relate to providing overdraft facilities, settling letters of credit (or discounting bills of exchange), purchasing, and selling securities, providing locker facilities, and paying and collecting credits.

33 The functions of the JSBs of Vietnam include the provision of commercial banking services for individuals and corporate clients; international clearing services and money transfer services; derivative products, such as futures, forwards, swaps, and options. Other operational functions of JSB include financial leasing activities and offering guarantee services, insurance services, and securities related services.

34 Direct influence of the government's planning legacy, which persisted throughout the reform period, includes directly interfering in credit institution activities, decisions on lending restructuring non-performing loans (NPLs), determining capital adequacy and ceilings as well as guaranteeing deposit insurance. Indirect government influence relates to a gradual build-up and strengthening of a non-governmental lobby for an independent central bank (Kovsted et al.: 2003).

35 These include deregulation of domestic interest rates on deposits and loans, liberalization of domestic financial markets, restructuring of Non-Performing Loans (NPL), particularly of State-Owned Enterprises (SOEs), and easing entry requirements for foreign-owned banking services as per the terms and conditions agreed to in the context of the country's membership in the World Trade Organization.

36 There were "nearly 1,500 companies listed in securities market (365 on Ho Chi Minh Stock Exchange, 376 on Hanoi Exchange and 772 on Upcom market with market capitalization of over 102 percent of GDP" by the end of 2018.

37 These include (a) the types of institutions – democratic, authoritative (centralized) or market-based; (b) decision-making processes – relative or absolute decentralization – the latter being the full devolution of power from centre to periphery; and (c) functions or division of roles and responsibilities for example between government and market institutions.

38 The Fatherland Front is a voluntary union of political parties, socio-political organizations, and individuals whose aim is to consolidate cohesion and solidarity between

the people and the party in the exercise of socialist democracy. It was established by National Assembly Law No.14/1999/QH10 of 12 June 1999. These entities are parallel but have "entwined hierarchies" (Datta and Mendizabal: 2018).

39 While Vision 2035 of Vietnam aims to make the country's economy fully market-based, with a significantly diminished role of the state in the economy, the 2016–2020 Socio-Economic Development Plan (SEDP) sets specific goals and targets for the country's future development (World Bank: 2016c, FAO 2017). The current SEDP is available at:
http: //pubdocs.worldbank.org/en/839361477533488479/Vietnam-SEDP-2016-2020.pdf.

40 For organizational structure and key functions, see https://en.vcci.com.vn/organizational-structure.

41 The Ease of Doing Business Index ranks countries against each other based on how conducive the regulatory environment is to business operation, with stronger protections of property rights. Overall, economies with a high rank (1 to 20) have simpler and more business-friendly regulations.

42 These include, for instance, in labour-intensive manufacturing such as textiles and apparel, leather and leather products, agriculture, fisheries, and forestry

43 These were often criticized for using Maoist strategies and techniques imported from China (Tuong: 2014).

Bibliographical references

ADB. (2017). *Country Operations Business Plan: Vietnam 2018–2020*. Institutional Document, November 2017. Asia Development Bank.

BBGV. (2018). *Vietnam-Infrastructure, Business Centre of the British Business Group Vietnam*. BBGV, Ho Chi Minh City.

Business Wire: Research and Markets. Research Report on Coffee Industry in Vietnam, 2017–2021: Robusta and Arabica are the Main Trees Planted in Vietnam - Research and Markets, May 2017. Available at: https://www.businesswire.com/news/home/20170505005264/en/Research-Report-Coffee-Industry-Vietnam-2017-2021-Robusta.

Chand, S., Duncan, R., and Quang, D. (2001). The Role of Institutions in the Development of Vietnam. *ASEAN Economic Bulletin*, 18(3), 276–288. http://www.jstor.com/stable/25773687.

CustomsNews. ASEAN's Principle of Consensus, 9 August 2017. Available at: https://customsnews.vn/aseans-principle-of-consensus-4290.html.

Datta, A., and Mendizabal, E. (2018). Political and Economic Transition in Vietnam and its Impact on Think Tank Traditions. On Think-Tank, Independent Research, Ideas and Advice. Available at: https://medium.com/@info_92670/political-and-economic-transition-in-vietnam-and-its-impact-on-think-tank-traditions-381ffd8ef303.

Dezan Shira & Associates. (2020). Vietnam Briefing: Growing Economic Cooperation between Japan and Vietnam. Available at: https://www.vietnam-briefing.com/news/growing-economic-cooperation-japan-vietnam.html/, accessed on 25 June 2020.

Electricity Vietnam (EVN) Annual Reports 2018 and 2020.

European Parliament. (2018). Fisheries in Vietnam, Research for PECH Committee, Policy Department for Structural and Cohesion Policies, European Parliament, PE 629.175, October 2018. Available at: https://www.europarl.europa.eu/RegData/etudes/STUD/2018/629175/IPOL_STU(2018)629175EN.pdf.

FAO. (2005). *Livestock Sector Brief (Livestock Information Sector Analysis) of Vietnam*. Food and Agriculture Organization (FAO).

FAO. (2017). *Country Programme Framework (CPF) for Vietnam for 2017–2021*. Food and Agriculture Organization (FAO).

FAO. (2018). *The State of Fisheries and Aquaculture: Meeting the Sustainable Development Goals*. Food and Agriculture Organization (FAO), Rome. Available at http://www.fao.org/3/i9540en/I9540EN.pdf.

FAO. (2019). *Globefish Highlights: A Quarterly Update on World Seafood Markets*. Food and Agriculture Organization (FAO).

General Statistics Office (GSO) of Vietnam. (2020). Education Statistics (Chapter or Section 10). Available at: https://www.gso.gov.vn/Default_en.aspx?tabid=491.

GGGI. (2018). Sweetening the Deal for Biomass Energy in Vietnam's Sugar Industry. Global Green Growth Institute (GGGI). Insight Brief 01, Vietnam, November 2018.

GIZ. (2017). Sugar Industry Directory of Vietnam 2017. Energy Support Programme Unit, Hanoi, Vietnam.

Hoai, A. (2018). cited in Pham Linh & Nguyen Huong (2020). The Supply Chain and Logistics of Vietnam in the Context of International Economic Integration. *International Business Research*, 13. Published by Canadian Center of Science and Education, May 27, 2020, 27–44.

Hoang, L., and Pham, H. (2016). An Analysis of Vietnamese Footwear Manufacturers' Participation in the Global Value Chain: Where They Are and Where They Should Proceed? *VNU Journal of Economic and Business*, 32(5E), 55–65.

Hostiou, N., Duy, K. P., Cesaro, J.-D., Thanh, H. T., Duteurtre, G., Tien, D. N., Bonnest, P., and Cournuts, S. (2016). The Transition of Animal Farming in Vietnam: From Semi-Subsistence to Commercial Systems. International Conference on Agri-chains and Sustainable Development.

International Coffee Organization. (2019). ICO Coffee Profile: Vietnam, No. ICC-124-9.

International Monetary Fund. (2018a). Article IV Consultation- Press Release, July 2018, IMF.

International Monetary Fund. (2018b). Staff Report No. 18/2015 prepared for the 2018 Article IV Consultations between the Fund and Vietnam. 24 May 2018, IMF.

International Telecommunication Union. (2017). *Global ICT Development Index 2017*. International Telecommunication Union (ITU). Available at: https://www.itu.int/net4/ITU-D/idi/2017/#idi2017economycard-tab&VNM.

International Telecommunications Union (ITU) Database. (2020). Available at: https://www.itu.int/en/ITU-D/Statistics/Pages/stat/default.aspx.

JICA. (2013). *Agricultural Transformation and Food Security 2040: ASEAN Region with a Focus on Vietnam, Indonesia, and Philippines*. Japanese International Cooperation Agency (JICA).

Kaila, H. (2017). Information and Communication Technology in Vietnam. In *Growth, Structural Transformation, and Rural Change in Vietnam: A Rising Dragon on the Move*. Edited by F. Tarp. UNU-WIDER Studies in Development Economics, ISBN 978-0-19-879696-1. Oxford University Press, Oxford. Available at: http://doi.org/10.1093/acprof:oso/9780198796961.001.0001.

Kim, A. T. N. (2017). Ocean Economics for Sustainable Fishery Development: Experience from Vietnam with Implications to Myanmar and Other Asian Developing Countries, a Presentation Titled, Delivered at the UNCTAD Asian Regional Workshop Held in Yangon, Myanmar, from 8 to 10 August 2017.

Kim, A. T. N., and Curtis, M. J. (2018). Balancing interests of actors in the ocean tuna value chain of Khanh Hoa, Province, Vietnam. *Marine Policy*, 98, 11–22. Available at: www.elsevier.com/locate/marpol.

King, R. G., and Levine, R. (1993). Finance and Growth: Schumpeter Might be Right. *Quarterly Journal of Economics*, 108(3): 717–737.

Kokko, A. (1998, December). Vietnam: Ready for Doi Moi II? *ASEAN Economic Bulletin*, 15(3) (in Southeast Asia's Economic Crisis: Origins, Lessons, and the Way Forward) December 1999, 319–327. Published by ISEAS-Yusof Ishak Institute. Stable URL: http://www.jstor.com/stable/25773546.

Kovsted, J., Rand, J., Tarp, F., Nguyen, D. T., Nguyen, V. H., and Thao, T. M. (2003). Financial Sector Reforms in Vietnam: Selected Issues and Problems. Discussion Paper in Economic Policy, Series No. 0301. Central Institution for Economic Management.

Kwak, S. (2019). Deconstructing the Multi-Layered Nature of Citizen Participation in Vietnam: Conceptual Connotations, Discourses of International Development, and the Country's Institutional Context. *Asian Journal of Political Science*, 27(3), 257–271.

Leather, Footwear and Handbag Association (LEFASO) of Vietnam. (2017). Statistics on Vietnam's Leather, Footwear and Handbag Exports and Markets.

Leh, A. T. (2017). Challenges and Opportunities in Aquaculture Development: Experience from Vietnam with Implications to Myanmar and Other Asian Developing Countries. A presentation delivered at the UNCTAD Asian Regional Workshop held in Yangon, Myanmar, from 8 to 10 August 2017.

Leung, S. (2009). Banking and Financial Sector Reforms in Vietnam. *ASEAN Economic Bulletin*, 26(1), 44–77.

Masina, P. (2002). Vietnam and the Regional Crisis: The case of "Late Latecomer". Brill, Leiden. Available at: http://www.brill.nl/.

Markussen, T., and Quang-Thanh, N. (2018). Economic and Non-Economic Returns to Communist Party Membership in Vietnam. WIDER Working Paper 2018/46. United Nations University, UNU-WIDER.

Masina, P. (2006). *Vietnamese Development Strategies*. Routledge Taylor and Francis Group, London.

Masina, P., and Cerimele, M. (2018). Patterns of Industrialization and the State of Industrial Labour in Post-WTO-Accession Vietnam. *European Journal of East Asian Studies*, 17, 289—323.

MIC (Ministry of Information and Communication of Vietnam). 2019. *White book: Vietnam Information and Communication 2019*. Information and Communication Publishing.

Ministry of Agriculture and Rural Development of Vietnam. (2020). Report on Coffee Processing Capacity of Vietnam. Hanoi, Vietnam.

Ministry of Education and Training of Vietnam. (2015). *Vietnam National Education For All 2015 Review*. Ministry of Education and Training, Vietnam.

Ministry of Transport. Vietnam National Transport Strategy Study (ITRANSS). Long Term Development Strategies for Year 2020. Road and Road Transport. Technical Report No. 5.

Nguyen, T. A., Luu, M. D., and Trinh, D. C. (2016). The Evolution of Vietnamese Industrialization. In *Manufacturing Transformation: Comparative Studies of Industrial Development in Africa and Emerging Asia*. Edited by C. Newman, J. Page, J. Rand, A. Shimelis, M. Soderbom, and F. Tarp. Chapter 12. UNU-WIDER Studies in Development Economics. Oxford University Press, Oxford, 236–276.

Nguyen, T. T., and Trinh, C. D. (2018). Slack Resources and Innovation in Vietnamese SMEs: A Behavioural, Stewardship, and Institutional Perspective. WIDER Working Paper 2018/78. United Nations University-WIDER, August 2018.

OECD. (2014). *Lessons from PISA for Korea, Strong Performers and Successful Reformers in Education*. OECD Publishing, Paris. https://doi.org/10.1787/9789264190672-en

OECD. (2020). Investment (GFCF) (Indicator). https://doi.org/10.1787/b6793677-en.

Phung, T. K. D., Visseren-Hamakers, J. I., and Arts, B. (2015). A Framework for Assessing Governance Capacity: An Illustration from Vietnam's Forestry Reforms. *Environment and Planning C: Politics and Space*, August 2015. http://doi.org/10.1177/0263774X15598325.

PricewaterhouseCoopers. (2014). *The Vietnamese Healthcare Industry: Moving to Next Level*. PWC-Vietnam Ltd, Vietnam.

Scott. (1995) in Nguyen, T. T. and Trinh, C. D. (2018). Slack Resources and Innovation in Vietnamese SMEs: A Behavioural, Stewardship, and Institutional Perspective. WIDER Working Paper 2018/78. United Nations University-WIDER, August 2018.

SRV (Socialist Republic of Vietnam). National Assembly Law No. 14/1999/QH10 of 12 June 1999. Legal Normative Documents. Available at: http://vbpl.vn/TW/Pages/vbpqen-toanvan.aspx?ItemID=928.

SRV (Socialist Republic of Vietnam). National Assembly Resolution No. 142/2016/QH13 Dated 12 April 2016 on Five-Year Socio-Economic Development Plan (SEDP) 2016–2020.

Spire. (2019). Spire Report on ICT Sector in Vietnam: Opportunities and Challenges. Spire Research and Consulting, 11 December 2019. Available at: https://www.spireresearch.com/wp-content/uploads/2019/12/Vietnam-ICT-sector-Report-Spire_.pdf.

SSC (State Securities Commission of Vietnam) and International Finance Corporation-IFC. (2019). Vietnam Corporate Governance Code of Best Practices for Public Companies. August 2019, SSC and IFC, The World Bank.

Statista. (2020). Online Data Base. Employment Distribution in Vietnam in 2019, by Industry. https://www.statista.com/statistics/1088567/vietnam-employment-distribution-by-industry/.

Sturgeon, T., and Zylberberg, E. (2017). Vietnam's Evolving Role in ICT Global Value Chains. http://doi.org/10.1596/978-1-4648-0996-5_ch9.

Tarp, F. (Ed.). (2017). *Growth, Structural Transformation, and Rural Change in Viet Nam: A Rising Dragon on the Move*. UNU-WIDER Studies in Development Economics, ISBN 978-0-19-879696-1. Oxford University Press, Oxford. Available at: http://dx.doi.org/10.1093/acprof:oso/9780198796961.001.0001.

The ASEAN Post. Construction Ahead for Vietnam. 28 September 2018. https://theaseanpost.com/article/construction-ahead-vietnam.

TMA Solutions, Infographics on Vietnam ICT Infrastructure. (2019). https://www.tmasolutions.com/files/infographic-vietnam-ict-infrastructure.pdf.

TrendEconomy. (2019). Vietnam: Imports and Exports of Sugars and Sugar Confectionery, 2008–2019.TrendEconomy. Annual International Trade Statistics by Country. Available at: https://trendeconomy.com/data/h2/Vietnam/17.

TrendEconomy. (2020).Vietnam Imports and Exports: Dairy Produce (Birds, Eggs, Natural Honey Edible Products of Animal Origin), 2008–2019. *Annual International Trade Statistics by Country*, 10 February 2020. Available at: https://trendeconomy.com/data/h2/Vietnam/04.

Tvet Vietnam (Trained in Vietnam). Human Capital is Vietnam's Strongest National Resource, 10 November 2019. Available at: https://www.tvet-vietnam.org/en/article/1733.human-capital-is-vietnam-s-strongest-national-resource.html.

Tuong, V. (2014). *Persistence Amid Decay: The Communist Party of Vietnam at 83*. Palgrave Macmillan. https://doi.org/10.1057/9781137347534.0006.

UNCTAD. (2017d). *Fishery Exports and the Economic Development of LDCs: Bangladesh, Cambodia, the Comoros, Mozambique, Myanmar, and Uganda*. United Nations, Geneva.

UNCTAD. (2020b). *Building Capacity in Least Developing Countries to Fully Harness the Potential of Fisheries and Aquaculture, Training Manual*. United Nations, Geneva.

UNCTAD Statistics (UNCTADstat). (2019, 2020). Available at: https://unctadstat.unctad.org/EN/Index.html.

UNDESA. (2019). World Population Prospect 2019. United Nations Department for Social and Economic Affairs Population Dynamics. Available at: https://population.un.org/wpp/.

UNDP. (2019). Human Development Report 2019: Inequalities in Human Development in the 21st Century Briefing note for Angola on the 2019 Human Development Report.

UNDP. (2019b). Human Development Report 2019: Inequalities in Human Development in the 21st Century, Briefing note for Vietnam on the 2019 Human Development Report.

UNESCO. (2015). Transforming Teaching and Learning in Asia and the Pacific.

UNESCO. (2020). UNESCO Database for Vietnam. Available at: http://uis.unesco.org/en/country/vn.

USDA (2019). United States Department of Agriculture. Foreign Agriculture Service. Vietnam Coffee Annual (2019) Report.

UNIDO. (2019). Vietnam Industry White Paper 2019: Manufacturing and Subsector Competitiveness.

Urban Development Management Center. (2016). Financing Transport Infrastructures in Ho Chi Minh City (Vietnam): Tools, Innovations and Challenges. Working Paper No. 2-2015, 2016.

Vietnam Briefing. Laying the Foundation for Growth: The Future of Vietnamese Infrastructure, 21 August 2020. https://www.vietnam-briefing.com/news/infrastructure-vietnam.html/.

Vietnam Investment Review. What Vietnam Stands to Gain from ICT, 16 February 2019. https://www.vir.com.vn/what-vietnam-stands-to-gain-from-ict-65667.html.

Vietnam Plus. Health Insurance Covers 87.62 Percent of Vietnam Population, 7 November 2018. Available at: https://en.vietnamplus.vn/health-insurance-covers-8762-percent-of-vietnam-population/141453.vnp.

Vuong, Q. H. (2019). The Financial Economy of Vietnam in an Age of Reform. In *Routledge Handbook of Banking and Finance in Asia 1986–2016*. Edited by U. Volz, P. Morgan, and N. Yoshino. Routledge, New York, 201–222.

WHO. (2014). Success Factors for Vietnam's Health Sector, Including Women's and Children's Health: Policy and Program Highlights from 10 Fast-Track Countries. Vietnam's report is available at: http://www.who.int/pmnch/successfactors/en/.

WHO and UNICEF. Joint WHO and UNICEF Estimates of Immunization Coverage of Vietnam (2019 Revision). Available at: https://www.who.int/immunization/monitoring_surveillance/data/vnm.pdf.

World Bank. (2004). *The Socialist Republic of Vietnam: Coffee Sector Report*. World Bank, Washington, DC. https://openknowledge.worldbank.org/handle/10986/14405 License: CC BY 3.0 IGO

World Bank. (2013). *Trade Facilitation, Value Creation, and Competitiveness: Policy Implications for Vietnam's Economic Growth*. The World Bank, Washington, DC.

World Bank. (2016a). *Transforming Vietnamese Agriculture: Growing More from Less*. The World Bank, Washington, DC.

World Bank. (2016b). *Poverty in a Rising Africa*. The World Bank, Washington, DC.

World Bank. (2016c). *The Role of the State in Viet Nam's Economic Development: Enhancing the Role of the State in Facilitating a More Competitive and Productive Economy*. The World Bank, Washington, DC.

World Bank. (2017a). Well Begun but Aiming Higher: A Review of Vietnam's Education Trends in the Past 20 Years and Emerging Challenges. Policy Research Paper 8112. Development Data Group. The World Bank Group.

World Bank. (2017b). Country Partnership Framework for the Socialist Republic of Vietnam for the period 2018–2022, May 4, 2017. Report No.111771- VN.

World Bank. (2018c). *Vietnam's Future Jobs: Leveraging Mega-Trends for Greater Prosperity*. The World Bank, Washington, DC.

World Bank. (2019a). Connecting Vietnam for Growth and Shared Prosperity. Vietnam Development Report, Hanoi, Hong Duc Publishing. World Bank Group, December 2019.

World Bank. (2020a). For Sub-Saharan Africa, Coronavirus Crisis Calls for Policies for Greater Resilience, 9 April 2020. World Bank Group. Available at: https://www.worldbank.org/en/region/afr/publication/for-sub-saharan-africa-coronavirus-crisis-calls-for-policies-for-greater-resilience.

World Bank. (2020b). World Bank Development Indicators (WBDI) Database: Vietnam (2020). Available at: https://data.worldbank.org/indicator/SL.AGR.EMPL.ZS?locations=VN.

World Bank. (2020c). Learning from Power Sector Reform Experiences: The Case of Vietnam. Policy Research Paper 9169. Energy and Extractives Global Practice. World Bank Group.

World Bank Blogs. Accelerating Vietnam's Paths to Prosperity, 21 February 2019. Published on Voices. Available at: https://blogs.worldbank.org/voices/accelerating-vietnams-path-prosperity.

World Bank Blogs. To Close Vietnam's Human Capital Development Gap, Look to Ethnic Minorities, 9 September 2019. Published on East Asia & Pacific on the Rise. Available at: https://blogs.worldbank.org/eastasiapacific/close-vietnams-human-capital-development-gap-look-ethnic-minorities.

World Bank Data. (2019). World Bank Open Data. https://data.worldbank.org/

World Bank Doing Business. (2020). *Comparing Business Regulations in 190 Economies*. World Bank Group. Available at: http://documents1.worldbank.org/curated/en/688761571934946384/pdf/Doing-Business-2020-Comparing-Business-Regulation-in-190-Economies.pdf.

World Economic Forum. (2019). *The Global Competitiveness Report 2019*. World Economic Forum (WEF), Geneva, Switzerland.

World Economic Forum and Global Alliance for Trade Facilitation. (2016). *The Global Enabling Trade Report 2016*. World Economic Forum (GEF) and Global Alliance for Trade Facilitation (GATF), Geneva, Switzerland.

World Education News Plus Reviews (WENR). Education in Vietnam, Asia-Pacific 8 November 2017. Available at: https://wenr.wes.org/2017/11/education-in-vietnam.

WTO. (2019). *World Trade Statistical Review 2019*. World Trade Organization., Geneva, Switzerland.

9 Policy Lessons from Vietnam for Countries of SSA

The preceding chapters reveal that internal engines and enablers of growth and transformation have played a critical role in in Vietnam. Vietnam is part of East Asia (specifically Southeast Asia), but it is a latecomer in the development process. Learning from successful economies of the region (front-runners), Vietnam has become the manufacturing, export, and investment hub in Asia and the developing world in a short period. These trends have also enabled the country to quickly catch up with newly industrialized economies in terms of trade, savings and investments, technology, innovation, finance, and R&D. East Asian economies (apart from China, Indonesia, Malaysia, and now Vietnam) have no known and commercially viable natural resources. Vietnam's experience also shows that natural resources are important for growth and transformation, if carefully harnessed and rents are fully captured within the economy. However, such resources are not decisive or determining factors for sustained growth and development. The only resource where most of the East Asian economies have comparative advantages is in abundant labour or human capital. Nonetheless, they managed to achieve significant transformation in parallel with substantially raising the standards of living of their population. The structural transformation seen in Vietnam is in contrast with the pessimistic views and expectations[1] that widely prevailed in the 1960s and 1970s about Asia's growth and transformation (Kanbur: 2018, Nayyar: 2019). Examining the growth and transformation paths of countries such as Vietnam is, therefore, critically important for understanding their development processes and growth paths. The emphasis should be on how they relieve binding constraints and unlock their development potential with substantial socioeconomic gains. The aim is to identify and synthesize specific policy lessons which can have practical and operational implications for the countries of SSA.

In drawing policy lessons, it is important to emphasize at least three key factors. First and foremost, Asia and Africa are entirely different continents not only in history, geography, climate, and demography but also in resource endowments, initial conditions, social and cultural contexts as well as institutions. Likewise, binding constraints and drivers of growth are by no means identical or similar: they vary across countries and economies. Therefore, there is no universal blueprint or "one-size-fits-all" policy approach to unlock binding constraints

DOI: 10.4324/9781003295334-9

to economic growth and development. Addressing country-specific constraints to development and tapping comparative advantages require specific solutions that are tailored to initial conditions of countries. Second, there is a tendency to draw lessons only from successful experiences, ignoring useful insights that can be gained from failed policies and strategies. This not only masks the reasons behind failures but also obliges nations to repeat the same mistakes time and again. It also misleads policymakers and practitioners to "pick national winners",[2] wasting scarce resources through inefficiency, rent-seeking behaviours, and misallocation. Such a process can also undermine the potential for growth in sectors considered losers or not winners. Any development strategy – whether industrial, trade, or agricultural – should avoid targeting sectors or firms that are considered winners from political perspectives and for short-term gains. Instead, policies should "deliver a clear long-term sense of direction to economic actors" (*Financial Times*, 28 March 2019). Picking winners and providing incentives (such as government subsidies) may also increase corruption and rent-seeking behaviours. This has been problematic, particularly in economies where there is a lack of regulation, accountability, and checks and balances, and where market information is scant, inadequate, or imperfect (Stigliz: 1996).

Finally (third), there has not been a single or uniform policy pursued in Vietnam or in East Asian economies. The assumption that success in Asia's star performers is due to a particular policy or strategy is grossly mistaken and misleading. Washington-based institutions, after decades of standard policy prescriptions to developing countries (particularly in Africa) have concluded that "no one formula or standard prescription had been decisive in East Asian development" (Leipziger and Thomas: 1993). Some countries have relied heavily on active government interventions more than others, often with varying outcomes. Thus, the sources, spread, and forms of growth as well as the drivers of such growth vary across East Asian economies, Vietnam, and SSA. Recognizing country heterogeneity means that diverse factors influence development experiences, and hence require country-specific approaches. As with the other East Asian economies, the key to success in Vietnam is pragmatic, self-discovery, and forward-looking policymaking. Policy pragmatism implies the ability of the state to learn quickly from failures with no ideological motivation in choosing a particular course of action (Leipziger and Thomas: 1993). Stiglitz (1996) on the other hand, relates pragmatism to diverse factors that make markets work for development. He argues that capital formation (including human capital), dynamic gains from exports, the state's ability to make markets work, and ensuring political stability are vital ingredients to a successful socioeconomic transformation in East Asia. Many other authors place emphasis on the relationships between historical factors such as resource endowments and colonial histories on the one hand, and their current institutions, policy choices, and development, on the other (Acemoglu et al.: 2005, Nayyar: 2006, Rodrik: 2013).

Learning from diverse development experiences also depends on pragmatic policy formulation and implementation which requires "technocratic bureaucracy". This has been part of the political mandate of policy reform and sustained implementation in most East Asian economies (Leipziger and Thomas: 1993), and now Vietnam. Technocracy also includes the important role of "policymakers' beliefs" in determining learning outcomes, which is particularly important in policy choices, for instance, about the relative merits of the market versus the state in transitioning towards a market-oriented economic system (Buera et al.: 2007). Equally important in learning is the role of a proactive Developmental State that ensures balanced distribution of productive assets (such as land and income), understands the limitations of markets, and articulates corrective measures with the aim to maximize societal gains (Stiglitz: 1996). Another perspective underlines the importance of knowledge at the heart of learning from successful and less successful experiences of nations (Fagerberg et al.: 2007). Accordingly, knowledge developed elsewhere and the capacity to fully exploit it are key determining factors of learning from others, irrespective of the origin of new knowledge. Self-discovery in terms of policy implementation, successes, and failures also assist countries in learning from their own experiences. It allows an understanding of what works, what does not, and why. The greatest value-added from learning from experimentation is the identification of comparative advantages (latent or revealed) and understanding key binding constraints to tapping such advantages. Poor institutions, weak private sector, lack of technology, and problematic access to and use of an affordable energy mix, can individually and collectively undermine the capacity to self-discovery, self-experimentation, and learning by doing. Such weaknesses inherent in the economies of SSA can also undermine the positive impact of incentives, productivity of factors of production, and production transformation. This means that "self-discovery" should be examined from a broader set of factors that impact the development trajectories of countries beyond the usual neoclassical model of economic growth as dependent on markets, institutions, and technology (Hausman and Rodrick: 2003).

The research and debates on drivers of development and learning are likely to continue in the future, given the presence of outstanding performers in some parts of the world amid colossal policy failures elsewhere. A recent analysis of learning from the experiences of East Asian economies underscores the centrality and complexity of technological learning and catch-up, together with the indispensability of beneficial interactions between the state and the private sector in building technological capabilities (Oqubay and Ohno: 2019). Emphasis here is on the critical role of technological learning at firm level, policy learning by the state, and "learning by doing, experimentation, emulation, innovation and leapfrogging" (Oqubay, 28 November 2019). Further research cautions policymakers in developing countries against the fallacy of creating a dichotomy between short-term (static) and long-term (dynamic) gains. For instance, an important lesson for Vietnam from the experiences of East Asia's Industrial Parks (IPs) is that, from the start, the latter countries focused on the long-term (dynamic) gains and development impact of IPs such as how best to foster linkages between Foreign Direct Investment (FDI) firms and domestic enterprises, create global networks, maximize spill-over effects, and technological learning (Alcorta and

Tesfachew: 2020). By learning from East Asian economies, Vietnam's well-formulated and implemented IPs have made important contributions in deriving long-term (dynamic) gains through production linkages, transfers of technology, knowhow and spill-over effects, and industrialization. This is the outcome of pragmatism and a forward-looking planning process that successful Asian economies adopted when formulating their industrialization and structural economic transformation strategies.

Despite variations in the approaches to learning from development experience, and irrespective of the emphasis placed on a particular set of drivers of growth, there is emerging consensus on: (a) notwithstanding the heterogeneity and diversity of driving factors behind socioeconomic development, nations can learn from each other; (b) the search for empirical evidence and plausible justifications as to why some countries prosper while others are still grappling with socioeconomic challenges begs continued exploration and examination; (c) drawing policy lessons from the growth and development paths of developed or industrialized nations is important for the latecomers and late latecomers to learn both from successful and less successful experiences (Alcorta and Tesfachew: 2020); (d) learning from successful development experience is neither inevitable nor automatic (Oqubay, 28 November 2019) but it is vitally important; and (e) transformation requires long-term visions and carefully sequenced policies and strategies combined with capable institutions and a vibrant private sector. Building on these useful conclusions, the following section discusses Vietnam's development experience and lessons for SSA.

9.1 Learning from Vietnam's Experience: Policy Lessons for SSA

In less than 35 years, Vietnam's economy has gone through transformation unprecedented in the recent history of nations. The GDP of the country reached USD 260 billion in 2019 from as little as USD 14 billion in 1980 – a 19-fold increase or 1,757 percent. The total value of international trade (imports and exports of goods and services) of the country reached about 236 percent of the GDP, making the country one of the most open economies in the world. These changes are not only quantitative; they are also qualitative and structural.

Vietnam's experience of the last decades shows that its success cannot be ascribed to one single driver or engine of growth. Rather, its sources are to be found in diverse sectors (agriculture, manufacturing, ICT, infrastructure, exports, service institutions, and human capital). These drivers and enablers together form the country's productive capacities, which have resulted in a profound structural transformation. Notwithstanding the relevance of each driver and engine of growth, Vietnam's experience shows the central role of the country's policymaking environment and the capacity of the state to recalibrate productive resources and growth-enabling factors in the implementation of policies and strategies. Such have been facilitated, guided, and governed by the following success factors.

9.1.1 *Pragmatic, Non-Confrontational, Non-ideological, Home-Grown Policies Matter*

Policymaking in post-1986 Vietnam has been pragmatic, flexible, and adaptive to changing circumstances and it is based on national consensus. Carefully sequenced reforms, policies, and strategies (Doi-Moi) have maximized welfare, building on earlier socialist income-distribution models. Consensus-based, results-oriented, and problem-solving policy coordination, experimentation, and emulation have contributed to sustaining the reforms and their effective implementation. Vietnam's policymakers embraced globalization with tacit, non-confrontational, and non-ideological rejection of the orthodoxy. Policy reforms have been gradual, carefully sequenced, and based on the country's development ambitions and visions. The distinction between political leadership and bureaucracy, though invisible or vague, has minimized political interference in economic decision-making. Vietnam has taken the best from the East Asian development model, while tacitly rejecting policy prescriptions from Washington-based institutions (but in a non-ideological way). For instance, Vietnam's policymakers agreed with some policy prescriptions (such as gradually reducing the role of State-Owned Enterprises (SOEs) in the economy but maintained their opposition to others (such as free or subsidized provision of universal access to education and health). Despite mounting criticism from mainstream fundamentalists (neoliberals), the Government of Vietnam also persisted with its expansionary monetary and fiscal policies to finance infrastructure and the provision of targeted state subsidies. That is, while accelerating the pace and depth of transformation, Vietnam effectively captured natural resources rent in transformative processes including subsidizing social and key economic sectors. Overall, its post-socialist Developmental State model guided markets and institutions to work for development by harnessing investments (domestic and FDI), channelling these to strategic sectors as well as providing targeted incentives. Through carefully designed strategies of integration to the global economy and multilateral trading system (WTO) as well as bilateral and regional trade agreements, Vietnam maximized trading opportunities both for its SOEs and the private sector. The country has laid a solid foundation for robust production and supply capacities before it negotiated bilateral trade agreements with the USA, Japan, and ASEAN and prior to joining the World Trade Organization (WTO). Unlike Vietnam, most African countries, particularly those in SSA, joined the WTO early on and accepted policy prescriptions from the custodians of free market policies (orthodoxy). They have also concluded bilateral and regional trade and investment agreements and granted Overseas Development Assistance (ODA), market access, and investment facilitation by major global economies. However, they still lack production, supply, and export capacities and failed to benefit from such multi-layer engagements.

9.1.2 Harnessing Natural Capital for Development Played an Important Role in Vietnam

Natural capital (such as land, mining, fisheries, forest, and water resources) is a key component of productive capacities. Vietnam prioritized key sectors and products in which it had comparative advantages and where the potential for domestic demand was high. Agricultural production such as rice, coffee, sugarcane, and livestock played an important role in ensuring food self-sufficiency, rural employment, exports, and providing input to the nascent industrial sector early in the reform process. Consequently, Vietnam has emerged from being a net food-importing and food-insecure nation into one of the top producers and exporters of food items (e.g., rice) in the world. Forestry and fishery as well as the discovery of mineral resources (oil, coal, zinc, and industrial metals) augmented its capacity to invest and sustain growth and reap benefits by financing infrastructure, ensuring regionally balanced growth, and investing in education, health, and healthcare services, with a focus on income-poor and rural communities. Government policies designed to ensure access to productive resources such as land (through land reforms and land-use rights) have played an important role in enhancing agricultural productivity, production, rural employment, and exports. Rural electrification from coal and the by-products of sugarcane processing were instrumental in the creation of off-farm employment, which now provides jobs to four out of five active individuals in rural areas.

The growth and expansion of agriculture served as a springboard for the county's industrial and manufacturing sector. This was done through conscious efforts and strategic thinking to exploit comparative advantages. Vietnam has invested heavily in the upstream stages of the value chains before joining downstream activities. In the leather and leather products sector, for example, initial efforts in the development of the sector were concentrated in enhancing the quality and quantity of livestock rearing. This was subsequently followed by the gradual improvement of slaughterhouses, building storage houses and tannery facilities for hides and skins. These were complemented further by parallel efforts in training farmers in animal husbandry, modernizing and marketing livestock resources, and building production linkages. Vietnam has taken time to learn and understand markets and quality requirements as well as what is happening in the global production and supply network in the leather and leather products sector, such as risks and uncertainties.

Like Vietnam, several countries in SSA[3] are endowed with large herds of livestock. However, poor quality and the spectre of devastating animal diseases, lack of scientific knowledge and veterinary medicine render the subsector economically unviable, environmentally unsustainable, and weak in fostering forward and backward linkages. For instance, Ethiopia is first in Africa and tenth in the world in cattle herds[4] – significantly larger than Vietnam's. However, the value of Ethiopia's average annual export of leather and leather products, between 2013 and 2017 was USD 135 million and employed a 21,000-strong work force (Grumiller et al.: 2019). This is a drop in the ocean when compared to Vietnam's annual average export of USD 18 billion and direct employment of 1.2 million people during the same period. The key bottlenecks for Ethiopia's leather sector are the poor quality of the livestock, lack of investment, and poor quality of hides and skins. The quality of hides and skins as inputs determines the quality of finished leather and leather products, which will be exported to high-end global markets. In addition to poor quality and lack of investment, misguided policies are also among the key factors undermining Ethiopia's beneficial integration into regional and global value chains in leather and leather products. Although leather and leather products account for nearly 64 percent of the country's manufacturing exports – more than 90 percent of which is by FDI enterprises (UNIDO: 2018b, Grumiller et al.: 2019), the contribution of the sector to Ethiopia's transformation remains extremely weak and low. The sector's contribution to exports, employment, FDI, and overall economic growth of Ethiopia is too small to have any meaningful impact on the country's competitiveness and economic transformation.

Contrary to the experience of Vietnam, natural capital (wealth) in SSA has entrenched commodity dependence, heightened vulnerability, and the exposure of these economies to the vagaries of external shocks, as well as reinforced rent-seeking and state capture behaviours (UNCTAD: 2013). A perverse role of natural capital in the socioeconomic development of SSA does not imply a resource curse. Rather, it clearly shows missed opportunities in harnessing natural capital or capturing productive resources to foster productive capacities, structural economic transformation, and achieve socioeconomic development. In most cases, weak policies and badly designed strategies are to blame. In Angola (Chapter 4), with the discovery of oil and other extractive minerals in the 1950s and full-scale commercialization of the extractive sector, the agriculture sector has been completely abandoned, changing the country from the largest producer of staple foods and coffee in southern Africa to a net food-importing and food-insecure nation in recent years. While Angola became the second largest producer and exporter of oil in SSA (after Nigeria) and the second largest exporter to China (after countries of the Middle East), the country is known for its vulnerability, macroeconomic instability, corruption, weak governance, and Dutch Disease. Angola's agricultural, manufacturing and services sectors suffered serious setbacks with the discovery of oil reserves and large-scale commercialization that have continued to attract an influx of FDI and liquid money (cash) into the economy. Such negative consequences have caused the overvaluation of the country's domestic currency (Kwanza) in relation to major global trading and investment currencies, which in turn led to a drop in exports, an increase in imports, job losses, and overall macroeconomic instability. Such a paradoxical situation, which usually follows the discovery of large-scale production and exports of oil, natural gas, and other minerals is not unique to Angola. Rather it is a wider phenomenon characterizing most extractive resource-driven economies of SSA. Overall, SSA suffers from bad micro- and macroeconomic policies, misguided strategies, lack of investment, absence of business plans, poor financial systems, and outdated land tenure systems (World Bank: 2016). These remain among the key constraints undermining socioeconomic relevance of vital sectors such as agriculture, mining, or manufacturing.

9.1.3 Building Human Capital Matters

Vietnam has used the rents from natural capital (natural resources wealth) to accelerate the formation of human capital. Building on the country's socialist system and placing education and health at the centre of Doi-Moi, its performance in the social sector has been outstanding, exceeding some of the top performers in East and Southeast Asia. The reform has been key to substantially enhancing public investment in education and health while introducing effective administrative (governance) structures. The outcome of these processes can be described as unparalleled in the recent development experiences of nations. Not only has Vietnam increased investment in education and health as a percentage of public expenditure or GDP, but it has also improved access, coverage, and quality. The country exceeded all expectations in literacy and numeracy, improving healthcare and the augmenting life expectancy of its citizens. As Stiglitz (1996) rightly noted, the ability of nations to acquire technology, attract FDI, foster innovation and R&D as well as turn the physical capital accumulation into development, largely depends on human capital formation. As elsewhere in East Asia, Vietnam's investment in human capital and creating a technology-savvy society has been a necessary condition to absorb advanced and highly complex technologies as well as to accelerate economy-wide productive capacities and structural transformation.

In SSA, investment in social sector has not been as substantial as in Vietnam. However, several countries of the region have increased their expenditure on education and health to foster human capital formation. However, the region's human capital component of productive capacities remains disappointingly low when compared to other developing regions (Chapter 3). The difference is that Vietnam's success in fostering human capital formation relates not only to the huge investments made in health and education but also to a series of institutional, regulatory, and operational reforms undertaken in the social sector as part of the country's overall reform processes. The outcomes of increased allocation of public investment and reforms in education and health are proof that state actions and institutional capabilities can provide public goods and foster productive state-society relations (North: 1991, Evans and Heller: 2018).

9.1.4 Consistent and Coherent Trade, Industrial, and Other Sectoral Policies Play a Vital Role

Export and investment-led policies were key to the success of most East Asian Newly Industrializing Countries (NICs). However, in the case of Vietnam it is the combination of export-led and carefully targeted Import Substitution (IS) strategies that worked well. While export-led strategies focused on labour-intensive manufacturing and value-added agricultural produce, IS strategies targeted agricultural products for which there is domestic demand (rice, livestock, fisheries, and sugar). Imports to the country were consciously designed to support industrialization and adding sophistication to the export basket. Electronics, electrical parts, telephone and computer parts, integrated circuits, refined petroleum, light rubberized (knitted) fabrics, and communications equipment have become the leading or top import items (*Vietnam Briefing*, 19 November 2018). Nearly 96 percent of inputs and intermediate goods to produce these complex products originate from Asian suppliers. Moreover, through various incentive schemes, Vietnam also attracted significant FDI inflows into its manufacturing and exports sector. Overall, the gradual but persistent shift from central planning to strategic planning played an important role. A deliberate strategy to enhance the role of the private sector in rural areas through various incentives and direct support (e.g., by rural electrification) have played a vital role in expanding off-farm job opportunities.

Vietnam has also demonstrated consistent and coherent policies in its integration into regional economic groupings (ASEAN) and the multilateral trading system (WTO), while tapping the potential in bilateral trade agreements with major global economic powerhouses such as the EU, USA, and Japan. Contrary to the experience of Vietnam, in the countries of SSA, the share of the manufacturing sector both in employment and GDP has continued to decline over the years (Chapter 4). The gap in socioeconomic performance and structural transformation between Vietnam and the countries of SSA is also evident from the comparative industrial ratio[5] (Figure 9.1).

In the early 2000s, Vietnam and SSA (average) had an equal industrial ratio. In subsequent years while SSA regressed, Vietnam continued to substantially increase its industrial and service share in the economy reaching a combined share of nearly 84 percent in 2018. Despite the continuous decline in the GDP share of manufacturing value-added, the average industrial ratio of SSA has increased after 2006, albeit more slowly than that of Vietnam. However, the

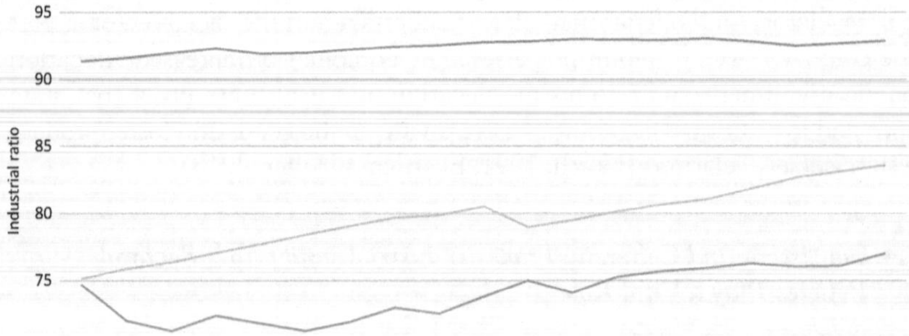

Figure 9.1 Industrial ratio in Vietnam and SSA (2000–2018).

Source: Computation from UN Statistics of National Accounts – analysis of main aggregates.

increase was only the result of the continued "servicification"[6] of the economies of SSA, where the GDP share of low-skill and low-value-added services has continuously increased in their economies. The overall qualitative and quantitative improvements in Vietnam's industrial and service ratio is the outcome of consistent and coherent industrial, trade, investment, and other sectoral policies and strategies. Learning from successful economies of East Asia, the state in Vietnam has become not only developmental but also entrepreneurial.

9.1.5 *Fostering Infrastructure, Energy, and ICT Connectivity Play an Important Role*

The transport and electricity infrastructure and an increasing role for ICT have served as enablers and accelerators of productive capacities and structural transformation in Vietnam, including in rural areas. These have also speeded up Vietnam's transformation to become an industrial hub and competitive exporter of manufacturing in the otherwise highly competitive and dynamic Asian region. The complete electrification of households, including in rural areas, has also been key in improving the efficiency of the delivery of services such as education, technical and vocational training, health, and ICT services. As discussed above, the energy sector has also had multiplier effects in expanding jobs and creating employment opportunities in the country.

Likewise, over the years, the expansion of transport infrastructure (road, air, railways, waterways, and maritime) have substantially improved Vietnam's regional and global export competitiveness and the country's participation in regional and global production and supply chains. The further deepening of Vietnam's economic transformation is aided by the increasing role of the ICT sector in the country's industrialization and modernization efforts. This was particularly key in helping Vietnam in moving towards the Fourth Industrial Revolution (Industry 4.0) as the country offers a highly trained and relatively cheaper labour force with rapidly expanding urbanization and growing middle class consumers. Overall, increasing public investment and FDI in transport, energy (electricity), and ICT infrastructures has boosted structural change as key to Vietnam's transformational growth and development. As can be observed from Figure 9.2, since 2008 Vietnam has even outclassed other developing countries in structural change, let alone SSA.

Among the components of productive capacities where the countries of SSA are significantly lagging are the energy, transport infrastructure, human capital, institutions and ICT components. These weaknesses have collectively undermined efforts to structurally change and transform SSA's economies. This adverse impact hinders or prevents quantitative and qualitative shifts and changes within and across their various sectors. Consequently, the performance of SSA in structural change is not only the lowest of all the developing regions but it is also deeply troubling, despite the region's increased partnership, including with China. The shifts witnessed in SSA in sectoral contributions to GDP are the wrong, mis-directing and misleading type of transformation as opposed to those observed in Vietnam and other Asian economies.

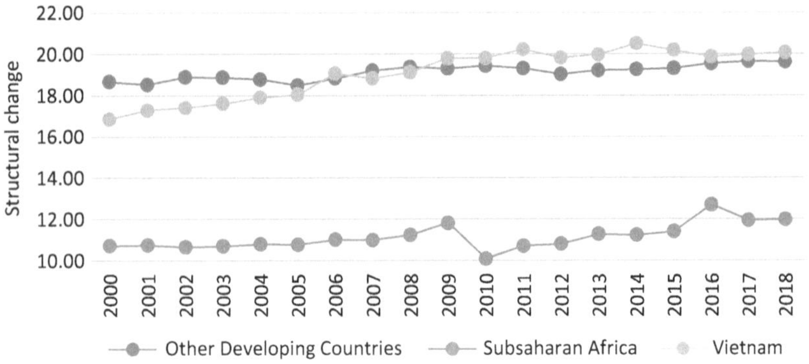

Figure 9.2 Structural change[7] in SSA, Vietnam, and other developing countries (2000–2018).

Source: UNCTAD's global Productive Capacities Index (PCI).

9.1.6 *Vigorous, Flexible, and Growth-Friendly Institutions Matter*

Vietnam followed centralized institutional arrangements, and (after 1986) mixed economy policymaking. Throughout these transitions, Vietnam's vibrant institutions have assisted in indigenous economic policy formulation and implementation which mobilized endogenous drivers of growth. The political leadership, the state machinery, educational, and R&D institutions, as well as technology centres, have functioned in unison and in tandem with market forces in recalibrating growth and transformation as part of the country's post-socialist Developmental State model. The tacit and conscious distinction between political leadership and the bureaucracy have been functioning well for the last three decades, with tangible socioeconomic outcomes.

Over the years, Vietnam has also gradually expanded the role of the private sector and civil society by fostering public-private dialogue and enacting growth-friendly policies, laws, and codes. The country's history of socialism has also fostered the culture of public mobilization and participation in socioeconomic development, which enhanced national ownership of policies and strategies at communal, provincial, and state levels. Vietnam's sustained and inclusive economic growth maximized societal welfare and improved the standards of living of the population. Despite widespread criticism and characterization of the country's regime as authoritarian, tangible welfare gains have greatly assisted in fostering trust, legitimacy, and mutual accountability between Vietnamese elite institutions, the bureaucracy, and the people at large. Socialist-era Mass Organizations, farmers associations, civil society entities, and professional associations were key in fostering social capital and creating synergy between elite political institutions and state machinery in mobilizing public action for implementation of policies and strategies. The government's support, including by enacting clear rules, regulations, and procedures for civic engagement at central, provincial, and community levels also enhances the participation of citizens in important political and economic decision-making.

In SSA, despite wide-ranging reforms of the 1980s and the 1990s (see Chapter 1), institutions remain too weak to enable formulating and implementing development policies. Externally prescribed policies may have contributed to improving political governance, managing conflicts, and rebuilding states (World Bank: 2000). However, the economic outcome remains bleak, fragile, and vulnerable to negative external shocks. The externalization of development policymaking in SSA and its heavy dependence on aid for development financing have improved policy formulation (or articulation). However, the capacity to effectively implement growth-friendly policies remains severely inadequate with "low-level equilibrium of poor institutional capability and ineffective economic transformation" (World Bank: 2000). International Financial Institutions (IFIs) have been consistently blamed for controlling SSA's economic policymaking. The country offices of IFIs were accused of effectively becoming "de facto ministries of finance, undermining sovereign policymaking in SSA" (Nyango'ro: 2002). Weak institutional capacities for policy formulation, implementation, and coordination in SSA are also the outcomes of a lack of financial and technical resources and core governance crises such as corruption, misallocation of scarce resources, inefficiency, and lack of political legitimacy (Nyango'ro: 2002).

9.1.7 *Strategic Integration into the Global Economy is Key to Maximizing Development Gains*

In parallel with its domestic efforts, Vietnam has also negotiated bilateral agreements with key trading partners such as the USA, Japan, the EU, and other regional and global players in trade and investment. The country has also concluded regional economic agreements (ASEAN) and joined a multilateral trade body (WTO). This means that Vietnam's strategic integration has not been limited to one country, region, or economy. China is also among the key partners of Vietnam as it is the main source of the country's imports. According to the Observatory of Economic Complexity (OEC) database (https://oec.world/en/profile/country/asvnm#top), in 2018, China was the largest source of Vietnam's imports, worth USD 83.3 billion, followed by South Korea (USD 48.6 billion), Japan (USD 15.6 billion), Thailand (USD 13 billion), and Singapore (USD 11.8 billion). Interestingly, while Vietnam's key export markets include other major countries and regions (e.g., the USA and EU), its imports are largely dominated by the Asian suppliers. That is, unlike SSA, Vietnam's sources of growth for trade, investment, and development partnership are highly diverse and its dependence on China is not substantial. In fact, in labour-intensive manufacturing exports Vietnam emerged as a competitor for China. Dependence on imports from the region and nearby countries, is strategically important in reducing the costs of imports (such as transport, insurance, and handling costs). It is also key in directing Vietnam's sources of imports towards countries of the region, with competitively lower costs of production, technological, and geographical proximity as well as sociocultural similarity. These are important features or conditions that facilitate Vietnam's acquisition of machinery and equipment as well as technologies that are affordable and relatively easy to disseminate, learn, and catch up with. Moreover, the financing infrastructure in Vietnam is largely from domestic resources (with a small portion from ODA and borrowing from multilateral and regional institutions such as the World Bank and the Asian Development Bank).

SSA's dependence on external finance (including from China) for infrastructure is becoming debt-creating in many countries of the region. While most of SSA, like other developing countries including Vietnam itself, are parts of China's Belt and Road Initiative (BRI), Vietnam is among the few countries that debate the operational modality, impact on sovereign (independent) decisions, effectiveness, value-added, transparency and sustainability of BRI[8] (Hiep: 2018). The way Vietnam relates to China is in terms of diversifying mutually beneficial relations or partnerships, not to create dependency. As such, Vietnam's approach towards China is more balanced, distanced, and nuanced than its seeming proximity would make it appear to be, which is worth examining.

The trade and development partnership between China and Vietnam has been consistently expanding. This positive trend is against seemingly uneasy political relationships, and Vietnam's approach towards diversified partnerships and broader integration into the regional and global economy. Vietnam also applies systems and techniques tested in China in public mobilization for political participation, civic duties, and engagements in economic activities, with close supervision of Chinese advisors (Tuong: 2014, Hackenesch and Bader: 2020). The post-socialist Developmental State model (see Bolesta: 2015, 2017) which has been successfully implemented in China is widely operationalized in the context of Doi-Moi in Vietnam and its strategic plans centred on a "socialist free-market system". For instance, in Vietnam, the pace of economic growth and integration in the global economic systems (e.g., WTO) was identical to China's in terms of strategy and intent. Strategically, both countries had a hidden or implicit policy of restricting domestic market access to foreign economic actors "by maintaining old and creating new entry barriers as well as manoeuvring around the WTO rules, which is motivated by economic nationalism" (Bolesta: 2015, 2017). In both China and Vietnam, the state has continued to play a major role not only in fostering centrally planned economic systems but also in guiding policy interventions and defining incentive schemes. Such heavy-handed involvement of the state is in line with policy lessons that the two countries inherited from earlier experiences of Northeast Asia (Japan, South Korea, and Taiwan), where the state played a dominant role of "guidance, selection and coordination over the private sector in channelling investments, encouraging industrial upgrading, avoiding waste of resources through unregulated competition, supporting export, etc." (Wade: 2003). Clearly, China and Vietnam, share similar best practices, policy lessons, and experiences as well as expanded partnerships with the vibrant and neighbouring economies – something which is very hard to achieve or find in SSA.

However, unlike SSA, there is no evidence of excessive dependence of Asian latecomers such as Vietnam on one market, economy, or development model for their socioeconomic development, capital accumulation, and the fostering of productive capacities and structural economic transformation. The discussions of the experience of Vietnam also show that, while the country's policymaking is centralized, implementation is very much decentralized, with clear delineation of functions and responsibilities between elite political institutions, the bureaucracy, and the public at large, which enhanced legitimacy, trust, and ownership of policies and strategies. This does not mean that there are not challenges or weaknesses. As with many developing countries, Vietnam still faces hurdles in its "liberalization" of the political system and institutions. For instance, the distinction in the roles and responsibilities of civil society, NGOs, and the country's Mass Organizations restricts their political or rights-based advocacy functions. This, in turn, may limit the liberty of citizens such as freedoms of speech or the right to organization, undermining accountability and transparency in the governance structures and processes. Despite these remaining challenges, Vietnam has made tremendous progress in achieving sustained and inclusive economic growth which is behind the country's improved socioeconomic wellbeing, aggregate income, and capital accumulation – all of which are critically important for fostering productive capacities and structural economic transformation. Vietnam's strategic integration into regional and multilateral trade is also consistent with its drive for industrialization and production transformation, which has greatly contributed to diversifying markets for its exports, maximizing trade and investment opportunities.

The key lesson from Vietnam's experience for the countries of SSA resides in the role of the post-socialist Developmental State, which not only created economy-wide capacities and capabilities, but also fostered social and institutional capital. Vietnam's state has particularly led the process of capital accumulation, value creation (and retention) – a role similar to the characteristic features of the East Asian Developmental State model and identical to an "entrepreneurial state" (Mazzucato: 2013). Not only has the state in Vietnam led "smart growth" but it has also ensured that such a growth is centred on productive capacities and structural transformation in a manner consistent with an "entrepreneurial state" (Mazzucato and Penna: 2016). This has been done by investing in risky areas such as agriculture and rural infrastructure. The private sector only finds "the courage to invest after an entrepreneurial State has made high-risk investments" (Mazzucato and Penna: 2016). In these all processes and as with in East Asian economies, Vietnam has clearly defied policy prescriptions from outside. It tacitly rejected the idea of confining the role of the state to correcting market failures as advocated by mainstream orthodoxy. Instead, the state has played a paramount role in formulating, sequencing, and directing home-grown policies and strategies towards transformational development.

In the following section, the implications of Vietnam's successful transformation for SSA will be discussed. The focus is to identify key elements for a "productive capacities–structural transformation" framework or roadmap for SSA.

9.2 Implications of Vietnam's Experience for Policymaking in SSA

Development policies and strategies pursued by SSA in the post-independence period have failed to deliver promises of inclusive and sustained socioeconomic transformation. This is despite huge potential in natural capital, increased international support measures, and the region's growing ties with China. Moreover, despite SSA's higher per capita income levels than their Asian peers in the 1960s and 1970s, investment in education, health, and production transformation has remained low in the former. With decades of lost opportunities, SSA's socioeconomic performance continues to be weak, fragile, and vulnerable to external economic shocks. When growth occurred, its sources have been enclave-based or commodity-driven, with little or no impact on job creation and poverty reduction. The region's pattern of growth has further entrenched commodity dependence, high export concentration, weak manufacturing sectors, and greater vulnerability to volatile financial and commodity markets. This is because of a lack of economy-wide improvements in productivity, value addition by domestic producers, and long-term structural economic transformation. This has also led to widening trade deficits, declining terms of trade, external indebtedness, excessive microeconomic and macroeconomic instability, and overall socioeconomic vulnerability to the vagaries of negative shocks. Most economies of SSA have also been under stress from the increased negative impact of climate change, continued political instability, and civil conflicts (IMF: 2019). The confluences of these negative trends have exacerbated and perpetuated SSA's underdevelopment, further compounding the challenges of achieving sustained and inclusive growth. The dire socioeconomic conditions of SSA and the lack of government capacity to improve and "expand collective goods such as education and health services" (Evans and Heller: 2018) have further eroded state legitimacy and worsened state–society relations. In situations where states or institutions are weak or conflict-stricken, mobilizing public action and resources towards development will become difficult. Such a predicament undermines the legal and institutional basis for sustained and inclusive growth and development. Unlike in East Asia and Vietnam, the role of the state in SSA has been further weakened by sacrificing policy independence to external influences or prescriptions and overdependence on external sources of finance for development. These lead to a lack of policy space in formulating and implementing development policies. Africa's states have remained bureaucratic, overly political, or traditional – lacking basic experience, expertise, and capacities to become developmental and, at the same time, entrepreneurial.

Amid weak productive capacities and declining socioeconomic trends, "rising China" has emerged as the main development partner of SSA. This partnership has been guided by principles of South-South cooperation.[9] Trade between SSA and China has boomed, and Chinese FDI and development finance flows to SSA have substantially and consistently increased over the last couple of decades. Contrary to the widely held view that Chinese FDI stock is concentrated in countries with natural (extractive) resources, the evidence presented in this book shows that Chinese investment is diversified and has increasingly been targeting countries with comparative advantages outside of the extractive sectors. However, even the increasingly positive and encouraging Africa-China ties have not altered the fundamentals or characteristic features of weak productive capacities and lack of structural transformation in SSA. On all measures and benchmarks of productive capacities, the performance of SSA remains sluggish or the weakest of all developing regions. The region's natural capital component has not contributed either to reverse persistent weakness in productive capacities and structural transformation. For instance, SSA's exports to China remain dominated by unprocessed primary commodities, while the surge in the region's imports from China has been in light or labour-intensive manufacturing products. Sadly, the huge natural capital wealth of the region has not been used to transform production structures. The natural endowment of SSA has not translated into socioeconomic wellbeing for the countries concerned.

As with all the measures of productive capacities, SSA's manufacturing value-added in GDP has been continuously declining. Similarly, Gross Fixed Capital Formation (GFCF) remained low and volatile. Such a poor performance has been further accentuated by the absence of changes in the merchandise export diversification and concentration indices over the years examined. There is also growing concern that Chinese lending can lead to increasing the overall external indebtedness of several countries of SSA. The assessment of Africa-China relations based on country-specific case studies (Chapter 6) confirms similar trends regarding the overall impact of partnership of SSA with China. Firm-level evidence also shows that, in SSA, productivity is low, technology acquisition and innovation is non-existent, and the overall competitiveness of firms remains too weak to become an engine of growth, productivity, and structural transformation. The region's firms particularly suffer from poor and inadequate electricity infrastructure, which is a direct reflection of the poor overall performance of SSA in the energy component of productive capacities. In sum, the findings and conclusions of this book contradict the expectation that Africa-China trade, finance, and investment relations will have qualitative impact and lead to the fostering of productive capacities and structural transformation in SSA. Although Africa-China trade and investment ties are "conditionally" development-friendly, they are not substantially different from those of the EU, the USA, and Japan in terms of qualitative impact on SSA. These all have entrenched further commodity dependence.

Notwithstanding the disappointing impact, there is no doubt that China-SSA relations have provided new impetus, dynamism, and added opportunities for SSA. To make such opportunities qualitatively different from SSA's long-standing exploitative relations with the West, a series of fundamental changes are necessary and concrete actions are urgently needed. Subsequent sections of this offer policy insights or options as to what SSA can do to maximize the potential benefits of the region's growing relationships with China. The arguments and evidence provided in this book show that the complex and intertwined trade and development challenges facing SSA are both causes and consequences of weak productive capacities and lack of structural economic transformation. Consequently, SSA will most likely continue to be economically underdeveloped and the locus of poverty. SSA's economies may remain the last frontier in the global fight against multidimensional poverty and underdevelopment in the 21st century. This is not to say that all is doomed and that the countries of SSA cannot hope to undo their socioeconomic stagnation, decline, marginalization, and overall underdevelopment. Nor is it to deny or underestimate the significant potential that the region holds for growth and transformation. Therefore, any discourse on the development of SSA should reckon with the region's abundant natural resources, its dynamic demographic trends[10] and the growing middle class[11] (Deloitte: 2015, *The Economist*, 28 March 2020). Capturing natural resource endowments in socioeconomic development and for converting SSA's demographic dividend into real economic opportunities, will require the fostering of productive capacities and structural economic transformation. These are sine qua non for sustained and inclusive economic growth with substantial job creation as well as accelerated and sustained poverty reduction.

Yet, enhancing productive capacities and structural economic transformation is not simple. Nor is it straightforward or automatic. It requires addressing complex development issues through carefully balanced and results-oriented decision-making. Such an approach calls for an extraordinary paradigm shift in formulating and implementing coherent, holistic, and comprehensive growth as well as development-friendly policies. Widely held views and assumptions that market forces provide ultimate responses to SSA's development problems, and that state institutions must enable market forces to work are shrouded in faulty reasoning and unsound arguments. There is emerging consensus that "business-as-usual" approaches can no longer be an option for productive transformation in SSA. This is not to suggest a single (universal) blueprint for the formulation and implementation of development policies in countries of SSA. There is no "one-size-fits-all" development (economic) policy approach. The specific focus areas (priorities), choice of a particular mix of policies and sequence of implementation, should be based on country-specific realities, key binding constraints to growth, and other initial conditions. Policies and strategies applied or implemented in East Asian economies and Vietnam may not be perfectly fitting or suitable for SSA's specific situations.

However, despite heterogeneity between countries and regions, the burden of primary responsibility for converting the growing economic, trade, and investment ties with China into meaningful transformation rests with countries (governments and peoples) of SSA. Learning from the successful experiences of Asia (particularly Vietnam), SSA must create conditions for productive transformation. What can the countries of SSA do to maximize or harness their growth and development potential as well as take advantage of their increasing ties with China to foster productive capacities and structural economic transformation? There are several and consequential actions that countries of SSA can undertake based on their overall socioeconomic circumstances. The following are key issues that merit serious consideration but not necessarily in the order in which they are discussed or articulated.

9.2.1 *Mindset Changes*

The starting point for putting in place new-generation policies in SSA should be to cultivate positive mindsets by radically altering the current political attitude about economic growth and development. There should be a conviction at the level of the political leadership of SSA that key determinants of growth and development are endogenous (internal to the economy). What is needed is a developmental and entrepreneurial state like in Vietnam. Making SSA's development largely driven by internal factors, rather than by external determinants, should be a priority in overall policymaking, vision, and thinking. At the level of policy thoughts, intents, and articulation, indigenous (home-grown), country-specific solutions should be sought to domestic development challenges. The conception and elaboration of policies should be to exploit comparative advantages and unlock binding constraints. Policies and strategies dependent or driven by external factors (resources and actors) can crowd out domestic "policy space" and undermine ownership capacities. Therefore, domestic policies and strategies should not be formulated based on financing expectations or handouts from outside as is currently the case in most countries of SSA. Nor should these countries succumb to or depend on policies imposed or prescribed from outside. This is not to discount the importance of complementary and favourable external factors. SSA's development experience thus far has shown that external factors and international support measures alone will not change socioeconomic realities on the ground.

Indeed, the performance of the most aid-dependent economies in SSA has remained the weakest when compared to least aid-dependent countries of Asia and Latin America throughout the last several decades. Likewise, despite preferential and favourable market access granted to the region by traditional and emerging development partners, SSA's share in global exports and FDI flows has remained marginal or continued to deteriorate. Moreover, wide-ranging externally prescribed and widely implemented policies in SSA have not delivered their intended results. Countries such as Vietnam and East Asian economies that eschewed externally imposed policy prescriptions have successfully transformed their economies with significant improvements in the living standards of their population in a relatively short period. Vietnam's experience with policy formulation and implementation shows that leadership should not be viewed only as an opportunity to exercise political power and legitimacy. It should, instead, be seen as a heavy responsibility to carefully manage risks or pitfalls and maximize opportunities through policy formulation, experimentation, emulation, and implementation. The political leadership and development policymakers of SSA must be assertive, visionary, and pragmatic in maximizing their partnership with China and with other partners – long-standing or emerging. They should also be in the driving seat and lead the way for their countries' socioeconomic transformation, primarily by exploiting their comparative advantages, unlocking binding constraints, and diversifying sources of economic growth.

9.2.2 A New Growth Narrative Is Needed for New-Generation Policies and Strategies

As part of the proposed change in political mindsets, it is necessary for SSA to redefine the institutional, regulatory, and policy imperatives of achieving higher economic growth. Preoccupation with the quantity of growth has its roots in a grossly mistaken assumption and widely shared notion that "a certain level of order" (Snowden and Boon: 2007), which exists in a few countries and generated impactful high economic growth for them, applies uniformly across the world. However, commodity-driven, and enclave-based economic growth (seen during 2002–2007), has not brought about meaningful changes or social outcomes such as poverty reduction. Instead of ensuring broad-based, sustained, and inclusive economy-wide growth, SSA's policymakers have been content with short-term gains in managing poverty. That is, political ambition in SSA has so far been to achieve higher economic growth without due attention to the source, form, and sustainability of growth. The objective of economic growth should go beyond managing poverty. It should, instead, focus on the form, source, and quality of growth, which is vital to address the root causes of underdevelopment by creating decent jobs, expanding aggregate income, fostering capital accumulation, and contributing to accelerated and sustained poverty reduction. Such growth is indispensable not only to make growth inclusive but also sustainable and transformational.

In Vietnam, the objective of growth has never been to manage poverty. Poverty reduction is not viewed as an end but seen primarily as a "resource" for further economic growth and development. Yet, the impact of growth on poverty reduction, capital accumulation, structural transformation, and overall improvements in the standard of living of the population of Vietnam is by far the greatest. Therefore, African countries should replace their existing policy approach by robust actions aimed at achieving better quality growth. The new approach to economic growth should be accompanied by a new political narrative anchored in pragmatism, forward-looking and determined efforts not only to generate quality growth but also to sustain it. Only with qualitatively different growth-friendly frameworks and narratives can SSA create the foundational conditions for sustained capital accumulation, economy-wide productive capacities, and structural transformation. Such qualitative changes should be complemented by effective income distribution or welfare-maximizing policies. Further strategies aimed at promoting better opportunities, facilitating economic empowerment, and mobilizing citizens for development are equally important to sustain growth and broaden its sources. In Vietnam (as in several East Asian economies) subsidized universal access to education and health services, infrastructure and ICT connectivity, electrification, and land-use rights all have significantly enhanced agricultural productivity, expanded off- and on-farm job opportunities with significant and sustained poverty reduction. Such interventionist policies have played vital roles in fostering productive capacities and structural transformation.

9.2.3 *Home-grown and Nationally Owned Policies Are Key*

Changes in the mindsets and attitudes alone are not enough in the articulation of new institutional and policy imperatives for development. There should be deliberate efforts to formulate and implement home-grown and country-owned policies and strategies. This should not be confined to macroeconomic stability or stabilization and deregulation policies only as those prescribed from outside. Implementation of new-generation domestic policies, which are strongly recommended in this book should be independent and free from external influences. They should be based on country-specific articulations of comparative advantage, identification of binding constraints, and realignment of interventions and incentive structures to relieve bottlenecks. Microeconomic and macroeconomic as well as sectoral policies (such as in agriculture, industry, infrastructure, investment, education, and health) must be nationally owned. They should be particularly oriented towards enhancing employment-intensity of growth and lay the foundation for fostering economy-wide productive capacities, capital accumulation, and structural transformation. Besides externally imposed policies, one further shortcoming in SSA's development policymaking process is the total lack of national deliberation and consensus on the content, depth, and breadth of reforms and overall direction of policies. Generally, policies are formulated top-down, and implementation is coordinated vertically. This impedes information flows and undermines the capacity and legitimacy of the state in mobilizing domestic finance, key stakeholders, and the public in the cause of development.

Against perceptions about Vietnam's system of governance, particularly in the West, Vietnam has developed a culture of dialogue (both formal and informal). This has helped in building national consensus on policy directions since the launch of the 1986 reform process. This was key in mobilizing the domestic resources and actions of the public and stakeholders (including private sector and civil society actors) in the country's development. In so doing, Vietnam has enhanced public investment in the education and health sectors, introduced new administrative (governance) structures through "publicly backed" reforms. These include the provision of free universal education and healthcare services, particularly to the urban poor and rural communities, often through state subsidies. There was also an understanding (even tacit consensus) that economic growth, job creation, and poverty reduction are key to the political survival and continuity of centralized but gradually market-oriented policies and strategies. High-quality growth that contributed to improved standards of living in Vietnam has been key to enhancing the legitimacy of the state and foster confidence and trust between the public, elite institutions, the bureaucracy, and the entire state machinery of the country.

9.2.4 *Investing in Human Capital Formation*

Human capital formation is a requisite for fostering productive capacities and structural transformation. It implies providing quality education and health services and enhancing the literacy, numeracy, and technical capacities of the labour force. Such vital social sectors are key to enhancing the productivity of the labour force that is needed for transformational growth and development. Public investment and incentives are necessary to expand education and health services in rural areas, less privileged urban centres, and provinces as well as communities in geographically inaccessible and remote areas. In SSA, poor education and health services undermine labour productivity, entrepreneurial and job-creating capacities. Without investing in human capital formation, it will be difficult to achieve sustained and inclusive growth (by physical capital accumulation only). The East Asian economies that have been leading the transformation process are not as endowed with natural resources as the countries of SSA. They used their only comparative advantages – an educated and well-trained labour force – to attract investment, facilitate technological capabilities, and foster R&D and innovation centres. The deep-dive analysis of Vietnam provided in the previous chapter, shows that the country has boosted investment in education and health in parallel with reforming the sector with outstanding gains in fostering human capital for its transformational development. Vietnam's significantly enhanced human capital has been leading and deepening the country's continued structural transformation, which is largely driven by ICT, digitization, export sophistication, investment (including FDI) – all of which are strategically pursued to usher in the new industrial revolution.

Contrary to Vietnam's experience, natural resource-rich countries of SSA (such as Angola) lag significantly behind the rest of the developing world in improving their human assets. Without raising the quality of human capital and matching the skills with the needs and requirements of the economy, it will be impossible to build productive capacities and transform economies. Botswana – a country that has been an outstanding performer in Africa, both in political governance and the delivery of quality social services – boasts a highly educated labour force. However, there is a mismatch between the educated labour force, and the skills needed by the economy of the country. The country now has one of the highest educated but unemployed labour force as the mining-dependent economy requires more technicians, engineers, and surveying specialists than lawyers, managers, and social scientists, which its universities have been producing in significant numbers.

9.2.5 Fostering Production and Supply Linkages

Carefully harnessing natural capital in countries that have such resource wealth (such as agriculture, forest, water, and mineral resources) is key to productive transformation. However, this requires the formulation and implementation of a wide range of mutually supportive and realigned policies and strategies. For instance, in countries with a potential in agriculture, policies and strategies should focus on enhancing the production and productivity of the sector. Addressing low and declining productivity and production in agriculture, requires strategic thinking, diagnosis, and holistic policy approaches that correct past policy failures, while transforming the sector. This can be done by identifying key binding constraints to the sector and redesigning incentive structures to unlock the potential of the sector. Such an approach can include fostering R&D and innovation in agriculture, diffusing new farm technologies, providing inputs, and expanding production techniques. Policymakers and their implementing institutions, as well as technical experts, must agree on priorities. This should be based on evidence and country-specific circumstances because incorrect identification of priorities and means to implement them can be too costly for the economies to bear. What is needed in SSA is enterprising the rural economy and the agricultural sector through the provision of social services and building infrastructure (roads, electricity, schools, and health centres), which are key to generating on- and off-farm jobs, for example, as Vietnam did.

There are several policy lessons that can be drawn from the experience of Vietnam in agricultural development by boosting investment in rural infrastructure such as transport, electricity, storage (warehouses), irrigation, drainage, and ICT services. This is crucial in fostering two-way sectoral linkages, creating rural employment, raising real income, and stimulating aggregate demand for rural non-farm produce and services. Vietnam's improved investment in agriculture has been pursued in alignment with other strategies aimed at expanding off-farm employment opportunities. These efforts include expanding financial, insurance, and marketing systems as well as disseminating agricultural market information. Expanding agri-processing, meeting international food safety, quality, social, and environmental standards as well as fostering linkages between farms and hospitality sector and other catering services are further effective ways of increasing farm production, productivity, employment, and income. The country's successful rural transformation and infrastructure (such as roads and electricity) were decisive in fostering agricultural production and productivity. Agriculture served as a springboard for the country to expand exports, incomes, and employment opportunities and combat rural poverty. Agriculture also served as a potential source of labour and capital for the growth and expansion of agri-processing and labour-intensive manufacturing. For instance, Vietnam's strategy in improving the quality of livestock and increasing investment in upstream parts of the value chains can also offer further policy lessons. These policy efforts of the country led to reduced imports of meat and increased exports of hides and skin, before hooking into downstream parts of the value chains. Moreover, Vietnam has gradually and significantly improved the availability of quality inputs which increased the country's competitive production and exports of leather and leather products as well as footwear. Unlike Vietnam, Ethiopia's latest efforts to harness its livestock potential began by attracting investment in the downstream parts of the value chain (establishing processing firms). This was before improving upstream segments of the leather and leather products of the leather value chain. The results are far less positive than expected (especially when compared with the huge quantity of livestock the country possesses). This has called into question the competitiveness and sustainability of the country's leather industry. Ethiopia's newly established processing firms continue to outsource raw materials or intermediate goods because of low-quality domestic supplies.

Moreover, in Vietnam, rents from petroleum, copper, coal, zinc, and other mineral resources have been used in boosting agricultural productivity and rural development by supporting the provision of targeted farm subsidies, financing transport and energy infrastructures, and ensuring the access of the rural poor to universal education and health services. Rents from the extractive sector also played a part in catalyzing balanced regional development and expanding domestic demand in Vietnam. Fiscal and monetary policies have equally enhanced important roles in physical and human capital formation by accelerating public investments in infrastructure and raising spending on education, vocational and technical training, and health services. Contrary to the case of Vietnam, in several countries of SSA, the agriculture, minerals, and manufacturing sectors failed to establish or catalyze inter- and intra-sectoral linkages and transformation. The discovery of oil and other precious minerals in Angola has in fact penalized the agricultural and manufacturing sectors. The extractive sector has accelerated the premature relocation of core productive resources such as labour and capital (investment) away from the vital sectors. It has also induced macroeconomic imbalances. In many economies of SSA, investment (both public and private) in agriculture is the lowest despite large proportion of their population residing in rural areas. In most of them, domestic credit to the agricultural sector is as little as 2 percent in total domestic credit disbursements (World Bank: 2000).

The development experience of Vietnam provides evidence that natural resource rents can help in acquiring technologies and fostering skills to funnel productive structures into higher value-added activities. This, in turn, results in higher incomes that fuel the demand and stimulate new investments, including in agriculture. Such virtuous relationships and linkages between natural resource wealth, capital accumulation, and structural transformation can lead to further development of new activities. These can further induce job creation, bring technological sophistication to exports, and allow countries to move away from traditional to more modern sectors, thereby intensifying the process of structural economic transformation.

9.2.6 *Supportive and Complementary Public and Private Investments*

Public and private investments should work hand in hand in the framework needed to foster productive capacities and structural economic transformation. The governments of SSA need to play a proactive role in promoting public investment in infrastructure and other public goods, irrespective of ownership. This is critically important given a weak and underdeveloped private sector, with severely limited capacity to invest in transformational growth and development. The primary aim of public investment should be to unlock key binding constraints on economic growth by identifying the sectors of spill-over effects. For instance, investing in infrastructure such as transport and electricity can boost growth, which in turn creates employment, income, and aggregate demand. Expanding income and local demand are vital, particularly for locally produced agricultural goods and labour-intensive manufactures. These are vital in attracting the private sector (domestic and foreign) and building trust in economic policymaking. This is important because public investment alone may not be sufficient to intensify the fostering of productive capacities and structural transformation. The private sector can play an important and complementary role in accelerating capital formation, technology transfer, innovation, and technological learning.

In SSA, large (usually foreign) firms tend to exploit all available opportunities to their advantage most of the time, at the expense of the domestic private sector (usually SMEs) and at the cost of overall development of the countries concerned. Countries rich in extractive resources also tend to provide lucrative incentives for foreign companies that invest in the exploitation of natural resources. In Vietnam, the mineral sector, including oil and coal, as well as the generation and distribution of electricity, remain fully or in part, in the hands of the state. Only in recent years has Vietnam allowed the domestic private sector to become an actor in the generation and distribution of electricity. Still today, Vietnam's SOEs are the largest stakeholders in the country's power generation and distribution. Instead of providing incentives and subsidies to firms engaged in the exploitation of extractive resources, SSA countries should endeavour to lure investments towards agriculture and labour-intensive manufacturing industries. They need to prioritize agri-processing and manufacturing sectors through the combination of incentives and integrating domestic firms into the global value chains. This should be pursued in parallel with attracting FDI. Governments in SSA should carefully negotiate the terms and conditions of investment particularly in attracting FDI. For instance, in Vietnam FDI firms are required to export rather than compete with local firms and enterprises. Moreover, governments in East Asia and Vietnam carefully negotiate with foreign firms to secure transfers of capital, technology, and knowhow, as well as hiring and training their nationals to work not only on assembly lines but also in management and quality jobs. Besides building their negotiating capacities, SSA's governments need to improve the institutional and regulatory frameworks governing private investments (both domestic and foreign). This should include efforts to improve transparency, accountability, competition, sound business procedures, and anticorruption laws. These are critically important in mobilizing investments (including FDI) and facilitating the acquisition of much needed capital, technology, and knowhow. They are also vital for creating opportunities for employment and export diversification. While the initial focus should be in agriculture or industry (manufacturing), the countries of SSA should gradually funnel FDI into infrastructure and the services sector such as the tourism, ICT, business, and financial sectors.

With the objective of enhancing the role of investment (including FDI) in industrialization and manufacturing, several countries of SSA have designed Export Processing Zones (EPZs), Industrial Parks (IPs) and industrial clusters. However, apart from Mauritius (Stiglitz: 2015) and South Africa, such efforts have not yet produced substantial benefits, particularly when compared with the costs of the facilities. Latecomers such as Rwanda lack effective business plans for the EPZs and IPs. Rwanda's EPZs and IPs currently accommodate more than 80 percent of foreign firms and account for more than 95 percent of exports (see Chapter 6). The only benefits from EPZs and IPs for Rwanda (and many countries of SSA) for the time being are attracting FDI, creating low-skill jobs, poverty reduction, and contributing to low-value exports. These are generally regarded as short-term benefits as opposed to long-term (dynamic) gains such as fostering production linkages and structural economic transformation (Alcorta and Tesfachew: 2020). Operational and policy lessons from the experience of Vietnam are that there is an urgent need to realign the objectives of the EPZs and IPs with those of national development plans and visions, focusing more on long-term development gains than short-term benefits.

9.2.7 *Capable, Independent, and Effective Institutions Matter*

There is a need for SSA to put in place institutional and regulatory frameworks that guide and facilitate the fostering of productive capacities and structural economic transformation. These are as important in SSA as they were in Vietnam. However, the notion of capable and effective institutions should go beyond market governance or facilitating the functioning of market institutions. They should also go beyond public administration, ensuring multiparty democracy, and managing routine state affairs such as maintaining law and order, security, and maximizing welfare to societies, though these too are important. Institutions should encompass capacities and capabilities to formulate and implement sectoral strategies and development policies centred on the fostering of productive capacities and structural economic transformation. This requires capacities to mobilize and efficiently allocate development resources and recalibrate regional and global opportunities for transformational development. Several SSA countries (such as Botswana, Ghana, Mauritius, and Senegal) built vibrant and effective governance systems and institutions, which have led to successive competitive democratic elections. However, these countries are still in a low-level equilibrium (poor socioeconomic outcome, weak productive capacities, lack of financial and technical resources) and are unable to foster institutions and structural transformation. In SSA, except for the relative successes in Mauritius, the challenge of fostering productive capacities and transforming economies remains elusive or daunting. Botswana's political governance has been credited for effectively stamping out corruption, instituting fiscal prudence, effectively capturing the natural resources wealth in the delivery of quality services (including education and health), ensuring democratic elections, and reducing extreme poverty over the years. However, the country's successive cycles of Economic Diversification Drives (EDD) have failed to materialize or translate into structural transformation. In fact, Botswana's dependence on exports and government revenues on a single commodity (diamonds) has increased over the years, instead of decreasing. Botswana remains one of the most vulnerable economies in the world to the vagaries of international commodity price swings and consequent external negative shocks. Moreover, Botswana's policies encourage and facilitate the participation of the private sector in the economic development of the country, whose role, thus far, has remained extremely low in terms of economic and employment contributions.

In parallel with instituting governance and democratic reforms, several SSA countries have also improved the quality of their development plans, strategies, or vision documents. This may have been due to the use of international consultancy industry and advisory services. Irrespective of the improved qualities and better articulation of policies and strategies, there is a wide gap between the aspirations or ambitions of the policies and their actual implementation. In most cases, financial, technical, and human resources are not adequate or aligned with the institutional mandates or assigned tasks. In other cases, dependence on international institutions and donors for financing policy implementation made such resources unpredictable and unsustainable. Furthermore, the growth of non-state actors (domestic and international NGOs or civil society actors) and their increasing role in externally funded development projects has raised questions about the competing and at times conflicting role of such entities in catalyzing development.

There is consensus on the important roles of civil society actors[12] in building post-conflict societies, fighting corruption, facilitating national consultations and dialogue, and acting as a balancing force in electoral or democratic governance processes. There are serious contentions as well regarding their role in development – especially when it comes to fostering economy-wide productive capacities and structural transformation for sustained and inclusive growth in SSA. It is critically important for the economies of SSA to confine civil society functions to areas where they have recognized experience, expertise, and comparative advantages. There is also a need to realign the functions of international NGOs with those based nationally. This may be key to resolving uneasy, (implicit) unfriendly historical relationships between the African polity, intelligentsia, and international civil society entities that often lack local knowledge, expertise, and experience, and yet attempt to impose imported values and norms on local stakeholders or citizens. Useful lessons can be discerned from the experiences of East Asian economies and that of Vietnam regarding the importance of effective and capable institutions including in the financial and banking sectors. In these economies, institutions have played a crucial role in leading the way for productive transformation. They facilitated the fostering of development-supportive R&D centres, enhancing knowledge creation and absorption. East Asian and Vietnam's institutions have been particularly successful in facilitating technology transfers, supporting innovation, and learning (including through financing), which are decisive for economic growth and catch-up.

Institutions are vital for leading and kick-starting productive transformation. However, creating useful institutions alone may not be enough if not matched by human and financial resources and an overall enabling environment. Institutions need independent decision-making powers, building mutual trust, respect (see Crespi: 2014) and recognition of their alternative views by policymakers and political leadership. Without all-round support and enabling environments, the capacity of SSA institutions to formulate alternative policy approaches and effectively implement strategies will continue to be inadequate. This in turn causes policy formulation and implementation in SSA to remain externally driven, undermining endogenous drivers of growth and production transformation. "Externalization" of development policymaking and implementation not only undermines independence and sovereign decision-making processes, but it also renders the ownership, accountability, legitimacy, and transparency of policies and their outcomes difficult. It will particularly make domestic institutions too weak to provide alternative views, correct market failures or distortions, and challenge the imposition of an externally financed neoliberal order.

9.2.8 *Infrastructure and ICT Connectivity as Development Enabler*

Productive capacities and structural transformation-supportive infrastructure and ICT connectivity are vital for attaining sustainable and inclusive growth in SSA. Hard infrastructures in transport, communications, power (electricity), schools, hospitals, clinics, water, and sanitation are critically important for development. These should be facilitated and complemented by soft infrastructure such as financial, ICT, quality and safety standards, rules, and regulations as well as skilled human resources. Weak and underfunded infrastructure is the outcome of policy failure, misaligned priorities, misallocation of resources. This is because weak states or institutions are unable to manage, maintain, and modernize the sector. Weak infrastructure also limits countries' capacities to mobilize productive investment (domestic and foreign), undermines industrialization, competitiveness, and the overall productive capacities of the economies. Poor infrastructure particularly hinders structural economic transformation by creating enclaves of economic activities (mostly clustered where infrastructure and related services exist) usually in urban centres. In most SSA countries, weak infrastructure connectivity has led to missed opportunities in economic diversification that would fully harness natural resources and rural development opportunities. In Angola, transport infrastructure is designed to support the natural resource (predominantly oil) sector. This has restricted Angola's capacity to diversify its economy away from the oil sector into manufacturing, agri-processing, horticulture, and fisheries. Each of these sectors requires a different set of transport infrastructure and trade logistics such as cold storage, laboratories, and quality control facilities. In most SSA countries, particularly countries without access to the sea (landlocked countries), poor infrastructure and ICT connectivity are among the reasons for high trade transport costs and the poor competitiveness of these economies. Vietnam and newly industrialized East Asian economies have managed to address infrastructure and connectivity barriers, while effectively tackling economic underdevelopment. In Vietnam, transport, electricity, and ICT infrastructure and connectivity served as enablers of productive capacities and accelerated structural economic transformation. The provision of reliable and affordable electricity has speeded up Vietnam's transformation into an industrial hub and competitive exporter of manufactured goods. This has also played an important role in expanding jobs and creating employment opportunities including in rural areas. Regarding the ICT sector, Vietnam has registered massive progress, not only in terms of access but also in driving the internet-based economy, which has been growing at about 40 percent a year (see the case study on Vietnam). Vietnam's energy, transport, and ICT infrastructures are development-oriented and transformation-accelerating. They are linked to industrialization (manufacturing) hubs, urban growth poles, and are carefully designed to facilitate an integrated rural development, fostering sectoral (forward and backward) linkages and the country's participation in regional and global production networks and value chains.

In SSA, limited resources are behind the weak investment in new and modern infrastructure. However, there is equally serious weakness in the maintenance and upgrading of existing infrastructure. This reflects weak policies, poor management, and governance, rather than a mere lack of financial resources. There is also misunderstanding about the role of infrastructure in formulating national policies, strategies, and visions. In the countries reviewed, there is more emphasis on ensuring wider access, often at the expense of using infrastructure as enabler of fostering productive capacities and in acceleration of structural economic transformation. This is the result of misguided infrastructure policies and strategies – precisely what Vietnam, for example, managed to avoid. Rwanda aspires to become an ICT hub in central Africa through internet connectivity and computer literacy. These are worthy initiatives. However, there is little or no use or application of ICT as an enabler of economic transformation. For instance, in SSA, the potential of ICT has not been fully harnessed for reducing business transaction costs, disseminating market information, easing business deals or transactions online, marketing products and services, improving the quality of designs for local labour-intensive manufacturing, and, above all, creating employment opportunities. Likewise, electricity policies in most of SSA are designed to improve access for households as opposed to most East Asian economies which exploited rural electrification for expanding off-farm job opportunities and kick-starting the agri-processing industry. Scaling up investment in infrastructure and ICT connectivity is vital for the economies of SSA.

9.2.9 Industrial Policy and Manufacturing Should Remain the Leitmotiv and Conduit for Structural Transformation

Historical and empirical evidence show that without industrialization and a competitive manufacturing sector, structural economic transformation hardly occurs. SSA's weak manufacturing sector and lack of economy-wide improvements provide a strong case for industrial policies in supporting the fostering of productive capacities and structural economic transformation. The current crises and disruption of manufacturing value and supply chains caused by the COVID-19 pandemic brought back the debates on the need for industrialization and manufacturing in SSA. With the pandemic, Personal Protective Equipment (PPE), facemasks, hand-gloves, and hand-sanitizers have become critically needed to contain the spread of the virus, saving lives and limiting the adverse impact on economic development. However, the production and supply of these life-saving labour-intensive manufactured goods was severely disrupted with the spread of the pandemic. This makes nations that usually rely on imports (such as those in SSA) extremely vulnerable and dependent on aid and handouts from abroad. For SSA countries, the impact of the pandemic on global production segments and export restrictions by some countries translated into a serious dilemma – for three important reasons. First, they cannot import PPE because of disruption of value chains and export restrictions by countries that used to produce these medical supplies for export. Second, they cannot quickly repurpose their domestic productive capacities to produce PPE because their productive capacities are weak or less developed. Finally, even when countries that have the productive capacities to do so began producing PPE in bulk for export in the aftermath of the outbreak, most SSA countries lacked the foreign exchange reserves to buy them. Therefore, the COVID-19 shock was a "wake-up call" for countries in SSA that when the chips are down, naturally, every nation becomes preoccupied with domestic needs and priorities. Therefore, lagging in productive capacities building could be detrimental not only to the process of structural transformation but also to the survival and wellbeing of citizens, particularly during unforeseen shocks and crises such as the current pandemic. This phenomenon underlines the urgency of building productive capacities and manufacturing capability in SSA more today than ever before.

The absence of the domestic production and supply of industrial goods in SSA is the result of failures of successive industrial policies pursued in these economies. Externally imposed market-led privatization and stabilization policies have weakened the capacity of states to foster industrialization. Therefore, SSA's policymakers and political leaders must regain their development policymaking autonomy in pursuing industrialization through carefully sequenced industrial policies. Governments in SSA must be free to promote industrialization through well-targeted state subsidies and supportive incentive structures. Companies that create decent jobs and add value to the economy and export structures (through diversification) should be identified, supported, and vigorously promoted. Nevertheless, care should be taken to ensure that industrialization is not pursued at the expense of other sectors with comparative advantages: it must be realigned with such advantages. In Vietnam (as in other East Asian economies), industrialization laid the foundation for harnessing the country's comparative advantages. The aim of promoting a labour-intensive manufacturing sector was to build a competitive sector based on a highly skilled and well-trained labour force in which Vietnam had comparative advantages over its competitors in the region, such as China and Thailand. What distinguishes Vietnam from the rest of the East Asian economies is the fact that the country's industrialization was also designed to harness the potential of natural resources (agriculture and mining) in parallel with labour-intensive (light) manufacturing. This is because, unlike several economies in East Asia, Vietnam has ample potential not only in abundant labour but also in agriculture, forestry, fishery, and mineral resources. This is an important lesson for economies of SSA to explore as these countries too have huge natural resources and a bulging youth population.

9.2.10 *A Dynamic and Competitive Export Sector Is Key to Fostering and Sustaining Structural Economic Transformation*

Discussions in earlier chapters stressed the importance of building a vibrant and competitive export sector not only as a source of foreign exchange but also for dynamic gains such as technology transfers, innovation, competitiveness, and learning. In Vietnam, exports and investment-led strategies brought about successful socioeconomic transformation. These were implemented in parallel with carefully selected and targeted IS strategies. This mixed and balanced approach has played a vital role in the country's accelerated structural socioeconomic change over the years. In contrast, the experience of SSA's commodity-dependent economies shows that they were unable to maximize the potential of trade for their economic growth and transformation. Instead, their dependence on the export of unprocessed commodities has increased over the years, making these economies more vulnerable and fragile than ever before.

This calls for renewed and vigorous efforts in export diversification and the need to define a long-term vision that maximizes the role of commodities as important sources and drivers of comparative advantages and structural transformation. This should include deliberate and targeted policies and strategies aimed at enhancing the participation of economies in SSA in regional and global commodity value chains in the sectors where they have comparative and competitive advantages. Fostering productive capacities and structural economic transformation in SSA also requires channelling rents from commodities to their socioeconomic development and transformation. This should include financing key infrastructure such as transport, electricity, and ICT, and fostering integrated rural development. Governments in SSA must also invest their natural resource wealth in transforming human capital (through public investment in education and health) and augmenting economy-wide capital accumulation.

9.2.11 *Fostering Broad Partnerships with Countries, Economies, and Institutions Plays a Complementary Role*

The countries of SSA enjoy historic, political and economic ties with the EU. These were cemented on and culminated in conventions and agreements negotiated in various rounds. These partnership frameworks, although based on negotiations between unequal economic and political powers, aimed to improve the socioeconomic, institutional, and political landscapes of African, Caribbean and Pacific (ACP) nations – a grouping that covers SSA countries. Development and humanitarian aid, technical assistance, market access, and investment facilitation support from the EU were central to EU-ACP partnership conventions and agreements. Nevertheless, these partnerships, as with all externally generated economic policies in SSA, have not delivered on their promises in terms of enhancing exports and facilitating FDI flows. Consequently, socioeconomic vulnerability, premature deindustrialization, and the continued deterioration of SSA's share in global trade and investment have continued unabated. As with the EU, the countries of SSA also developed expanded trade and investment partnerships with the USA through (the Africa Growth and Opportunity Act – AGOA), with Japan (the Tokyo International Conference on African Development – TICAD), and China (the Forum on China-Africa Cooperation – FOCA). All these partnerships and frameworks, as well as several regional and bilateral trade and investment agreements, have certainly brought growing optimism and opportunities, but unfortunately, they have not led to substantial socioeconomic transformation in SSA. SSA's increasing trade and investment ties with China are not outcomes of trade creation but more of trade diversion from West to East.

Therefore, an overriding need for the countries of SSA is to strive to formulate and implement a home-grown indigenous development agenda, driven by endogenous growth factors. Learning from the case of Vietnam, SSA should build productive and supply capacities in parallel with intensifying partnerships for trade, investment, and economic growth. As with previous partnership agreements, the current Africa-China trade, investment, and development finance ties have only brought about quantitative shift in trade and investment away from traditional partners (EU, USA, Japan) towards China. Such a quantitative change has not created more trade and investment opportunities for a structural economic transformation of countries of SSA. Harnessing trade and investment opportunities, including those arising from China's engagement in Africa, requires building production and supply capabilities, not least in manufacturing and knowledge-intensive service sectors. How Vietnam has leveraged bilateral, regional, and multilateral trade and economic agreements for trade and investment creation, diversification, and better adapted economic structures, should provide practical and operational lessons for a new policymaking vision in SSA.

Notes

1 In his most influential book – *The Asian Drama: An Inquiry into the Poverty of Nations* – published in 1968, Gunnar Myrdal describes Asia as an economically stagnant region (Kanbur, R: 2018, Nayyar: 2019).

2 Here, picking winners should not be mixed up with Import Substitution (IS) strategies but rather it refers to selective government interventions, targeting of industries or firms that are strategically viewed as important to lead economic growth and transformation.

3 These are Botswana, Burkina Faso, Cameroun, Chad, Ethiopia, Kenya, Lesotho, Madagascar, Mali, Namibia, Nigeria, Senegal, Somalia, Sudan, Tanzania, and Zambia (World Bank: 2000).

4 UNIDO 2018b and Grumiller et al. (2019) estimate that Ethiopia had about 57.83 million head of cattle; 28.04 million sheep, and 28.61 million goats (livestock population), and produces about 8 million pieces of cattle hide, 12 million sheep skins, and 8 million goat skins annually.

5 The industrial ratio is the average ratio of the shares of manufacturing to services in GDP in a year. It is an aggregate measure of the performance of the two sectors and an indicator of the degree of structural economic transformation.

6 The term "servicification" is used in recent economic literature, including by UNCTAD, to describe trends towards a disproportionate increase in the share of the service sector (usually low-skill and low-technology services) in an economy.
7 UNCTAD's Productive Capacities Index (PCI) measures structural change by using composite indicators consisting of the Merchandise Export Concentration Index, Economic Complexity Index, Gross Fixed Capital Formation, and industrial ratio.
8 The dispute between China and Vietnam over the South China Sea has further compounded concerns about Belt and Road Initiative (BRI), and consequently, Vietnam is still cautious about the value-added BRI, although it has formally supported the tenets (Hiep: 2018).
9 This is sometimes interpreted as meaning less political conditionality, non-interference in the domestic affairs of states, friendship, and solidarity in development. It can also mean reciprocal and mutually beneficial relationships where both partners are assumed to be reaping equal or proportional benefits.
10 In 2019, the Population of SSA was estimated at 1.1 billion (www.woldbankdata.org) and forecast to reach 2.5 billion by 2050 (https://population.un.org/wpp/).
11 Deloitte estimated that in 2013 the middle class of SSA was about 375 million (34 percent of the population), and is forecast to reach 500 million by 2030.
12 Broadly defined to include domestic and international Non-Governmental Organizations (NGOs), non-profit organizations, independent professional associations, academic and research institutions, social media communities, diaspora associations, etc. (World Economic Forum, 2013, and Africa Development Bank 2012).

Bibliographical references

Acemoglu, D., Johnson, S., and Robinson, A. J. (2005). Institutions as a Fundamental Cause of Long-Run Growth. National Bureau of Economic Research (NBER), Working Paper 10481. Available at: http://www.nber.org/papers/w1048.

Alcorta, L., and Tesfachew, T. (2020). Special Economic Zones and Export-Led Growth: An Industrial Policy Imperative. In *The Oxford Handbook of Industrial Hubs and Economic Development*. Edited by A. Oqubay, and J. Y. Lin. Chapter 18 pp 323–344. Oxford University Press. Oxford, U.K.

Bolesta, A. (2015). *China and Post-Socialist Development*. Published by Policy Press. Bristol, U.K. February 2015.

Bolesta, A. (2017). The Post-Socialist Developmental State in Asia. In *Post-Communist Development: Europe's Experiences, Asia's Challenges*. Edited by A. Bolesta. Collegium Civitas, Warsaw. pp 11–36.

Buera, J. F., Monge-Naranjo, A., and Primiceri, E. G. (2007). Learning the Wealth of Nations, September 2007.

Crespi, G. (2014). *Rethinking Productive Development: Sound Policies and Institutions for Economic Transformation*. Inter-American Development Bank (IDB), Palgrave Macmillan. New York, USA.

Deloitte. (2015). The Deloitte Consumer Review of Africa: A 21st Century View. Deloitte. Available at: https://www2.deloitte.com/content/dam/Deloitte/ng/Documents/consumer-business/the-deloitte-consumer-review-africa-a-21st-century-view.pdf.

Dezan Shira & Associates. (2020). Vietnam Briefing: Growing Economic Cooperation between Japan and Vietnam. https://www.vietnam-briefing.com/news/growing-economic-cooperation-japan-vietnam.html/, accessed on 25 June 2020.

Economic and Financial Survey. (2019). *Regional Economic Outlook*. IMF, April 2019.

Evans, P., and Heller, P. (2018). The State and Development. WIDER Working Paper 2018/112. September 2018. United Nations University, UN-WIDER, ISSN 1798-7237. ISBN 978-92-9256-554-1.

Fagerberg, J., Srholec, M., and Knell, M. (2007). The Competitiveness of Nations: Why Some Countries Prosper While Others Fall Behind. *World Development*, 35, 1595–1620. https://doi.org/10.1016/j.worlddev.2007.01.004.

Financial Times. (2019). Industrial Policy is Not Just About Picking Winners, 28 March 2019. https://www.ft.com/content/9a6568a2-4f15-11e9-9c76-bf4a0ce37d49.

Grumiller, J., Raza, W., Alexander, R., and Yilma, T. (2019). *Value Chain Analysis for Leather Products from Ethiopia*. CBI Netherlands, Austrian Foundation for Development Research (Final Report) 20 February 2019.

Hackenesch, C., and Bader, J. (2020). The Struggle for Minds and Influence: The Chinese Communist Party's Global Outreach. *International Studies Quarterly*, 1–11. Available at: https://doi.org/10.1093/isq/sqaa028.

Hausman, R., and Rodrik, D. (2003). Economic Development as Self-Discovery. National Bureau of Economic Research, Working Paper No.8952. DOI:10.3386/w8952.

Hiep, L. H. (2018). The Belt and Road Initiative in Vietnam: Challenges and Opportunities, ISEAS Yusof Ishak Institute, ISSN 2335-6677. Available at: http://hdl.handle.net/11540/8138.

International Monetary Fund. (2019). Sub-Saharan Recovery Amid Elevated Uncertainty. Regional Economic Outlook, International Monetary Fund, Washington, DC.

Leipziger, D. M., and Thomas, V. (1993). *The Lessons of East Asia: An Overview of Country Experience*. *A World Bank Publication*. The World Bank, Washington, DC.

Kanbur, R. (2018). Gunnar Myrdal and Asian Drama in Context, Center for Economic Policy Research (CEPR), 9 March 2018.

Mazzucato, M. (2013). Debunking the Market Mechanism: A Response to John Kay. *Political Quarterly*, 84(4), 444–447.

Mazzucato, M., and Penna, C. (2016). Beyond Market Failures: The Market Creating and Shaping Roles of State Investment Banks. *Journal of Economic Policy Reform*, 19(4), 305–326. SPRU working paper version. Available at: http://www.sussex.ac.uk/spru/documents/2014-21-swps-mazzucato-and-penna.pdf.

Nayyar, D. (2006). Development through Globalization. UNU-WIDER Research Paper No. 2006/29, March 2006. United Nations University.

Nayyar, D. Learning from a Half-Century of Economic Development in Asia. UNU-WIDER Policy Brief, 3/19. Available at: https://www.wider.unu.edu/sites/default/files/Publications/Policy-brief/PDF/PB2019-3-Learning-from-a-half-century-of-economic-development-in-Asia.pdf.

North, C. D. (1991). Institutions. *The Journal of Economic Perspectives*, 5(1), 97–112. http://links.jstor.org/sici?sici=0895-309%28199124%295%3A1%3C97%3AI%3E2.0.CO%3B2-W.

Nyango'ro, J. (2002). Globalization, the State and Economic Development in Africa. In *Globalization, the Third World State and Poverty Alleviation in the Twenty-First Century*. Edited by B. IkubolaJeh Logan. Chapter 6. ASHGATE, Aldershot, 76–88.

Oqubay, A. (Blog). (2019). About Learning, OECD, 28 November 2019, 19th International Economic Forum on Africa, 29 November 2019, available at: https://oecd-development-matters.org/2019/11/28/how-do-nations-learn-why-development-is-first-and-foremost-about-learning/.

Oqubay, A., and Ohno, K. (2019). *How Nations Learn: Technological Learning, Industrial Policy, and Catch-Up*. Oxford University Press, Oxford.

Rodrik, D. (2013). Structural Change, Fundamentals, and Growth: An Overview. Institute for Advanced Study, September 2013 (revised).

Snowden, J. D., and Boone, E. M. (2007). A Leader's Framework for Decision Making. *Harvard Business Review*. Available at: http://www.hbr.org.

Stiglitz, J. (1996). Some Lessons from the East Asian Miracle. *The World Bank Research Observer*, 11(2), 151–177. http://www.jstor.com/stable/3986429.

Stiglitz, J. (2015). The Mauritius Miracle. Available at: http://www.project-syndicate.org/commentary/stiglitz136/English.

The Economist Magazine. (2020). Africa's Population Will Double by 2050. But the Education of More African Girls Means it Might Peak Sooner than Most People Expect. Special Report, 28 March 2020. Available at: https://www.economist.com/special-report/2020/03/26/africas-population-will-double-by-2050.

Tuong, V. (2014). *Persistence Amid Decay: The Communist Party of Vietnam at 83*. Palgrave Macmillan. https://doi.org/10.1057/9781137347534.0006.

UNCTAD. (2013). *World Investment Report*. United Nations, New York and Geneva.

UNIDO. (2018b). *Ethiopia's Leather Sector: Current Status and Future Prospects*. Available at: https://www.unido.org/sites/default/files/files/2018-8/Ethiopian%20Leather%20Sector-Current%20status%20and%20future%20prospects.pdf.

Wade, R. (2003). Governing The Market: Economic Theory and the Role of Government in East Asian Industrialization. Princeton University Press, USA.ISBN:978069117294. November 2003.

World Bank. (2000). *Can Africa Claim the 21st Century? April 2000*. The World Bank, Washington, DC.

World Bank. (2016). Africa's Pulse: Global Economic Weakness Continues to be a Drag on Africa's Economic Growth. April 2016.

Index